Advances in Chinese Document and Text Processing

Series on Language Processing, Pattern Recognition, and Intelligent Systems

Editors

Ching Y. Suen
Concordia University, Canada
parmidir@enes.concordia.ca

Lu Qin
The Hong Kong Polytechnic University, Hong Kong
csluqin@comp.polyu.edu.hk

Published

Vol. 1 Digital Fonts and Reading
edited by Mary C. Dyson and Ching Y. Suen

Vol. 2 Advances in Chinese Document and Text Processing
edited by Cheng-Lin Liu and Yue Lu

Forthcoming

Vol. 3 Social Media Content Analysis: NLP and Beyond
edited by Kam-Fai Wong, Wei Gao, Wenjie Li and Ruifeng Xu

Vol. 4 Computational Linguistics, Speech and Image Processing for Arabic Language
edited by Neamat El Gayar and Ching Y. Suen

Series on Language Processing, Pattern Recognition, and Intelligent Systems — Vol. 2

Advances in Chinese Document and Text Processing

Edited by

Cheng-Lin Liu
Institute of Automation, Chinese Academy of Sciences
Beijing, China

Yue Lu
East China Normal University
Shanghai, China

World Scientific

NEW JERSEY • LONDON • SINGAPORE • BEIJING • SHANGHAI • HONG KONG • TAIPEI • CHENNAI • TOKYO

Published by

World Scientific Publishing Co. Pte. Ltd.
5 Toh Tuck Link, Singapore 596224
USA office: 27 Warren Street, Suite 401-402, Hackensack, NJ 07601
UK office: 57 Shelton Street, Covent Garden, London WC2H 9HE

British Library Cataloguing-in-Publication Data
A catalogue record for this book is available from the British Library.

Series on Language Processing, Pattern Recognition, and Intelligent Systems — Vol. 2
ADVANCES IN CHINESE DOCUMENT AND TEXT PROCESSING

ISBN 978-981-3143-67-8

Printed in Singapore

Preface

This book is a collection of invited chapters by experts in Chinese document and text processing, and is part of a series on Language Processing, Pattern Recognition, and Intelligent Systems. The chapters introduce the latest advances and state-of-the-art methods for Chinese document image analysis and recognition, font design, text analysis and speaker recognition.

Chinese texts and document images have different characteristics from the scripts of Western languages such as Roman script. Typically, Chinese texts have no space between words. This makes the word segmentation and text semantic parsing difficult. In document images, the texts are in bitmap form and need pattern recognition technology to convert them into electronic form. In addition to the difficulty of word segmentation (which implies word-level recognizer is not feasible), the large number of character classes (nearly 10,000 Chinese characters are frequently used) also poses a challenge in character recognition and document analysis.

Since the 1960s, there have been many works contributed to Chinese character recognition and document analysis, as well as Chinese text analysis and speech recognition. In the early stage of research, Chinese character recognition was usually treated as an isolated character classification problem. Nowadays, the recognition of single characters, even handwritten characters, has gained large improvements. Accuracies as high as over 97% can be achieved for handwritten Chinese characters using deep convolution neural networks (CNNs) when training with large number of samples. Handwritten text line recognition (a.k.a. character string recognition) is also in good progress by combining CNNs with over-segmentation or directly using recurrent neural networks. The techniques in text analysis and speech recognition are providing inspirations to document recognition, or directly used in document recognition. For example, statistical language models are widely used in document recognition for utilizing the linguistic context.

This edited volume contains 10 chapters. Handwritten Chinese character recognition and text line recognition are at the core of document image analysis (DIA), and therefore, are addressed in four chapters for different scripts (online characters, offline characters, ancient characters, and text lines). Two chapters on character recognition pay much attention to deep convolutional neural networks (CNNs), which are widely used and performing superiorly in various pattern recognition problems. A chapter describes a large handwriting database consisting of both online and offline characters and text pages. Postal mail reading and writer identification, addressed in two chapters, are important applications of DIA. There are also three chapters discussing font typefaces, text parsing and speaker recognition, respectively.

The collection can serve as a useful reference for students and engineers in Chinese document and text processing and their applications.

Contents

Chapter 1

Characteristics of English, Chinese, and Arabic Typefaces

Ching Y. Suen, Shima Nikfal, Bing Zhang and Jehan Janbi

Centre for Pattern Recognition and Machine Intelligence,
Concordia University, Montreal, Quebec H3G 1M8, Canada
suen@cenparmi.concordia.ca

This study attempts to identify the personalities associated with various fonts. We focused on the English typefaces and their personality traits. By conducting a font survey, 71 participants rated the 6 personality traits (Legible, Artistic, Formal, Sloppy, Readable, and Attractive) of 24 English typefaces using a modified five point Likert Scale. For the Chinese and Arabic fonts, we present their typographical characteristics against the English typefaces. Personalities associated with them are presented in tables and the characteristics of Chinese and Arabic typefaces are compared with the English counterparts.

1. Introduction

Since the first reported study in 1920 by Berliner (as cited in Davis & Smith, 1933), the connotative role of typography has been a frequently-researched topic in business, psychology, design, and education. According to the psychologists, typography is defined as the "art of using typeface, layout, and color to convey the meaning of text" (Smart *et al.*, 2000), or as "the form, spacing, and layout of words and sentences in the text of a written or displayed communication message" (McCarthy & Mothersbaugh, 2002). In general, typography is the tool that creates words from characters for example 26 basic in English on paper or screen.

Typefaces are usually classified according to overall appearance and unique typographical features which influence the nature of the typefaces and make them more suitable for some purposes such as (serif, sans serif, display, etc.) or proportionality of the typeface. The combination of appearance and typographical features guided typographers using personality traits to describe typefaces ("less cuddly, more assertive", Berry, 2004). Typographers and designers are often interested in the typeface personality or "typographic allusion" which refers to "the capacity of a typestyle to connote meaning over and above the primary meaning which is linguistically conveyed by words" (Lewis & Walker, 1989).

Brumberger (2003) describes that the "content and purpose of the text should dictate the design of a document, and that form, including typography, should express the content just as the verbal text itself expresses content". Within communications research, many experts suggest that typefaces can convey mood, attitude, and tone while having a distinct persona based on the font's unique features. Each document should be rendered in a font that connects the mood, purpose, intended audience, and context of the document.

The existing research on typography is related to readability and legibility issues. But only a few studies are focused on typefaces and their perceived personas perhaps because typography has generally been considered transparent.

1.1. *The purpose of this chapter*

This study looks at typeface persona, and explores the persona profiles for a series of typefaces. The main concern in this study is on the persona of typefaces to determine whether or not participants consistently attribute 6 tangible personality traits to the 24 chosen English fonts, and to what degree the English fonts could convey these traits.

1.2. *Literature review of typeface personality studies*

Morrison (1986) notes that legibility is often a primary concern in typeface selection. However, most common typefaces perform reasonably well in terms of legibility (Suen *et al.*, 2010; Suen & Komoda, 1986; Lee *et al.*, 2008). Part of the typeface selection process should include the goal of "communicating an affective message" (Morrison, 1986).

Psychologists, typographers, document designers, and graphical artists have all had a similar opinion that a typeface has a "connotative or affective dimension". This dimension carries many aliases: typographic allusion, atmospheric value, typeface personality, rhetorical appropriateness, etc. (Bartram, 1982; Lewis & Walker, 1989; Schriver, 1996; Zachrisson, 1965). In spite of the many terms used to describe the affective quality of a typeface, their meanings are generally the same. In other words, typographers are often interested in the typeface personality which refers to the capacity of a type style to imply meaning over and above the primary meaning which it conveys linguistically by words (Bartram, 1982; Lewis & Walker, 1989; Schriver, 1996; Zachrisson, 1965).

Many empirical studies on typeface personalities have been conducted in the field of psychology over a long period of time. An earlier study that was conducted by Poffenberger and Franken (1923), identified 5 atmospheric values such as cheapness, dignity, economy, luxury, and strength for 29 typefaces. The term "atmospheric value" was used to describe the affective quality of a typeface. Another similar study that was conducted subsequently by Spencer (1969), concluded that typefaces can be grouped under three headings pertaining to atmospheric value: luxury/refinement, economy/precision and strength. Davis and Smith (1933) asked participants to indicate which typeface would best express feelings on a scale of 1 to 24. These early studies all used rank-order methodologies (typefaces were ranked on the adjectives) that led researchers to conclude that readers do attribute personality traits to typefaces.

Kostelnick (1990) exposed that the concept of typeface personalities conveying messages, beyond what can be expressed within the text, is not novel. In the 2nd century, serif typefaces were used as "symbols of the empire" while sans serif typefaces were used as "symbols of the republic" (Bringhurst, 1996). Tschichold (1991) found that different typefaces can contain different personas and that the characteristics of a typeface should match the meaning of the text. Also, visual characteristics can have a strong effect that goes beyond the effects of legibility and readability Kostelnick (1990).

Quite a few researchers have matched physical characteristics with typeface personas. For example, round series are “friendly” while squared serifs are “official” (Parker, 1997, p. 60). Also, typefaces with light weights are “delicate, gentle and feminine” while typefaces with heavy weights are “aggressive and masculine” (White, 1988; Baylis, 1955).

Several researchers have attempted to give particular personas to specific typefaces. Kostelnick *et al.*, (1998) assigned “bookish and traditional” to Times New Roman; “dramatic and sophisticated” to Bodoni MT and “corpulent and jolly” to Goudy. In another research study conducted by Shunshan and Wright (1994), Garamond was labeled as “graceful, refined and confident” and Century Schoolbook was labeled as “serious yet friendly”. Shaikh *et al.* (2006) investigated the relationship between 20 fonts with fifteen personality traits. Experimental results suggested that 20 fonts can be represented in five groups, which were labeled based on their common personality traits (serif, sans serif, display, script/funny, and monoscaped). The uses of this data were appropriate for some onscreen document types. Serif and sans serif typefaces were generally more appropriate than display and script faces for reading materials.

However, on the topic of typefaces, there were discrepancies among rating scores within the previous studies. Each of the above-stated researchers determined the inconsistencies between rating scores of typeface personality traits. These discrepancies could have been due to the differences in participants, based on gender, age or other demographics factors. Moreover, little research has evaluated user perceptions of what fonts maybe appropriate for digital displays. Therefore, in this study, we examined the visual expressions of digital English typefaces and their personality traits.

1.3. *Participants*

A total of 71 participants (39% male, 61% female) completed the survey. Participants are Concordia students from different countries. Approximately 51% of participants were 20–29 years old, and 40% of participants were between 30–39. Only 2% of participants were above the age of 40 and the other 7% participants were below 20 years old.

Regarding educational background, 26% of participants stated they have a Bachelor's Degree, 35% of participants reported they have a Master's Degree and 28% reported they have a Doctorate. The educational background of the remaining 11% participants includes high school and junior college/technical college education.

1.4. *Materials*

The 24 typefaces used throughout the online survey are shown in Figure 1. The fonts chosen included samples of serif fonts (Kino Mt, Berlin Sans FB, Arial & Helvetica), sans serif fonts (Poor Richard, Garamond, Centaur, Times New Roman, Footlight Mt light & Belwe Lt BT), decorative fonts (Chiller, Play bill, Jokerman, Harington, Harry Portter, Broadway & Snap ITC), and display fonts (Onxy, Impac, Bernard MT Condensed, Kebal, Bauhaus 93, Rockwell & Cooper Black). The complete listing and classification of typefaces is represented in (Design Tutor, 2002).

These 24 fonts have been widely used in different applications. Some of them are popular for advertising such as Cooper Black and Impact. Others, such as Times New Roman and Arial, are standard fonts mainly used in books and newspapers (Li & Suen, 2010). Each font reveals a difference in design characteristics such as x-height, ascender, descender, and other features. We computed the characteristics including x-height, ascender and descender for the 24 typefaces based on the procedure described in (Zramdini & Ingold, 1998). We grouped the typefaces into 3 categories, small (S), medium (M) and large (L), by using the characteristic values we computed. By analyzing these values, we were able to find the thresholds to successfully separate the typefaces into these 3 groups.

Belwe Lt BT	Chiller
Arial	Broadway
Garamond	Rockwell
Poor Richard	Jokerman
Play bill	Kabel
Helvetica	Bauhaus 93
Snap ITC	Harry Potter
Berlin Sans FB	Harrington
Bernard MT Condensed	Onyx
Footlight MT Light	Kino MT
Times New Roman	Centaur
Cooper Black	Impact

Figure 1. Typefaces used in the survey.

1.5. *Results*

In order to explore the distribution of rating scores for each typeface based on each personality trait, we analyzed the histogram of rating scores of each typeface. From the analysis, we noticed that the histograms of rating scores displayed normal shape distribution.

We calculated the mean values, minimum values, maximum values and standard deviations of rating scores of each typeface based on each personality trait. Mean values of the rating scores for the 24 typefaces with their abbreviations related to 6 personality traits are listed in Table 1. These data are sorted based on typeface abbreviations and the top 3 typefaces most associated with each of the 6 personality traits are highlighted.

2. Chinese Character Characteristics Compared with English

2.1. *Overview*

In this section, we are focusing on the characteristics of Chinese characters, and comparing them with those of English letters and words. We extracted these Chinese characteristics from character structures, character components and strokes, involving the serif, sans serif and calligraphy typefaces.

In Figure 2, there are the samples of some common Chinese typefaces, including the serif, sans serif and calligraphy fonts. Based on these samples, we can better describe the characteristics of Chinese characters.

Table 1. Mean values of rating scores for 24 typefaces related to 6 personality traits.

Typeface	Abbreviation	Personality Traits					
		Legible	Artistic	Formal	Sloppy	Readable	Attractive
Arial	Al	**4.51**	2.07	**4.28**	1.48	**4.55**	3.01
Bauhaus 93	Bh93	2.89	2.77	1.86	2.39	2.99	2.55
Belwe Lt BT	BLB	4.06	2.87	2.96	1.83	4.04	3.04
Bernard MT Condensed	BMC	3.87	2.37	3.44	1.82	4.01	2.75
Berlin Sans FB	BSF	3.89	2.63	2.93	1.75	4.13	3.17
Broadway	Bw	2.97	3.04	2.07	2.41	2.93	2.61
Cooper Black	CB	3.73	2.75	2.77	1.96	3.93	3.01
Chiller	Cl	2.97	3.39	1.48	**2.94**	3.32	2.75
Centaur	Cr	4.35	2.38	3.96	1.56	4.54	3.14
Footlight MT Light	FL	3.97	2.77	3.28	1.70	4.20	**3.45**
Garamond	Ga	**4.56**	2.24	**4.27**	1.63	**4.79**	**3.38**
Harry Potter	HP	2.49	**3.68**	1.31	**2.87**	2.62	2.54
Harrington	Hr	3.34	**3.89**	2.01	2.41	3.41	**3.66**
Helvetica	Ht	**4.51**	2.11	**4.27**	1.61	**4.55**	3.01
Impact	Ip	4.20	1.79	3.89	1.58	4.30	2.65
Jokerman	Jm	2.63	**3.87**	1.39	**2.79**	2.92	3.04
Kabel	Kb	4.11	2.41	3.25	1.55	4.31	2.72
Kino MT	KM	3.00	2.99	1.87	2.27	3.17	2.66
Onyx	Ox	3.00	2.27	2.69	2.25	3.11	2.17
Play bill	Pb	3.15	2.41	2.46	2.14	3.34	2.38
Poor Richard	PR	3.80	3.45	2.76	2.07	3.99	**3.62**
Rockwell	Rw	4.35	2.41	3.83	1.62	4.41	3.13
Snap ITC	SITC	2.69	**3.82**	1.37	**2.99**	2.72	3.11
Times New Roman	TNR	**4.46**	2.11	**4.34**	1.45	**4.62**	3.08

Font	ACRONYMS	Font	ACRONYMS
微软简楷体	WRJKT	方正卡通	FZKT
华文中宋	HWZS	微软雅黑	WRYH
方正宋三	FZSS	迷你简毡笔黑	MNJZBH
方正准圆	FZZY	方正隶书	FZLS
方正仿宋	FZFS	汉仪综艺体简	HYZYTJ
微软简中圆	WRJZY	迷你简丫丫	MNJYY
方正魏碑	FZWB	方正黑体	FZHT
迷你简雪君	MNJXJ	微软简标宋	WRJBS
汉仪凌波体简	HYLBTJ	经典平黑简	JDPHJ

Figure 2. Chinese typeface samples.

2.2. *Relative baseline feature*

Unlike the English letter x-height feature, Chinese characters have a relative baseline, and almost all characters are displayed above this line. Firstly, we introduce the English x-height feature (Figure 3), and then we present an example of the Chinese baseline (Figure 4).

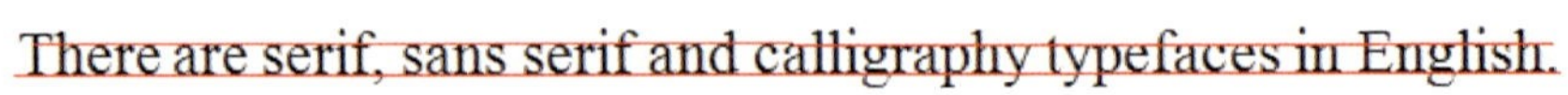

Figure 3. x-height sample.

The x-height definitely exists in English; there is no exception to the x-height rule. We can see that, all the English letters are displayed according to the two red lines. Actually, the typographical structure of text lines is determined by the height of letter x. Different typefaces have different x heights, affecting their performance in legibility.

However, in Chinese, the letter x does not exist. Almost all Chinese characters are written above a horizontal line. Here is an example.

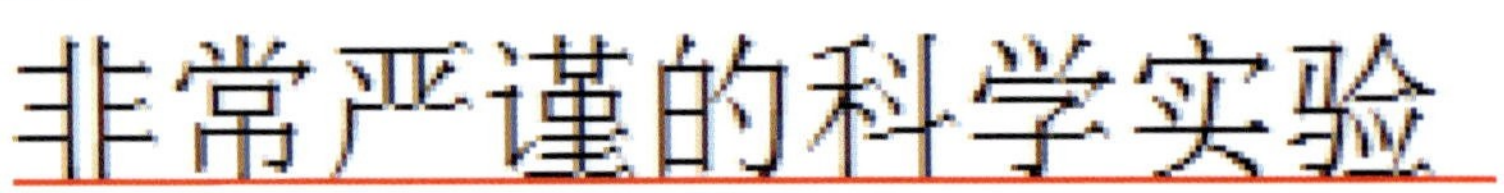

Figure 4. Chinese baseline.

Though different characters have different designs, they can all be listed above a baseline. However, the baseline of Chinese characters is relative, and not all the characters follow this rule, because of the features of the character components. We can see the red circle in Figure 5, the peripheral part crosses the baseline. Thus, we can only say, the baseline of Chinese character is relative, rather than an absolute feature.

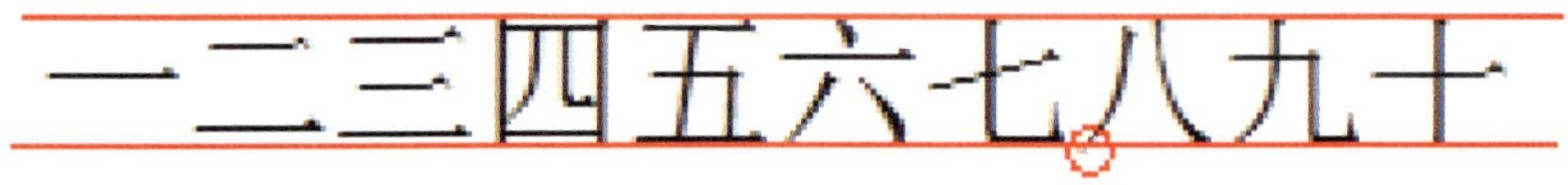

Figure 5. Baseline exception example.

2.3. *Squared character feature*

Unlike English letters, which has ascenders and descenders, Chinese characters are all square in shape. Here is another example.

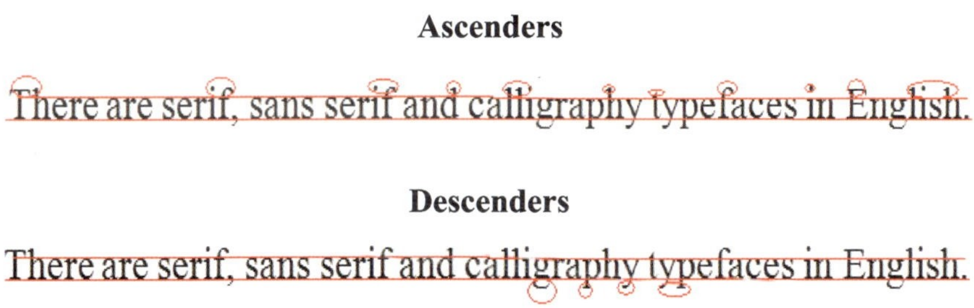

Figure 6. Example of English ascender and descender proportion.

Figure 7. Some square Chinese characters.

Through Figures 6 and 7, we can easily tell the design difference between these two classes. Though some single Chinese characters have the ascender or descender components, they cannot be counted as an obvious feature to tell their differences. For example, the character 大. It looks like having an ascender part above the horizontal line, however, when this character 大 is compared with character 天, the ascender part is gone, because the upper horizontal line in 天 has the same height as the character 大. Thus, in summary, ascenders and descenders could not be counted as a feature in Chinese.

2.4. *Weight detection*

The weight of font is reflected by the density of black surfaces on the white background. This density is extracted from the horizontal profile p'h (Figure 8) in an equation listed below.

Figure 8. Horizontal projection profiles.

It is computed on the central part of the line located between Hupper and Hbase, in order to be independent of the text line structure, *dn* is thus defined by:

$$dn = \frac{1}{n}\sum_{x=1}^{n} p'h[x]$$

This is a common feature in both Chinese and English, and both of them use this feature to tell the density of blackness. And this feature is related to the legibility of typefaces as well.

2.5. *Serif / sans serif / script*

In Chinese, there are still serif, sans serif and script typefaces, and each category has obvious characteristics. However, there are typefaces across the serif and sans serif boundaries, and they exist as a unique category. Some samples are shown below:

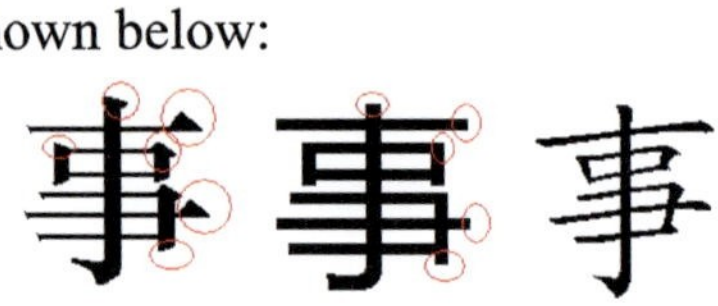

Figure 9. Serif, sans serif, and unique typeface samples.

In Figure 9, the third one is a character of WRJKT, which represents the unique typeface compared with serif and sans serif typefaces. Weibei Ti, Li Ti, etc. all belong to this kind of typefaces. Compared with the calligraphy typefaces such as MNJYY and HYZYTJ, these typefaces look much more formal and legible. However, English letters only have serif, sans serif and calligraphy typefaces.

2.6. *Structure design*

Unlike the English horizontal way, whose words are composed of letters along a horizontal line in one dimensioned array, Chinese characters comprise of components according to the specific relations, like two dimensional building blocks. An example of Chinese structure is shown in Figure 10.

Figure 10. Chinese structure design.

In this character, we can assume all the components could be taken off and replaced according to the Chinese structural rules. For example, if we put another two strokes on this character, it would become another character 乘. And if we put some more strokes, it would become a new character 剩.

2.7. *Stroke contrast*

Serif typeface has stroke contrast on the Heng and Shu (horizontal vs. vertical lines) to highlight the serif design. However, sans serif typefaces adopt the consistent width on both Heng and Shu. This feature is similar to that in English typeface design.

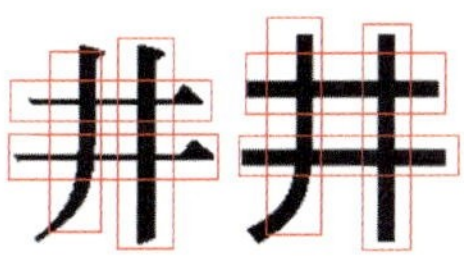

Figure 11. Samples of stroke contrast of the serif and sans serif typefaces.

However, the unique category of Chinese typefaces is kind of different. Serif typeface has the stroke contrast on Heng and Shu, but unique category has the contrast on different parts of the same stroke. For example:

Figure 12. Samples of the unique typeface WRJKT show the contrast on the same stroke as if they are drawn with a brush.

It is clear that in the left character, the width of the lowest horizontal stroke varies. And all the stroke widths of the right character are different as well. Here is another example; we can easily see the differences.

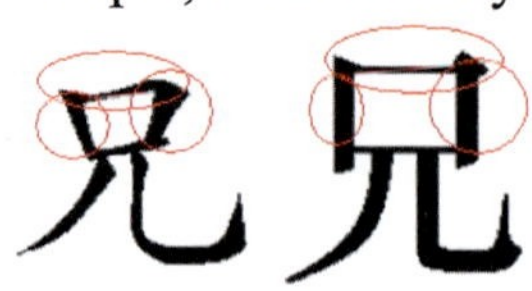

Figure 13. The strokes marked by red circles are the main differences.

2.8. *Design proportion*

This difference mainly comes from the producers. Different companies have different tiny designs of the same typefaces, and these tiny differences represent their design. Here is an example in English to illustrate this design. Through this example, we can easily understand what the design is about, and then we will find the same features in Chinese typefaces.

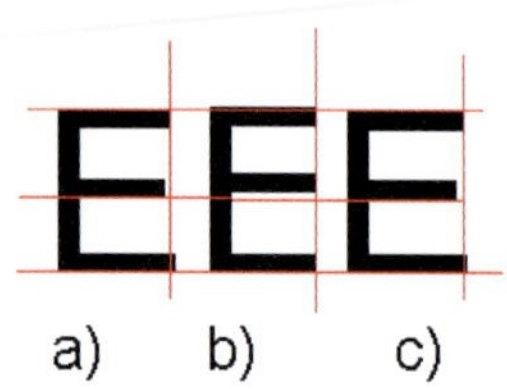

Figure 14. All the three letters Es belong to the same typeface, but they are produced by different companies. We can see the differences in their design based on the red lines.

Through the above example, we can easily see the differences between the following Chinese characters:

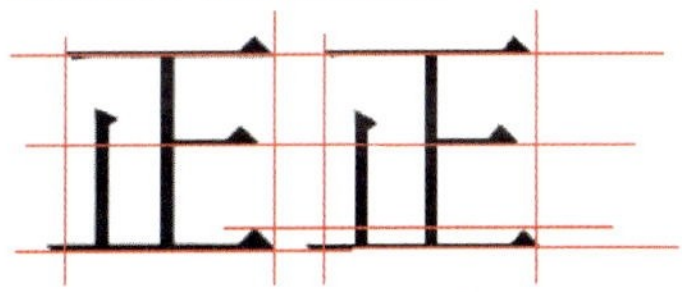

Figure 15. Samples of the same SongTi typefaces, but from different companies.

Though they are almost the same, character a) is much stronger than character b), because the vertical strokes in a) are wider than those in character b).

2.9. *Width to height ratio*

Although all Chinese characters look like square blocks, different typefaces have different width and height ratios. After measuring the 18 typefaces which were used in the experiment, we obtained the following result:

Table 2. Font height, font width and the ratio between height and width of eighteen fonts. Height and width unit in millimeter.

Abbreviation	Font	Height	Width	Ratio between height and width
WRJKT	微软简楷体	26.1	21.8	1.2168
FZKT	方正卡通	24.42	24.25	1.017
HWZS	华文中宋	27.33	25.08	1.0979
WRYH	微软雅黑	28	27.17	1.0387
FZSS	方正宋三	27.25	24.58	1.1337
MNJZBH	迷你简毡笔黑	26.67	25	1.0728
FZZY	方正准圆	26.33	27	0.9812
FZLS	方正隶书	17.8	24	0.7186
FZFS	方正仿宋	26.3	21.2	1.2581
HYZYTJ	汉仪综艺体简	27.08	26.83	1.0138
WRJZY	微软简中圆	26.17	24.67	1.0654
MNJYY	迷你简丫丫	23.33	21.5	1.0913

Table 2. (*Continued*)

Abbreviation	Font	Height	Width	Ratio between height and width
FZWB	方正魏碑	22.58	20	1.1427
FZHT	方正黑体	26.67	24.92	1.078
MNJXJ	迷你简雪君	26.17	19.92	1.337
WRJBS	微软简标宋	27.75	22.83	1.2934
HYLBTJ	汉仪凌波体简	26.17	24.42	1.0803
JDPJH	经典平黑简	27.25	25.42	1.078

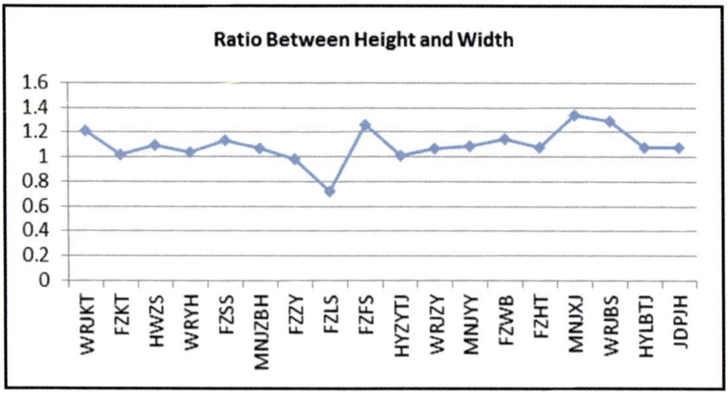

Figure 16. Ratio between the height and the width for the eighteen fonts.

2.10. *Character spacing*

We measured the default space between every pair of characters of the six fonts which were used in our research experiment II, and measured their character widths and heights as well by the projection method. Chinese printed characters can be segmented easily without using any complicated segmentation method, according to the neat character spaces between them.

To measure the spaces, widths and heights of Chinese characters in different typefaces, we used the full cover structures, for the characters with this structure could cover all the main features of Chinese characters, while maintaining the font's original design. The character boundary was just what we needed to measure. Because the heights and widths of Chinese characters were not similar, and the spaces between every pair of characters were different as well, the space value itself would not reflect any useful information. Therefore, we chose the following character to space ratio to represent the differences in space.

$$\text{space distance} = (\text{character width})/(\text{character space})$$

Table 3. Statistics related to typeface space between character pairs.

Font	Height (mm)	Width (mm)	character space (mm)	character area (mm2)	space area (mm2)	character/space
WRJKT	26.10	21.80	10.27	568.98	268.05	2.12
HWZS	27.33	25.08	6.55	685.44	179.01	3.83
WRYH	28.00	27.17	4.64	760.76	129.92	5.86
FZSS	27.25	24.58	5.73	669.81	156.14	4.29
FZWB	22.58	20.00	11.82	451.60	266.90	1.69
FZHT	26.67	24.92	6.82	664.62	181.89	3.65

Compared with Chinese characters, English letters also have similar characteristics, named as letter-spacing and word spacing. After measuring the spacing, we can still find the same result that the letter spacing and word spacing are different according to the different typefaces.

2.11. *Counter design & inner design*

These characteristics mainly come from the detailed design, and normally based on the same category, e.g. FZHT and WRYH. These two typefaces belong to the same category HeiTi. However, they have obvious differences on the counter design and inner design.

Counter: the white space enclosed by a letterform, whether wholly enclosed, as in d or o, or partially, as in c or m. Here are some examples:

Figure 17. Counter design samples: 1) FZHT, and 2) WRYH.

In this example, we can see that the WRYH has more inner space than FZHT, and obviously the counter design is different.

After the statistical analysis and feature analysis, we found that too much inner spacing did not attract readers. Inversely, participants preferred the original features.

2.12. *Stem and cap height design*

Stem: a main stroke that is more or less straight, not part of a bowl. The letter o, for example, has no stem; the letter l consists of stem and serif only.

Capital Y has two diagonal strokes and a vertical stem (Figure 18). We use capital Y to illustrate this design characteristic.

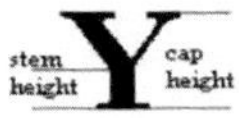

Figure 18. Stem height and Cap height of capital "Y".

Typeface designers are interested in the design of the stem height of Y. If the vertex is too low, the Y will be top heavy. However, if the vertex is too high, the space between the arms will be too small, and the gesture of the arms will look timid. In general, the stem of a serif capital Y should fall between 35–50% of the capital height.

This conclusion also fits for Chinese. In Chinese, we have many such characters, like 丫, 羊, 干 etc. And this feature can also improve or reduce the legibility of the specific Chinese characters.

2.13. *Junction points*

Junction point is one of the most important and useful features in the recognition procedure, especially in Chinese character recognition procedure. Because in Chinese, there are many similar characters with little difference, and the only way to tell these characters apart may be a junction point. Firstly, we illustrate what the junction point is, and then we give an example to distinguish two similar characters by the junction point feature.

Figure 19. All the junction points are marked by red circles.

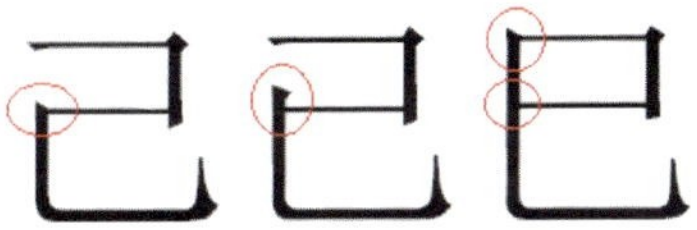

Figure 20. Very similar Chinese characters with little difference. By the number of junction points, it is easy to distinguish them.

2.14. *Stroke ending*

Stroke ending is another important and useful feature in the recognition procedure. Meanwhile, it is a popular feature used in the OCR. Here is an example to illustrate what the ending point is.

Figure 21. All the ending points are marked by the red circles.

2.15. *Curve*

Same as English letters, Chinese characters also have curvy strokes and these curves play an important role in the recognition process. Firstly, we illustrate the curve definition, and then we make a comparison. Illustration is shown below:

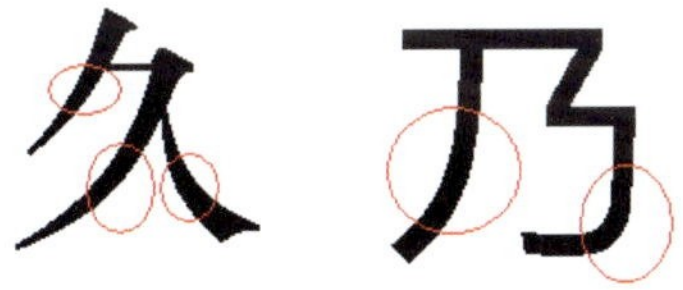

Figure 22. Curve sample in Chinese characters.

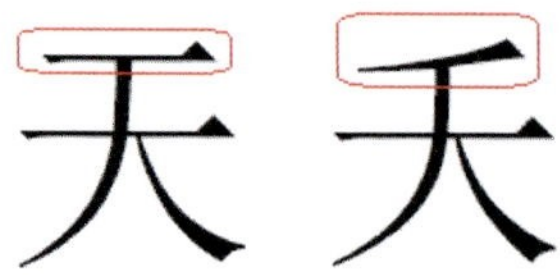

Figure 23. Two similar characters differentiated by a curve stroke.

Normally, this feature would be more important in human recognition than in machine OCR. Because the marked stroke is the only difference between these two characters, after comparison by the human eyes. However, machines can extract the projection features as reference to recognize these characters.

3. Comparing Arabic with Latin Font Characteristics

3.1. *Overview*

In desktop publishing design, the typographical choices will contribute to achieve or break the intended goal of the design. Typography is not only a way of representing information. It can play a role to enhance and to emphasize the message in the content. The professional typography invites reader as well as pleasures them to keep them reading. A well designed typography will maximize the legibility and consequently the readability of typed text.

Latin and Arabic scripts are the most common scripts used around the world. The Latin alphabet has been used in many languages such as English, French, German, Spanish, Italian...etc. While, the Arabic alphabet has been used by many other languages including Arabic, Farsi, Pashto Urdu, Dari, Punjabi...etc. This section highlights the differences and similarities between the Latin and Arabic scripts as well as their typographical characteristics. It is important for typography designers, who are interested in designing typography for both scripts, to determine the most important characteristics and which may influence their design and help them to obtain desired harmonization. Initially, we will compare the two script characteristics and point out the major differences. Then, in the next section we shall describe the anatomy of Arabic type and

Latin type. After that, we shall mention several points which can be considered in the design process.

3.2. *Feature of Arabic script compared to Latin script*

Direction of writing

The writing in Latin and Arabic scripts is going in opposite directions. The writing direction in Arabic starts from the right side toward the left side. Whereas numerals are written from left to right (Oweis, 2005). Unlike Latin script, where the writing direction moves from left to right even for the numerics.

Different forms of letters

Letters can take different forms when they are used in both scripts. In Latin, letters can be used in upper or lower case forms, whereas in Arabic, there is no such upper and lower case form. According to the cursively and connectivity nature of Arabic scripts, there are four different forms for the same letter depending on its position in a word e.g. isolated, initial (joined only on the left), middle (joined on both sides) and final (joined only on the right). Many Arabic letters simply lose their tails for the middle and final forms. A few letters change their shapes completely (AbiFares, 2007). Table 4 lists the different forms of Arabic letters.

Connectivity and cursiveness

The letters of Latin and Arabic scripts are used differently to form words. In Latin writing, letters can be used as independent characters or they can be connected in cursive style. With advance of technology and industrial revolution, the trend of using Latin letters in isolation has become dominated because of their higher legibility. The cursive style may be used just for authentic or imitating handwriting style. Unlike Arabic, there is no distinction between printing and handwriting. Only the cursive style is allowed. Letters that can be joined are always joined up in both handwritten and printed forms of Arabic. This is making the main portions of letters that form words emphasized on a horizontal line. Not all Arabic letters have the same connectivity rules. The connectivity of the letter differs according to its position in the word. In general, a letter will be joined only from the left side if it is the first letter of the word. If the letter is the last letter of the word, it will be joined only from the right side. The letter will be joined from both sides if its position is in the middle of the word. This case of connectivity rule is not the same for all letters. Six letters are never being joined from the left side even if they are positioned in the middle or the beginning of a word. Those letters are “أ ، د ، ذ ، ر ، ز ، و”. Table 4 lists all letters and their shapes in isolated form and in their initial, middle and final forms respectively.

Table 4. Different forms of Arabic letters.

Letter Name	Transliteration	Pronunciation & English Equivalent	Contextual forms			
			final	Middle	Initial	Isolated
alif	*Ā*	-	ـا	-	-	ا
baa	*B*	B as in bake	ـب	ـبـ	بـ	ب
taa	*T*	T as in take	ـت	ـتـ	تـ	ت
thaa	ṯ	th as in thin	ـث	ـثـ	ثـ	ث
jiim	Ǧ	j as in joke	ـج	ـجـ	جـ	ج
Haa	ḥ	no equivalent	ـح	ـحـ	حـ	ح
khaa	ḫ (also *kh*, *x*)	no equivalent	ـخ	ـخـ	خـ	خ
daal	*d*	d as in day	ـد	-	-	د
dhaal	ḏ (also *dh*, *ð*)	th as in this	ـذ	-	-	ذ
raa	*r*	r as in car	ـر	-	-	ر
zaay	*z*	z as in zeal	ـز	-	-	ز
siin	*s*	s as in snake	ـس	ـسـ	سـ	س
shiin	*š* (also *sh*)	sh as in shake	ـش	ـشـ	شـ	ش
Saad	ṣ	emphatic s	ـص	ـصـ	صـ	ص
Daad	ḍ	emphatic d	ـض	ـضـ	ضـ	ض
Taa	ṭ	emphatic t	ـط	ـطـ	طـ	ط
DHaa	ẓ	emphatic dh	ـظ	ـظـ	ظـ	ظ
ayn	ʿ	no equivalent	ـع	ـعـ	عـ	ع
ghayn	*ġ* (also *gh*)	no equivalent	ـغ	ـغـ	غـ	غ
faa	*f*	f As in face	ـف	ـفـ	فـ	ف
gaaf	*q*	emphatic k	ـق	ـقـ	قـ	ق
kaaf	*k*	k as in key	ـك	ـكـ	كـ	ك
laam	*l*	l as in leaf	ـل	ـلـ	لـ	ل
miim	*m*	m as in make	ـم	ـمـ	مـ	م
nuun	*n*	n as in none	ـن	ـنـ	نـ	ن
haa	*h*	h as in hat	ـه	ـهـ	هـ	ه
waaw	*w* / *ū* / *aw*	w as in wake	ـو	-	-	و
yaa	*y* / *ī* / *ay*	y as in yell	ـي	ـيـ	يـ	ي

Ligatures

Ligature occurs where two or more letters are joined as a single glyph. In Latin, some ligatures are stylistically used when consecutive letters collide to each other. The replaced glyph will improve the appearance of those letters such as fi ligature in Table 5. Other ligatures are used to represent new letters such as œ in French (Strizver, 2010; William, 2008).

Table 5. Ligatures used in Latin.

Without Ligatures	Ligatures
fl	ﬂ
fi	ﬁ
oe	œ
ae	Æ

In Arabic script, using ligatures is very common. One of the most used ligatures is ﻻ. In Table 6 below, other used ligatures are optional and they are mostly used for stylish purposes.

Table 6. Stylish ligatures used in Arabic.

Without Ligatures	Ligatures
الله	ﷲ
محمد	ﷴ
نبي	نبي
يثرب	يثرب
سرائي	سرائي

Diacritical marks

Diacritics are signs that are merged to existing letters to create new compound glyphs that represent new phonemes, or change in pronunciation. They can place above, below through the letter or any position around the letter (Turčić, Koren, Uglješić & Rajković, 2010; Hssini & Lazrek, 2011). In Latin, they are used in all Latin languages except English. They are used in languages whose phonetics use sounds that do not exist in Latin. Table 7 lists those diacritical marks classified according to their positions.

Table 7. Diacritical marks used in Arabic.

Position	Name	Shape	Example
Above	Fathah	◌َ	دَ
	Tanwin fathah	◌ً	اً
	Dammah	◌ُ	خُ
	Tanwin dammah	◌ٌ	مٌ
	Suku	◌ْ	سْ
	Shaddah	◌ّ	مّ
	hamzah	◌ٔ	أ
	Maddah	◌ٓ	آ
	Dagger alif	◌ٰ	هٰذَا
	waslah	◌ٱ	ٱ
Below	kasrah	◌ِ	فِ
	Tanwin kasrah	◌ٍ	تٍ
	hamzah	◌ٕ	إ

In Arabic script, there are different types of diacritical marks that are used for the same purposes as Latin. The essential diacritic mark is dots that are used to represent new letters for other languages that use the Arabic alphabet. One dot is a measurement unit marked by the feather of the used calligraphy pen (Hssini & Lazrek, 2011). The semantic role of a diacritic dot is such that certain letters are characterized by the presence, number and positions of these dots. For example, the basic glyph ٮ several letters according to the number of diacritic dots which appear above or below it: ب, ت and ث.

In addition, only three long vowels are written which are ا و ي. When the ambiguity appears, short vowels can be attached to the base consonants represented by diacritic signs. It helps to provide high phonetic accuracy pen (Hssini & Lazrek, 2011). The list of possible used signs for Arabic is presented in Table 8.

Table 8. Diacritical marks used in Latin.

Position	Name	Shape	Example
above	acute	ˏ	Ú
	Double acute	˝	ő
	grave	ˋ	è
	Double grave	̏	ȁ
	Circumflex	ˆ	â
	Caron	ˇ	č
	Breve	˘	ĕ
	Macron	¯	ō
	Ring	˚	ů
	Dot	˙	ċ
	Umlaut	¨	ü
	Tilde	~˜	ũ
	Comma	‘	ģ
below	Ogonek	˛	ą
	cedilla	¸	ç
	Comma	,	ķ
through	Slash	⁄	ȼ
	bar	-	ħ

3.3. *Anatomy of characters*

Arabic script (AbiFares, 2001; AbiFares, 2007; Oweis, 2005):

- Tooth: The short vertical strokes in Arabic letters that are joining and extending upwards from the baseline, as in the initial or medial positions of the letters ‘baa’ (ب), ‘taa’ (ت) and ‘Siin’ (س).
- Loop: The part of an Arabic letter that is shaped like a loop which encloses a counter, as in the medial position of the letter ‘faa’ (ف) in cursive type styles.
- Ascender: The part of some letters that extends above the tooth and loop-heights, as in the letters ‘Taa’ (ط), ‘alif’ (ا) and ‘kaaf’ (ك).
- Descender: The bottom part of the letterforms in isolated (free-standing) and final shape variations, as in the letters ‘Saad’ (ص), ‘ayn’ (ع), ‘waaw’ (و), ‘raa’ (ر), ‘nuun’ (ن) and ‘Haa’ (ح). The descender is located under the baseline.

- Bowl: The elliptical or round form of letters, such as ‘Haa’ (ح) and ‘ayn’ (ع).
- Stem: The main stroke of letterforms that is normally straight and is not part of a *bowl* (defined above).
- Knot: The part of a letter that is filled and closed such as the middle position of the letter ‘ayn’ (ع) in the cursive style.
- Eye: The enclosed counters in letters such as ‘waaw’ (و) and ‘Saad’ (ص).
- Shoulder: The flat horizontal stroke that is located above the bowl part of letters such as ‘khaa’ (خ) and ‘Haa’ (ح).
- Head: The elliptical or round form of letters such as the ‘ayn’ (ع).
- Ending strokes (Tail)
    - Slack Tail: The ending of the letterforms in isolated (free-standing) variations that are terminated with a straight stroke that extended vertically below the baseline, as in the letter ‘miim’ (م).
    - Stiff Tail: The ending of the letterforms in isolated (free-standing) variations that is terminated with a sharp curved stroke that extends below the baseline, as in the letter ‘waaw’ (و).
    - Curled (curved) Tail: The ending of the letterforms in isolated (free-standing) variations that are terminated with an upwards curling stroke, as in the letter ‘nuun’ (ن).
    - Flat tail: The ending of the letterforms in isolated (free-standing) variations, with a flat stroke that extends horizontally along the baseline, as in the letters ‘baa’ (ب) and ‘taa’ (ت).

Figure 24. Anatomy of Arabic letters.

Latin Script (Strizver, 2010; William, 2008; Gelderman, 1999; Bringhurst, 1992; Alsaiari, 2009):

- Arm: The upper horizontal or diagonal stroke that is attached on one side and free on the other side as in letter (K, E).
- Ascender: The part of lower case letters that extend above the height of lower case letter x as in letters (b, d, f, h, k, l, t).
- Cross bar: The horizontal stroke across the middle of uppercase letters such as (A, H).
- Bowl: The curved stroke of the character that enclosed a space which is then called counter as in letters (b, B, d, D, g, o).

- Counter: The partially or fully circular or curved negative space within character as in letters (C, g, o).
- Descender: The part of lower case characters that extends below the baseline as in letters (j, p, q, y, g).
- Ear: The small stroke on the upper right side of the bowl as in letter (g).
- Link: The stroke that connects the top and lower portions of character as in double-story letter (g).
- Loop: The lower enclosed counter of double-storey (g) that is connected to the upper portion by a link.
- Serif: The short extension from the upper and lower ends of main strokes of letters. It can take different shapes such as rounded, bracketed, cupped etc.
- Shoulder: The curved stroke as in letters (r, n, m, h).
- Spine: The curved main stroke of letter (S).
- Stem: The main vertical stoke or straight diagonal stroke of letter that has no vertical.
- Stroke: Any curved or straight line of a character.
- Tail: The descender of letter Q or j and the diagonal stroke of the bottom of R.
- Terminal: The final stroke, straight or curved, of a letter that doesn't end with serif as in letter (e, t).

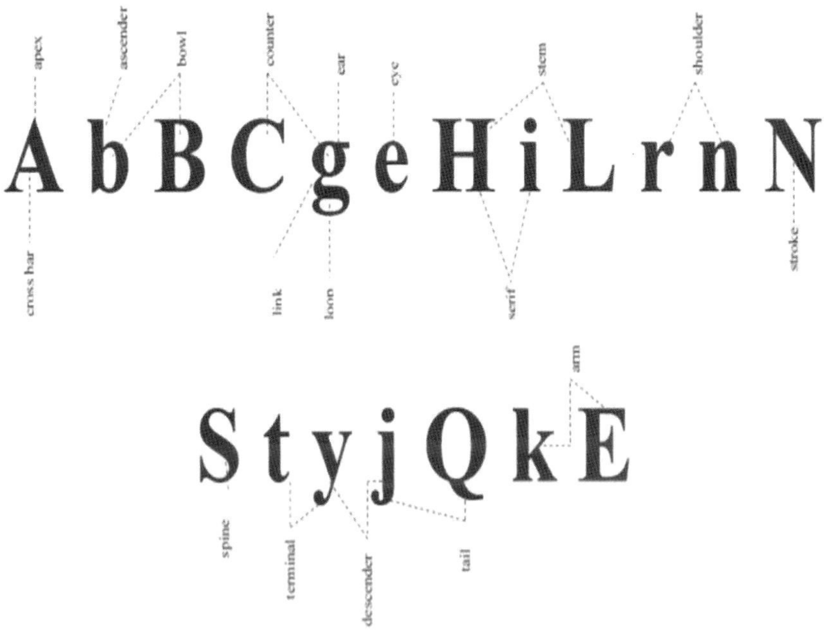

Figure 25. Anatomy of Latin letters.

3.4. *Design considerations*

Arabic and Latin scripts use Cartesian space differently. In Latin, the Cartesian space is divided into three areas while in Arabic scripts it is divided into five areas. Therefore, the design considerations of both scripts are different as listed below (AbiFares, 2001):

Figure 26. Division of Cartesian space for Latin.

For Latin

Determining the basic dimensions which are the cap height, the x-height, the ascender and the descender height. Cap height is the height of letters in upper case form (William, 2008) and x-height is the height of letter x in small case form. Ascender is the height of letter above x-height which is not necessary the same as cap height. While descender is the height of letter under the baseline.

- Starting by lower case letter 'n' to determine the proportion of the character width to x-height.
- The overall color of the font is determined by the ratio of the thickness of the stroke to the counter forms (ratio of dark to light).
- Determine the angle of axis and the stress which is the angle through the thinnest parts of the curve.
- Determine whether to use serif or not and their size and shape.
- Shape of curved strokes and straight strokes and how they will be connected.

For Arabic

Determining the basic dimensions which are the loop height, the tooth-height, the ascender and the descender heights:

- Starting by lowercase letter 'س' to determine the proportion of the character width to character height.
- Determine the thickness of strokes and their contrast which is the ratio of thickest to the thinnest part of the curved stroke.
- The overall color of the font is determined by the ratio of the thickness of the stroke to the counter forms (ratio of dark to light).
- Determine the shape of curved strokes and straight strokes and how they will be connected (AbiFares, 2001; Elyaakoubi & Lazrek, 2005).

Figure 27. Division of Cartesian space for Arabic.

References

[1] AbiFares, H. S. (2001). *Arabic Typography: A Comprehensive Sourcebook.* London: Saqi book.

[2] AbiFares, H. S. (2007). *Typographic Matchmaking*. Singapore: BIS & Khatt Foundation.

[3] Alsaiari, A. A. (2009). Arabic Typography: A Survey. *IJECS/IJENS*, **9**(10), 16–22.

[4] Bartram, D. (1982). Perception of semantic quality in type: differences between designers and non-designers. *Information Design Journal*, **3**(1), 38–50.

[5] Baylis, C. H. (1955). Trends in typefaces. *Printer's ink*, **252**(5), 44–46.

[6] Berry, J. D. (2004). *The Microsoft ClearType Font Collection*. Seattle, WA: Microsoft Corporation.

[7] Bringhurst, R. (1992). *The Elements of Typographic Style*. Vancouver: Hartley & Marks Publishers.

[8] Brumberger, E. R. (2003). The rhetoric of typography: The persona of typeface and text. *Technical Communication*, **50**(2), 206–223.

[9] Davis, R. C. & Smith, H. J. (1933). Determinants of feeling tone in typefaces. *Journal of applied Psychology*, **17**(6), 742–764.

[10] DesignTutor (2002). DesignTutor guide to Microsoft fonts. *Design Tutor Magazine*, **8**, 1–7.

[11] Dyson, M. & Suen, C. Y. (2015). *Digital Fonts and Reading*. Singapore: World Scientific.

[12] Elyaakoubi, M. & Lazrek, A. (2005). Arabic scientific e-document typography. In *5th International Conference on Human System Learning*, pp. 241–252.

[13] Gelderman, M. (1999). A short introduction to font characteristics. Retrieved from: http://www.ntg.nl/maps/22/16.pdf.

[14] Hssini, M. & Lazrek, A. (2011). Design of arabic diacritical marks. *IJCSI International Journal of Computer Science*, **8**(3), 262–271.

[15] Kostelnick, C. (1990). The rhetoric of text design in professional communication. *The Technical Writing Teacher*, **17**(3), 189–202.

[16] Kostelnick, C., Roberts, D. D. & Dragga, S. (1998). *Designing Visual Language: Strategies for Professional Communicators*. New York: Longman.

[17] Lee, D. S., Shieh, K. K., Jeng, S. C. & Shen, I. H. (2008). Effect of character size and lighting on legibility of electronic papers, *Displays*, **29**(1), 10–17.

[18] Lewis, C. & Walker, P. (1989). Typographic influences on reading. *British Journal of Psychology*, **80**, 241–257.

[19] Li, Y. & Suen, C. Y. (2010). Typeface personality traits and their design charactcristics, in *Proceedings of the 9th IAPR International Workshop on Document Analysis Systems*, Boston.

[20] McCarthy, M. S. & Mothersbaugh, D. L. (2002). Effects of typographic factors in advertising-based persuasion: A general model and initial empirical tests, *Psychology and Marketing*, **19**(7–8), 663–691.

[21] Morrison, G. R. (1986). Communicability of the emotional connotation of type, *Educational Communications and Technology Journal*, **34**(4), 235–244.

[22] Oweis F. (2005). *Pocket Guide to Arabic Script*. New York: Hippocrene Books.

[23] Parker, R. C. (1997). *Looking Good in Print* (3rd ed). North Carolina: Ventana Communications Group.

[24] Poffenberger, A. T. & Franken, R. B. (1923). A study of the appropriateness of typefaces. *Journal of Applied Psychology*, **7**, 312–329.

[25] Schriver K. A. (1996). *Dynamics in Document Design*. New York: Wiley.

[26] Shaikh, A. D., Chaparro, B. S. & Fox, D. (2006). Perception of fonts: Perceived personality traits and uses. *Usability News*, **8**(1), 1–6.

[27] Shunshan, R. and Wright, D. (1994). *Desktop Publishing by Design*. Redmond, WA: Microsoft Press. Smart, K. L., Rice, J. C. & Wood, L. E. (2000). Meeting the needs of users: toward a semiotics of the web. In *Proceedings of IEEE Professional Communication Society International, SIGDOC*, pp. 593–605.
[28] Spencer, H. (1969). *The Visible Word* (2nd ed.). New York: Lund Humphries in association with the Royal College of Arts.
[29] Strizver, I. (2010). *Type Rules!: The Designer's Guide to Professional Typography*. New Jersey: John Willey & Sons.
[30] Suen, C. Y. & Komoda, M. K. (1986). Legibility of digital type-fonts and comprehension in reading. In *Text Processing and Document Manipulation*, Cambridge University Press, pp. 178–187.
[31] Suen, C. Y., Nikfal, S., Li, Y., Zhang, Y. & Nobile, N. (2010). Evaluation of typeface legibility based on human perception and machine recognition. In *Proceedings of ATypI Conference*, Dublin, Ireland.
[32] Tschichold, J. (1991). *Graphic Arts and Book Design: Essays on the Morality of Good Design (Classic Typography Series)*. Washington: Hartley & Marks.
[33] Turčić, M., Koren, A., Uglješić, V. & Rajković, I. (2010). Design and positioning of diacritical marks in latin typefaces. *Journal for Printing Science and Graphic Communications*, **22**, 3–15.
[34] White, J. V. (1988). *Graphic Design for the Electronic Age: Manual for Traditional and Desk Top Publishing*: Watson-Publications and Xerox Press.
[35] William, R. (2008). *The Non-Designer's Design and Type Books* (Deluxe Ed.). Berkeley: Peachip Press.
[36] Zachrisson, B. (1965). *Studies in the Legibility of Printed Text*. Stockholm: Almqvist and Wiksell.
[37] Zramdini, A. & Ingold, R. (1998). Optical font recognition using typographical features. *IEEE Transactions on Pattern Analysis And Machine Intelligence*, **20**(8), 877–882.

Chapter 2

Chinese Handwriting Database Building and Benchmarking

Cheng-Lin Liu, Fei Yin, Da-Han Wang, Qiu-Feng Wang, Liang Xu and Xu-Yao Zhang

National Laboratory of Pattern Recognition,
Institute of Automation of Chinese Academy of Sciences,
Beijing 100190, China
{liucl, fyin, xyz}@nlpr.ia.ac.cn

This chapter introduces a series of online and offline Chinese handwriting datasets built by the Institute of Automation of the Chinese Academy of Sciences (CASIA), containing samples of isolated characters and handwritten texts. The samples were produced by 1,020 writers using Anoto pen on papers, such that both online trajectory data and offline image data were obtained. The offline samples and online samples are stored in the offline database CASIA-HWDB and the online database CASIA-OLHWDB, respectively. Both the CASIA-HWDB and the CASIA-OLHWDB are divided into six datasets, three for isolated characters (versions 1.0–1.2) and three for handwritten texts (versions 2.0–2.2). The (either online or offline) datasets of isolated characters contain about 3.9 million samples of 7,356 classes (7,185 Chinese characters and 171 alphanumerics and symbols), while the datasets of handwritten texts contain about 5,090 pages and 1.35 million character samples. Each dataset is segmented and annotated at character level, and is partitioned into standard training and test sets. We suggest using the databases for research of handwritten document segmentation, character recognition, text line recognition, document retrieval, writer adaptation and writer identification. The generalization ability of the datasets was demonstrated in a preliminary evaluation of isolated character recognition. Based on the datasets and an additional test set, we held three competitions of handwritten character and text line recognition in conferences CCPR 2010, ICDAR 2011 and ICDAR 2013. The competition results show constant progress over time and offer benchmarks for Chinese handwriting recognition research.

1. Introduction

Handwritten character recognition and document analysis have been studied intensively since the 1960s. Many effective methods and algorithms have been proposed and successful applications have been found in diverse areas. However, the recognition of unconstrained handwriting remains a great challenge: the performance of text line segmentation, word/character segmentation and recognition is still behind the human recognition capability. For the design and evaluation of handwriting recognition algorithms and systems, the availability of large-scale, unconstrained handwriting database is very important. For Chinese handwriting recognition, because of the large number of character classes (over 5,000 characters are frequently used), a large sample database is more demanding.

In the past decades, a number of databases in different languages have been published and have significantly benefited the research. Most of the databases are of offline data (images converted from paper documents). Among them are the CENPARMI digits dataset,[1] CEDAR database of English words and characters,[2] NIST handprinted forms and characters database,[3] IAM English sentence database,[4] Japanese Kanji character databases ETL8B and ETL9B, Korean database PE92,[5] Indian database of ISI,[6] Arabic databases,[7] Farsi databases,[8] Chinese databases HCL2000[9] and HIT-MW,[10] and so on. Databases of online handwritten data (trajectory data of strokes) are not so popular because the collection of online data relies on special devices like digitizing tablet, tablet PC and digital pen. Among them are the UNIPEN project,[11] the Japanese online handwriting databases Kuchibue and Nakayosi,[12] and the very recent Chinese online handwriting databases SCUT-COUCH2009[13] and HIT-OR3C.[14] The French database IRONOFF contains both online and offline data, collected by attaching paper on digitizing tablet during writing.[15]

A general trend of handwriting recognition is the transition from isolated character recognition to script recognition and from constrained writing to unconstrained writing. The existing Chinese handwriting databases do not satisfy this trend: they are either too neat in writing quality or not large enough. The offline databases HCL2000 and previous CASIA (a subset of a large dataset collected by the Institute of Automation of CAS around 1990), both containing isolated character images of 3,755 categories, have been reported test accuracies higher than 98%,[16,17] indicating low challenge. Some large datasets were used only privately.[18] The database HIT-MW is the first one of Chinese handwritten texts, but has only 853 page images containing 186,444 characters, and the text images were not segmented and annotated. The online database SCUT-COUCH2009 consists of 11 datasets of isolated characters (Chinese simplified and traditional, English letters, digits and symbols), Chinese Pinyin and words. It is comprehensive and large, but all the samples were produced by only 195 writers. Another online database HIT-OR3C contains character sample of 6,825 categories produced by 122 persons and handwritten texts of 10 articles produced by 20 persons.

This chapter introduces a new series of Chinese handwriting datasets built by the National Laboratory of Pattern Recognition (NLPR), Institute of Automation of Chinese Academy of Sciences (CASIA). The handwritten samples were produced by 1,020 writers using Anoto pen on papers, such that both online and offline data were obtained. The samples include both isolated characters and handwritten texts (continuous scripts). We collected data from writers from 2007 to 2010, and completed the segmentation and annotation of the data in 2010. A portion of online handwritten characters in the database called CASIA-OLHWDB1 (now called as CASIA-OLHWDB1.0), have been released at ICDAR 2009.[19] The new series include six datasets of online data and six datasets of offline data, in each case, three for isolated characters (versions 1.0–1.2) and three for handwritten texts (versions 2.0–2.2). The offline datasets and online datasets are stored in the offline database CASIA-HWDB and the online database CASIA-OLHWDB, respectively. In either online or offline case, the datasets of isolated characters contain about 3.9 million samples of 7,356 classes (7,185 Chinese characters and 171 alphanumerics and symbols), and the datasets of handwritten texts contain about 5,090 pages and 1.35 million character samples. All the data has been segmented and annotated at character level, and each dataset is partitioned into standard training and test sets.

Because of the large category set, availability of both characters and page images, annotation level and writer-specific storage of our datasets, we suggest that they can be used for research of handwritten document segmentation, character recognition, text line recognition, document retrieval, writer adaptation and writer identification. To demonstrate the generalization ability of the datasets, we conducted a preliminary evaluation of isolated character recognition to show that character classifiers trained with the CASIA datasets generalize well to previous datasets.

A preliminary description of our databases was presented in Ref. 20 and the data has been used for training classifiers in the Chinese

Handwriting Recognition Competitions in CCPR2010,[21] ICDAR2011[22] and ICDAR2013.[23] This paper extends the description with more details of database building, analysis and adds the results of preliminary evaluation. We also summarize the results in the competitions to show the constant progress in this field.

In the rest of this chapter, we describe the data collection settings in Section 2, the annotation process in Section 3, the statistics of datasets in Section 4, and give suggestions of database usage for research in Section 5, present a preliminary evaluation in Section 6, summarize the competition results in Section 7, and finally, conlcude the paper in Section 8.

2. Data Collection Settings

For handwriting data collection, we should first specify the target characters and texts to write, design template pages for writing, and after writing, segment and label the characters using annotation tools.

2.1. *Character sets*

We requested each writer to write a set of isolated characters (in given form with considerable spacing) and five pages of continuous texts (given texts without format constraints). The isolated characters cover the most frequently used characters in daily life, most of the texts are from Internet news and a few are from ancient poems.

The total number of Chinese characters is very large, e.g., the standard set GB18030-2000 contains 27,533 characters, which are not yet exhausted. We estimate that the number of daily used characters is about 5,000, which is almost the maximum that ordinary educated people can recognize. Many characters of low frequencies are used only for the names of persons and places or in ancient Chinese language. For our handwriting data collection, we compiled a character set based on the standard sets GB2312-80 and Modern Chinese Character List of Common Use (Common Set in brief).[24] The GB2312-80 contains 6,763 Chinese characters, including 3,755 in level-1 set and 3,008 in level-2 set. The Common Set contains 7,000 Chinese characters. Both the two sets have an appreciable number of characters that are unfamiliar to ordinary people. We nevertheless collected the union of the two sets, containing 7,170 characters, for possible recognition of practical documents.

We also referred to the Frequency List of Ref. 25 to validate our character set. We extracted the 7,000 leading characters (accumulating 99.995% of frequency) in the Frequency List and analyzed the intersection with the GB2312-80 and the Common Set. From Table 1, we can see that the three sets are largely overlapping. The difference set of Frequency List from the other two sets consists mostly of traditional Chinese characters while the other two sets contain only simplified characters. We therefore took the union of GB2312-80 and Common Set, and further added 15 characters that we met in our reading experience, to make a target set of 7,185 Chinese characters. In addition to the Chinese characters, we also collected a set of 171 symbols, including 52 English letters, 10 digits, and some frequently used punctuation marks, mathematics and physical symbols. The total number of character classes is thus $7,185 + 171 = 7,356$.

Table 1. Intersection statistics of three character sets.

Intersection	#characters
GB2312-80 & Common	6,593
GB2312-80 & Frequency	6,494
Common & Frequency	6,452
Intersect three sets	6,393

For collecting handwritten texts, we asked each writer to hand-copy five texts. We compiled three sets of texts (referred to as versions V1–V3), mostly downloaded from news Web pages except there are five texts of ancient Chinese poems in both V1 and V2. Each set contains 50 texts, each containing 150–370 characters. The three sets were used in different stages of handwriting data collection. The texts in each set were further divided into 10 subsets (referred to as templates T1–T10), each containing five texts to be written by one writer. Our analysis in Section 4 show that less than 0.15% of characters in the texts are out of the 7,356 classes of our isolated character set. This implies a character classifier trained using our isolated character datasets is sufficient to be used in handwritten text recognition.

2.2. *Data collection*

We collected handwriting data in three stages using three sets (versions) of templates. Each set has 10 templates to be written by 10 writers. A template has 13–15 pages of isolated characters and five pages of texts. For a template set, the isolated characters are divided into three groups:

symbols, frequent Chinese and low frequency Chinese. The symbols are always on the first page, followed by Chinese characters. The first six templates of a set print the same group of frequent Chinese characters in six different orders by rotating six equal parts, and the last four templates print the low frequency Chinese characters in four different orders. We rotated the same group of characters because people write a large number of characters with gradually changing quality in different time intervals. Rotation guarantees that each character is written equally in different time intervals. In addition, each template has five pages of different texts, which were printed on the pages following the isolated characters.

The three sets (versions) of templates are summarized in Table 2. V1 and V3 have the same set of isolated characters. The number of isolated Chinese characters in V1 and V3 is actually 7,184, not 7,185, because the templates of V1 were designed earliest. The templates of V3 inherited the isolated character set of V1 and updated the texts. The isolated Chinese character set of each version is split into a frequent set (in T1–T6) and a non-frequent set (in T7–T10). The frequent set of V1 and V3 is actually the level-1 set of GB2312-80, which was commonly taken as a standard set of Chinese character recognition research.

Table 2. Summary of templates. In each row, pages/symbols/Chinese are for one template, while texts/chars are for multiple templates.

Version	Template	#pages	#symbols	#Chinese	#texts/chars
V1	T1–T6	20	171	3,755	30/7,464
	T7–T10	19	171	3,429	20/4,918
V2	T1–T6	20	171	3,866	30/7,802
	T7–T10	18	171	3,319	20/5,196
V3	T1–T6	20	171	3,755	30/9,039
	T7–T10	19	171	3,429	20/6,016

For handwriting data collection using Anoto pen, all the template pages were printed on papers with dot pattern. On the printed template pages, each isolated character was written in the space below the pre-printed character, and each text was written on a separate page with the template text printed in the upper part. During writing, the online (temporal) data (coordinates, time and pressure of sampled stroke points) were recorded by the Anoto pen and later transmitted to computers. For offline data collection, the handwritten pages were scanned (in resolution of 300DPI) to obtain color images, which were segmented and labeled using annotation tools. Figure 1 shows two scanned pages of isolated characters and handwritten text, respectively.

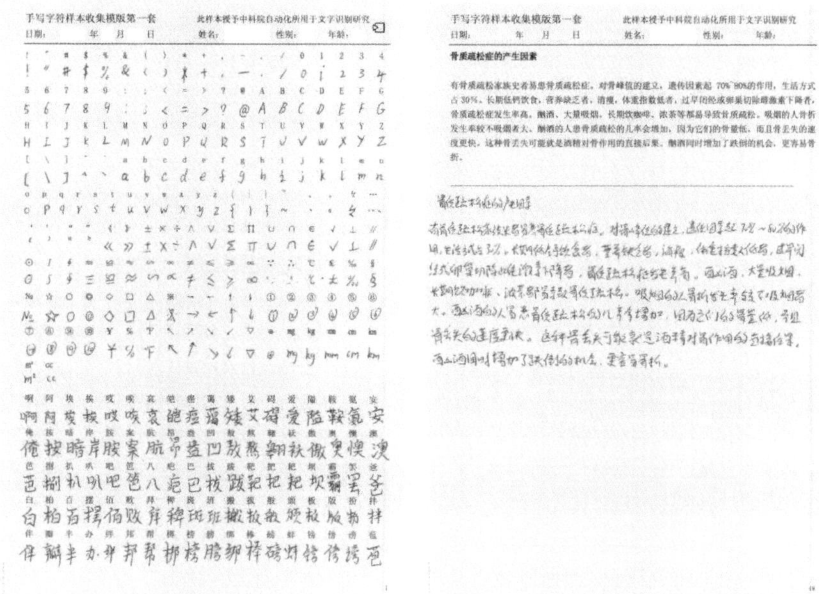

(a) (b)

Figure 1. Scanned pages of isolated characters and handwritten text.

3. Data Annotation

For segmenting and labeling characters in the online trajectory data and offline page images, we prepared annotation software tools and hired some people to process the data. We have different processing steps for online and offline data, and different steps for isolated character data and handwritten text data. In the following, we mainly describe the steps for offline data, while the steps for online data are similar.

For preparing annotation, the transcript characters (in GB codes) of each page (either online or offline, either isolated character or text) are ordered in the same layout as the handwritten page. For each page, the transcript (stored in a text file) has the same number of lines as the handwritten page, and the corresponding lines in the transcript and the handwriting have the same number of characters.

3.1. *Annotation of offline data*

From a scanned handwritten page, we need to first separate the handwritten characters from the background dots (pre-printed Anoto dot pattern) and the printed characters. We used two linear discriminant analysis (LDA) classifiers for pixel classification to separate the characters from background dots and separating handwriting from printed characters, respectively. The training data was extracted from some page images by global gray-scale thresholding and interactive removal of printed characters. For separation between characters and background, each pixel is extracted six features: the RGB values of the pixel and the average RGB values in 3×3 neighborhood. For separation between handwritten and printed characters, the pixel features are the RGB values and the average RGB values in a larger neighborhood. After two steps of pixel classification, the pixels of handwritten characters are stored in a gray-scale image, which then undergoes character segmentation and labeling. Figure 2 shows a handwritten text image extracted from the scanned page of Figure 1(b).

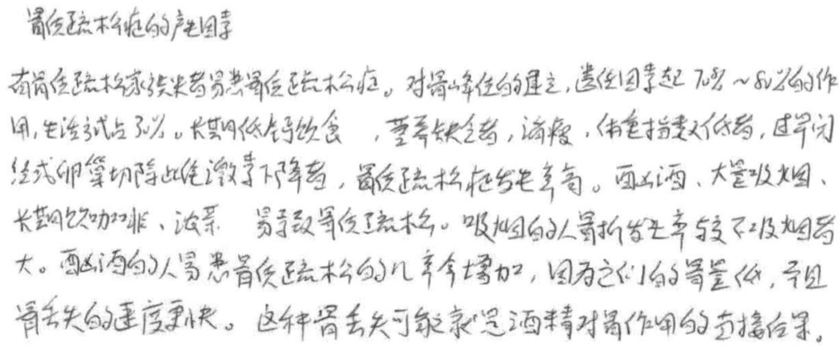

Figure 2. A handwritten text image extracted from scanned page by removing background and printed characters.

For pages of isolated characters, since the handwritten characters are approximately evenly placed with large gaps, we simply segmented the lines according to horizontal projection and segmented the characters according to between-character gaps. If the number of lines or the number of characters in each line is inconsistent with the transcript, the human operator will be reminded to correct the segmentation errors. The character labels in the transcript will then be attached to the segmented characters. Mis-written characters were labeled with a special tag by the human operator.

For pages of handwritten texts, we used the annotation tool developed by our group.[26] The handwritten document image is first segmented into text lines using a connected component clustering-based algorithm, and mis-segmented text lines are corrected by the human operator. For each text line, the handwritten line image (sequence of connected components) is matched with the transcript character string, whereby the connected components are grouped into characters and each character is aligned with a character (as label) in the transcript string. For separating touching characters (two or more characters contained in the same connected component), we used some heuristics to find candidate segmentation points, which are verified in transcript mapping. After transcript mapping, mis-segmentation and mis-labels were corrected by human operators and mis-written characters were labeled with a special tag. Figure 3 shows an example of character segmentation and labeling by transcript mapping.

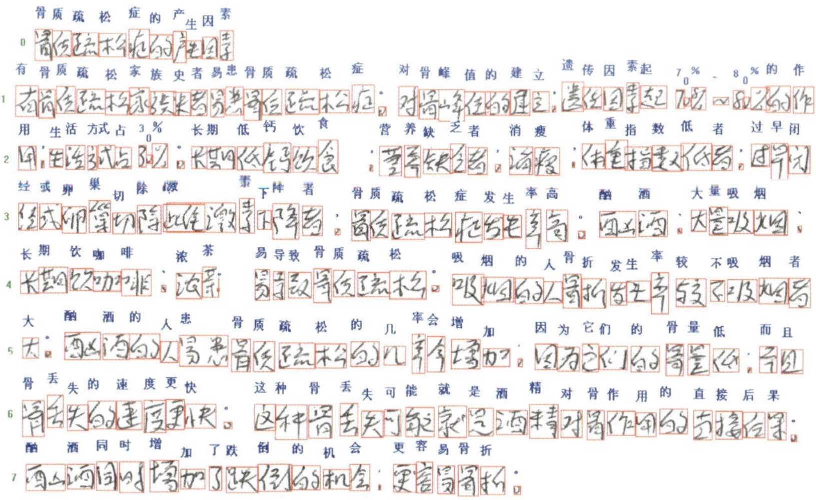

Figure 3. Annotation result by text line transcript mapping for the image of Figure 2. Each segmented character image is attached a label above it.

In both isolated characters and handwritten texts, when a written character is different from the corresponding character in the transcript, this is a kind of mis-writing, but if the written character is a legal character, we still retain it and attach its true class label.

3.2. *Annotation of online data*

The segmentation and labeling of isolated characters in online data (as described in Ref. 19) is similar to that for offline data. The main difference is that, in addition to the spatial information, the temporal information of pen lift between adjacent strokes is also used for text line and character segmentation.

The annotation of online handwritten text pages is also similar to that for offline data. A difference is that the online handwriting data recorded by Anoto pen does not mix any preprint information, and the pen lift information is used to better segment text lines and characters. For separating connected characters (two or more characters are connected without pen lift between them), selected strokes are split by combining spatial and temporal information.

3.3. *Data format*

We stored all the annotated data in writer-specific files named after the index number of writers. The online isolated character samples of each writer are stored in a file named xxx.POT (xxx is the writer index), and the offline character samples are stored in a file named xxx.GNT. A POT file stores multiple online character samples sequentially. Each sample has a record for total number of bytes, the class label (4-byte GB code), the number of strokes, and sequence of (x, y) coordinates of stroke points with (-1,0) denoting pen lift. A GNT file stores multiple gray-scale character images sequentially. Each image has a record for total number of bytes, the class label (2-byte GB code), the width and height, and the bitmap (one byte per pixel). The gray-scale image has background pixels uniformly labeled as 255, and so, can be easily converted to binary image.

The handwritten text data are stored in files one per page, named after writer index-page number. The page number ranges in 16–20 for templates T1–T6 of V1–V3, 15–19 for templates T7–T10 of V1 and V3, and 14–18 for templates T7–T10 of V2. The online text data of a page is stored in a file named xxx-Pyy.PTTS (yy is the page number), and the offline text data of a page is stored in a file named xxx-Pyy.DGR. A PTTS file first stores all the strokes of a page, each stroke as a sequence of (x, y) coordinates, then comes the number of lines and the records of lines. The record of a line includes the number of strokes and the index numbers of strokes, and then the number of characters and the records of characters. The record of a character includes its label (4-byte GB code), number of strokes and the index numbers of strokes. For offline data, a DGR file stores the sequence of text line images. The record of a text line includes the number of characters and the label (2-byte GB code), position and image of each character. From the records of text lines and characters, both the online and offline page layout can be easily recovered.

4. Statistics of Datasets

Until 2010, we collected the online and offline handwriting data of 1,280 writers, among which 760 used the templates of V2, 520 used the templates of V1 and V3 (see Table 2). We divided the isolated character samples of V2 into two datasets: (regardless of online/offline) DB1.0 (templates T1–T6) and DB1.2 (templates T7–T10). The online version of DB1.0, CASIA-OLHWDB1.0 in full name, is the one that we released in 2009.[19] The 420 writers in DB1.0 were selected from the original 456 writers according to the percentage of legally written characters.[19] Similarly, for DB1.2 we selected 300 writers of high percentage of legal characters from the original 304 writers of V2 templates T7–T10. We formed isolated character datasets DB1.1 and DB1.3 from the data of V1 and V3. The writers of DB1.1 include the 66 writers of V1 templates T1–T6 and selected 234 writers from the original 246 writers of V3 templates T1–T6. The writers of DB1.3 include the 44 writers of V1 templates T7–T10 and selected 156 writers from the original 164 writers of V3 templates T7–T10. Note that V1 and V3 have the same templates of isolated characters but different texts.

Having formed the isolated character datasets DB1.0–1.3, we formed the handwritten text datasets DB2.0–2.3 using the text data of the same writers of DB1.0–1.3. Specifically, the DB2.0 contains the handwritten text data of 420 writers of V2 templates T1–T6, DB2.2 contains the handwritten text data of 300 writers of V2 templates T7–T10, DB2.1 contains the handwritten text data of 66 writers of V1 templates T1–T6 and 234 writers of V3 templates T1–T6, and DB2.3 contains the handwritten text data of 44 writers of V1 templates T7–T10 and 156 writers of V3 templates T7–T10. Note that DB2.1 and DB2.3 have more diverse texts than DB2.0 and DB2.2, because they were constructed from two sets of templates V1 and V3.

In total, we obtained eight datasets for either online or offline handwriting: isolated character datasets DB1.0–1.3 and handwritten text datasets DB2.0–2.3. Totally 1,220 writers contributed the data: 420 writers for DB1.0 and DB2.0, 300 writers for DB1.1 and DB2.1, 300 writers for DB1.2

and DB2.2, and 200 writers for DB1.3 and DB2.3. The set of Chinese characters in DB1.0 (3,866 classes) and that of DB1.1 (3,755 classes, level-1 set of GB2312-80) both consist of high frequency Chinese characters, and they have a large overlap of 3,740 characters. Thus, it is appropriate to use DB1.0 and DB1.1 for benchmarking isolated character recognition. The set of Chinese characters in DB1.2 (3,319 classes) is a disjoint set of DB1.0, and is a good supplement to DB1.0 and DB1.1 for training character classifiers for very large category set. The union of Chinese character classes in DB1.0–1.2 has 7,185 classes.

Since the isolated character datasets DB1.0–1.2 are sufficient for character recognition of very large category set, we release DB1.0–1.2 and their corresponding handwritten text datasets DB2.0–2.2 for academic research. The handwritten sample data in these datasets was contributed by 1,020 writers. We keep the DB1.3 and DB2.3, containing handwriting data of 200 writers, for private and industrial purposes.

The released datasets of online data are named as OLHWDB1.0–1.2 (isolated characters) and OLHWDB2.0–2.2 (handwritten texts). The released datasets of offline data are named as HWDB1.0–1.2 (isolated characters) and HWDB2.0–2.2 (handwritten texts). The numbers of writers, character samples (including symbols and Chinese character samples/classes) of the isolated character datasets are summarized in Table 3. We can see that for either online or offline data, the three datasets have about 3.9 million character samples and the number of Chinese character classes is as large as 7,185. Including the 171 symbol classes, the total number of classes is 7,356.

Table 3. Statistics of isolated character datasets.

Dataset	#writers	#character samples		
		total	symbol	Chinese/#class
OLHWDB1.0	420	1,694,741	71,806	1,622,935/3,866
OLHWDB1.1	300	1,174,364	51,232	1,123,132/3,755
OLHWDB1.2	300	1,042,912	51,181	991,731/3,319
Total	1,020	3,912,017	174,219	3,737,798/7,185
HWDB1.0	420	1,680,258	71,122	1,609,136/3,866
HWDB1.1	300	1,172,907	51,158	1,121,749/3,755
HWDB1.2	300	1,041,970	50,981	990,989/3,319
Total	1,020	3,895,135	173,261	3,721,874/7,185

In the handwritten text datasets, each writer originally contributed five pages of texts. Due to the occasional failure of online trajectory data capturing, low intensity of strokes in scanned image or our mistakes in managing the data, some pages of online or offline data of a few writers were lost. So, OLHWDB2.2 contains the online data of 299 (not 300) writers, HWDB2.0 contains the offline data of 419 (not 420) writers, and the average number of pages retained per writer is also smaller than five. The numbers of writers, pages, lines and segmented character samples/classes are summarized in Table 4. We can see that for either online or offline data, the three handwritten text datasets contain nearly 1.35 million segmented characters and the number of character classes involved is over 2,600. DB2.1 involves more character classes than DB2.0 and DB2.2 because it was constructed from two sets of templates V1 and V3 and has 60 different texts, while DB2.0 and DB2.2 have 30 and 20 different texts, respectively. Though the online and offline data were produced by the same writers using the same templates, the number of character classes differs considerably (2,655 vs 2,703) between online and offline data. This is because the online and offline datasets have different missing pages, and even from the same handwritten text page, the online and offline data may have different missing characters (trajectory capturing failure and low intensity of scanning happen asynchronously) and different mis-labeling. However, the differing classes have very few samples.

Ordinary texts mostly consist of high frequency characters, but there are still a few rare characters in the handwritten text datasets. Some of the characters are even beyond the set of 7,356 classes of our isolated character datasets. We call these samples as out-of-class (OOC) samples. The numbers of OOC samples are shown in Table 4. Compared to the total number of character samples, the number of OOC samples (3,947 in total) is very small, occupying only 0.146% of the segmented characters.

Table 4. Statistics of handwritten text datasets. OOC: out-of-class samples.

Dataset	#writers	#pages	#lines	#character/#class	#OOC
OLHWDB2.0	420	2,098	20,574	540,009/1,214	1,283
OLHWDB2.1	300	1,500	17,282	429,083/2,256	225
OLHWDB2.2	299	1,494	14,365	379,812/1,303	581
Total	1,019	5,092	52,221	1,348,969/2,655	2,088
HWDB2.0	419	2,092	20,495	538,868/1,222	1,106
HWDB2.1	300	1,500	17,292	429,553/2,310	172
HWDB2.2	300	1,499	14,443	380,993/1,331	581
Total	1,019	5,091	52,230	1,349,414/2,703	1,859

5. Recommendations of Usage

The CASIA series of Chinese handwriting datasets have some favorable merits for handwriting recognition research: (1) That online and offline data were produced concurrently by the same group of writers enables recognition by combining online and offline data; (2) Both isolated character data and handwritten text data are available; (3) The storage of data samples in writer-specific files enables utilizing writer's individuality in recognition and writer identification; (4) The offline samples are recorded in gray-scale images, which enables accurate analysis of handwriting features.

We concede that the diversity of texts in the CASIA databases is not large, especially, the datasets DB2.0 and DB2.2, involving a large number of 720 writers, cover only 50 different texts. The dataset DB2.1 covers 60 different texts but involves a smaller number of 300 writers. Nevertheless, the diversity of texts does not influence the validity of handwritten text recognition performance if the language model is not estimated from the texts of the handwriting database. Actually, the language model is necessarily to be estimated from a general text corpus of huge size (usually tens of million characters).

For using the datasets for research, we recommend standard partitioning into training and test sets, and propose some research scenarios.

5.1. *Data partitioning*

We previously partitioned the OLHWDB1.0 dataset into a training set of 350 writers and a test set of 70 writers.[19] For uniform ratio in different datasets, we later reset the ratio of training writers and test writers as 4:1. The same partitioning of writers is taken between online and offline datasets and between isolated characters and handwritten texts datasets. In the following, we detail the partitioning of DB1.0–1.2, while DB2.0–2.2 follow the same partitioning of writers.

Following our previous file naming of OLHWDB1.0, the writers were numbered in deceasing order of re-substitution accuracies and divided into three grades. From each grade, 1/5 of writers are randomly selected for testing and the remaining 4/5 writers are used for training. We provide the users the lists of writer index numbers for training data and test data. The offline dataset HWDB1.0 (with the same writers as OLHWDB1.0) follows the same partitioning.

For the datasets DB1.1 and DB1.2, we did not sort the writers according to the writing quality or recognition accuracy, but directly selected a percentage of writers randomly from each template (T1–T6 of V1 and V3, T7–T10 of V2) such that different templates have the same ratio of training and test writers. Since the templates T1–T6 of V1 and the templates T1–T6 of V3 have the same set of isolated characters and we did not differentiate V1 and V3 in partitioning the writers, the text templates in V1 and V3 (for datasets DB2.1 and DB2.2) do not necessarily have the same ratio of training and test writers in the partitioning. For the datasets DB1.1 and DB1.2, DB2.1 and DB2.2, both the training writers and test writers are indexed as consecutive numbers, unlike that the index numbers of test writers in DB1.0 are not consecutive in 1–420.

The distribution of writers in different templates in datasets DB1.0–1.2 is shown in Table 5. We can see that the training set and test set of each dataset have approximately same number of writers for different templates. The handwritten text datasets DB2.0–2.2 have the same writers with DB1.0–1.2, but OLHWDB2.2 has a missing training writer of template V2-T9, and the HWDB2.0 has a missing test writer of template V2-T3.

Table 5. Distribution of templates in datasets.

Dataset	Partition	Templates		#writers per template	total
DB1.0	Train	V2	T1–T6	55:52:54:57:57:61	336
	Test	V2	T1–T6	14:14:14:14:14:14	84
DB1.1	Train	V1	T1–T6	9:8:8:10:9:9	53
		V3	T1–T6	31:32:32:30:31:31	187
	Test	V1	T1–T6	2:3:3:1:2:2	13
		V3	T1–T6	8:7:7:9:8:8	47
DB1.2	Train	V2	T7–T10	60:60:60:60	240
	Test	V2	T7–T10	15:15:15:15	60

5.2. *Research scenarios*

Based on the CASIA series of handwriting datasets, some typical research tasks of handwritten document analysis can be performed. Our recommendations are as follows.

5.2.1. *Handwritten document segmentation*

The segmentation of (either online or offline) handwritten documents into text lines is a challenge since the handwritten text lines are often curved, skewed and sometimes interfered. Our datasets contain handwritten text pages produced by a large number of writers without instructions of format. There are 5,092 online text pages and 5,091 offline text pages in total. All the pages have ground-truths of text lines, and hence, are convenient for training and evaluating text line segmentation algorithms.

5.2.2. *Handwritten character recognition*

This is a traditional problem, but is not solved yet. The accuracy of unconstrained handwritten character recognition is yet to be improved, either as alone or used in character string recognition. For either online or offline handwritten character recognition, our datasets contain large number of samples of alphanumeric characters and symbols (171 classes, nearly 1,020 samples per class), and particularly, Chinese characters of large category set (7,185 classes). If the research focus is isolated Chinese character recognition, we recommend to use the datasets DB1.0 and DB1.1. The Chinese character set of DB1.1 (3,755 classes as in the level-1 set of GB2312-80) is commonly used in Chinese character recognition research. The DB1.0 has 3,740 Chinese character classes overlapping with the DB1.1, such that each of these 3,740 classes has nearly 720 samples. Merging the samples of 3,755 classes in DB1.0 and DB1.1 enables classifier training with large sample set and the evaluation of variable sample size.

5.2.3. *Text line recognition*

Character string recognition is the central task of handwritten text recognition because characters cannot be reliably segmented prior to character recognition. In Chinese handwriting, this amounts to text line recognition because a text line cannot be segmented into words prior to recognition. A feasible approach for character string recognition of large character set is the integrated segmentation-recognition approach based on over segmentation. Candidate characters are generated in over segmentation and are then verified by character classifier, language model and geometric context model. The isolated character datasets DB1.0–1.2 can be used to train a character classifier of large category set (7,356 classes). The geometric context model can be estimated from the training documents in DB2.0–2.2, and the language model is generally estimated from a corpus of pure texts. Finally, the performance of text line recognition is evaluated on the test documents in DB2.0–2.2. The text lines in our datasets have been segmented and labeled at character level, such that character segmentation performance can also be evaluated.

Handwritten text recognition can also be performed at page (or paragraph) level by combining the contextual information of multiple lines.

5.2.4. *Handwritten document retrieval*

The handwritten text pages in our datasets have been segmented into text lines and labeled at character level. In addition to text line segmentation and text line recognition research, the datasets can also be used for document retrieval, including keyword spotting, handwritten text categorization and content-based retrieval. The researcher can utilize the text line segmentation ground-truth in the datasets to focus on the retrieval task. As for text line recognition, document retrieval algorithms are recommended to be trained on the training documents in DB2.0–2.2, and evaluated on the test documents in DB2.0–2.2.

5.2.5. *Writer adaptation*

A merit of our datasets is that all the samples are stored in writer-specific files named after the writer index number. This ensures that all the samples in the same file are from the same writer and the writer index of each sample is known. This facilitates the research and evaluation of writer adaptation, which is necessary in handwriting recognition because even a large set of training samples cannot guarantee covering all writing styles and the writing style of a writer may vary in different writing conditions. Our datasets can be used for both supervised adaptation (on labeled samples) and unsupervised adaptation (on unlabeled/test samples). When a set of characters are written by the same writer (as in a handwritten text line or a page), the style consistency among characters (or called style context)[27] can help adapt the recognizer. Writer adaptation is particularly useful when we apply character classifiers trained with the isolated character samples to character string recognition, because the writing style of a character varies considerably from isolation to linguistic context.

5.2.6. *Writer identification*

In our datasets, each writer has five handwritten text pages. Though the multiple pages of a writer were written with little time interval, different pages of a writer still show certain degree of within-class style variation. We can perform experiments to judge whether two pages are from the same writer or not (writer verification) or classify a test page to a nearest reference page of known writer (writer identification). We can extract either text-dependent or text-independent features for writer verification/identification. The handwritten text datasets DB2.0–2.2 cover 22 unique templates (V2 templates T1–T10, V1 templates T1–T6 and V3 templates T1–T6) and 110 unique texts. The match of writers of different templates is totally text-independent. For the writers of the same template (five texts), the match between pages of same text is text-dependent, while the match between different texts is text-independent.

6. Preliminary Evaluation

To demonstrate the generalization ability of our datasets, we performed experiments of isolated handwritten Chinese character recognition by cross testing DB1.1 with previous datasets. Our isolated character datasets DB1.1 have Chinese character samples of 3,755 classes, as the level-1 set of GB2312-80 (also called GB1). There have been other datasets for samples of this character set, such as the previous CASIA offline handwritten Chinese character database[17,28] (called CASIA0.1 hereon), the HCL2000 database,[9] the online databases SCUT-COUCH2009[13] and HIT-OR3C.[14] The offline character database HCL2000 contains normalized character images of standard size, which precludes algorithm design for the important normalization step. Hence, we cross tested our offline dataset HWDB1.1 with the CASIA0.1, which contains 300 character samples per class. For online character recognition, the GB1 dataset of SCUT-COUCH2009 (called SCUT-GB1 hereon) contains 188 samples per class, and the HIT-OR3C contains character samples of 122 writers. The bigger dataset of SCUT-GB1 was cross tested with our dataset OLHWDB1.1.

In offline handwritten Chinese character recognition, we implemented the normalization-cooperated gradient feature extraction method[28] combined with pseudo two-dimensional normalization by line density projection interpolation,[29] and used the modified quadratic discriminant function (MQDF)[30] for classification. The 512D feature vector was reduced to 160D by Fisher linear discriminant analysis (FLDA), the MQDF uses 50 principal eigenvectors per class and the unified minor eigenvalue was selected by holdout cross validation on training data. From the HWDB1.1, the 897,758 samples of 240 specified training writers were used for training, and the 223,991 samples of the remaining 60 writers were used for testing. From the CASIA0.1, the 938,750 samples of 250 writers were used for training and the 187,750 samples of 50 writers were use for testing. Since the

CASIA0.1 has only binary images, we used binarized images rather than the gray-scale images from HWDB1.1.

The test accuracies of offline character recognition are shown in Table 6. We can see that when the training data and test data are from the same dataset, HWDB1.1 obtained test accuracy 87.87% and the CASIA0.1 obtained a high accuracy 98.54%. This indicates that the new dataset HWDB1.1 is much more challenging. When testing using classifier trained with a different dataset, the test accuracy of CASIA0.1, 96.49%, drops slightly compared to its highest accuracy 98.53%. However, the test accuracy of HWDB1.1 drops drastically from 87.87% to 78.36%. This indicates that the new dataset HWDB1.1 has better generalization ability in the sense that the classifier trained on it generalizes well to the previous dataset CASIA0.1.

Table 6. Cross test accuracies of offline handwritten character recognition.

	Training data		
	HWDB1.1	CASIA0.1	1.1+0.1
HWDB1.1	87.87%	78.36%	87.83%
CASIA0.1	96.49%	98.53%	98.61%

In online handwritten Chinese character recognition, we implemented the normalization-cooperated direction feature extraction method of Ref. 31 combined with pseudo two-dimensional bi-moment normalization, and also used the MQDF for classification. Feature dimensionality reduction and MQDF parameter learning follow the way of offline character recognition as above. From the OLHWDB1.1, the 898,573 samples of the 240 training writers were used for training, and the 224,559 samples of 60 writers were used for testing. From the SCUT-GB1, we followed[13] to randomly select 20% samples per class (141,188 in total) for testing and the remaining 564,752 samples for training.

The test accuracies of online character recognition are shown in Table 7. We can see that when the training data and test data are from the same dataset, OLHWDB1.1 obtained test accuracy 92.22% and the SCUT-GB1 obtained test accuracy 94.96%. This indicates that the new dataset OLHWDB1.1 is more challenging than the SCUT-GB1. When testing using classifier trained with a different dataset, the test accuracy of SCUT-GB1, 92.62%, drops slightly compared to 94.96%. One the contrary, the test accuracy of OLHWDB1.1 drops considerably from 92.22% to 84.31%. This indicates that the new dataset OLHWDB1.1 has better generalization ability in the sense that the classifier trained on it generalizes well to a different dataset SCUT-GB1 (GB1 set of SCUT-COUCH2009).

Table 7. Cross test accuracies of online handwritten character recognition.

	Training data		
	OLHWDB1.1	SCUT-GB1	CASIA+SCUT
OLHWDB1.1	92.22%	84.31%	92.50%
SCUT-GB1	92.62%	94.96%	95.68%

In addition, some recognition results using the databases CASIA-HWDB and CASIA-OLHWDB have been published. The evaluation of online and offline isolated Chinese character recognition methods on DB1.0 and DB1.1 can be found in Ref. 32. Results of offline and online Chinese handwritten text recognition can be found in Refs. 33 and 34, respectively. Some works of handwritten keyword spotting have been done on the offline database[37] and online database[38] as well.

7. Competition Results

Based on the databases CASIA-HWDB and CASIA-OLHWDB, we organzied three competitions of Chinese Handwriting Recognition in CCPR 2010,[21] ICDAR 2011,[22] and ICDAR 2013,[23] respectively. In addition to the released datasets DB1.0–DB1.2 and DB2.0–2.2, we also prepared test datasets of 60 additional writers for evaluation in competitions. The competition test datasets were kept private until the ICDAR 2013 competition, and were published after that for research purpose. The competition test sets of isolated characters contain 224,590 online samples and 224,419 offline samples, both within the 3,755 classes of GB2312-80 level-1 set. The test set of handwritten texts has 300 pages, containing 3,432 text lines. The online text dataset has 91,576 characters of 1,375 classes, while the offline text dataset has 91,563 characters of 1,385 classes. The character class sets were not published in the competitions, so, the recognition systems must consider larger character set like the whole set of 7,356 classes in CASIA-HWDB/OLHWDB. The competition participants mostly used the published CASIA-HWDB/OLHWDB databases for training classifiers.

For isolated character recognition, the performance metric is the correct rate of character classification. For handwritten text recognition, the segmented text lines were presented to the recognizers, and performance was evaluate in respect of character correct rate (CR) and accurate rate

(AR). To calculate, the recognition output text of each text line is aligned with the ground-truth by dynamic programming. Then, the percentage of correctly aligned ground-truth characters is the CR, and the percentage of (correctly aligned characters minus inserted characters) is the AR.

The CCPR 2010 competition received nine systems from four groups for participating two tasks (online and offline isolated character recognition). The ICDAR 2011 competition received 25 systems from eight groups participating four tasks (isolated character recognition and text line recognition). The ICDAR 2013 competition received 27 systems from 10 groups participating five tasks (isolated character recognition and text line recognition, as well as character classification with given feature data).

In Table 8, we list the correct rates of the best performing systems in three competitions and other published results on the same test dataset. Comparing the best results of three competitions, we can see constant progress of performance over time. Particularly, the offline character recognition accuracy was improved from 89.99% in 2010 to 94.77% in 2013, the online character recognition accuracy was improved from 92.39% in 2010 to 97.37% in 2013, the offline text recognition accuracy was improved from 77.26% in 2011 to 88.76% in 2013, and the online text recognition accuracy was improved from 94.33% in 2011 to 95.03% in 2013. The best performing isolated character recognizer in both 2011 and 2013 was deep convolutional neural network (CNN) for both offline and online recognition. In 2010, both the offline and online character recognizer used traditional direction feature extraction and MQDF classifier. The CNN outperfoms the traditional methods by a large margin, but it needs huge number of training samples (usually via distorting existing samples) and the computation cost is high in both training and testing. In handwritten text recognition, all the systems used integrated segmentation-recognition approach based on over-segmentation. The best offline text recognizer in both 2011 and 2013 used an MQDF classifier, while the online text recognizer in 2011 and 2013 used a neural network classifier.

Among the published results, the isolated character recognition results of Liu *et al.*[32] were obtained using traditional methods. The offline text line recognition method of Wang *et al.*[33] was re-evaluated on the competition test set to give the result as in Table 8, which remains the best so far. The online recognition result of Zhou *et al.*[34] on the competition test set was obtained before the competition 2013, and remains competitive to the best competition result. Both the methods of Refs. 33 and 34 use integrated segmentation-recognition framework, with elaborate classifier design and context fusion.

The availability of public datasets triggered research in the field, and the recognition performance is still improving since 2013. Particularly, improved versions of deep neural networks are being used in handwritten Chinese character recognition to update the state of the art. Some recent results can be found in Chapter 3 and Chapter 4 in this book.

Table 8. Correct rates of best performing systems in competitions 2010, 2011 and 2013.

Competition	Offline isolated	Online isolated	Offline text	Online text
2010	89.99%	92.39%	N/A	N/A
2011	92.18%	95.77%	77.26%	94.33%
2013	**94.77%**	**97.37%**	88.76%	**95.03%**
Liu *et al.*[32]	92.72%	95.31%		
Wang *et al.*[33]			**90.22%**	
Zhou *et al.*[34]				94.62%

8. Conclusion

We introduced a new series of online and offline Chinese handwriting datasets. The datasets contain online and offline data produced concurrently by the same group of writers using Anoto pen, and are grouped into an offline database CASIA-HWDB and an online database CASIA-OLHWDB. We collected both isolated character samples and handwritten texts, without style constraint imposed on the writers. The datasets are large in the sense that there are as many as 1,020 writers and either the online or offline isolated character datasets contain about 3.9 million samples of 7,356 classes, and the number of character samples in the online/offline handwritten text datasets is about 1.35 million. All the data has been segmented and labeled at character level for the ease of training and evaluation in research. The generalization ability of the new datasets was demonstrated in experiments of isolated character recognition by cross testing with previous datasets. Based on the databases, we organized three competitions of Chinese Handwriting Recognition, and released additional test datasets for competitions. The competition results show constant progress of performance over time and can be taken as benchmarks for research. All these datasets are free for academic research[a], and available for industrial use based on license agreement.

[a]Application forms for using the CASIA databases can be found at http://www.nlpr.ia.ac.cn/databases/handwriting/Home.html

References

1. C. Y. Suen, C. Nadal, R. Legault, T. A. Mai, L. Lam, Computer recognition of unconstrained handwritten numerals, *Proc. IEEE*, **80**(7): 1162–1180, 1992.
2. J. Hull, A database for handwritten text recognition research, *IEEE Trans. Pattern Analysis and Machine Intelligence*, **16**(5): 550–554, 1994.
3. P. J. Grother, NIST Special Database 19: Handprinted Forms and Characters Database, 1995, http://www.nist.gov/srd/upload/nistsd19.pdf
4. U.-V. Marti, H. Bunke, The IAM-database: An English sentence database for offline handwriting recognition, *Int. J. Document Analysis and Recognition*, **5**(1): 39–46, 2002.
5. D.-H. Kim, Y.-S. Hwang, S.-T. Park, E.-J. Kim, P. S.-H, S.-Y. Bang, Handwritten Korean character image database PE92, *IEICE Trans. Information and Systems*, **E79-D**(7): 943–950, 1996.
6. U. Bhattacharya, B. B. Chaudhuri, Databases for research on recognition of handwritten characters of Indian scripts, *Proc. 8th ICDAR*, Seoul, Korea, 2005, pp. 789–793.
7. V. Märgner, H. El Abed, Databases and competitions: Strategies to improve Arabic recognition, In *Arabic and Chinese Handwriting Recognition*, S. Jaeger and D. Doermann (Eds.), LNCS Vol. 4768, Springer, 2008, pp. 82–103.
8. F. Solimanpour, J. Sadri, C. Y. Suen, Standard databases for recognition of handwritten digits, numerical strings, legal amounts, letters and dates in Farsi language, *Proc. 10th IWFHR*, La Baule, France, 2006, pp. 3–7.
9. H. Zhang, J. Guo, G. Chen, C. Li, HCL2000 — A large-scale handwritten Chinese character database for handwritten character recognition, *Proc. 10th ICDAR*, Barcelona, Spain, 2009, pp. 286–290.
10. T. H. Su, T. W. Zhang, D. J. Guan, Corpus-based HIT-MW database for offline recognition of general-purpose Chinese handwritten text, *Int. J. Document Analysis and Recognition*, **10**(1): 27–38, 2007.
11. I. Guyon, L. Schomaker, R. Plamondon, M. Liberman, S. Janet, UNIPEN project of on-line data exchange and recognizer benchmarks, *Proc. 12th ICPR*, Jerusalem, 1994, Vol. II, pp. 29–33.
12. K. Matsumoto, T. Fukushima, M. Nakagawa, Collection and analysis of on-line handwritten Japanese character patterns, *Proc. 6th ICDAR*, Seattle, USA, 2001, pp. 496–500.
13. L. Jin, Y. Gao, G. Liu, Y. Li, K. Ding, SCUT-COUCH2009 — A comprehensive online unconstrained Chinese handwriting database and benchmark evaluation, *Int. J. Document Analysis and Recognition*, **14**(1): 53–64, 2011.
14. S. Zhou, Q. Chen, X. Wang, HIT-OR3C: An opening recognition corpus for Chinese characters, *Proc. 9th IAPR Int. Workshop on DAS*, Boston, USA, 2010, pp. 223–230.
15. C. Viard-Gaudin, P. M. Lallican, S. Knerr, P. Binter, The IRESTE On/Off (IRONOFF) dual handwriting database, *Proc. 5th ICDAR*, Bangalore, India, 1999. pp. 455–458.
16. H. Liu, X. Ding, Handwritten character recognition using gradient feature and quadratic classifier with multiple discrimination schemes, *Proc. 8th ICDAR*, Seoul, Korea, 2005, pp. 19–23.

17. C.-L. Liu, Handwritten Chinese character recognition: Effects of shape normalization and feature extraction, In *Arabic and Chinese Handwriting Recognition*, S. Jaeger and D. Doermann (Eds.), LNCS Vol. 4768, Springer, 2008, pp. 104–128.
18. Q. Fu, X. Ding, C. Liu, A new AdaBoost algorithm for large scale classification and its application to Chinese handwritten character recognition, *Proc. 11th ICFHR*, Montreal, Canada, 2008, pp. 308–314.
19. D.-H. Wang, C.-L. Liu, J.-L. Yu, X.-D. Zhou, CASIA-OLHWDB1: A database of online handwritten Chinese characters, *Proc. 10th ICDAR*, Barcelona, Spain, 2009, pp. 1206–1210.
20. C.-L. Liu, F. Yin, D.-H. Wang, Q.-F. Wang, CASIA online and offline Chinese handwriting databases, *Proc. 11th ICDAR*, Beijing, China, 2011, pp. 37–41.
21. C.-L. Liu, F. Yin, D.-H. Wang, Q.-F. Wang, Chinese Handwriting Recognition Contest 2010, *Proc. 2010 Chinese Conf. Pattern Recognition*, Chongqing, 2010.
22. C.-L. Liu, F. Yin, Q.-F. Wang, D.-H. Wang, ICDAR 2011 Chinese handwriting recognition competition, *Proc. 11th ICDAR*, Beijing, China, 2011, pp. 1464–1469.
23. F. Yin, Q.-F. Wang, X.-Y. Zhang, C.-L. Liu, ICDAR 2013 Chinese handwriting recognition competition, *Proc. 12th ICDAR*, Washington D.C., 2013, pp. 1095–1101.
24. Modern Chinese Character List of Common Use (XianDai HanYu TongYong ZiBiao), http://wenke.hep.edu.cn/gfhz/html/tyzb4.asp
25. Character Frequency List of Modern Chinese, http://lingua.mtsu.edu/chinese-computing/statistics/index.html
26. F. Yin, Q.-F. Wang, C.-L. Liu, A tool for ground-truthing text lines and characters in off-line handwritten Chinese documents, *Proc. 10th ICDAR*, Barcelona, Spain, 2009, pp. 951–955.
27. P. Sarkar, G. Nagy, Style consistent classification of isogenous patterns, *IEEE Trans. Pattern Analysis and Machine Intelligence*, **27**(1): 88–98, 2005.
28. C.-L. Liu, Normalization-cooperated gradient feature extraction for handwritten character recognition, *IEEE Trans. Pattern Analysis and Machine Intelligence*, **29**(8): 1465–1469, 2007.
29. C.-L. Liu, K. Marukawa, Pseudo two-dimensional shape normalization methods for handwritten Chinese character recognition, *Pattern Recognition*, **38**(12): 2242–2255, 2005.
30. F. Kimura, K. Takashina, S. Tsuruoka, Y. Miyake, Modified quadratic discriminant functions and the application to Chinese character recognition, *IEEE Trans. Pattern Analysis and Machine Intelligence*, **9**(1): 149–153, 1987.
31. C.-L. Liu, X.-D. Zhou, Online Japanese character recognition using trajectory-based normalization and direction feature extraction, *Proc. 10th IWFHR*, La Baule, France, 2006, pp. 217–222.
32. C.-L. Liu, F. Yin, D.-H. Wang, Q.-F. Wang, Online and offline handwritten Chinese character recognition: Benchmarking on new databases, *Pattern Recognition*, **46**(1): 155–162, 2013.

33. Q.-F. Wang, F. Yin, C.-L. Liu, Handwritten Chinese text recognition by integrating multiple contexts, *IEEE Trans. Pattern Analysis and Machine Intelligence*, **34**(8): 1469–1481, 2012.
34. X.-D. Zhou, D.-H. Wang, F. Tian, C.-L. Liu, M. Nakagawa, Handwritten Chinese/Japanese text recognition using semi-Markov conditional random fields, *IEEE Trans. Pattern Analysis and Machine Intelligence*, **35**(10): 2484–2497, 2013.
35. D.-H. Wang, C.-L. Liu, X.-D. Zhou, An approach for real-time recognition of online Chinese handwritten sentences, *Pattern Recognition*, **45**(10): 3661–3675, 2012.
36. X.-Y. Zhang, C.-L. Liu, Writer adaptation with style transfer mapping, *IEEE Trans. Pattern Analysis and Machine Intelligence*, **35**(7): 1773–1787, 2013.
37. L. Huang, F. Yin, Q.-H. Chen, C.-L. Liu, Keyword spotting in unconstrained handwritten Chinese documents using contextual word model, *Image and Vision Computing*, **31**(12): 958–968, 2013.
38. H. Zhang, D.-H. Wang, C.-L. Liu, Character confidence based on n-best list for keyword spotting in online Chinese handwritten documents, *Pattern Recognition*, **47**(5): 1904–1916, 2014.

Chapter 3

CNN Based Handwritten Character Recognition

Song Wang, Li Chen, Chunpeng Wu*, Wei Fan, Jun Sun and Satoshi Naoi

Fujitsu R & D Center, Beijing, China
**Department of Electrical and Computer Engineering, University of Pittsburgh, USA*

Handwritten character recognition is one of the most challenging task in pattern recognition since the character appearance varies according to different writers, writing styles and noise. Through decades of research, traditional methods have reached the limit while the emergence of deep learning technologies provide a new way to break such limit. In this chapter, a CNN-based handwritten character recognition system is introduced and it achieved the beyond human performance on handwritten Chinese character recognition task. This system contains sample generation, CNN model and voting, which are introduced in detail and analyzed experimentally. The analysis has shown that the simple CNN model can be improved to a large extent under the framework of this system.

1. Introduction

As shown in Figure 1(a), there are often two main steps of traditional method for isolated character (digits, Chinese, Arabic, etc.) recognition:[1–3] the feature extraction and classification. Usually, the character feature is designed or chosen manually, such as contour feature,[4] gradient feature[5] and image keypoint[6] (SIFT,[7] SURF,[8] etc.). Those empirical features will determine the recognition rate to a large extent. For classification, most of the off-the-shelf classifiers can be employed, for example, the MQDF,[9] SVM[10] and MLP.[11] In the past decades, this framework was widely used in OCR research.

The traditional ways were fundamentally changed when the deep learning technologies emerged. Both the feature extraction and classification can be done automatically within the deep neural networks. In other words, the

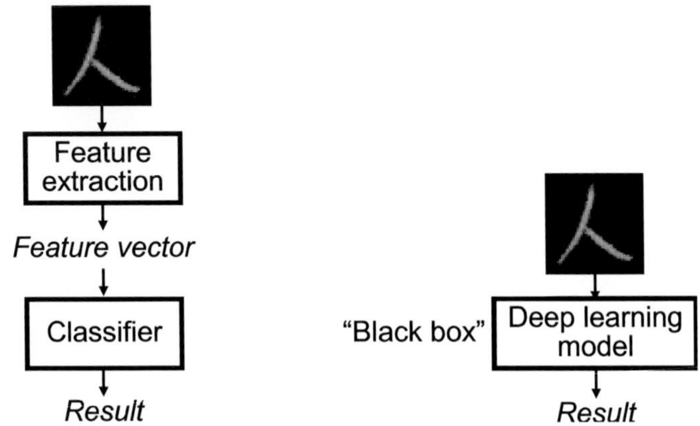

(a) Traditional method.

(b) Deep learning.

Figure 1. Comparison of character recognition methods.

deep neural networks can be seen as "black box". As shown in Figure 1(b), we just need to input the character images and then the recognition results are obtained. The superior performance of deep learning proved that this "black box" is able to learn better representation of characters than handcrafted features.

1.1. *Development of deep learning*

The deep learning research is derived from traditional artificial neural networks (ANN),[12–14] which has a history of more than 70 years. However, because of the development status of the computers, the ANN research was limited to shallow models (usually less than three layers) for a long time. Until recently, with the help of high-performance computers, especially the GPU-based servers, the training of deep neural networks becames possible. Different types of deep neural networks have been proposed, such as Stacked Auto-Encoder (SAE),[15,16] Deep Believe Network (DBN),[17] Convolutional Neural Network (CNN),[18] PCA Network (PCANet),[19] and Deep Sparse Coding (DeepSC).[20] Simply by extending the network scale and layer number, the deep neural networks have achieved the state-of-the-art performance on various tasks.

1.2. *CNN for image understanding*

Among the deep learning models, CNN is the most popular for image understanding. Compared with other models, CNN has achieved the state-of-the-art performance on different image based detection and recognition tasks, such as image recognition,[21,22] human face recognition[23] and human pose estimation.[24]

The great success of CNN on image understanding is mainly due to the fact that CNN can take full advantage of the image characteristics. First, as we know, an image is a kind of structured data representation. In the image, each pixel is strongly correlated to its neighborhood but has little relationship to those pixels far away. This locality principle is well reflected by the local connectivity strategy of CNN. As shown in Figure 2, in CNN, each neuron is only connected to a small local set of the neurons (called the local receptive field) of the previous layer. Second, different parts of the image usually share similar properties, such as texture and brightness. Similarly, the weight sharing strategy of CNN also has such characteristic. In CNN, the local receptive fields (can be seen as "parts") share the same set of parameters. The above features of CNN make it the best choice for image understanding tasks.

1.3. *Character recognition by CNN*

The character recognition can be seen as a special image classification task, thus for which CNN is also a powerful tool. A lot of trials have been made to implement CNN for both handwritten character recognition[25–27] and scene character recognition.[28,29,29]

As mentioned above, as a kind of deep learning model, CNN is able to learn better representation of character shapes automatically and achieve higher recognition rate. One example of the feature extraction by CNN is visualized in Figure 3. As can be seen from those feature maps, the character features (contour, stroke width, etc.) are emphasized in different ways. Similarly, in the handcrafted feature design, the character contour and stroke are also widely used. The difference is that, the numerous weights of CNN can create more complex and flexible feature description for characters. In this feature space, the character class is more compact. Although this advantage is demonstrated by the state-of-the-art performance of CNN on character recognition, the theoretical explanation still needs future investigation.

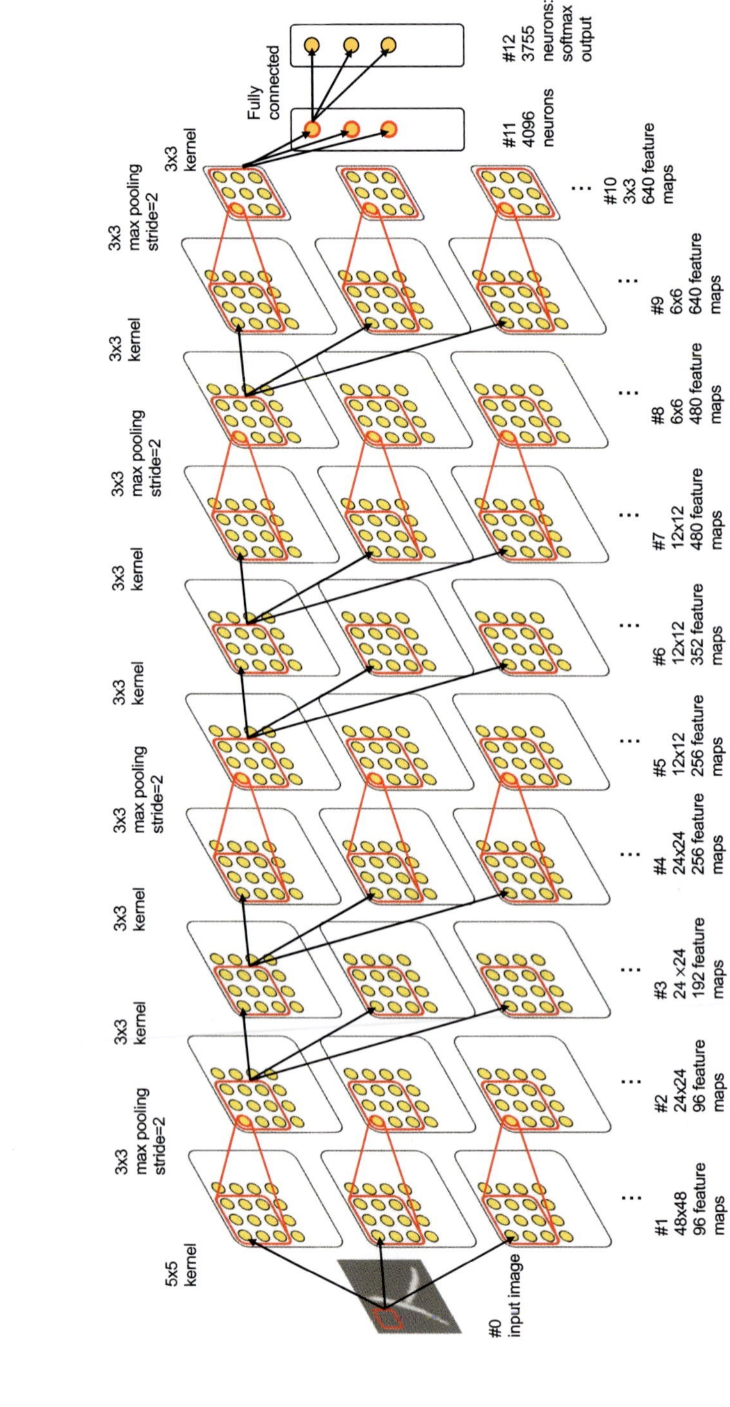

Figure 2. CNN model for handwritten Chinese character recognition.

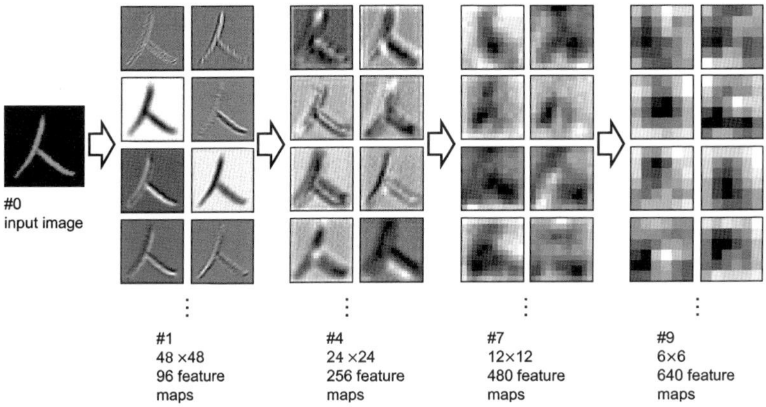

Figure 3. Visualization of the CNN feature maps.

Because of the cursive writing style, the handwritten character recognition is always considered as a difficult problem. In order to improve the traditional recognition method, many researchers have made great efforts on normalization, feature design and classifier optimization. However, when the traditional method reaches its limit, even a little progress is hard to get (under the traditional framework). Therefore, the emergence of CNN provides a brand new way to make the breakthrough for this problem. According to this trend, in this chapter, a handwritten character recognition system based on CNN is introduced.

2. Overview of the CNN-Based Handwritten Character Recognition System

As an off-the-shelf classifier, CNN is very easy to use. In general, we only need to prepare the character image data and select a proper network structure. Then, the CNN can learn the feature extraction and classification automatically. Simply by doing this, a relatively high recognition rate can be obtained (compared with traditional methods). Nevertheless, if we want to pursue the state-of-the-art performance, there are a lot of issues need to be considered. For example, the CNN model of larger scale usually has better performance but requires a large number of training samples. Therefore, in order to improve the CNN model, we need to apply proper sample generation methods. Another issue is the training tricks of CNN. We should study different training tricks and find the efficient ones especially for handwritten

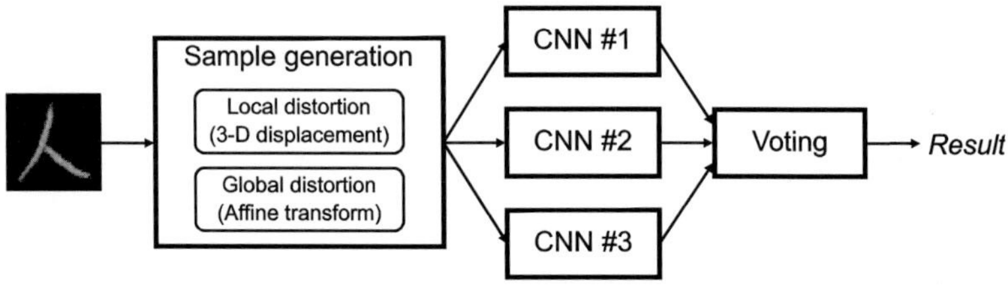

Figure 4. Framework of the CNN-based handwritten character recognition system.

character recognition. In the proposed CNN-based handwritten character recognition system, we have addressed all these issues and given proper solutions for them.

2.1. *The framework of the system*

The general framework of the system is shown in Figure 4. In the system, there are mainly three modules: the sample generation (random distortion), CNN model and voting. Those modules are described as follows.

- Sample generation: the purpose of this module is to provide enough training samples for CNN training. As mentioned above, in order to train a large-scale CNN model sufficiently, we need large quantity of samples. The sample generation is realized through random distortion of character images, which includes both local (3-D displacement) and global (affine transformation) distortions.
- CNN model: as the main module of the system, the structure of the CNN model is designed according to the properties of handwritten characters. Besides, several training tricks of CNN are also employed. Those tricks are efficient in improving the CNN for handwritten character recognition.
- Voting: after multiple CNN models are trained independently, the recognition results are combined through some voting strategy to achieve better accuracy.

Compared with the simple CNN classifier, this system can achieve much higher recognition rate. This is proved by the experimental results on handwritten character datasets (which are shown in the following sections). The sample generation, training tricks and voting all have their own contributions to the performance of the system. Specifically, the sample generation and the training tricks can improve the recognition rate by about 1%. When using three CNN models for voting, the recognition rate can be improved by about 0.5%. In conclusion, the potential of the CNN classifier can be fully developed by the proposed framework. Therefore, the state-of-the-art performance of the system can be expected.

2.2. *Recognition beyond human*

It is well-known that the handwritten character recognition is very easy for human but extremely difficult for machines. In the past decades, many researchers have been trying to improve the methods for handwritten character recognition. However, the progress was slow and the performance of those methods was limited. Before the deep learning emerged, no one believe that the machine learning methods can surpass human on the character recognition task. Based on the powerful CNN classifier, the proposed system finally achieved such goal. One interesting point is that, when people tried to teach machines how to recognize characters (traditional methods), the performance of the machine was always far away from human. In contrast, when we let the machine to learn the recognition by itself (deep learning), the performance of which becames even better than human. Therefore, although the deep learning has been criticized for lacking of theoretical explanation, it does provide us a more promising direction.

We have tested the system on two different handwritten character datasets: the MNIST and CASIA-HWDB 1.1.[30] MNIST is a well-known dataset of handwritten digits (10 classes), which has been widely used for machine learning and pattern recognition research. Compared with MNIST, the CASIA-HWDB is a much more difficult dataset, which contains 3,755 classes of commonly used Chinese characters.[a] Moreover, in CASIA-HWDB there are only 299 samples per class while in MNIST there are about 6,000 samples per class. The lack of samples makes the handwritten Chinese character recognition even harder.

The comparison results of human and the system are shown in Table 1. The error rate of human on MNIST and CASIA-HWDB are about 0.2%[31] and 3.87%,[32] respectively. Meanwhile, the corresponding error rates of the proposed system were 0.21% and 3.79%. The system has achieved better performance on CASIA dataset. On MNIST, the performance of the system is also very close to human. This is a quite large breakthrough for

[a]The full CASIA-HWDB 1.1 contains 7,356 classes of characters, which includes 7,185 Chinese characters and 171 symbols (English letters, digits, etc.). In the experiments, we only used the 3,755 Chinese characters of level-1 set, which are most commonly used in Chinese.

Table 1. Error rate (%) of human and proposed system on handwritten character recognition.

	MNIST	CASIA-HWDB
Human	≈0.2	3.87
Proposed system	0.21	3.79

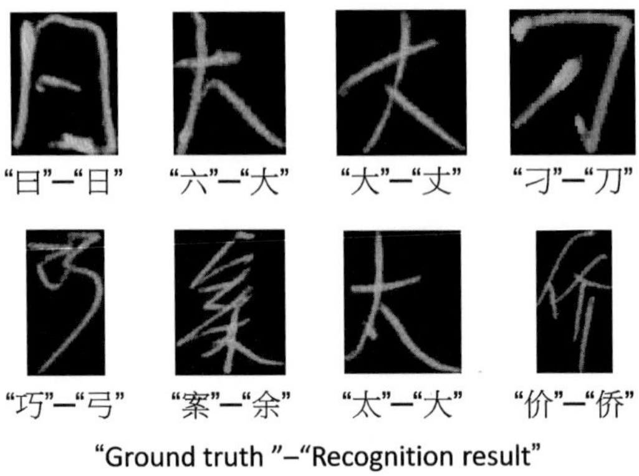

Figure 5. Recognition errors of the system. The first character shows the ground truth and second character shows the recognition result.

handwritten character recognition. Finally, with the help of deep learning, the machine can achieve human-level recognition rate of characters. Especially for the Chinese character recognition task, even a person still needs years of training. Now the machines can do it better than skilled people!

Error analysis is very helpful to reveal how and why machine can outperform human in recognition tasks. The misrecognized samples are shown in Figure 5. First, we can see that the ground truth and recognition result of the characters of the first row are very ambiguous. For example, the "曰" and "日" have the same structure but different aspect ratio. Such difference is very hard to be detected from the handwritten samples. Generally, for those ambiguous characters, we cannot expect CNN to recognize them without any contextual information. Second, the characters of the second row also have corresponding ambiguous character. However, we can find the stable difference from the local part. For example, compared with "大", the "太" has an extra point on the left bottom part. Therefore, although these two characters are globally similar, it is possible to distinguish them from the small local difference. For CNN, if we can design a network structure which can emphasize such local differences, then the errors like these characters can be corrected.

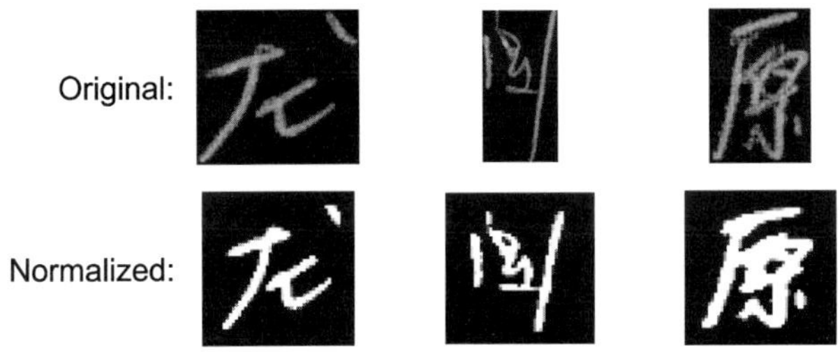

Figure 6. The normalization of character images.

In summary, the performance of the CNN-based handwritten character recognition system indicates that the deep learning technology can significantly improve the character recognition method. Besides, the success of the system on CASIA-HWDB (which only contains limited training samples per class) also proves the importance of the rest modules of the framework, such as the sample generation and voting strategy. The detailed methodology and effect of those modules are introduced in the following sections.

3. Random Distortion for Sample Generation

Before introducing the methodology of the random distortion, we should clarify that in our system there is no normalization employed for the character images. This is easy to understand because the random distortion and normalization are in some sense contradictory. As shown in Figure 6, in traditional methods, the normalization is used to reduce the variance of the character images and then the classification difficulty can also be reduced.[4,5,33] In contrast, the CNN is a very powerful classifier, thus the more variant the character images are, the more recognizable information it can learn. Our experimental results also proved such conclusion. That is, the system has better performance without any normalization process.

As shown in Figure 4, in the system, there are two kinds of random distortion: the local distortion and global distortion. The local distortion aims to add distortion at the local part of the character. Based on the original sample, the new similar samples are generated. Compared with the local distortion, the global distortion changes the character image globally. After global distortion, the specific character shape remains almost the same while the perspective of which changes. Actually, the diverse perspective is common to see when capturing the character images. The global distortion is just used to simulate such situation.

In the system, a 3-D displacement method is employed to realize the local distortion, which can be seen as an extension of the 2-D displacement (X and Y dimension on image).[25] It is claimed that the 2-D displacement can simulate the uncontrolled oscillations of the hand muscles during writing. In 3-D displacement, besides the X and Y dimension, we added the gray value as the third dimension. This is because that we believe the displacement of the gray value can simulate the complex light condition when the handwritten character image is captured. Finally, with the gray value, each point of the image can be seen as a 3-D vector. Assume $\mathbf{p} = (x, y, g)$ is a certain point of the original image, x, y, g are the X, Y coordinates and gray value of which, respectively. Then, a small displacement $\mathbf{\Delta p} = (\Delta x, \Delta y, \Delta g)$ is added to p and we have

$$p' = p + \Delta p = (x + \Delta x, y + \Delta y, g + \Delta g),$$

where p' is the point of the generated image.

As shown in Figure 7, the process of the local distortion is as follows.

- Step 1: a displacement field is first generated randomly, in which the Δx, Δy and Δg are limited to a small range to avoid unreasonable change.
- Step 2: apply Gaussian smoothing to the generated displacement field. By doing this, the stroke of the generated image can be continuous and natural.
- Step 3: add the displacement field to the original image and then a new generated image is obtained. Since the image data is discrete, a bilinear interpolation is employed to generate the new image.

Compared with the original image, the generated image is similar but has some difference at certain local part. Obviously, with the local distortion, we can increase the diversity of the training samples.

The implementation of the global distortion is quite simple, which is just the random affine transformation. This is because usually the character size is not large enough to generate obvious perspective transformation[34,35] when capturing by camera or scanner. Therefore, affine transformation is enough to simulate the real situations. As shown in Figure 8, the parameters of the affine transformation are generated randomly within a certain range and then the transformation is applied to the original image. The global distortion is another important way to increase the diversity of the training samples.

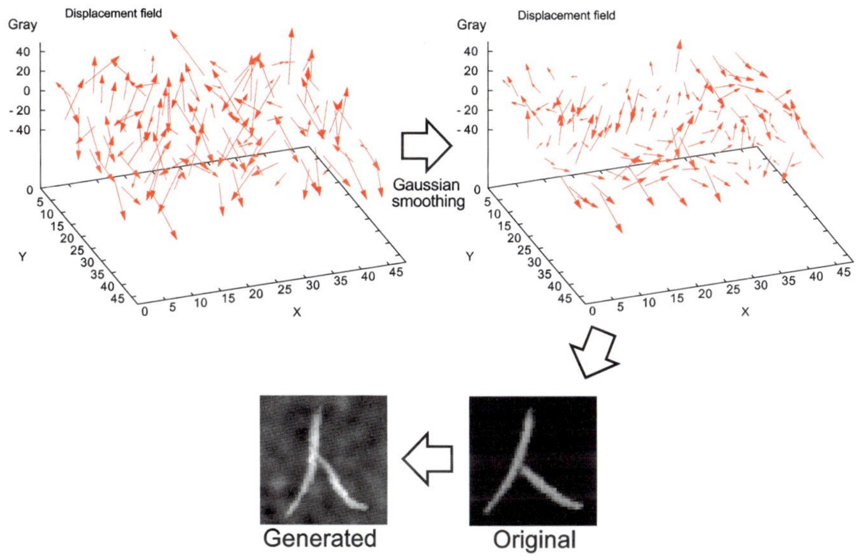

Figure 7. 3-D displacement for local distortion.

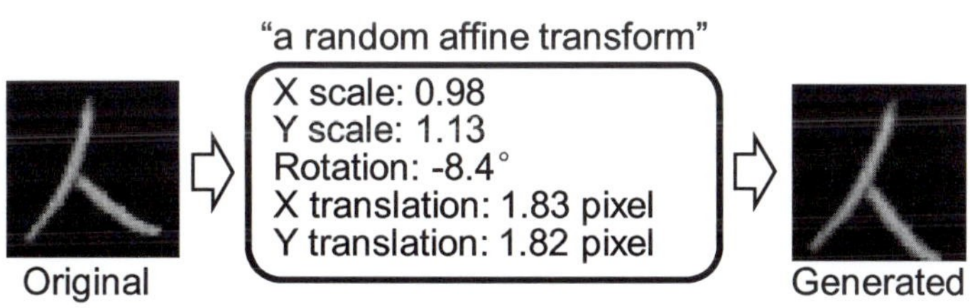

Figure 8. Affine transform for global distortion.

The experimental analysis of the effect of the random distortion is shown in Figure 9. Since the multi-model voting of the system is an independent module, all the comparison experiments were conducted on single CNN model for less computational cost. Besides, all the experimental analysis were based on the CASIA dataset since it is more challenging. The experimental analysis of the following sections were also based on single CNN model. From the experiments we can see that the random distortion is very effective in improving the performance of the single CNN model. When the local distortion was integrated, the error rate decreased from 4.96% to 4.28%. Moreover, when the global distortion was also integrated, the error rate further decreased to 4.15%.

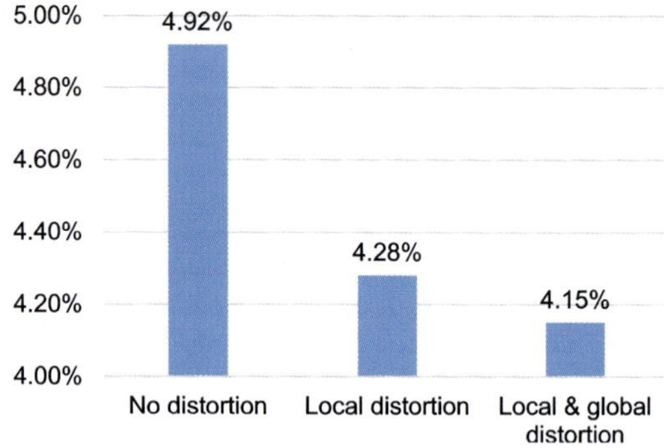

Figure 9. CNN error rates of different random distortions on CASIA.

In summary, the diversity of the training samples can influence the performance of the CNN model to a large extent. In the system, the local and global distortion are employed for sample generation, which can increase the diversity of the training samples from different ways. The experimental analysis indicates that the random distortion is important for the system to achieve beyond human performance on handwritten character recognition.

4. Training Tricks of CNN Model

The great success of deep learning has attracted many researchers to contribute in this field. Many regularization methods for training have been proposed, such as dropout,[36] dropconnect,[37] maxout,[38] stochastic pooling[39] and network in network.[40] Besides, the alternatively training[41] is also proposed and which is effective especially for CNN on handwritten character recognition. Another problem of CNN training is the vanishing gradient problem. When the CNN has many layers, the gradients propagated to the lower layers are extremely small, thus those layers cannot be trained during the training. In order to solve this problem, the multi-supervised training[22,42] is proposed. Although the above methods are lack of theoretical explanation (called training "tricks"), they are able to improve the deep learning classifiers significantly. In the system, the multi-supervised training, dropout and alternatively training are employed for better performance.

The framework of the multi-supervised training is shown in Figure 10. In order to enhance the gradients propagated to the lower layers, extra output layers are connected to layers of different depth. In the training, those

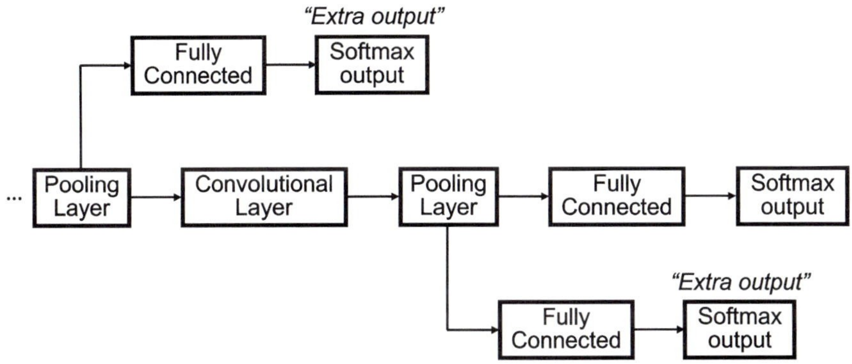

Figure 10. Multi-supervised training.

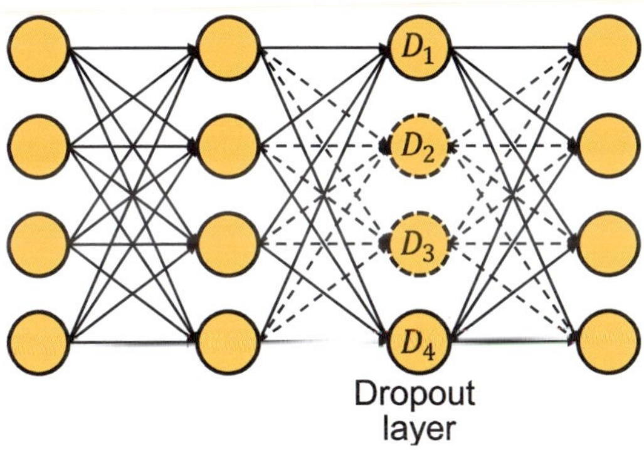

Figure 11. The process of dropout.

extra output layer also generate error for backpropagation. Consequently, the lower layers can be trained with gradients from different output layer. In the system, the CNN structure used for Chinese character recognition is shown in Figure 2. Obviously, this is a very deep structure, which has as many as twelve layers in total. Without the multi-supervised training, such deep network even cannot converge during the training.

The process of the dropout is shown in Figure 11. In the training, for a certain layer, a number of neurons are selected randomly. In the next iteration, the values of those neurons are set to 0 all the time. As a result, all the connections to those selected neurons are disabled. In other words, those selected neurons are removed from the network temporarily. Hence, in the next iteration, only a sub-structure of the network is trained. After

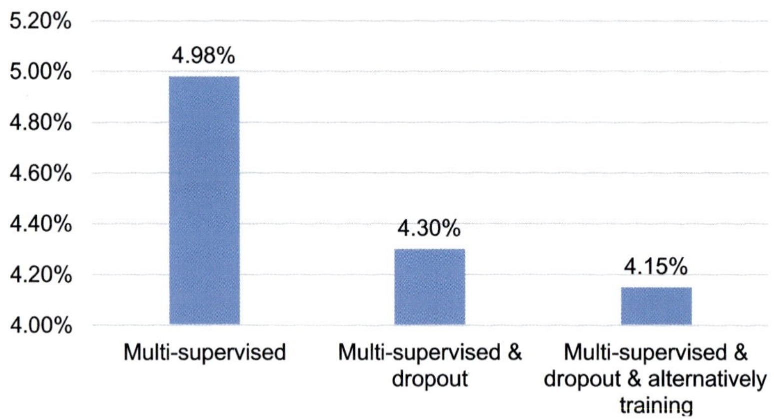

Figure 12. CNN error rates of different tricks on CASIA.

the iteration is finished, we will change the selected neurons (while the number remains the same) and repeat the same process. Through dropout, we can force the different parts of the network to be fully trained, which is important to explore the potential of the network for classification task.

The alternatively training is similar to dropout, which also aims to fully train each part of the network. First, a layer is selected randomly from the network. Second, in the next few iterations, the learning rate of the selected layer is set to 0. Different from dropout, the selected layer will still work during the training. Of course, the weights of the selected layer will not update since the learning rate is 0. After a few iterations, we will change the selected layer and repeat the process. The alternatively training is also effective in improving the performance of the CNN model.

Both of the dropout and alternatively training are efficient for improving the CNN training. The difference is that the dropout is usually used only for fully connected layers while the alternatively training can be used for all layers. Therefore, it is possible to combine both tricks by applying them to different layers.

As shown in Figure 2, for multi-supervised training, we add two extra output layers and which are connected to Layer #5 and Layer #8. Besides, the dropout is used at the fully connected layer while the alternatively training is used at the rest of the layers. We have conducted an experimental analysis of the three training tricks and the results are shown in Figure 12. Since the network cannot converge without the multi-supervised training, the result of the multi-supervised training is then used as the baseline. The error rate of multi-supervised training was only 4.98%. When the dropout was employed, the error rate decreased to 4.30% and when the alternatively training was also employed, the error rate further decreased to 4.15%. For single CNN model, this improvement is very impressive.

In conclusion, the training tricks are somehow important for improving the CNN model. Through the experiments we can see that these tricks (multi-supervised training, dropout and alternatively training) employed in the system are very effective. Moreover, these tricks can be used at the same time and each of which has its own contribution to the performance of the system. This point is also essential for the usage of the tricks since sometimes one trick may conflict with other tricks.

5. Model Scale and Input Image Size

Two important issues related to the performance of the single CNN model are the model scale and input image size. Generally speaking, for CNN, the larger scale can generate higher recognition rate. It is the same situation for the input image size. However, in the real application, we need to consider not only the recognition rate but also the computational cost. Besides, the relationship between the scale, the image size and the recognition rate is not simply linear. With the increase of the scale and input image size, the benefit of which will become less.

First, the experimental analysis of the influence of the model scale is shown in Figure 13. We have tested the single CNN model of three different scales: small, middle, and large. The CNN of large scale is shown in Figure 2. Compared with the large scale, the CNN of middle scale has one layer (Layer #3) less. Accordingly, the numbers of feature maps of the following layers are also reduced. The feature map numbers of Layer #4, #5, #6, #7, #8, #9, #10 are 192, 192, 256, 352, 352, 480, 480, respectively. Similarly, the small scale has two layers less (Layer #3 and Layer #6) and the corresponding reduced feature map numbers for the layers. The error rates of the small, middle and large scale are 5.09%, 4.54% and 4.15%, respectively. Clearly, with larger scale, the better performance can be obtained. However, the improvement from middle to large is smaller than the improvement from small to middle, which illustrates the above viewpoint of benefit reduction.

Second, the experimental analysis of the influence of the image size is shown in Figure 14. We have also tested three different input size: 32×32, 40×40 and 48×48. For different input size, the structure of the CNN model

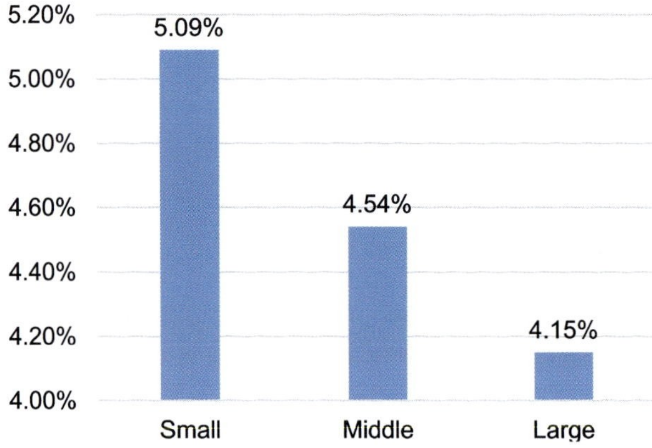

Figure 13. CNN error rates of different scales on CASIA.

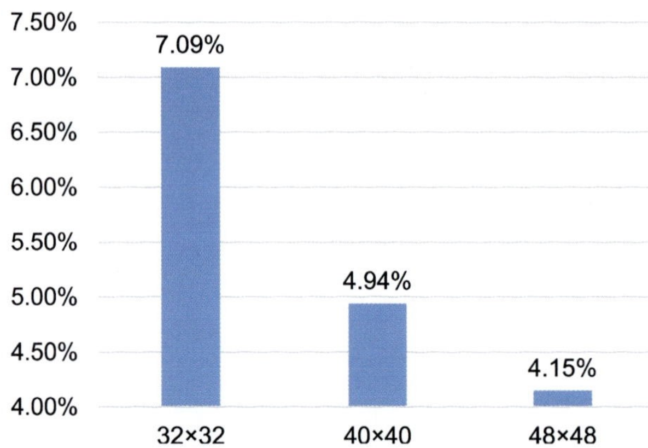

Figure 14. CNN error rates of different input image sizes on CASIA.

is the same. However, the size of the feature maps are changed according to the input image size. From small to middle, the error rate decreased dramatically from 7.09% to 4.94%. In contrast, from middle to large, the error rate was only decreased by about 0.8%. This observation is just like the experimental analysis of the model scale. Consequently, we may draw a similar conclusion that when the input image size is large enough to show the character details, the benefit from size increase will become much less.

In conclusion, the model scale and input image size can directly influence the performance of the CNN model. Although the larger scale and image size can bring higher recognition rate, they also require more com-

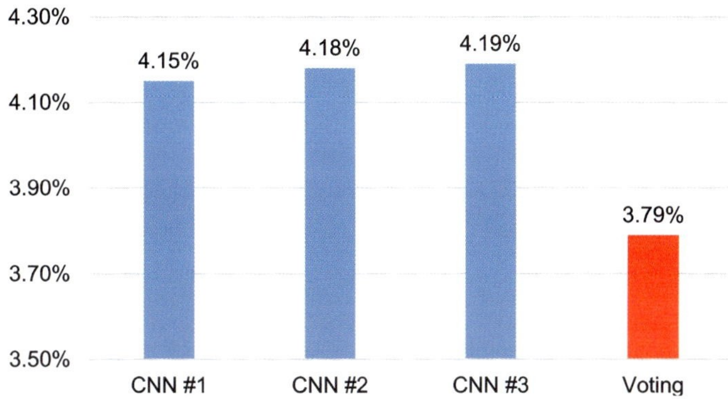

Figure 15. Error rates of single CNN models and voting on CASIA.

putational resource. Therefore, in the real application, we have to find a balance between the performance and the computational cost to build the recognition system.

6. Multi-Model Voting

The multi-model voting of the CNN has been widely used[21,27,43] and which is based on such fact: the separately trained CNN models of the same structure can be seen as different classifiers. This is because the training of CNN is not a convex optimization problem, each trained CNN is actually a local optimum solution. Moreover, in the system each training image has a random distortion process before sent into CNN, there is no two exact same images used all through the training. Consequently, simply by using a voting of different CNN models, the system can achieve better performance.

The experimental analysis of the multi-model voting is shown in Figure 15. The average error rate of three CNN models is 4.17%. Clearly, compared with the single CNN model, when three models were used to vote for the final recognition result, the error rate decreased from 4.17% to 3.79%. Similar to the model scale and input image size, the more models used for voting, the better performance the system has. Meanwhile, we have to solve the higher computational cost problem. Consequently, just as the selection of the model scale and input image size, we have to find the balance between the number of models and the computational cost.

7. Conclusion

Through the above analysis, we can see that although the CNN is a powerful classifier, it still needs to work under proper framework to achieve the state-of-the-art performance on handwritten character recognition. In the proposed system, according to the character characteristic, we have designed and tested proper strategies to improve the performance of CNN, such as sample generation, special training tricks and multi-model voting. As a result, the proposed system achieved the beyond human performance on handwritten Chinese character recognition. Besides, the probabilities for further improvements of CNN are also revealed through the proposed system. The simple way is to enlarge the network scale or input image size and more advanced way is to modify the sample generation methods, training scheme and network structure.

Besides the performance, it is also very important to extend the application of CNN to more character recognition tasks. For example, except for the isolated handwritten Chinese character recognition, it is also worth to try CNN on handwritten Chinese string recognition, which is also seen as a very difficult task. There is some proposed framework[44] for this task and in which the traditional classifier is used. Although such framework already had great performance, just like the isolated task, the usage of powerful CNN classifier can further improve its performance. With the help of CNN, even beyond human performance can be expected.

Finally, based on deep learning technologies, we hope the character recognition research can generate more promising results. Meanwhile, the accumulation of the feature design from the traditional research may also help us to use the deep learning models better. Although now the deep learning models are used as "black box", they may also benefit from such experience. For example, in the proposed system, we may design better strategy of sample generation according to the existing empirical features. We believe that the interaction between the new powerful classifier and the traditional research is the key point for solving the character recognition problems.

References

1. C.-L. Liu, K. Nakashima, H. Sako, and H. Fujisawa, Handwritten digit recognition: benchmarking of state-of-the-art techniques, *Pattern Recognition*, **36**(10), 2271–2285 (2003).

2. C.-L. Liu, F. Yin, D.-H. Wang, and Q.-F. Wang, Online and offline handwritten Chinese character recognition: Benchmarking on new databases, *Pattern Recognition*, **46**(1), 155–162 (2013).
3. L. Lorigo and V. Govindaraju, Offline Arabic handwriting recognition: a survey, *IEEE Transactions on Pattern Analysis and Machine Intelligence*, **28**(5), 712–724 (2006).
4. C.-L. Liu, K. Nakashima, H. Sako, and H. Fujisawa, Handwritten digit recognition: investigation of normalization and feature extraction techniques, *Pattern Recognition*, **37**(2), 265–279 (2004).
5. C.-L. Liu, Normalization-cooperated gradient feature extraction for handwritten character recognition, *IEEE Transactions on Pattern Analysis and Machine Intelligence*, **29**(8), 1465–1469 (2007).
6. S. Uchida and M. Liwicki, Part-based recognition of handwritten characters. In *2010 International Conference on Frontiers in Handwriting Recognition (ICFHR)*, IEEE, 2010, pp. 545–550.
7. D. G. Lowe, Distinctive image features from scale-invariant keypoints, *International Journal of Computer Vision*, **60**(2), 91–110 (2004).
8. H. Bay, T. Tuytelaars, and L. Van Gool, Surf: Speeded up robust features. In *Computer vision — ECCV 2006*, Springer, 2006, pp. 404–417.
9. F. Kimura, K. Takashina, S. Tsuruoka, and Y. Miyake, Modified quadratic discriminant functions and the application to Chinese character recognition, *IEEE Transactions on Pattern Analysis and Machine Intelligence*, (1), 149–153 (1987).
10. C. J. Burges, A tutorial on support vector machines for pattern recognition, *Data Mining and Knowledge Discovery*, **2**(2), 121–167 (1998).
11. D. E. Rumelhart, G. E. Hinton, and R. J. Williams, Learning representations by back-propagating errors, *Cognitive Modeling*, **5** (1988).
12. W. S. McCulloch and W. Pitts, A logical calculus of the ideas immanent in nervous activity, *The Bulletin of Mathematical Biophysics*, **5**(4), 115–133 (1943).
13. D. Hebb, *The Organization of Behavior*. New York: Wiley, 1949.
14. F. Rosenblatt, The perceptron: A probalistic model for information storage and organization in the brain, *Psychological Review*, **65**(6), 386–408 (1958).
15. J. Masci, U. Meier, D. Ciresan, and J. Schmidhuber, Stacked convolutional auto-encoders for hierarchical feature extraction. In *Artificial Neural Networks and Machine Learning*, Springer, 2011, pp. 52–59.
16. P. Vincent, H. Larochelle, I. Lajoie, Y. Bengio, and P.-A. Manzagol, Stacked denoising autoencoders: Learning useful representations in a deep network with a local denoising criterion, *The Journal of Machine Learning Research*, **11**, 3371–3408 (2010).
17. G. Hinton, S. Osindero, and Y.-W. Teh, A fast learning algorithm for deep belief nets, *Neural Computation*, **18**(7), 1527–1554 (2006).
18. Y. LeCun, L. Bottou, Y. Bengio, and P. Haffner, Gradient-based learning applied to document recognition, *Proceedings of the IEEE*, **86**(11), 2278–2324 (1998).

19. T.-H. Chan, K. Jia, S. Gao, J. Lu, Z. Zeng, and Y. Ma, PCANet: A Simple Deep Learning Baseline for Image Classification?, arXiv preprint arXiv:1404.3606 (2014).
20. Y. He, K. Kavukcuoglu, Y. Wang, A. Szlam, and Y. Qi, Unsupervised Feature Learning by Deep Sparse Coding, arXiv preprint arXiv:1312.5783 (2013).
21. A. Krizhevsky, I. Sutskever, and G. E. Hinton, Imagenet classification with deep convolutional neural networks. In *Advances in Neural Information Processing Systems*, 2012, pp. 1097–1105.
22. C. Szegedy, W. Liu, Y. Jia, P. Sermanet, S. Reed, D. Anguelov, D. Erhan, V. Vanhoucke, and A. Rabinovich, Going deeper with convolutions, arXiv preprint arXiv:1409.4842 (2014).
23. Y. Taigman, M. Yang, M. Ranzato, and L. Wolf, Deepface: Closing the gap to human-level performance in face verification. In *2014 IEEE Conference on Computer Vision and Pattern Recognition (CVPR)*, IEEE, 2014, pp. 1701–1708.
24. J. J. Tompson, A. Jain, Y. LeCun, and C. Bregler, Joint training of a convolutional network and a graphical model for human pose estimation. In *Advances in Neural Information Processing Systems*, 2014, pp. 1799–1807.
25. P. Y. Simard, D. Steinkraus, and J. C. Platt, Best practices for convolutional neural networks applied to visual document analysis. In *2013 12th International Conference on Document Analysis and Recognition*, Vol. 2, p. 958, IEEE Computer Society (2013).
26. D. C. Ciresan, U. Meier, L. M. Gambardella, and J. Schmidhuber, Convolutional Neural Network Committees for Handwritten Character Classification, pp. 1135–1139, IEEE (Sept. 2011).
27. D. Ciresan, U. Meier, and J. Schmidhuber, Multi-column deep neural networks for image classification. In *2012 IEEE Conference on Computer Vision and Pattern Recognition (CVPR)*, IEEE, 2012, pp. 3642–3649.
28. T. Wang, D. J. Wu, A. Coates, and A. Y. Ng, End-to-end text recognition with convolutional neural networks. In *2012 21st International Conference on Pattern Recognition*, IEEE, 2012, pp. 3304–3308.
29. I. J. Goodfellow, Y. Bulatov, J. Ibarz, S. Arnoud, and V. Shet, Multi-digit number recognition from street view imagery using deep convolutional neural networks, arXiv preprint arXiv:1312.6082 (2013).
30. C.-L. Liu, F. Yin, D.-H. Wang, and Q.-F. Wang, CASIA Online and Offline Chinese Handwriting Databases, pp. 37–41 (Sept. 2011).
31. Y. Lecun, L. D. Jackel, H. A. Eduard, N. Bottou, C. Cartes, J. S. Denker, H. Drucker, E. Sackinger, P. Simard, and V. Vapnik, Learning Algorithms For Classification: A Comparison On Handwritten Digit Recognition. In *Neural Networks: The Statistical Mechanics Perspective*, World Scientific, 1995, pp. 261–276.
32. F. Yin, Q.-F. Wang, X.-Y. Zhang, and C.-L. Liu, Icdar 2013 Chinese handwriting recognition competition. In *12th International Conference on Document Analysis and Recognition*, IEEE, 2013, pp. 1464–1470.
33. C.-L. Liu, M. Koga, H. Sako, and H. Fujisawa, Aspect ratio adaptive normalization for handwritten character recognition. In T. Tan, Y. Shi, and

W. Gao (Eds.), *Advances in Multimodal Interfaces (ICMI 2000)*, Lecture Notes in Computer Science, Vol. 1948, Springer, 2000, pp. 418–425.

34. T. Wakahara, Y. Kimura, and A. Tomono, Affine-invariant recognition of gray-scale characters using global affine transformation correlation, *IEEE Transactions on Pattern Analysis and Machine Intelligence*, **23**(4), 384–395 (2001).
35. T. Nakai, K. Kise, and M. Iwamura, Use of Affine Invariants in Locally Likely Arrangement Hashing for Camera-Based Document Image Retrieval. In H. Bunke and A. L. Spitz (Eds.), *Document Analysis Systems VII*, Vol. 3872 LNCS, Springer, 2006, pp. 541–552.
36. N. Srivastava, G. Hinton, A. Krizhevsky, I. Sutskever, and R. Salakhutdinov, Dropout: A Simple Way to Prevent Neural Networks from Overfitting, *J. Mach. Learn. Res.* **15**(1), 1929–1958 (2014).
37. L. Wan, M. Zeiler, S. Zhang, Y. L. Cun, and R. Fergus, Regularization of Neural Networks using DropConnect, 2013, pp. 1058–1066.
38. I. J. Goodfellow, D. Warde-Farley, M. Mirza, A. Courville, and Y. Bengio, Maxout Networks, arXiv:1302.4389 [cs, stat] (Feb. 2013).
39. M. D. Zeiler and R. Fergus, Stochastic Pooling for Regularization of Deep Convolutional Neural Networks, arXiv:1301.3557 [cs, stat] (Jan. 2013).
40. M. Lin, Q. Chen, and S. Yan, Network in Network, arXiv:1312.4400 [cs] (Dec. 2013).
41. C. Wu, W. Fan, Y. He, J. Sun, and S. Naoi, Handwritten Character Recognition by Alternately Trained Relaxation Convolutional Neural Network, *International Conference on Frontiers in Handwriting Recognition*, 2014.
42. C.-Y. Lee, S. Xie, P. Gallagher, Z. Zhang, and Z. Tu, Deeply-Supervised Nets, arXiv:1409.5185 [cs, stat] (Sept. 2014). arXiv: 1409.5185.
43. D. Ciresan, U. Meier, J. Masci, and J. Schmidhuber, Multi-column deep neural network for traffic sign classification, *Neural Networks*, **32**, 333–338 (Aug. 2012).
44. Qiu-Feng Wang, Fei Yin, and Cheng-Lin Liu, Handwritten Chinese text recognition by integrating multiple contexts, *IEEE Transactions on Pattern Analysis and Machine Intelligence*, **34**(8), 1469–1481 (2012).

Chapter 4

Online Handwritten Chinese Character Recognition: From a Bayesian Approach to Deep Learning

Lianwen Jin*, Weixin Yang, Ziyong Feng and Zecheng Xie

School of Electronics and Information,
South China University of Technology,
381 Wushan Road, Guangzhou 510640, China
**lianwen.jin@gmail.com*

In this chapter, we introduce two approaches for online handwritten Chinese character recognition (OHCCR). The first is the traditional statistical learning approach based on Bayesian decision rules, and the second is a new deep learning approach that uses convolutional neural networks (CNNs). Several traditional domain-specific processing technologies are introduced, including nonlinear normalization, addition of imaginary strokes, elastic meshing for character image partition, 8-directional feature extraction, and a new feature extraction method called path of signature feature maps. Then we describe in detail a deep learning-based method for OHCCR using CNNs. We present the network structure of our OHCCR-CNN model, into which different domain-specific knowledge layers are embedded. A learning algorithm named DropSample is developed for CNNs, and a hybrid serial-parallel deep CNN (DCNN) ensemble model for OHCCR is described. Experimental results showed that the proposed hybrid serial-parallel DCNN and DropSample training methods achieve state-of-the-art results on three widely used public datasets (CASIA-OLHWDB 1.0, CASIA-OLHWDB 1.1, and the ICDAR 2013 handwritten Chinese character recognition competition dataset). Finally, some future research directions and topics are discussed.

1. Introduction

With the popularization of smartphones and tablets that use touch-based interfaces, the accurate and robust recognition of handwritten Chinese characters is becoming a critical part of many pen-based applications [1]–[3]. The widespread use of touch screens and the development of handwriting recognition technologies mean that text input is no longer limited to the keyboard. Indeed, handwritten input is becoming increasingly popular, especially in China. According to a market survey conducted by iMedia Research in 2015 [4], about 12.5% of users prefer handwriting out of all the input methods available on Chinese mobile phones. This is the second highest after Pinyin (76.5%) and is much higher than voice input (5.2%) and Chinese stroke input (3.1%) [8]. If we assume there are 500 million smartphone users in China [5], this suggests that more than 60 million people would prefer to use handwritten input. This indicates that handwritten input is becoming more and more important for mobile phones and devices.

Online handwritten Chinese character recognition (OHCCR) is a challenging problem because of its large-scale vocabulary (as many as 6,763 classes in the GB2312-80 standard, 27,533 classes in the GB18010-2000 standard, and 70,244 classes in the GB18010-2005 standard), diversity of handwriting styles (each individual may have his/her own handwriting characteristics), similar and confusable Chinese characters, and so on. Combined with the wide range of applications of OHCCR, these challenges have attracted the attention of many researchers. This problem has been extensively studied for more than 40 years [1]–[3][11][12]. During the past decade, many statistical approaches have been developed and applied to handwritten character recognition. These have become the most popular approaches because of their simplicity and robustness [6]. Among these, the modified quadratic discriminant function (MQDF) [7], which is based on Bayesian decision rules, and its variants [9][10][83][84] have been extremely successful. The MQDF plays a very important role in many high-accuracy classifiers [8]–[11]. With the power of this quadratic classifier, state-of-the-art recognizers can achieve more than 98% recognition accuracy on certain constrained databases [9][13][14]. However, for unconstrained handwriting recognition, recent studies suggest that the recognition accuracy falls to less than 95.3% on realistic unconstrained OHCCR databases using traditional MQDF-based approaches [11]. This shows that the problem of unconstrained OHCCR is far from being completely solved.

Despite the tremendous efforts and successful applications for the past four decades, OHCCR remains a major challenge. Numerous methods for dealing with confusing characters or cursive handwriting have been proposed. Among them, classification methods using new technologies such as discriminative feature extraction [21] and discriminative learning quadratic discriminant function (DLQDF) [9][84] have achieved better performance levels, with very low test error rates of 4.72% and 5.15%, respectively, on two challenging datasets (CASIA-OLHWDB1.0 and CASIA-OLHWDB1.1) [11]. However, such results are still somehow far from the human perceptron performance.

A traditional isolated OHCCR method typically contains the following three steps:

(1) Preprocessing of an input handwritten character (e.g., linear or nonlinear normalization (NLN) [15], addition of imaginary strokes [16]–[20], etc.);

(2) Feature extraction and dimension reduction (e.g., 8-directional feature extraction [19], discriminative directional feature extraction [21], etc.);

(3) Classification via machine learning methods (e.g., MQDF [8]–[11], hidden Markov model [22], etc.).

Under the traditional framework using a statistical learning classifier such as MQDF, preprocessing and feature extraction usually play a crucial role. Some widely used key technologies include NLN methods [15], data augmentation using distorted sample generation [23]–[25], 8-directional feature extraction [19], and dimension reduction with linear discriminant analysis (LDA) [21]. All of these domain-specific technologies occupy a significant position in traditional OHCCR. However, very limited progress has been reported in recent years in terms of both novel feature extraction methods and novel preprocessing technologies under the traditional OHCCR framework. It seems that traditional HCCR approaches, such as MQDF-based methods, have reached a bottleneck, with no significant progress reported in recent years.

Meanwhile, deep learning methods such as convolutional neural networks (CNNs), deep belief networks (DBNs), deep neural networks, and deep recurrent neural networks [27]–[36] have recently been shown to be very effective technologies for various computer vision tasks. Hence, such approaches have attracted a considerable amount of research and industry attention. Among them, CNNs [32][33] have been extensively investigated in recent years. Owing to the availability of large-scale training data, new training technologies such as Dropout [28] or DropConnect [29], and advances in computing hardware such as GPUs [31], traditional CNNs have been extended with deeper architectures [34]–[36], advanced training techniques, and effective learning algorithms [30][37]. This has enabled CNNs to successfully overcome various challenges posed by computer vision and pattern recognition problems. Consequently, significant breakthroughs have been achieved in image recognition [27][28][35][36], facial recognition [38][39], handwriting recognition [46]–[49], pose recognition [40], text detection, and natural scene image recognition [41]–[45]. Furthermore, deep CNNs (DCNNs) with different structures have been successfully applied to the field of HCCR [48]–[51]. Deep learning methods provide an alternative end-to-end solution to HCCR without any dedicated feature extraction or preprocessing technique, and enable potentially much higher performance.

The International Conference on Document Analysis and Recognition (ICDAR) 2011 HCCR competition [21] reported the first successful application of CNN for large-vocabulary HCCR. In this competition, the systems developed by IDSIA, a Swiss artificial intelligence institute, won first place for offline Chinese character recognition and fourth place for online Chinese character recognition. The IDSIA team used a CNN for handwritten character recognition and reported their results in various studies [46]–[48]. Among them, the multi-column deep neural network (MCDNN) model [48] achieved significant success in several image recognition tasks, including online and offline HCCR. However, MCDNN is a simple average voting ensemble model composed of several standard CNNs. Furthermore, it is worth mentioning that the performance of MCDNN for online Chinese character recognition is still inferior to some traditional methods, such as DLQDF [11] and compact MQDF [10]. It is interesting to observe that DCNN models continued their success by winning the online and offline HCCR competitions at ICDAR 2013 [50]. The sparse CNN (DeepCNet) model proposed by

Graham [49][55] won the online HCCR competition, with an accuracy rate of 97.39% [50], and a team from Fujitsu won the offline HCCR competition, with an accuracy rate of 94.77%. In 2014, Wu *et al.* [54] further improved the performance of offline HCCR to 96.06%, based on the voting of four alternately trained relaxation CNNs. In 2015, the records for both the online and offline ICDAR competition dataset were broken by a research group from South China University of Technology, who used a new DCNN structure and advanced training techniques [56]–[58]. The new state-of-the-art results for the online and offline ICDAR HCCR datasets were 97.51% and 96.64%, respectively, which were obtained using CNN-based approaches. This demonstrates the promising performance and potential ability of deep learning methods.

In this chapter, we first introduce traditional technologies for OHCCR, including methods for preprocessing, feature extraction, data augmentation, imaginary stroke techniques, and classifier design based on Bayesian decision rules. We then present a CNN-based approach for OHCCR in Section 3 (we called this the OHCCR-CNN model). OHCCR-CNN combines traditional domain-knowledge techniques with DCNNs to achieve very promising results for OHCCR. Comparative experimental results are given and analyzed in Section 4. Conclusions and future research directions are discussed in Section 5.

2. Online HCCR under a Bayesian Statistical Learning Framework

2.1. *General framework for OHCCR*

Figure 1 shows a typical flowchart for an OHCCR system. The main modules are preprocessing, feature extraction, dimensionality reduction, and classifier design. The preprocessing module usually includes resampling, normalization, shape correction, and so on. Feature extraction plays an important role in the overall OHCCR system. To date, the most effective and widely used features are directional feature patterns. Among these, 8-directional feature extraction is one of the most commonly used features for OHCCR because it has an outstanding ability to express directional stroke change patterns, which are known to be very useful for distinguishing different categories of handwritten

Chinese characters. The dimensionality reduction module is typically used to make the extracted features more compact and to find a better subspace to which the original feature vectors can be projected. This makes it much easier for the recognizer to classify the feature vectors. Finally, the MQDF classifier is used to make the final classification output [7]. MQDF is based on Bayesian decision rules, which are known to be an excellent statistical learning approach, especially for HCCR.

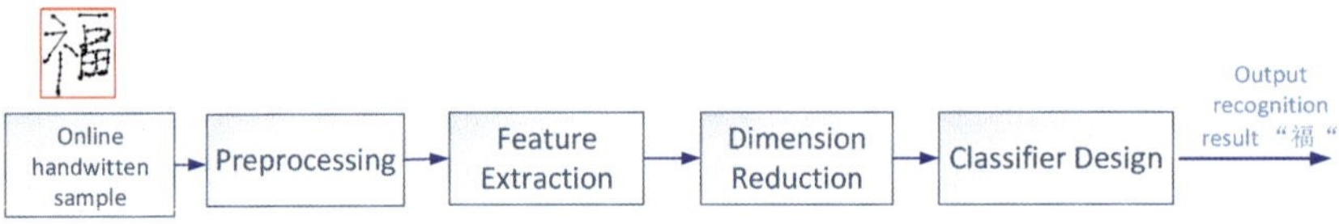

Figure 1. Typical flowchart for an OHCCR system.

2.2. *Preprocessing*

2.2.1. *Normalization*

The normalization process regulates the shape, size, and position of character images, thus reducing the shape variation between images of the same class. In general, there are two categories of normalization: linear and nonlinear. Linear normalization transforms the input character images into a standard size, giving a fixed dimensionality for classification. NLN corrects shape variations and distortion. Shape normalization with NLN has been found to increase the accuracy of HCCR systems. In the field of character recognition, a large number of effective normalization methods have been proposed. In possibly the first paper to address the shape normalization problem, Casey [59] proposed moment normalization (MN) for alphanumeric characters. Tsukumo and Tanaka [60] and Yamada *et al.* [61] proposed an NLN method using line density equalization, and Liu *et al.* [62] developed bi-moment normalization, which performs slightly better than MN. Centroid-boundary alignment (CBA) uses quadratic curve fitting to align the centroid and the physical boundaries. Liu and Marukawa [63] proposed a modified CBA to enable the inner density to be deformed. A pseudo two-dimensional NLN (P2DNLN) method has been developed to overcome the insufficient shape restoration capability of one-dimensional NLN

[64]. To reduce the computational cost of P2DNLN, Liu and Marukawa [65] developed a new P2DNLN method using line density projection interpolation (LDPI).

In general, normalization is performed by transforming the input handwritten character images to a standard image plane, so that the normalized images have the same size and less shape distortion. Let (x, y) be the coordinates of an input character image and (x', y') be the coordinates of the normalized image. The normalization is performed by the following mapping function:

$$
\begin{aligned}
x' &= f_x(x) \\
y' &= f_y(y)
\end{aligned}
\tag{1}
$$

where $f_x(\bullet)$ and $f_y(\bullet)$ are two mapping functions.

Suppose the width and height of the input character images are W_1 and H_1, and the width and height of the normalized output character images are W_2 and H_2, respectively. The mapping functions for linear normalization are then given by

$$
\begin{aligned}
f_x(x) &= \frac{W_2}{W_1} x \\
f_y(y) &= \frac{H_2}{H_1} x
\end{aligned}
\tag{2}
$$

For line density equalization-based NLN [61], the mapping functions are given by

$$
\begin{aligned}
f_x(x) &= W_2 \sum_{u=0}^{x} h_x(u) \\
f_x(x) &= H_2 \sum_{v=0}^{y} h_y(v)
\end{aligned}
\tag{3}
$$

where $h_x(u)$ and $h_y(v)$ are the line density histograms in the x and y directions, respectively. These can be computed as follows:

$$h_x(u) = \frac{p_x(u)}{\sum_x p_x(u)}$$
$$h_y(v) = \frac{p_y(v)}{\sum_y p_y(v)} \tag{4}$$

where $p_x(x)$ and $p_y(y)$ are the line density projections onto the x and y axes, respectively.

By carefully designing different mapping functions according to different shape normalization rules (e.g., moment-based, pseudo 2D density equalization), we can perform different types of NLN in a similar way.

2.2.2. *Data augmentation with deformation transformation*

A number of researchers have demonstrated that data augmentation techniques can improve the classifier performance. Commonly used affine transformations include translation, scaling, rotation, flipping, and shearing [25][67]. However, affine transformations act on the global region of the character image and cannot change the density distribution of the local strokes. To overcome the insufficient local distortion capability of affine transformations, we should design a sample generation technique that accounts for the characteristics of handwritten Chinese characters.

Let an online handwritten Chinese character image be represented as

$$C = \{p_1, p_2, \cdots, p_n\} \tag{5}$$

where $p_i = (x_i, y_i)$ denotes the coordinates of the ith point of the online trajectories and n is the total number of handwriting points. After the deformation transformation, the Chinese character can be rewritten as

$$C_D = \mathcal{D}(C) = \{\mathcal{D}(p_1), \mathcal{D}(p_2), \mathcal{D}(p_3) \cdots \mathcal{D}(p_n)\} \tag{6}$$

$$\mathcal{D}(p_i) = (x, y) + (f_x(x, y), f_y(x, y)) \tag{7}$$

where $\mathcal{D}$ is a type of displacement vector and $f_x(x, y)$, $f_y(x, y)$ are mapping functions. In fact, the deformation transformation method essentially redistributes image pixels according to the mapping functions. We can use different mapping functions to realize this deformation. However, the deformation approach must retain the original topological structure and satisfy the specific boundary conditions of the handwritten Chinese characters. In this study, we introduce a deformable transformation method to realize the style transformation [23]. As we can transform the image in both the x and the y directions, the transformation is given by

$$\begin{cases} \mathcal{D}(x_i) = x_i + f(x_i) \\ \mathcal{D}(y_i) = y_i + f(y_i) \end{cases} \tag{8}$$

where $f(x_i), f(y_i)$ are mapping functions. Without loss of generality, x and y are normalized to the interval [0, 1].

The following nonlinear trigonometric function is used to realize the transformation:

$$f(x) = x + \eta \cdot x[\sin(\pi\beta x + \alpha)\cos(\pi\beta x + \alpha) + \gamma] \tag{9}$$

where α and β are constants and η is a deformation parameter. In order to avoid the deformation of image boundary and retain a smooth image curve, we must satisfy the following boundary conditions:

$$\pi\beta x + \alpha|_{x=0} = a, \tag{10}$$

$$\pi\beta x + \alpha|_{x=1} = b, \tag{11}$$

$$f(0) = 0,\ f(1) = 1. \tag{12}$$

From (10) to (12), we get

$$\alpha = a, \tag{13}$$

$$\beta = \frac{b-a}{\pi}, \tag{14}$$

$$\gamma = -\sin b \cos b. \tag{15}$$

On the basis of these results, we can rewrite the mapping function as

$$\mathcal{D}(x_i) = x_i + \eta_1 x_i\{[\sin(b_1 - a_1)x_i + a_1][\cos(b_1 - a_1)x_i + a_1] - \sin b_1 \cos b_1\} \tag{16}$$

$$\mathcal{D}(y_i) = y_i + \eta_2 y_i\{[\sin(b_2 - a_2)y_i + a_2][\cos(b_2 - a_2)y_i + a_2] - \sin b_2 \cos b_2\} \tag{17}$$

where $0 \le a_1 \le b_1 \le 1$, $0 \le a_2 \le b_2 \le 1$, and η_1, η_2 denote the deformation parameters in the x and y directions, respectively.

In general, with a suitable selection for the values of a, b, η, we can perform 24 types of deformation processing for a given handwritten Chinese character, as shown in Figure 2.

Figure 2. Twenty-four types of deformation processing for the handwritten Chinese character '埃'.

2.2.3. *Imaginary stroke technique*

In practice, stroke connection is widely adopted by humans to accelerate their writing speed. However, this tendency leads to considerable shape distortion compared with neatly written characters. To recognize cursive characters with connected strokes and neatly written characters without increasing the standard character patterns, Okamoto *et al.* [16]–[18] proposed the imaginary stroke technique, which has been proved to be very effective for OHCCR [19][20].

Imaginary strokes are pen-moving trajectories in the pen-up state that are created to simulate the possible stroke connections formed during rapid cursive writing. Figure 3 shows some examples of characters with imaginary strokes.

Figure 3. Illustration of imaginary strokes.

In general, the imaginary stroke technique simulates the human's stroke connection habit and unifies different writing styles to a certain degree. Therefore, it can result in better performance than when imaginary strokes are not added.

Nevertheless, because the original character patterns are disturbed by these imaginary strokes, the imaginary stroke processing can introduce unwanted similarity between characters that are in fact distinguishable. Hence, it is recommended that imaginary strokes should be used in conjunction with the original strokes in an appropriate manner [20].

2.3. *Feature extraction*

2.3.1. *Region partition with the meshing technique*

To extract statistical features for online Chinese handwritten samples, the meshing method usually partitions a character image into a set of small regions (e.g., 8×8). It partitions the region of the character images with imaginary grids. If linear grids equally partition the character images, this is a linear meshing (illustrated in Figure 4(a)). However, as the character styles produced by different writers vary significantly, linear meshing does not always perform well. To overcome this disadvantage, we can construct a global elastic meshing and a local meshing [68] (illustrated in Figures 4(b) and (c)). These produce a global or local distribution of the black pixels in each row and column, respectively.

Image histograms under linear meshing and elastic meshing are illustrated in Figure 5. As shown in the figure, elastic meshing produces a uniformly distributed histogram. Therefore, it can shape and standardize the handwritten character images and is intolerant of a character's local deformation and stretching, which are caused by different writing styles.

(a) (b) (c) (d)

Figure 4. Linear meshing and global elastic meshing: (a) 8×8 linear meshing; (b) 8×8 global elastic meshing; (c) 8×8 local elastic meshing; (d) more examples of global elastic meshing.

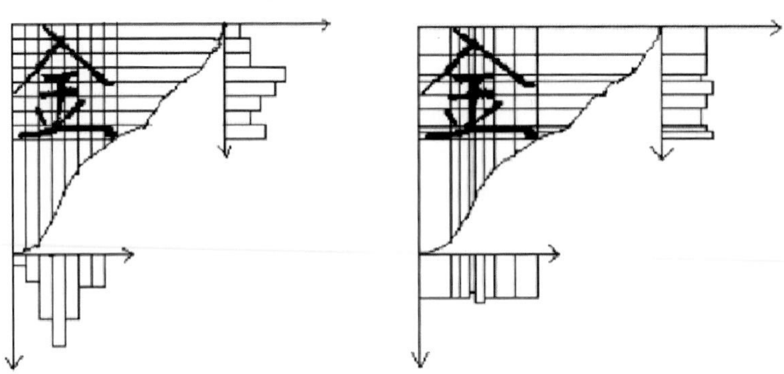

(a) (b)

Figure 5. Histograms of linear and elastic meshing: (a) linear meshing; (b) elastic meshing.

2.3.2. *8-directional feature extraction*

The 8-directional feature [19] is widely used in HCCR because of its outstanding ability to express stroke directions. In this technique, features are extracted from each online trajectory point based on eight 2D directions, and eight pattern images are then generated accordingly. Although the technique can be simplified to four directions or expanded to 16, eight affords a reasonable balance between storage requirements and precision.

To extract the 8-directional features, the technique has to apply several processing steps to an input online handwritten Chinese character sample. These include linear normalization, addition of imaginary strokes, nonlinear shape normalization, equidistance resampling, and smoothing. The result is a 64×64 normalized online character sample. The 8-directional features are then computed for each online trajectory point, and, consequently, 8-directional pattern images are generated. Finally, a 512-dimensional vector of raw features is formed.

In summary, the 8-directional features are given by the following steps:

1) Linear normalization: The original character trajectories are normalized to a fixed size of 64×64 using an aspect-ratio-preserving linear mapping.
2) Addition of imaginary strokes: The imaginary stroke technique is applied for each consecutive stroke pair.
3) Resampling: The sequence of online points in each stroke (including all imaginary strokes) of a character is resampled as a sequence of equidistant points.
4) Smoothing: The trajectory sequence is smoothed by a mean filter.
5) Extraction of the directional vector of each trajectory point: Given a stroke point P_j, its direction vector $\vec{V_j}$ is defined as follows:

$$\vec{V_j} = \begin{cases} \overrightarrow{P_j P_{j+1}} & \text{if } P_j \text{ is a start point} \\ \overrightarrow{P_{j-1} P_{j+1}} & \text{if } P_j \text{ is a internal point} \\ \overrightarrow{P_{j-1} P_j} & \text{if } P_j \text{ is an end point.} \end{cases}$$

6) Projection: The directional vector $\vec{V}_j$ is projected onto two of the 8-directional axes to generate an eight-dimensional direction code at each trajectory point.
7) Blurring: The character image is divided into 8×8 subblocks using fixed or elastic meshing. Within each subblock, the eight-dimensional direction codes are blurred by a Gaussian filter, resulting in a 512-dimensional feature.
8) Transformation: A variable transformation $y = x^{0.5}$ is applied to each element of the extracted feature vector to make its distribution more Gaussian-like.

2.3.3. *Signature of path features*

Path signatures, pioneered by Chen [103] in the form of iterated integrals, can be used to solve any linear differential equation and uniquely express a path with a finite length. The path-signature feature was first introduced to the recognition of online handwritten characters by Graham [49], who achieved very impressive performance. Essentially, the zeroth, first, and second iterated integrals correspond to the 2D bitmap, the direction, and the curvature of the pen trajectory, respectively.

Consider a time interval $[T_1, T_2] \subset \mathbb{R}$ and the writing plane $W = \mathbb{R}^2$. A pen stroke can be expressed by a continuous function $P: [T_1, T_2] \to W$. Given the intervals $[t_1, t_2] \subset [T_1, T_2]$ and $k \in \mathbb{N}^*$, the kth iterated integral of P is the 2^k-dimensional vector defined by

$$P_{t_1,t_2}^k = \int_{t_1 < u_1 < \cdots < u_k < t_2} 1 dP_{u_1} \otimes \cdots \otimes dP_{u_k} . \tag{18}$$

Conventionally, the $k = 0$ iterated integral denotes the original input, $k = 1$ represents the path displacement, and $k = 2$ denotes the path curvature. By increasing the value of k, we can extract higher levels of path information. However, the dimension of the iterated integrals increases rapidly. Therefore, we use the truncated form:

$$S(P)_{t_1,t_2}^n = (1, P_{t_1,t_2}^1, P_{t_1,t_2}^2, \ldots, P_{t_1,t_2}^n). \tag{19}$$

The iterated integrals P_{t_1,t_2}^k in (19) can be calculated by

$$\begin{aligned} &P_{t_1,t_2}^0 = 1,\ P_{t_1,t_2}^1 = \Delta_{t_1,t_2},\ P_{t_1,t_2}^2 = (\Delta_{t_1,t_2} \otimes \Delta_{t_1,t_2}) / 2!, \\ &P_{t_1,t_2}^3 = (\Delta_{t_1,t_2} \otimes \Delta_{t_1,t_2} \otimes \Delta_{t_1,t_2}) / 3!,\ \ldots, \end{aligned} \tag{20}$$

where $\Delta_{t_1,t_2} := P_{t_2} - P_{t_1}$ denotes the path displacement. At this stage, each point along the path can generate a set of signature values at the truncated level n. The dimension of $S(P)$ is $2^{n+1} - 1$ (i.e., the number of feature maps).

For better observation, we fill the pen's trajectory with the respective signature values at each level from $k = 0,\ldots, 3$, and set the background pixels to 0. We then apply image histogram equalization for each feature map (see the visualization for this in Figure 6). Each row corresponds to the handwriting feature maps contributed by a writer. Each column can be regarded as a specific descriptor that extracts special information (e.g., the direction or curvature) from the original path.

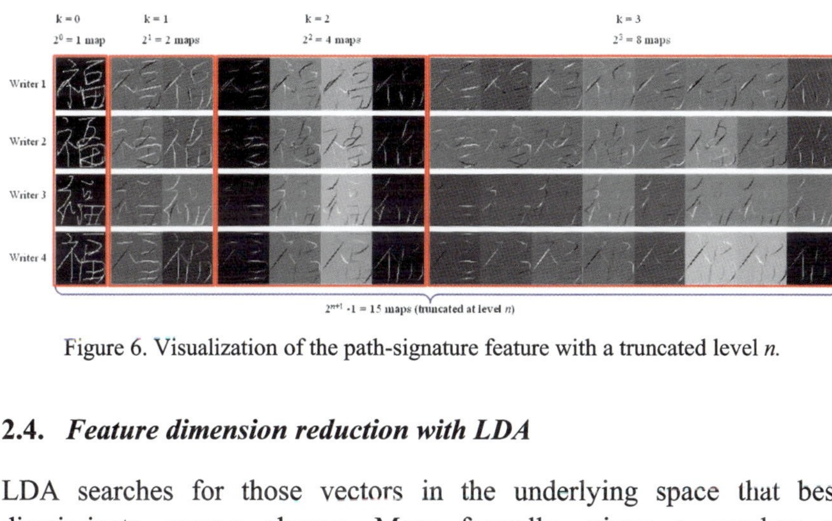

Figure 6. Visualization of the path-signature feature with a truncated level n.

2.4. *Feature dimension reduction with LDA*

LDA searches for those vectors in the underlying space that best discriminate among classes. More formally, given a number of independent features that describe the data, LDA creates a linear combination of these features that yields the largest mean differences between the desired classes. Mathematically speaking, for all samples of all classes, we define two measures: (i) the within-class scatter matrix, given by

$$S_w = \sum_{j=1}^{c} \sum_{i=1}^{N_j} (x_i^j - \mu_j)(x_i^j - \mu_j)^T \tag{21}$$

where x_i^j is the ith sample of class j, μ_j is the mean of class j, c is the number of classes, and N_j is the number of samples in class j; and (ii) the between-class scatter matrix

$$S_b = \sum_{j=1}^{c} (\mu_j - \mu)(\mu_j - \mu)^T \tag{22}$$

where μ represents the mean of all classes.

The goal of LDA is to maximize the between-class measure while minimizing the within-class measure. One way to do this is to maximize the ratio $\det|S_b| / \det|S_w|$. If S_w is a non-singular matrix, then the ratio is maximized when the column vectors of the projection matrix W_{lda} are the eigenvectors of $S_w^{-1} S_b$.

Modified linear discriminant analysis improves the performance of LDA by compensating for the error in the estimation of S_w. If the covariance matrix for class j is denoted as

$$\Sigma_j = \frac{1}{N_j} \sum_{i=1}^{N_j} (x_i^j - \mu_j)(x_i^j - \mu_j)^T, \tag{23}$$

then S_w can be denoted using Σ_j as

$$S_w = \sum_{j=1}^{c} N_j \Sigma_j. \tag{24}$$

Taking the eigen-decomposition, we can rewrite Σ_j as

$$\Sigma_j = \mathrm{B}_j \Lambda_j \mathrm{B}_j^T, \tag{25}$$

where $\Lambda_j = diag(\lambda_{j1},...,\lambda_{jd})$, with λ_{jk} $(k = 1,2,\ldots,d)$ being the eigenvalues (ordered in decreasing order) of Σ_j, and $\mathrm{B}_j = [\beta_{j1},...,\beta_{jd}]$, with β_{jk} $(k = 1,2,\ldots,d)$ being the ordered eigenvectors. B_j is orthonormal (unitary) such that $\mathrm{B}_j \mathrm{B}_j^T = I$.

To compensate for the estimation error of Σ_j with finite sample sizes, we use $\tilde{\Lambda}_j$ to replace Λ_j and reconstruct Σ_j as $\tilde{\Sigma}_j = \mathrm{B}_j \tilde{\Lambda}_j \mathrm{B}_j^T$, where $\tilde{\Lambda}_j = diag(\lambda_{j1},...\lambda_{jm},\delta_j,...\delta_j)$ with

$$\delta_j = \frac{1}{d-m} \sum_{k=m+1}^{d} \lambda_{jk}. \tag{26}$$

Thus, the reconstructed within-class scatter matrix becomes

$$\tilde{S}_w = \sum_{j=1}^{c} N_j \tilde{\Sigma}_j. \tag{27}$$

In Chinese character recognition applications, $\tilde{S}_w$ is usually a non-singular matrix. Hence, the desired ratio is maximized when the column vectors of the projection matrix W_{mlda} are eigenvectors of $\tilde{S}_w^{-1} S_b$.

2.5. *MQDF classifier*

Based on Bayesian decision rules that classify the input pattern to the class of maximum *a posteriori* probability, the quadratic discriminant function (QDF) is obtained under the assumption of multivariate Gaussian density for each class. The MQDF proposed by Kimura *et al.* [7] introduces the Karhunen-Loeve (K-L) transform to the QDF and smooths the minor eigenvalues to improve the computational efficiency and classification performance.

According to Bayes's rule, *a posteriori* probability is computed by

$$P(\omega_i \mid x) = \frac{P(\omega_i)p(x \mid \omega_i)}{p(x)}, \quad i = 1, \ldots, M, \tag{28}$$

where M is the number of classes, $P(\omega_i)$ is the a priori probability of class ω_i, $p(x \mid \omega_i)$ is the class probability density function, and $p(x)$ is the mixture density function. As $p(x)$ is independent of class, the numerator of (28) can be used as the discriminant function for classification:

$$g(x, \omega_i) = P(\omega_i)p(x \mid \omega_i). \tag{29}$$

Assume the probability density function of each class is a multivariate Gaussian:

$$p(x \mid \omega_i) = \frac{1}{(2\pi)^{\frac{D}{2}} |\Sigma_i|^{\frac{1}{2}}} \exp[-\frac{(x-\mu_i)^T \sum_i^{-1} (x-\mu_i)}{2}], \tag{30}$$

where μ_i and Σ_i denote the mean vector and covariance matrix of class ω_i, respectively, and D is the dimension of μ_i. We can insert (30) into (29) and take the negative logarithm and omit the common terms under equal a priori probabilities to obtain the QDF:

$$g_0(x, \omega_i) = (x-\mu_i)^T \sum_i^{-1} (x-\mu_i) + \log|\Sigma_i|. \tag{31}$$

The QDF can be used as a distance metric in the sense that the class of minimum distance is assigned to the input pattern.

Using a K-L transform, the covariance matrix can be diagonalized as

$$\Sigma_i = \Phi_i \Lambda_i \Phi_i^T, \tag{32}$$

where $\Lambda = diag[\lambda_{i1}, \ldots, \lambda_{iD}]$, with $\lambda_{ij}\,(j = 1, \ldots, D)$ being the eigenvalues (ordered in decreasing order) of Σ_i, and $\Phi_i = [\phi_{i1}, \ldots, \phi_{iD}]$, with

ϕ_{ij} (j = 1, …, D) being the ordered eigenvectors. Φ_i is orthonormal (unitary) such that $\Phi_i^T \Phi_i = I$.

According to (32), the QDF can be rewritten in terms of eigenvectors and eigenvalues as

$$\begin{aligned} g_0(x,\omega_i) &= [\Phi_i^T(x-\mu_i)]^T \Lambda_i^{-1}\Phi_i^T(x-\mu_i) + \log|\Lambda_i| \\ &= \sum_{j=1}^{D} \frac{1}{\lambda_{ij}}[\phi_{ij}^T(x-\mu_i)]^2 + \sum_{j=1}^{D}\log\lambda_{ij}. \end{aligned} \tag{33}$$

By replacing the minor eigenvalues with a constant δ_i, we obtain the MQDF as

$$\begin{aligned} g_1(x,\omega_i) &= \sum_{j=1}^{K} \frac{1}{\lambda_{ij}}[\phi_{ij}^T(x-\mu_i)]^2 \\ &\quad + \sum_{j=K+1}^{D} \frac{1}{\delta_i}[\phi_{ij}^T(x-\mu_i)]^2 + \sum_{j=1}^{K}\log\lambda_{ij} \\ &\quad + (D-K)\log\delta_i \\ &= \frac{1}{\delta_i}\left\{ \|x-\mu_i\|^2 - \sum_{j=1}^{K}(1-\frac{\delta_i}{\lambda_{ij}})[\phi_{ij}^T(x-\mu_i)]^2 \right\} \\ &\quad + \sum_{j=1}^{K}\log\lambda_{ij} + (D-K)\log\delta_i \end{aligned} \tag{34}$$

where K denotes the number of dominant eigenvectors. The above uses the invariance of Euclidean distance:

$$d_E(x,\omega_i) = \|x-\mu_i\|^2 = \sum_{j=1}^{D}[\phi_{ij}^T(x-\mu_i)]^2. \tag{35}$$

In training the QDF classifier, the patterns' eigenvalues are always underestimated because of the limited sample set. In addition, the minor eigenvalues become a type of unstable noise, which affects the classifier's robustness. Smoothing them in the MQDF classifier not only improves classification performance, but also reduces the computation time and storage space required for the parameters.

The parameter δ_i can be set to a class-independent constant [7] or a class-dependent constant calculated as the average of the minor eigenvalues [9]. In practice, we observed superior performance when setting the constant to be class independent rather than class dependent. The same result was also found in Refs. [14][84]. Thus, we set this parameter to be a class-independent constant and optimize its value by holdout cross-validation on the training data.

To date, the MQDF is one of the best statistical learning methods for OHCCR. During recent years, there has been considerable improvement in the MQDF-based classifier for HCCR, such as DLQDF [84], a compact version of MQDF [10], large-margin minimum classification error training of MQDF [102], and perceptron learning of MQDF [83].

3. OHCCR-CNN: An End-to-End Approach for OHCCR using Deep Convolutional Neural Networks

3.1. *Brief introduction to CNNs*

CNNs [32][33] are hierarchical neural networks that extract local features by convoluting the input with a group of kernel filters. The resulting convolutional feature maps are then activated, subsampled (denoted as pooling), and filtered to the next layer, as shown in Figure 7. Unlike the traditional multilayer perceptron, the convolutional layer locally connects input units to the output unit through a topological structure and shares the weights (kernel filters) with each connection. This type of connection makes CNN more suitable for images, which need fewer parameters, and is consistent with the local receptive field theory [34] in cognitive science. In this section, we briefly introduce the CNN algorithm.

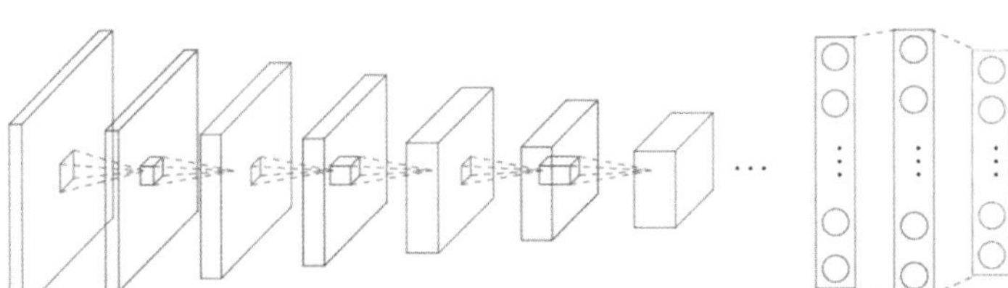

Figure 7. Illustration of a deep CNN. Red cuboids represent convolutional layers, blue cuboids represent pooling layers, red bars with circles represent fully connected layers, and green bar with circles represents the softmax layer.

3.1.1. *Convolutional layer*

Let $x_i^l \in \mathbb{R}^{M_l \times M_l}$ represent the ith feature map in the lth layer. The jth kernel filter in the lth layer connected to the ith map in the $(l-1)^{th}$ layer is denoted as $k_{ij}^l \in \mathbb{R}^{K_l \times K_l}$, and the set of index maps M_j is defined as $\{i \mid i^{th}$ map in the $(l-1)^{th}$ layer map connected to the jth map in the lth layer$\}$. The convolution operation can be written as

$$z_j^l = \sum_{i \in M_j} x_i^{l-1} * k_{ij}^l + b_j^l, \tag{36}$$

where $*$ denotes the convolution operation, $z_j^l \in \mathbb{R}^{M_l \times M_l}$ is the output feature map, and $b_j^l \in \mathbb{R}^{M_l \times M_l}$ is the bias matrix. Figure 8 illustrates the convolution operation for $K_l = 3$, $M_1 = \{1,3\}$. As shown in this figure, the output map is just connected to the first and third input maps.

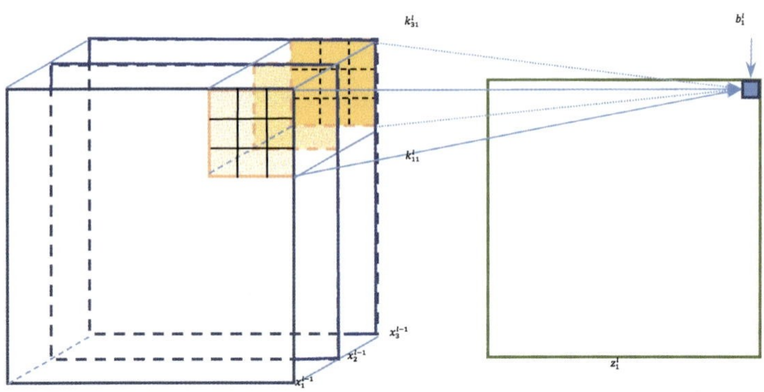

Figure 8. Convolution operation.

In Ref. [33], it was found that only certain input feature maps need to be connected to the output map. Hence, we define the index map set to represent the connection relationship. In current models, however, all input maps are connected to the output maps. Thus, the index set is insignificant, and we can convert the convolution operation to matrix multiplication. We set the input as a tensor $x^{l-1} \in \mathbb{R}^{M_{l-1} \times M_{l-1} \times C_{l-1}}$, which means x^{l-1} has C_{l-1} feature maps of size $M_{l-1} \times M_{l-1}$. The kernel filter is also denoted as a tensor $k^l \in \mathbb{R}^{K_l \times K_l \times C_{l-1} \times C_l}$, which means that k^l has C_l filters of size $K_l \times K_l$ and C_{l-1} channels. We write the tensor k^l as the matrix $w^l \in \mathbb{R}^{K_l^2 C_{l-1} \times C_l}$ and take $K_l \times K_l$ patches from x^{l-1} to vectorize and concatenate the matrix $x_{col}^{l-1} \in \mathbb{R}^{K_l^2 C_{l-1} \times M_l^2}$. Thus, we can use matrix multiplication to compute the outputs:

$$z_{col}^l = \left(w^l\right)^T x_{col}^{l-1} + b^l, \tag{37}$$

where $z_{col}^l \in \mathbb{R}^{C_l \times M_l^2}$. After reshaping the matrix z_{col}^l, we can obtain the desired output as the tensor $z^l \in \mathbb{R}^{M_l \times M_l \times C_l}$.

After the convolution operation, the output units are fed into an activation function, such as the sigmoid function or hyperbolic tangent function. However, in recent years, rectified linear units (ReLUs) [70] have become more popular, as the error rate decreases faster using stochastic gradient descent [34]. The ReLU activation function is defined as

$$f(z) = \max(0, z). \tag{38}$$

3.1.2. *Pooling layer*

The pooling operation mainly achieves spatial invariance and reduces the resolution of the feature maps. Typically, the pooling operation is used in a non-overlapping feature map [47]. The pooling equation can be written as

$$x_i^l = pool(x_i^{l-1}), \tag{39}$$

where $pool(\cdot)$ computes the maximum or average value of each $n_l \times n_l$ region in map x_i^{l-1}. Figure 9 shows the non-overlapping max-pooling of x_i^{l-1} with a pooling size of 2. We use different colors to indicate the different pooling regions in feature map x_i^{l-1}.

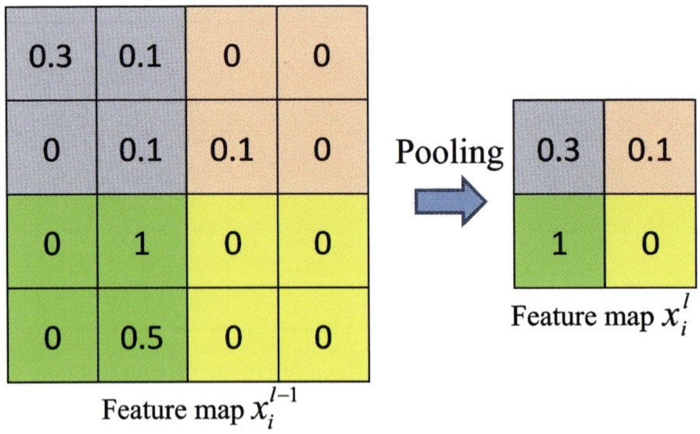

Figure 9. Max-pooling.

3.1.3. *Softmax layer and loss function*

Softmax regression is an effective method for multi-class classification problems. Suppose we have T categories and denote the training data for each category as (x_i^{l-1}, y_i), $i = \{1, \ldots, N\}$, where $x_i^{l-1} \in \mathbb{R}^d$ and $y_i \in \mathbb{R}$ are the feature vector and label, respectively. The softmax function is employed as the top layer of the CNN. This is defined as

$$\text{softmax}_t(x_i^{l-1}) = \frac{\exp(\theta_t^T x_i^{l-1})}{\sum_{m=1}^{T} \exp(\theta_m^T x_i^{l-1})}, \tag{40}$$

where $\sum_{m=1}^{T} \exp(\theta_m^T x_i^{l-1})$ is a normalization factor. Finally, CNNs minimize the following cross-entropy loss function:

$$J(W) = -\frac{1}{N}\left[\sum_{i=1}^{N}\sum_{t=1}^{T} 1\{y_i = \text{t}\} \log(\text{softmax}_t(x_i^{l-1}))\right], \tag{41}$$

where W denotes the CNN parameters and $1(\cdot)$ is an indicator function.

The loss function $J(W)$ can be minimized using mini-batch stochastic gradient descent (SGD) during the CNN training process. Mini-batch SGD uses small batches of data selected from the dataset to stochastically train the CNN. This can provide effective solutions to difficult problems, especially the training of a CNN, which is a highly non-convex problem. SGD is explained in Algorithm 1.

Algorithm 1. Mini-batch SGD

input: training set $\mathcal{X} = \{(\mathbf{x}_1, \mathrm{y}_1), \ldots, (\mathbf{x}_N, \mathrm{y}_N)\}$, initialized parameters W, learning rate $\eta(t)$

1: $t \leftarrow 0$
2: **while** not converged **do**
3: $t \leftarrow t+1$
4: Fetch mini-batch data $\mathcal{X}' \subset \mathcal{X}$
5: Forward the CNN and calculate the loss $J(W)$
6: Calculate $\nabla W = \frac{\partial J(W)}{\partial W}$ by backpropagation
7: Update$W = W - \eta(t) \cdot \nabla W$
8: **end while**
9: **output**W

3.1.4. *Platforms for training CNNs*

Unlike other machine learning algorithms, CNN takes a long time to train because of the huge number of parameters, deep structure, and large amount of training data. Originally, CNNs were trained on clusters [71]. However, some developers have implemented the entire framework on GPUs and made the platform open source, which has enhanced the popularity of CNNs. ConvNet[a] was the first open source GPU implementation, developed by Alex Krizhevsky, and won first prize in the ImageNet Large Scale Visual Recognition Challenge 2012 (ILSVRC2012). Caffe[b] is a widely used deep learning framework that is efficient and modular, and the Torch[c] scientific computing framework for machine learning algorithms includes a fast convolution implementation. CXXNet[d] is an efficient scheme for multi-GPUs that can achieve linear speed-up. Theano[e] is a Python library for deep learning research that makes it easy to define, optimize, and evaluate mathematical expressions. DIGIT[f] is an interactive deep learning GPU system for training CNNs and visualizing the results and parameters without coding.

[a]https://code.google.com/p/cuda-convnet/
[b]http://caffe.berkeleyvision.org/
[c]http://torch.ch/
[d]https://github.com/dmlc/cxxnet/
[e]http://deeplearning.net/software/theano/
[f]https://developer.nvidia.com/digits

3.2. *Domain knowledge-enhanced DCNN for OHCCR*

In recent years, DCNNs have achieved noteworthy success in HCCR, beating benchmark performances by wide margins [47][48][50]. Graham [49] first proposed a variant of CNN called DeepCNet, which won first place in the ICDAR 2013 Chinese Handwriting Recognition Competition [50]. DeepCNet takes advantages of the sparsity of the input layer and the slow convolutional and max-pooling layers; this slow speed allows more spatial information to be retained, thus improving the generalization ability.

Our OHCCR-CNN architecture adopts a similar structure to DeepCNet, but is much thinner and consists of a domain-specific knowledge layer that is used to process and embed useful knowledge (Figure 10). Previous studies have shown that the incorporation of domain-specific knowledge, such as path-signature feature maps [50], can achieve highly successful OHCCR. This inspired us to adopt some of the domain knowledge described in Section 2 in our OHCCR-CNN model. In particular, we consider deformation transformation [23]–[25], NLN [15], imaginary stroke maps [16], 8-directional feature maps [19], and path-signature feature maps [72].

After the domain-specific knowledge layer, the architecture contains six convolutional layers, the first five of which are followed by max-pooling. The size of the convolutional filters is 3×3 in the first layer and 2×2 in the subsequent layers. The convolution stride is set to 1. Max-pooling is carried out over a 2×2 pixel window, with a stride size of 2. Finally, a stack of convolutional layers is followed by two fully connected (FC) layers containing 480 and 512 nodes, respectively. The number of convolutional filter kernels is much less than that in Ref. [49]; our model has 80 in the first layer, and then it increases in steps of 80 after each max-pooling, resulting in a total of 3.8 million parameters, far fewer than the 5.9 million used in Ref. [49]. ReLU activation functions [70] are used for the neurons in the convolution and FC layers, and softmax is used for the output layer.

We render the input image into a 48×48 bitmap embedded in a 96×96 grid. Thus, the architecture of our OHCCR-CNN model can be represented as follows:

Input96×96-M×96×96-80C3-MP2-160C2-MP2-240C2-MP2-320C2-MP2-400C2-480N-512N-Output,

where *M* denotes the number of input channels, that varies from 1 to 30, depending on the number of different types of domain knowledge incorporated. Note that the domain-specific knowledge methods only play a role in the input to the network and therefore produce only a minimal increase in the computational burden.

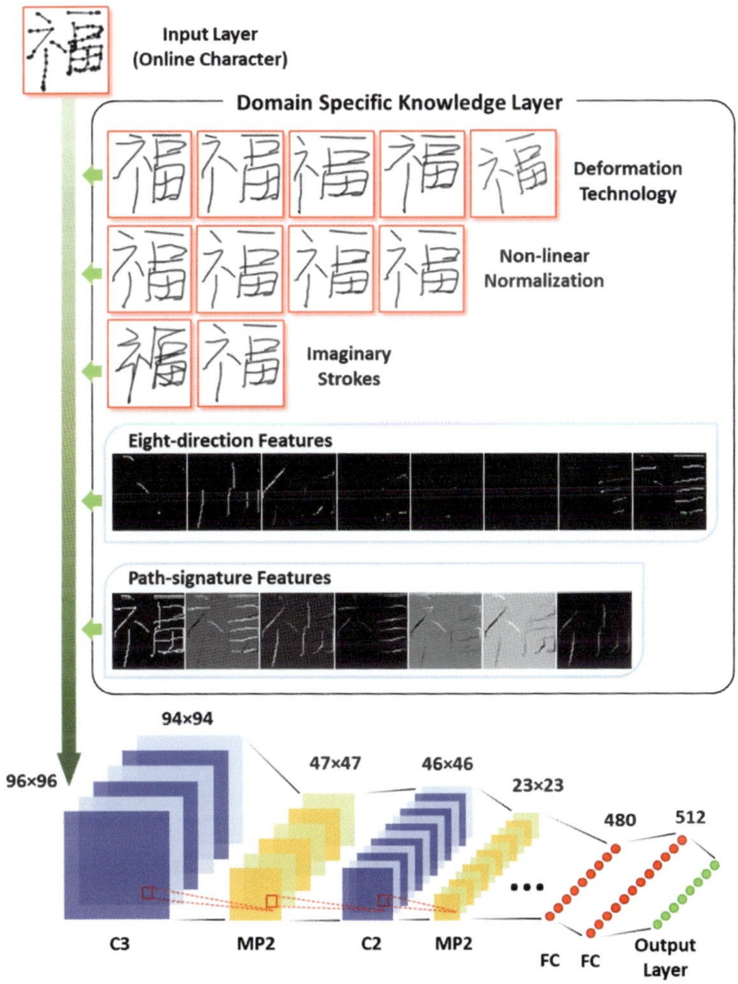

Figure 10. Illustration of a DCNN for OHCCR.

3.3. *Efficient training of CNN using a new algorithm named DropSample*

The performance of current CNNs is highly dependent on the greedy learning of model parameters based on a properly designed network architecture with abundant training data. Most CNN models treat all training samples uniformly during the learning process. However, we have found that the error reduction rate during the learning process is initially high, but decreases after a certain number of training iterations. This may be because most of the samples are well trained after a certain number of iterations; thus, the error propagation in adapting the network parameters is low, whereas confusable samples, which are difficult to learn and account for a relatively low ratio of the training dataset, do not have a high likelihood of contributing to the learning process. Some previous CNNs consider this phenomenon as a signal to manually reduce the learning rate or as a criterion for early stopping [73], thereby neglecting the potential of the confusing samples that have not been sufficiently well learned.

Inspired by the theory of Leitner's [74] learning box from the field of psychology, we introduce a new training method, called DropSample [57], to enhance the efficiency of the CNN learning process. We use DropSample to solve the challenge of OHCCR. Leitner's learning box is a simple implementation of the principle of spaced repetition for learning [75], which incorporates increasing intervals of time between subsequent reviews of previously learned material to exploit the psychological spacing effect. Although the principle of spaced repetition is useful in many contexts, it requires learners to acquire a large number of items and retain them in memory indefinitely. A direct application of Leitner's learning box theory is that material that is difficult to learn will appear more frequently and material that is easy to learn will appear less frequently, with difficulty defined according to the ease with which the user is able to produce the correct learning response. The DropSample training method proposed in this chapter adopts a similar concept to the design of a learning algorithm for CNN. According to the principles of DropSample, each training sample is assigned to a box with a quota function that is dynamically adjusted according to the classification confidence given by the CNN softmax output. After a learning iteration, samples with high confidence are placed in a box with low appearance probability, whereas those with low confidence are placed in another box with high appearance probability. Thus, the latter group are more likely to appear being selected as the training data in the next iteration. A small amount of noisy data (e.g., mislabeled samples and outliers) always exists in the training dataset, and such data may prevent the network from achieving high prediction accuracy. Noisy data should therefore be placed in a box with low appearance probability, allowing them to be gradually eliminated.

3.3.1. *Basic idea of DropSample*

We usually encounter three problems during the training of CNNs for large-scale pattern recognition tasks:

(1) Although the problem of heavy computation in CNN training can be solved using GPU-based massive parallel processing [76], CNN training with an extremely large amount of training data for large-scale classification remains a time-consuming process. This is because the CNN has to learn millions or even billions of parameters, and convolution produces a large number of additional computations compared with traditional fully connected shallow neural networks [32].

(2) After a certain number of training epochs (e.g., after five to ten training epochs), the training error decreases very quickly. As discussed above, this may be because most of the samples are well recognized after a certain number of training epochs; thus, the error propagation in adapting the network parameters is low. However, confusable samples, which are difficult to learn and account for a relatively low ratio of the training set, do not have a high chance of being selected for the training process. Some CNNs treat this phenomenon as a signal for early stopping [73], thereby neglecting the potential of the confusable samples that have not been sufficiently well learned and ignoring the proper processing of noisy samples (such as mislabeled samples or outliers).

(3) Despite great efforts to train and clean the dataset collection, many databases include a significant number of mislabeled and very noisy samples. Figure 11 shows some examples from the widely used CASIA-OLHWB OHCCR dataset [77]. Although the mislabeled and noisy samples constitute a minority of the overall dataset, they should not

be tolerated because the error reduction rate will gradually decrease and start to oscillate after a number of training epochs. Thus, mislabeled and very noisy samples might be harmful because the strong error feedback produced by these samples will backpropagate from the output layer to previous layers and interfere with the entire network.

Figure 11. Examples of very noisy samples, mislabeled samples, and outliers from the CASIA-OLHWDB dataset. The given label of each example is shown in the upper left corner. (a) and (b) comprise very noisy samples or outliers, whereas (c) and (d) comprise mislabeled samples or outliers. Examples of (a) and (c) were taken from CASIA-OLHWDB 1.0, whereas (b) and (d) were from CASIA-OLHWDB 1.1.

Inspired by these observations, we propose a new DCNN training solution to address the three problems mentioned above [57]. The proposed DropSample method sorts the training dataset into groups and uses the softmax output to dynamically adjust the selected quotas of samples in different groups. The output layer uses a k-way softmax activation function to generate a probability distribution over the n classes. According to a previous study, the softmax output of CNNs can be regarded as a confidence measurement of the CNN classification output [37]. In the case of training using DropSample, samples with high confidence are placed in a box with low appearance probability, and those with low confidence are discarded so that the remaining samples can be frequently reviewed in the network.

Suppose that we have m training samples (x_i, y_i). The input vectors are $(n+1)$-dimensional. Batch gradient descent is used to train a DCNN with k-way softmax in the output layer. The hypotheses of softmax can be written as

$$h_{\theta_j}(x_i) = \frac{\exp(\theta_j^T x_i)}{\Sigma_{l=1}^k \exp(\theta_l^T x_i)} \quad (j = 1, 2, \ldots, k), \tag{42}$$

where θ_j denotes the weights and bias corresponding to the jth output. The loss function $J(\theta)$ can be written in cross-entropy form with a regularization term as

$$J(\theta) = -\frac{1}{m}\left[\sum_{i=1}^{m}\sum_{j=1}^{k} 1\{y_i = j\} \log \frac{\exp(\theta_j^T x_i)}{\Sigma_{l=1}^k \exp(\theta_l^T x_i)}\right] + \frac{\lambda}{2}\sum_{i=1}^{k}\sum_{j=0}^{n}\theta_{ij}^2. \tag{43}$$

Its partial derivative (known as the "error term") with respect to θ_j is given by

$$\nabla_{\theta_j} J(\theta) = -\frac{1}{m}\sum_{i=1}^{m}\left[x_i(1\{y_i = j\} - p(y_i = j \mid x_i; \theta))\right] + \lambda\theta_j, \tag{44}$$

where p is the probability distribution of the softmax output, $1\{\cdot\}$ is the indicator function, and λ is a penalty factor. Thus, one gradient descent iteration updates the parameters as

$$\theta_j := \theta_j - \alpha\nabla_{\theta_j} J(\theta) \quad (j = 1, 2, \ldots, k), \tag{45}$$

where α is the learning rate of the parameters.

The error term in (44) can be split into three groups based on the softmax output. Let p_i be the probability of the predicted class of the ith sample. Let T_1 and T_2 be the thresholds for p_i that roughly separate m training samples into three groups, M_1, M_2, and M_3, corresponding to the well-recognized group ($T_2 < p_i \le 1$), the confusing group ($T_1 \le p_i \le T_2$), and the noisy group ($0 \le p_i < T_1$), respectively. Thus, (44) can be rewritten as

$$\begin{aligned}
\nabla_{\theta_j} J(\theta) &= E_1 + E_2 + E_3 + \lambda\theta_j \\
&= -\frac{1}{m}\left\{\sum_{i_1 \in M_1}\left[x_{i_1}(1\{y_{i_1} = j\} - p(y_{i_1} = j \mid x_{i_1}; \theta))\right]\right. \\
&\quad + \sum_{i_2 \in M_2}\left[x_{i_2}(1\{y_{i_2} = j\} - p(y_{i_2} = j \mid x_{i_2}; \theta))\right] \\
&\quad \left. + \sum_{i_3 \in M_3}\left[x_{i_3}(1\{y_{i_3} = j\} - p(y_{i_3} = j \mid x_{i_3}; \theta))\right]\right\} + \lambda\theta_j,
\end{aligned} \tag{46}$$

where E_1, E_2, and E_3 represent the suberror terms corresponding to the three abovementioned sample groups, respectively. These groups can be explained as follows.

(1) Well-recognized group M_1: Given that the values of the probability distribution p for a well-recognized sample are similar to those of the indicator function, the parameter θ_j obtains a small update from the suberror term E_1 according to (45) and (46). Well-recognized samples are less useful for improving the network because they produce very low error feedback. Therefore, it is reasonable to reduce their likelihood of selection as training data in the next training iteration.

(2) Confusing group M_2: In contrast, a confusing sample has a relatively decentralized softmax probability distribution. Neither the probability value of the predicted class nor the probability values of similar classes can be ignored because both have an obvious effect on E_2. Moreover, in the feature space, confusing samples often appear near the decision boundary and exert an influence on boundary optimization. Therefore, the adaptive quotas of the confusing samples, which reflect their opportunity for selection as training data, should be increased to achieve fast, reinforced learning.

(3) Noisy group M_3: It is sometimes useful to acquire a large amount of feedback by backpropagation from the suberror terms. However, an exception arises in the case of noisy samples, which often produce a larger suberror term E_3 than E_1 or E_2. These samples should be excluded from the training process, but not initially. This is because the network itself will find it difficult to identify heavily noisy or mislabeled samples during the early training epochs. Moreover, the noisy samples can be regarded as noise to enhance the regularization of the DCNN in the initial stage of training [37].

3.3.2. *Implementation of DropSample*

Each sample in the training dataset is allocated an equal initial quota, fixed to 1, and an updating function is then defined to change this quota according to the softmax output. A sample's quota represents its probability of it being selected as a training sample.

We develop a quota-updating strategy as

$$q_i^t = q_i^{t-1} f(p_i^t), \tag{47}$$

where $f(\cdot)$ denotes the quota-updating function, p_i^t is the softmax probability of the predicted class given by the ith sample at the tth updating iteration, and q_i^t is the adaptive quota of the ith sample at the tth updating iteration. This update equation accounts for the previous updating quota, thus preventing excessively fast quota adjustment. After a few epochs, the quota gradually absorbs information from the previous training results. Therefore, a well-recognized sample has a low quota resulting from excellent performance every time it is selected.

In practical applications, the function $f(\cdot)$ can be manually fitted to certain requirements or tasks. Here, we present an exponential piecewise function given by

$$f(p_i^t) = \begin{cases} 1-\exp(-\gamma p_i^t) & 0 \le p_i^t < T_1 \\ 1-\exp(-\beta(1-p_i^t)) & T_2 < p_i^t \le 1, \\ 1/q_i^{t-1} & \text{otherwise} \end{cases} \tag{48}$$

where β and γ are the slope factors. A higher value of β or γ indicates a steeper gradient to the function. The three equations in (48) correspond to the three training groups M_1, M_3, and M_2, respectively. The parameters were determined empirically as $\beta = 400$, $\gamma = 600$, $T_1 = 1/k$, and $T_2 = 0.99$. The threshold T_1, which defines the boundary of the noisy samples, is set to $1/k$ because this is equivalent to the random guess probability of k classes. We consider a sample to be very noisy if the probability of its labeled class is lower than this threshold after a certain number of mini-batch training iterations.

DropSample does not actually drop samples from the training set; instead, it provides adaptive quotas for samples, thus dynamically adjusting their chance of selection as training data. Moreover, as the DropSample technique is independent of the network architecture, it is highly flexible and can be extended to other deep models such as a network in a network [36], DBN [78], and stacked auto-encoder [79].

The DropSample training algorithm is summarized in Algorithm 2.

Algorithm 2 DropSample training algorithm

Input: training set $X = \{(x_i, y_i)\}, i = 1, ..., m$ of *k* classes.

Output: network parameters ϑ.

Initialization: iteration $t \leftarrow 0$; learning rate $\alpha(t)$; quota parameters $q_i^0 \leftarrow 1, \forall i$;

quota-updating function f_1; $\beta = 400$, $\gamma = 600$, $T_1 = 1/k$, $T_2 = 0.99$.

1: **while** not converged **do**

2: $P^t = (q_1^t / Z^t, ..., q_m^t / Z^t)^{\mathrm{T}}$ where $Z^t = \sum_{i=1}^{m} q_i^t$

3: $t \leftarrow t + 1$ sample a mini-batch from *X* based on p^t

4: forward propagation: get the softmax output of the predicted class p_i^t

5: backpropagation: calculate error term $\nabla_\theta J(\theta) = E_1 + E_2 + E_3 + \lambda\theta$

6: update network parameters $\theta = \theta - \alpha(t)\nabla_\theta J(\theta)$

7: calculate quota-updating function $f_1(p_i^t)$

8: **if** $0 \le p_i^t < T_1$, $f_1(p_i^t) = 1 - e^{-\gamma p_i^t}$

9: **else if** $T_2 < p_i^t \le 1$, $f_1(p_i^t) = 1 - e^{-\beta(1 - p_i^t)}$

10: **else** $f_1(p_i^t) = 1 / q_i^{t-1}$

11: update quota parameters $q_i^t \leftarrow q_i^{t-1} f_1(p_i^t)$

12: **end while**

3.4. *Hybrid serial-parallel ensemble of DCNN for OHCCR*

Given that a set of networks offers many ways to represent different types of domain knowledge, using them in combination can be expected to produce better performance (e.g., MCDNN [47]). In view of this, we present an ensemble strategy called hybrid serial-parallel (HSP) [56], as illustrated in Figure 12. When a sample enters the HSP-DCNN system, the domain knowledge-based processing extracts feature maps for the following DCNNs. The input passes through a DCNN, producing a recognition decision if the predicted probability of this DCNN output is greater than a predefined threshold *T*. Otherwise, the input is sent to the next DCNN with corresponding feature maps from the sample, and this continues until either the threshold has been met or it fails to be output by the last network. If none of the DCNN output predictions is greater than the threshold, the final recognition decision is based on the average output of all the DCNNs. In essence, this proposed HSP classifier ensemble strategy takes advice from the best-qualified expert, while referring the hardest choices to the group to decide as a whole. Experiments suggest that this method demonstrates better results and is computationally less expensive than a simple voting or averaging procedure.

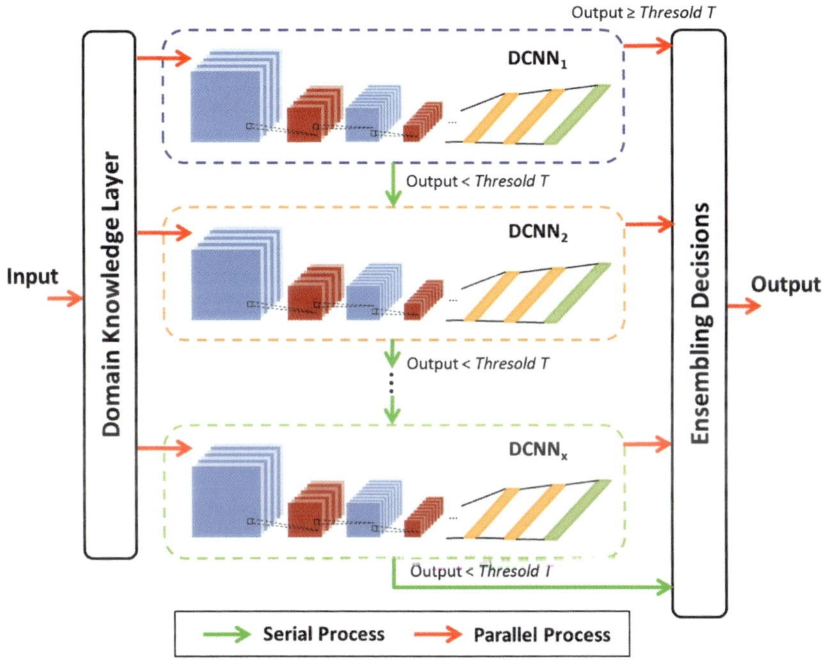

Figure 12. Illustration of the HSP-DCNN architecture.

4. Experimental Results

4.1. *Experimental database*

We used the CASIA-OLHWDB 1.0 (DB 1.0) and CASIA-OLHWDB 1.1 (DB 1.1) [77] databases, which were set up by the Institute of Automation at the Chinese Academy of Sciences. DB 1.0 contains 3740 Chinese characters in the GB2312-80 standard level 1 set (GB1) obtained from 420 writers (336×3740 samples for training, 84×3740 for testing). DB 1.1 contains 3755 classes in GB1 obtained from 300 writers (240×3755 samples for training, 60×3755 for testing).

The database for the ICDAR 2013 HCCR competition [50] comprises three datasets for isolated characters (CASIA-OLHWDB 1.0–1.2). All data have been annotated at the character level. The test dataset, which was published after the competition, was obtained from 60 writers who were not considered in DB 1.0–DB 1.2. In our experiments, we used only a combination of DB 1.0 and DB 1.1 to evaluate the ICDAR 2013 HCCR competition dataset because the classes of DB 1.2 are outliers of the 3755 classes in GB1.

4.2. *Investigation of the effectiveness of domain-specific knowledge*

To ensure a fair comparison, we used the baseline method (denoted as Bitmap in Table 1) to train the CNN by directly rendering an online handwritten Chinese character as an offline bitmap (single feature map) as a training sample, without using any domain-specific knowledge [47]. We then designed nine OHCCR-CNNs (denoted as A–I in Table 1) to intensively evaluate the performance achieved by the addition of different domain-specific knowledge to the baseline network. The experimental results for DB 1.1 are summarized in Table 1.

From the results shown in Table 1, we can see that the OHCCR-CNNs with path-signature features clearly enhanced the Bitmap by adding online information. Network C using Sign.2 was better than Network B using Sign.1 and was cost-effective compared with Network D using Sign.3 in terms of the number of feature maps. Similarly, all other networks with different domain knowledge outperformed the baseline CNN by a clear margin. Network E with DT gave slightly better results than Network C with Sign.2, although the improvement was more obvious in our preliminary small-scale experiments. Network F with the LDPI NLN [15] performed worse than Network C, although it gave better results than the other approaches in our preliminary experiments with small categories of training samples. It was found that additional DT can extend the coverage of possible handwriting styles, especially when the data are insufficient. Thus, we retain the DT domain knowledge for further use by the ensemble model. Network G with 8-directional features produced better results than the baseline and Network C, indicating that the additional features offer extra statistical information on stroke direction to enhance the performance of the baseline CNN. Network H with imaginary strokes embedded in an online character showed an obvious improvement, indicating that the imaginary stroke technique is useful. Integrating all the domain knowledge (referred to as fusion) except NLN to Network I achieved a significant improvement, which indicates that domain-specific knowledge is very useful for improving CNNs for HCCR.

Table 1. Recognition rates (%) of different domain-specific knowledge on CASIA-OLHWDB 1.1.

Network	Domain-specific methods*	Recognition rate (%)
A	**Baseline**: Bitmap (no domain knowledge)	93.99
B	Bitmap+Sign.1	95.95
C	Bitmap+Sign.2	96.12
D	Bitmap+Sign.3	96.12
E	Bitmap+Sign.2+DT	96.13
F	Bitmap+Sign.2+NLN	95.81
G	Bitmap+Sign.2+8 Dir	96.22
H	Bitmap+Sign.2+IS	96.33
I	**Fusion**: Bitmap+Sign.2+DT+8 Dir+IS	**96.39**

* Five types of domain-specific knowledge were used, namely, the path of signature feature maps (denoted as Sign.x), deformation transformation, nonlinear normalization, 8-directional feature maps, and the imaginary strokes. Please see Sections 2.2–2.3 for details about these domain knowledge processes.

4.3. *Investigation of the DropSample training method*

We applied the DropSample training method to nine experiments with different combinations of domain knowledge. The results are presented in Table 2 and Figure 13.

Table 2 shows that, for all experimental settings with different types of domain knowledge, the DCNN trained with DropSample consistently outperformed the DCNN that was not trained with DropSample.

Table 2. Recognition rates (%) for training with or without DropSample on CASIA-OLHWDB 1.1.

Network	Domain-specific methods	Without DropSample	With DropSample
A	**Baseline**: Bitmap	93.99	94.20
B	Bitmap+Sign.1	95.95	96.08
C	Bitmap+Sign.2	96.12	96.26
D	Bitmap+Sign.3	96.12	96.30
E	Bitmap+Sign.2+DT	96.13	96.27
F	Bitmap+Sign.2+NLN	95.81	96.08
G	Bitmap+Sign.2+8 Dir	96.22	96.34
H	Bitmap+Sign.2+IS	96.33	96.44
I	**Fusion**: Bitmap+Sign.2+DT+8 Dir+IS	96.39	96.55

Figure 13. Real-time web demo of the OHCCR-CNN online handwritten character recognition system [82].

4.4. *Investigation of HSP-DCNNs*

Given a set of CNN models with different domain knowledge and training with and without DropSample, it is useful to combine various domain knowledge types to achieve better performance. As shown in Table 3, our ensemble methods include voting, averaging, and the proposed HSP-DCNNs. Note that the HSP-DCNNs significantly outperformed the single network by a wide margin and achieved better results than other previous ensemble strategies. Our HSP-DCNNs attained a high recognition rate of 97.33% on DB1.0, 97.06% on DB1.1, and 97.51% on the ICDAR 2013 competition dataset, representing relative test error reductions of 53%, 51%, and 58%, respectively, compared with the baseline. As shown in Table 4, our final results are superior to those from state-of-the-art methods including an MQDF-based method (DLQDF [11]), MCDNN [47], and DeepCNet [49].

Table 3. Recognition rates (%) of the single network and the ensemble on the three CASIA-OLHW datasets.

Database	**Single Network**			**Ensemble (Nets A–I)**		
	Baseline	Fusion	Training with DropSample	Voting	Average	HSP-DCNNs
CASIA-OLHWDB 1.0	94.32	96.71	**96.93**	97.26	97.32	**97.33**
CASIA-OLHWDB 1.1	93.99	96.39	**96.55**	96.99	97.05	**97.06**
ICDAR 2013 competition DB	94.12	96.93	**97.23**	97.43	97.51	**97.51**

Table 4. Comparison of different methods on the three CASIA-OLHW datasets.

Database	Published State-of-the-Art Performance (%)				
	MQDF based	MCDNN [47]	DeepCNet [49]	Our Single DCNN	Our Ensemble
CASIA-OLHWDB 1.0	95.28 [11]	94.39	N/A	96.93	**97.33**
CASIA-OLHWDB 1.1	94.85 [11]	N/A	96.42	96.55	**97.06**
ICDAR 2013 competition DB	92.62⁺ [83]	N/A	97.39*	97.23	**97.51**

*The result of the winner of the ICDAR 2013 HCCR competition. Note that the number of parameters of DeepCNet (5.9 million) is much larger than that of our single DCNN (3.8 million).
⁺This result was submitted by the HIT team [50] using the PL-QMDF classifier [83].

We also evaluated the time consumption of different ensemble methods at the testing stage. As shown in Table 5, the proposed HSP-DCNN is much faster than the voting or averaging ensemble strategies. With the HSP strategy, approximately 84% of the test samples can be recognized from the first OHCCR-CNN with no need for further testing, accounting for its reduced time cost.

Table 5. Comparison of time consumption at the testing stage.

Testing (with GPU)	Single Network		DCNN Ensembling (A–H)		
	Baseline	Fusion	Voting	Averaging	HSP-DCNN
Time per Sample (ms)	2.40	3.50	28.10	28.08	6.22

4.5. *Evaluation of large-scale OHCCR*

We further extended the CNN architecture to recognize as many as 10,081 classes of a mixture of handwritten Chinese characters, English letters, numerals, and symbols. The 10,081 classes of characters included 6763 simplified Chinese characters in the GB2312-80 standard, 5401 traditional Chinese characters in the Big5 standard, 52 English letters (26 uppercase and 26 lowercase), 10 standard numerals (0–9), 165 symbols, and 937 additional rarely used Chinese characters. Note that 3247 characters are common to both GB2312-80 and Big5; thus, there were 10,081 different classes of characters in all. The OHCCR-CNN architecture we used can be written as 96×96Input-M×96×96-100C3-MP2-200C2-MP2-300C2-MP2-400C2-MP2-500C2-MP2-600C2-1024FC-10081Output. This is similar to that presented in Section 3, but with more convolution kernels. We used around 10 million data samples for training and 2 million data samples for validation, mainly obtained from the SCUT-COUCH dataset [80] and the CASIA-OLHWDB [77] dataset, together with some in-house datasets. It took approximately 2 weeks to train and optimize this OHCCR-CNN system[g], as shown in Figure 13. Testing was conducted on another 827,685 samples selected at random from seven datasets (see Table 6); these samples were not included in the training or validation datasets. The results are summarized in Table 6. It can be seen that, despite the very large number of classes (10,081), the OHCCR-CNN model achieved a very promising average recognition rate of 97.74% across seven datasets. This reflects the robust and excellent classification ability of the OHCCR-CNN with DropSample and domain knowledge enhancement.

Table 6. Performance of large-scale unconstrained handwritten character recognition on seven databases.

Test Set	DB 1.0 [77]	DB 1.1 [77]	DB 1.2 [77]	SCUT-COUCH [80]	HKU [19]	In-house Dataset	863 [81]	Total
Number of Samples	143,600	98,235	79,154	161,166	120,863	184,089	40,578	827,685
Recognition Rate (%)	96.70	96.05	97.24	98.62	97.73	98.42	99.72	97.74

5. Conclusion and Discussion

In this chapter, we have described two approaches to solve the OHCCR problem, namely, the traditional method based on Bayesian statistical learning and a new deep learning method with dedicated CNNs. In the

[g]A real-time web demo of this OHCCR-CNN online handwritten character recognition system is available at http://www.deephcr.net/.

traditional method, the state-of-the-art classifier is based on MQDF using Bayesian decision principles. Under this framework, preprocessing and feature extraction are vitally important. The performance of MQDF systems depend heavily on the proper use of domain-specific preprocessing such as NLN and imaginary strokes, and handcrafted features such as the 8-directional features. In contrast, the DCNN-based method provides an alternative novel end-to-end OHCCR method that does not involve traditional processing techniques such as NLN or any explicit handcrafted feature extraction. Although using a pure end-to-end CNN model such as the MCDNN [48] can achieve fairly good performance, domain-specific processing such as the extraction of the signature of path feature maps is still very useful. Embedding this domain-specific knowledge into the CNN framework produced very promising results. We showed that most domain knowledge-based processing methods in the field of OHCCR can enhance the DCNN via suitable representation and flexible integration.

We also introduced a new training method, DropSample, for CNN-based OHCCR through the efficient use of training samples. DCNNs trained with the DropSample technique focus on confusing samples, selectively ignore well-recognized samples, and effectively avoid the interference caused by noisy samples. The recognition rates of OHCCR-CNN trained with DropSample significantly exceeded those of state-of-the-art methods on three publicly available datasets (CASIA-OLHWDB 1.0, CASIA-OLHWDB 1.1, and the ICDAR 2013 HCCR competition dataset). Compared with the previous best results using MQDF-based approaches on CASIA-OLHWDB 1.0 (95.28%), CASIA-OLHWDB 1.1 (94.85), and ICDAR 2013 (92.62%), our HSP-DCNN deep learning model achieved recognition rates of 97.33%, 97.06, and 97.51%, respectively.

Furthermore, we showed that the OHCCR-CNN can be extended to deal with very large scale handwritten character recognition involving 10,081 classes of characters, achieving a very promising average recognition rate of 97.74% across seven open testing datasets.

It is clear that the emergence of novel deep learning technologies such as CNN, as well as proper yet simple incorporation with traditional domain-specific knowledge processing, can achieve very high accuracies for realistic unconstrained handwritten datasets such as SCUT-COUCH, as well as very promising results for cursive unconstrained datasets such as CASI-OLHWDB. Nevertheless, many challenging problems have received less attention and remained unsolved. We believe that there are still many research topics worthy of further study in the field of OHCCR. For example,

(1) Writer adaptation: For real-world applications, it is impossible to collect training data for an HCCR system that covers all writing styles. Hence, user experiences with many handwriting input method editors are unsatisfactory, especially for cursive writing styles. An obvious way of increasing the recognition accuracy for a particular user, is to adapt a writer-independent recognizer to an individual's writing style. This can be done by first training an initial general-purpose classification model on a generic writer-independent dataset and then tuning this for a particular writer using specific incremental data. This process is also known as writer adaptation or personalized handwriting recognition [85]. In recent years, there has been increasing research interest in this topic (e.g., [86]–[88]).

(2) Rotation-free OHCCR: According to a new national standard in China for HCCR systems, Chinese handwriting recognition software for text input should be able to recognize a character written with a rotational distortion of up to ±45°. However, to the best of our knowledge, no currently available software can meet this requirement. Although some researchers have tried to address this problem [90]–[94], the rotation-free online recognition of handwritten Chinese characters remains an open problem.

(3) New deep learning model for OHCCR: In this chapter, the deep learning model we reported for OHCCR was a CNN, which is one of various models in the field of deep learning. Although recent studies have reported the successful design or application of other models for handwritten character recognition (such as DNN [95] and the BLSTM recurrent neural network model [96][97]), the potential of such models or their variants has not been completely explored and their performance achieved so far is inferior to that of CNNs for OHCCR. Furthermore, some new deep learning

models such as deep reinforcement learning and DQN [98][99] may shed light on new ways to solve the problems of OHCCR.

(4) Building compact and fast CNN for real-time large-scale OHCCR: Compared with traditional methods, some excellent CNN models for OHCCR face the problem that they are neither fast nor compact enough. Moreover, most current studies limit the problem of OHCCR to 3755 classes (which is just the number in the GB2312-80 level character set). For a practical, usable OHCCR system, more than 10,000 classes should be considered. However, very few studies have reported on such a scale [57][88]. To date, there is no publicly available dataset that contains more than 10,000 classes (e.g., there are as many as 27,533 classes in the GB18010-2000 standard). Building a fast and compact CNN for large-scale problems in real-time applications is a practical issue that is worthy of attention.

(5) Development of a uniform learning and recognition platform for multi-task and multi-language character recognition: Humans have the ability to process multitask pattern recognition problems [100][101]. For example, the human brain vision system not only can recognize printed characters or handwritten characters, but also can distinguish different categories of objects, faces, persons, and so on. Thus, it is possible to design a uniform general-purpose pattern recognition platform that can handle multitask character recognition problems (e.g., printed, handwriting, different languages, etc.) such that the system can automatically learn some common knowledge and share it among different tasks to build a more robust and complex system.

(6) As the isolated OHCCR problem has been solved to some extent, we suggest that more attention should be paid to more challenging problems, such as unconstrained handwritten text-line recognition [104], overlay multi-character recognition [105], automatic mixture recognition of isolated characters/text lines/overlay texts, paragraph-level online handwritten text understanding and retrieval, and so on.

Acknowledgments

This work was supported in part by the National Natural Science Foundation of China (grant no.: 61472144), the National Science and Technology Support Plan (grant nos.: 2013BAH65F01 and 2013BAH65F03), and GDUPS (2011).

References

[1] C. Liu, S. Jaeger and M. Nakagawa, Online recognition of Chinese characters: The state-of-the-art, *IEEE Trans. Pattern Analysis and Machine Intelligence*, **26**(2), 198–213 (2004).

[2] M. Cheriet, N. Kharma, C. Liu and C. Suen, *Character recognition systems: A guide for students and practitioners* (Wiley, 2007).

[3] R. Plamondon and S. N. Srihari, On-line and off-line handwriting recognition: A comprehensive survey, *IEEE Trans. Pattern Analysis and Machine Intelligence*, **22**(1), 63–84 (2000).

[4] iiMedia Research, 2014Q3 Report of input methods for mobile phone in China market, [EB/OL]. http://www.iimedia.com.cn/, 2015-01-08.

[5] http://www.emarketer.com/Article/2-Billion-Consumers-Worldwide-Smartphones-by-2016/1011694, accessed on Dec. 11, 2014.

[6] A. K. Jain, R. P. W. Duin and J. Mao, Statistical pattern recognition: A review, *IEEE Trans. Pattern Analysis and Machine Intelligence*, **22**, 4–37 (2000).

[7] F. Kimura, K. Takashina, S. Tsuruoka and Y. Miyake, Modified quadratic discriminant functions and the application to Chinese character recognition, *IEEE Trans. Pattern Analysis and Machine Intelligence*, **9**(1), 149–153 (1987).

[8] H. Liu and X. Ding, Handwritten character recognition using gradient feature and quadratic classifier with multiple discrimination schemes, *Proc. 8th ICDAR*, 2005, pp. 19–23.

[9] C.-L. Liu, High accuracy handwritten Chinese character recognition using quadratic classifiers with discriminative feature extraction, *18th Int. Conference on Pattern Recognition*, 2006, pp. 942–945.

[10] T. Long and L. W. Jin, Building compact MQDF classifier for large character set recognition by subspace distribution sharing, *Pattern Recognition*, **41**(9), 2916–2925 (2008).

[11] C.-L. Liu, F. Yin, D.-H. Wang and Q.-F. Wang, Online and offline handwritten Chinese character recognition: benchmarking on new databases, *Pattern Recognition*, **46**(1), 155–162 (2013).

[12] H. Fujisawa, Forty years of research in character and document recognition — an industrial perspective, *Pattern Recognition*, **41**(8), 2435–2446 (2008).

[13] C. Liu and X. Zhou, Online Japanese character recognition using trajectory-based normalization and direction feature extraction, *Proc. International Workshop, Frontiers Handwriting Recognition*, 2006, pp. 217–222.

[14] H. Liu and X. Ding, Handwritten character recognition using gradient feature and quadratic classifier with multiple discrimination schemes, *Proc. International Conf. Document Analysis and Recognition*, 2005, pp. 19–23.

[15] C. L. Liu and K. Marukawa, Pseudo two-dimensional shape normalization methods for handwritten Chinese character recognition, *Pattern Recognition*, **38**(12), 2242–2255 (2005).

[16] M. Okamoto, A. Nakamura and K. Yamamoto, On-line handwriting character recognition method with directional features and directional change features, *Proc. 4th Int'l Conf. Document Analysis and Recognition*, **2**, 926–930 (1997).

[17] M. Okamoto, A. Nakamura and K. Yamamoto, Direction-change features of imaginary strokes for on-line handwriting character recognition, *Proc. 10th Int'l Conf. Pattern Recognition*, 1998, pp. 1747–1751.

[18] M. Okamoto and K. Yamamoto, On-line handwriting character recognition using direction change features that consider imaginary strokes, *Pattern Recognition*, **32**(7), 1115–1128 (1999).

[19] Z. L. Bai and Q. Huo, A study on the use of 8-directional features for online handwritten Chinese character recognition, *Proc. 8th Int'l Conf. Document Analysis and Recognition*, 2005, pp. 262–266.

[20] K. Ding, G. Deng and L. W. Jin, An investigation of imaginary stroke technique for cursive online handwriting Chinese character recognition, *Proc. 10th Int'l Conf. Document Analysis and Recognition*, 2009, pp. 531–535.

[21] C. L. Liu, R. Mine and M. Koga, Building compact classifier for large character set recognition using discriminative feature extraction, *Proc. 8th Int'l Conf. Document Analysis and Recognition*, 2005, pp. 846–850.

[22] H. J. Kim, K. H. Kim, S. K. Kim and J. K. Lee, On-line recognition of handwritten Chinese characters based on hidden Markov models, *Pattern Recognition*, **30**(9), 1489–1500 (1997).

[23] L. W. Jin, J. C. Huang, J. X. Yin and Q. H. He, A novel deformation on transformation and its application to handwritten Chinese character shape correction, *Journal of Image and Graphics*, **7**(2), 170–175 (2002).

[24] F. Yin, M. K. Zhou, Q. F. Wang and C. L. Liu, Style consistent perturbation for handwritten Chinese character recognition, *Proc. 12th Int'l Conf. Document Analysis and Recognition*, 2013, pp. 1051–1055.

[25] K. C. Leung and C. H. Leung, Recognition of handwritten Chinese characters by combining regularization, Fisher's discriminant and distorted sample generation, *Proc. 10th Int'l Conf. Document Analysis and Recognition*, 2009, pp. 1026–1030.

[26] Q. Huo, Y. Ge and Z. Feng, High performance Chinese OCR based on Gabor features, discriminative feature extraction and model training, *ICASSP*, 2001, pp. 1517–1520.

[27] G. E. Hinton and R. R. Salakhutdinov, Reducing the dimensionality of data with neural networks, *Science*, **313**(5786), 504–507 (2006).

[28] G. E. Hinton, N. Srivastava, A. Krizhevsky *et al.*, Improving neural networks by preventing co-adaptation of feature detectors. arXiv preprint arXiv: 1207.0580, 2012.

[29] L. Wan, M. Zeiler, S. Zhang *et al.*, Regularization of neural networks using DropConnect, *Proc. 30th Int'l Conf. Machine Learning*, 2013, pp. 1058–1066.

[30] Y. Bengio, P. Lamblin, D. Popovici *et al.*, Greedy layer-wise training of deep networks, *Advances in Neural Information Processing Systems*, **19**, 153 (2007).

[31] J. D. Owens, M. Houston, D. Luebke *et al.*, GPU computing, *Proc. IEEE*, **96**(5), 879–899 (2008).

[32] Y. LeCun, B. Boser, J. S. Denker *et al.*, Handwritten digit recognition with a back-propagation network, *Advances in Neural Information Processing Systems*, 1990.

[33] Y. LeCun, L. Bottou, Y. Bengio *et al.*, Gradient-based learning applied to document recognition, *Proc. IEEE*, **86**(11), 2278–2324 (1998).
[34] A. Krizhevsky, I. Sutskever and G. E. Hinton, ImageNet classification with deep convolutional neural networks, *Advances in Neural Information Processing Systems*, 1097–1105 (2012).
[35] C. Szegedy, W. Liu, Y. Jia *et al.*, Going deeper with convolutions. arXiv preprint arXiv:1409.4842, 2014.
[36] M. Lin, Q. Chen and S. C. Yan, Network in network. arXiv preprint arXiv:1312.4400, 2013.
[37] G. Montavon, G. Orr and K. Müller, Neural networks: Tricks of the trade, LNCS Vol. 7700, Springer, 2012.
[38] Y. Taigman, M. Yang, M. A. Ranzato *et al.*, DeepFace: Closing the gap to human-level performance in face verification, *Proc. 2014 IEEE Conf. Computer Vision and Pattern Recognition*, 2014, pp. 1701–1708.
[39] Y. Sun, Y. Chen, X. Wang and X. Tang, Deep learning face representation by joint identification-verification, *Advances in Neural Information Processing Systems*, 2014, pp. 1988–1996.
[40] A. Toshev and C. Szegedy, DeepPose: Human pose estimation via deep neural networks. arXiv preprint arXiv: 1312.4659, 2013.
[41] T. Wang, D. J. Wu, A. Coates and A. Y. Ng, End-to-end text recognition with convolutional neural networks, *Proc. 21st Int'l Conf. Pattern Recognition*, 2012, pp. 3304–3308.
[42] A. Coates, B. Carpenter, C. Case et al., Text detection and character recognition in scene images with unsupervised feature learning, *Proc. 11th Int'l Conf. Document Analysis and Recognition*, 2011, pp. 440–445.
[43] M. Jaderberg, A. Vedaldi and A. Zisserman, Deep features for text spotting. In ECCV, 2014, pp. 512–528.
[44] A. Bissacco, M. Cummins, Y. Netzer and H. Neven, PhotoOCR: Reading text in uncontrolled conditions, *Proc. 2013 IEEE Int'l Conf. Computer Vision*, 2013, pp. 785–792.
[45] M. Jaderberg, K. Simonyan, A. Vedaldi and A. Zisserman, Synthetic data and artificial neural networks for natural scene text recognition. arXiv preprint arXiv: 1406.2227, 2014.
[46] D. C. Cireşan, U. Meier, L. M. Gambardella *et al.*, Convolutional neural network committees for handwritten character classification, *Proc. 11th Int'l Conf. Document Analysis and Recognition*, 2011, pp. 1135–1139.
[47] D. C. Cireşan, U. Meier and J. Schmidhuber, Multi-column deep neural networks for image classification, *Proc. IEEE Conf. Computer Vision and Pattern Recognition*, 2012, pp. 3642–3649.
[48] D. C. Cireşan and J. Schmidhuber, Multi-column deep neural networks for offline handwritten Chinese character classification. arXiv preprint arXiv:1309.0261, 2013.
[49] B. Graham, Sparse arrays of signatures for online character recognition. arXiv preprint arXiv:1308.0371, 2013.
[50] F. Yin, Q. F. Wang, X. Y. Zhang *et al.*, ICDAR 2013 Chinese handwriting recognition competition, *Proc. 12th Int'l Conf. Document Analysis and Recognition*, 2013, pp. 1464–1470.
[51] C. Wu, W. Fan, Y. He *et al.*, Handwritten character recognition by alternately trained relaxation convolutional neural network, ICFHR, 2014.

[52] C.-L. Liu, F. Yin, Q.-F. Wang and D.-H. Wang, ICDAR 2011 — Chinese Handwriting Recognition Competition, ICDAR, 2011.
[53] F. Yin, Q.-F. Wang, X.-Y. Zhang and C.-L. Liu, ICDAR 2013 — Chinese Handwriting Recognition Competition, ICDAR, 2013.
[54] C. Wu, W. Fan, Y. He *et al.*, Handwritten character recognition by alternately trained relaxation convolutional neural network, ICFHR, 2014.
[55] B. Graham, Spatially-sparse convolutional neural networks, arXiv 2014.
[56] W. Yang, L. Jin *et al.*, Improved DCNN for online HCCR using domain-specific knowledge, accept to appear in *ICDAR 2015*.
[57] W. Yang, L. Jin *et al.*, DropSample: A new training method to enhance deep convolutional neural networks for large-scale unconstrained handwritten Chinese character recognition, arXiv 2015.
[58] Z. Zhong, L. Jin and Z. Xie, High performance offline handwritten Chinese character recognition using GoogLeNet and feature maps, accept to appear in *ICDAR 2015*.
[59] R. G. Casey, Moment normalization of handprinted characters, *IBM J. Res. Dev.*, **14**(5), 548–557 (1970).
[60] J. Tsukumo and H. Tanaka, Classification of handprinted Chinese characters using nonlinear normalization and correlation methods, *Proc. 9th Int'l Conf. Pattern Recognition*, 1988, pp. 168–171.
[61] H. Yamada, K. Yamamoto and T. Saito, A nonlinear normalization method for handprinted Kanji character recognition — line density equalization, *Pattern Recognition*, **23**(9), 1023–1029 (1990).
[62] C.-L. Liu, H. Sako and H. Fujisawa, Handwritten Chinese character recognition: alternatives to nonlinear normalization, *Proc. 7th Int'l Conf. Document Analysis and Recognition*, **3**, 524–528 (2003).
[63] C.-L. Liu and K. Marukawa, Global shape normalization for handwritten Chinese character recognition: a new method, *Proc. 9th Int'l Workshop Frontiers in Handwriting Recognition*, 2004, pp. 300–305.
[64] T. Horiuchi, R. Haruki *et al.*, Two-dimensional extension of nonlinear normalization method using line density for character recognition, *Proc. 4th Int'l Conf. Document Analysis and Recognition*, **2**, 511–514 (1997).
[65] C.-L. Liu and K. Marukawa, Pseudo two-dimensional shape normalization methods for handwritten Chinese character recognition, *Pattern Recognition*, **38**(12), 2242–2255 (2005).
[66] A. Krizhevsky, I. Sutskever and G. E. Hinton, ImageNet classification with deep convolutional neural networks, *Proc. Neural Information Processing Systems*, 2012, pp. 1106–1114.
[67] M. D. Zeiler and R. Fergus, Visualizing and understanding convolutional networks, ArXiv preprint arXiv:1311.2901, 2013.
[68] L.-W. Jin and G. Wei, Handwritten Chinese character recognition with directional decomposition cellular features, *Journal of Circuit, System and Computer*, **8**(4), 517–524 (1998).
[69] D. H. Hubel and T. N. Wiesel, Receptive fields of single neurons in the cat's striate cortex, *J. Physiology*, **148**, 574–591 (1959).
[70] V. Nair and G. E. Hinton, Rectified linear units improve restricted Boltzmann machines, *Proc. Int'l Conf. Machine Learning*, 2010, pp. 807–814.
[71] A. Coates, B. Huval, T. Wang, D. J. Wu, B. C. Catanzaro and A. Y. Ng, Deep learning with COTS HPC systems, *ICML* **3**, 1337–1345 (2013).

[72] K. T. Chen, Integration of paths: A faithful representation of paths by noncommutative formal power series, *Trans. of the American Mathematical Society*, 1958, pp. 395–407.
[73] L. Prechelt, Early stopping — but when? in *Neural Networks: Tricks of the Trade*, 1998, pp. 55–69.
[74] S. Leitner, *So lernt man lernen: Der WegzumErfolg* (*Learning to learn: The road to success*), (Herder, Freiburg, 1972).
[75] A. D. Baddeley, *Human Memory: Theory and Practice* (Psychology Press, 1997).
[76] P. Y. Simard, D. Steinkraus and J. C. Platt, Best practices for convolutional neural networks, *Proc. 12th Int'l Conf. Document Analysis and Recognition*, **2**, 958–958 (2003).
[77] C. L. Liu, F. Yin, D. H. Wang *et al.*, CASIA online and offline Chinese handwriting databases, *Proc. 11th Int'l Conf. Document Analysis and Recognition*, 2011, pp. 37–41.
[78] G. E. Hinton, L. Deng, D. Yu *et al.*, Deep neural networks for acoustic modeling in speech recognition: The shared views of four research groups, *IEEE Signal Processing Magazine*, **29**(6), 82–97 (2012).
[79] P. Vincent, H. Larochelle, Y. Bengio and P. A. Manzagol, Extracting and composing robust features with denoising autoencoders, *Proc. 25th International Conference on Machine Learning*, 2008, pp. 1096–1103.
[80] L. W. Jin, Y. Gao, G. Liu *et al.*, SCUT-COUCH2009: A comprehensive online unconstrained Chinese handwriting database and benchmark evaluation, *International Journal on Document Analysis and Recognition*, **14**(1), 53–64 (2011).
[81] Y. L. Qian, S. X. Lin, Q. Liu *et al.*, Design and construction of HTRDP corpus resources for Chinese language processing and intelligent human-machine interaction, *Chinese High Technology Letters*, **15**(1), 107–110 (2005).
[82] SCUT gPen Handwritten Character Recognition Demo, http://www.deephcr.net/ (accessed on July 6, 2015).
[83] T.-H. Su, C.-L. Liu and X.-Y. Zhang, Perceptron learning of modified quadratic discriminant function, *Proc. 11th Int'l Conf. on Document Analysis and Recognition*, 2011, pp. 1007–1011.
[84] C.-L. Liu, H. Sako and H. Fujisawa, Discriminative learning quadratic discriminant function for handwriting recognition, *IEEE Trans. Neural Networks*, **15**(2), 430–444 (2004).
[85] L. Jin, K. Ding and Z. Huang, Incremental linear discriminant analysis for writer-adaptive online Chinese handwriting recognition, *Neural Computing*, **73**(10), 1614–1623 (2010).
[86] X.-Y. Zhang and C.-L. Liu, Writer adaptation with style transfer mapping, *IEEE Trans. on Pattern Analysis and Machine Intelligence*, **35**(7), 1773–1787 (2013).
[87] J. Du, J.-S. Hu, B. Zhu, S. Wei and L.-R. Dai, Writer adaptation using bottleneck features and discriminative linear regression for online handwritten Chinese character recognition, *Proc. ICFHR-2014*.
[88] J. Du, J.-F. Zhai, J.-S. Hu, B. Zhu, S. Wei and L.-R. Dai, Writer adaptive feature extraction based on convolutional neural networks for online handwritten Chinese character recognition, Accepted to appear in *ICDAR 2015*.
[89] GB/T18790-2010: Requirements and test procedure of on-line handwriting Chinese character recognition system.

[90] T. Long and L. Jin, A novel orientation free method for online unconstrained cursive handwritten Chinese word recognition, *Proc. Intl. Conf. Pattern Recognition*, 2008, pp. 1–4.

[91] S. Huang, L. Jin and J. Lv, A novel approach for orientation free Chinese character recognition, *Proc. ICDAR-2009*, 2009, pp. 1136–1140.

[92] T. He and Q. Huo, A character-structure-guided approach to estimating possible orientations of a rotated isolated online handwritten Chinese character, *Proc. ICDAR-2009*, 2009, pp. 536–540.

[93] S. Huang, A study on recognition for rotated isolated on-line handwritten Chinese character, Master Thesis (in Chinese and supervised by Professor Lianwen Jin), South China University of Technology, China, 2010.

[94] J. Du and Q. Huo, Designing compact classifiers for rotation free recognition of large vocabulary online handwritten Chinese characters, *Proc. ICASSP-2012*, 2012, pp. 1721–1724.

[95] J. Du, J.-S. Hu, B. Zhu, S. Wei and L.-R. Dai, A study of designing compact classifiers using deep neural networks for online handwritten Chinese character recognition, *Proc. ICPR-2014*.

[96] K. Chen, Z.-J. Yan and Q. Huo, A context-sensitive-chunk BPTT approach to training deep LSTM/BLSTM recurrent neural networks for offline handwriting recognition, accept to appear in *ICDAR 2015*.

[97] R. Messina and J. Louradour, Segmentation-free handwritten Chinese characters recognition with LSTM-RNN, accepted to appear in *ICDAR 2015*.

[98] M. L. Littman, Reinforcement learning improves behaviour from evaluative feedback, *Nature*, **521**, 445–451 (28 May 2015).

[99] V. Mnih, K. Kavukcuoglu, D. Silver *et al.*, Human-level control through deep reinforcement learning, *Nature*, **518**, 529–533 (26 February 2015).

[100] A. Evgeniou and M. Pontil, *Multi-task Feature Learning*, NIPS, 2007.

[101] K. Swersky, J. Snoek and R. P. Adams, Multi-task Bayesian optimization, NIPS, 2013.

[102] Y. Wang and Q. Huo, Sample-separation-margin based minimum classification error training of pattern classifiers with quadratic discriminant functions, *Proceedings of ICASSP*, 2010, pp. 1866–1869.

[103] K. T. Chen, Integration of paths — A faithful representation of paths by noncommutative formal power series, *Trans. of the American Mathematical Society*, 1958, pp. 395–407.

[104] Q. F Wang, F. Yin and C. L. Liu, Handwritten Chinese text recognition by integrating multiple contexts, *IEEE Trans. PAMI*, **34**(8), 1469–1481 (2012).

[105] Y. F. Lv, L. L. Huang and C. L. Liu, Learning-based candidate segmentation scoring for real-time recognition of online overlaid Chinese handwriting, *Proceedings of ICDAR*, 2013, pp. 74–78.

Chapter 5

Historical Chinese Character Recognition Using Transfer Learning

Liangrui Peng and Jixiong Feng

Tsinghua National Laboratory for Information Science and Technology, Department of Electronic Engineering, Tsinghua University, Beijing, 100084, China

{plr, fengjx}@ocrserv.ee.tsinghua.edu.cn

Historical Chinese document recognition technology is important for facilitating full-text digitization projects for digital libraries. One of the most important steps in this process is historical Chinese character recognition. This chapter presents a transfer learning framework for historical Chinese character recognition to solve the problem of an insufficient number of labeled training samples. Two transfer learning schemes, namely, linear Style Transfer Mapping (STM) and Gaussian Process Style Transfer Mapping (GP-STM), are described. The GP-STM method extends the STM method to a non-linear transfer learning scheme by incorporating a Gaussian process and kernel functions. The experimental results on test samples show that the recognition rate increases when using the proposed transfer learning framework and that the GP-STM method outperforms the STM method.

1. Introduction

Because China has a unique history that has been continuously recorded for thousands of years, rich and vital collections of historical Chinese documents are treasures of the nation's cultural heritage. Historical Chinese documents, which are sometimes called ancient Chinese books, are usually paper books or documents that were written in the Chinese language before the collapse of the last imperial dynasty (the Qing Dynasty), in 1912 [1]. Statistics indicate that historical Chinese documents that are preserved in various libraries and institutions in China amount to more than 30 million volumes and items, including over 2.5 million volumes of rare books. For many historical reasons, including cultural exchanges and wars, approximately 3 million ancient Chinese books are possessed by approximately 100 overseas libraries and institutions in Japan, Europe, North America, and other locations. For example, the Dunhuang historical documents are an important representation of the Chinese culture and cover the period from the 4th to the 11th centuries. The originals of these valuable manuscripts are preserved not only in China but also in the United Kingdom, France, Japan, and other countries. For many years, access to these materials of exceptional value was reserved for only a small number of privileged scholars.

With digital library technologies, it is possible to provide scholars and the general public with convenient and timely access to online catalogs, images and even full-text content of historical Chinese documents. As part of a groundbreaking international collaboration, International Dunhuang Projects (IDP) [2] aims to make the information and images from all manuscripts, paintings and textiles from Dunhuang and the archaeological sites of the Eastern Silk Road freely available on the Internet. Currently, an increasing number of electronic catalogs and digital images of Dunhuang manuscripts are accessible on the websites of participating libraries and institutions. However, the full-text content of these valuable resources is not yet available.

One of the ultimate goals of digitizing historical Chinese documents is to provide researchers with a full-text retrieval function. However, the construction of full-text resources requires not only an abundance of skilled human resources for proofreading, but also higher financial costs and related technological support. Many Chinese and foreign companies and institutions have developed several electronic versions of Chinese classics, including full-text resources [1]. A well-known example is the Electronic Version of Siku Quanshu (Wenyuange Edition), which was published by Digital Heritage Publishing Ltd. in Hong Kong [3] and includes electronic catalogs, images, full-text content resources and various useful tools, such as an online dictionary. Siku Quanshu was compiled between 1773 and 1782 during the Qing Dynasty, and it includes more than 3,460 titles up to the time of its compilation. There are approximately 2.3 million pages and approximately 800 million Chinese characters in Siku Quanshu. The character set includes nearly 32,000 Chinese character codes. Seven manuscript copies were made, but only three copies survived; one of these copies was the Wenyuange Edition and was originally preserved in the Forbidden City in Beijing and is currently in Taiwan. The full-text digitization of Siku Quanshu was conducted with Optical Character Recognition (OCR) technology to reduce the burden of keying tasks. The OCR system processes Siku Quanshu with regular layout and writing styles. This work was one of the earliest efforts in the field of historical Chinese document recognition research.

Many historical Chinese documents were created in different writing styles and in different historical periods. Therefore, special research efforts are needed to develop key technologies for historical Chinese document recognition, including preprocessing, layout analysis, character segmentation, and character recognition.

In this chapter, we will address the most challenging problems of historical Chinese character recognition, which is crucial to the full-text digitization of historical Chinese documents.

1.1. *Challenges for historical Chinese character recognition*

Historical Chinese character recognition can be viewed as a branch of offline handwritten Chinese character recognition. Several reasons why historical document recognition is more challenging than conventional printed or handwritten Chinese character recognition include the larger character set, the variety of writing styles, and the degradation of image quality. Historical Chinese character recognition has also suffered from an insufficient number of labeled training samples.

(1) Larger Character Set
Unlike alphabet scripts, Chinese characters number in the tens of thousands, although many of them are minor graphic variants that are encountered only in historical texts. For the traditional Chinese characters that are currently used in several districts, including Taiwan, Hong Kong and Macau, there are 5,401 Level-1 characters and 7,652 Level-2 characters in the BIG5 code standard [4], which is also a subset of the basic CJK Unified Ideograph blocks in the Unicode standard. The Kangxi Dictionary was the standard Chinese dictionary during the 18th and 19th centuries and was compiled under the supervision of the most famous Qing Dynasty Emperor, Kangxi Emperor. This dictionary contains more than 50,000 characters, although approximately 40% of them are graphic variants. All characters in the Kangxi Dictionary are included in the Unicode standard. Obviously, a large character set is a basic feature of historical Chinese character recognition. It may be feasible for historical Chinese character recognition to support the most commonly used characters and also to provide a self-learning function

when other characters are encountered during the digitization process.

(2) Various Writing Styles

Historical Chinese documents were mainly written with pen-brushes or woodblock printing. Throughout Chinese history, there have been dozens of major writing styles. For certain manuscripts, one or more writing styles were adopted, e.g., most Dunhuang manuscripts, especially Buddhist texts, were written in Kaishu, or "regular script." By contrast, other manuscripts were mainly written in the cursive Xingshu, or "running script." In addition, different writers had unique writing styles. Using practical samples, Figure 1 provides an example of different writing styles. The various writing styles create more challenges for recognition. On the one hand, when we use characters of one style to train the classifier and apply it to recognize characters of another style, the mismatch in writing styles results in a much higher error rate. On the other hand, when the training set contains different styles, the differences in classes increase, which makes it more difficult to train a high-performance omni-font classifier.

Figure 1. Examples of characters written in different styles.

(3) Degradation of image quality

The degradation of image quality and noise can be severe in historical Chinese documents because of the aging of paper and inappropriate preservation. An example is shown in Figure 2. Preprocessing steps are needed to manage these difficult situations.

(4) Lack of training samples

It is difficult and time-consuming to manually label the text codes of the samples. The operators must master knowledge of historical Chinese characters with a large character set. Many historical Chinese characters had different variants in different periods and regions: e.g., some special character variants exist only in Dunhuang manuscripts. Some variants were caused by clerical errors. Many obsolete characters and variants must be identified or verified by experts. The additional requirements for preprocessing and character segmentation make the sample collecting process even more difficult.

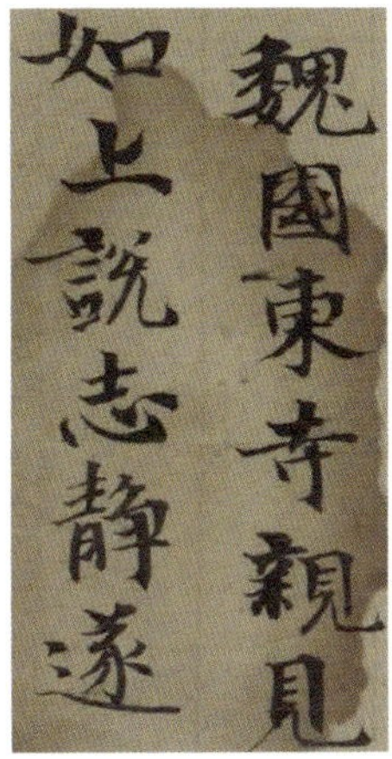

Figure 2. Example of noisy sample.

1.2. *Samples*

There are several publicly available handwritten character datasets for modern simplified Chinese, such as HCL2000 [5], HIT-MW [6], and CASIA-HWDB [7]. However, currently, no historical Chinese character samples are publicly available. Therefore, it is a fundamental step in building a dataset for experiments.

For research purposes, the National Library of China provided us with historical Chinese document images, mainly from Dunhuang manuscripts and local genealogy collections. We selected approximately 600 pages to make labeled character image samples for our experiments, including 160 pages from Dunhuang and 440 pages from local genealogies. The samples from the digitized local genealogies already had full-text ground-truth, as well as character positions on the images. Examples of character samples from local genealogies are shown in Figure 3.

Figure 3. Example of character samples from local genealogies.

For the samples from Dunhuang manuscripts, we manually labeled both character positions and ground-truth text codes. The geometrical positions of characters on a page were manually labeled in rectangles and saved to a file according to the reading order of the text, as shown in Figure 4(b). The reading order was vertical and from right to left. The character positions were marked by rectangles, which was suitable for regular writing styles. For more complex situations of touched characters, it was necessary to represent the character bounding boxes by using polygons. The text codes for characters on a page were manually input to a text file, which is shown in Figure 4(c). With information about the original page image, character positions and text codes, the character images on a page were extracted and saved to a character sample file. Examples of character samples are shown in Figure 4(d).

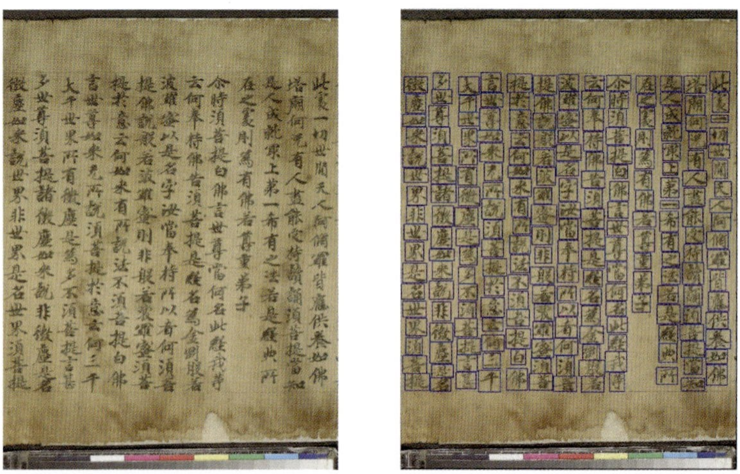

(a) Original image (b) Manually labeled character positions

此處一切世間天人阿脩羅皆應供養如佛
塔廟何況有人盡能受持讀誦須菩提當知
是人成就最上第一希有之法若是經典所
在之處則為有佛若尊重弟子
尔時須菩提白佛言世尊當何名此經我等
云何奉持佛告須菩提是經名為金剛般若
波羅蜜以是名字汝當奉持所以者何須菩
提佛說般若波羅蜜則非般若波羅蜜須菩
提於意云何如來有所說法不須菩提白佛
言世尊如來无所說須菩提於意云何三千
大千世界所有微塵是為多不須菩提言甚
多世尊須菩提諸微塵如來說非微塵是名
微塵如來說世界非世界是名世界須菩提

(c) Ground-truth of text contents

(d) Examples of character image samples

Figure 4. Example of extracting character samples for Dunhuang manuscripts.

1.3. *Related work*

In one of the earliest works on historical Chinese character recognition, a dynamic sample learning method, which was proposed by Ma *et al.* [8], was used to build the character recognition dictionary in a step-by-step manner during the digitization procedure of the Siku Quanshu project.

In recent years, historical document recognition in various scripts has attracted the attention of some researchers. The related scripts include Chinese, Latin, Arabic, and Mongolian. The resulting research has addressed preprocessing, word spotting [9], text-line extraction [10], character/word segmentation [11]–[14], character/word recognition [15][16], and system implementation [17][18]. For historical Chinese document recognition, one of the most essential research areas is historical Chinese character recognition.

Although historical Chinese character recognition has suffered from an insufficient number of labeled training samples that apply to a large character set and various writing styles, printed traditional Chinese character samples can be used for historical Chinese character recognition. A typical approach is to find common features between characters from historical documents and printed characters, such as in multitask learning [19][20]. Another approach is to view this problem in the transfer learning framework to project the features or classifier parameters from one domain to another [21][22], which is widely performed in speech recognition [20].

Style transfer mapping (STM) was first applied to online handwritten Chinese character recognition [23]. By using a linear transformation, writer-specific and class-independent features were mapped to a style-free space and then recognized by a writer-independent classifier. Inspired by this work, we applied STM to historical Chinese character recognition [16]. Because STM is a linear regression model, which may make it insufficient to handle variations of historical Chinese characters, we further incorporated the Gaussian process model [24] to extend the STM method [25].

The Gaussian process model is a probabilistic discriminative model for regressions [26]–[28]. In this approach, the transformation from one domain to another domain is non-linear. Linear regression models can be regarded as special cases of the Gaussian process model [26]. In addition, the parameters of the Gaussian process can be learned from multiple tasks [29][30], and kernels of the Gaussian process can also be learned [31].

In this chapter, we focus on transfer learning methods for historical Chinese character recognition. The STM and GP-STM methods are described in Section 2. The framework of transfer learning is presented in Section 3.

The experimental results are reported in Section 4. Section 5 provides the conclusion and suggestion for future work.

2. Method

2.1. *Linear style transfer mapping*

Linear STM assumes that different writing styles can be transformed by linear or affine transformation [23]. The feature vector for character i in the source style is denoted as $\mathbf{s}_i$; in the target style, it is denoted as $\mathbf{t}_i$. Let n be the number of style pairs $(\mathbf{s}_i, \mathbf{t}_i), i = 1, ..., n$. The source dataset is defined as

$$\mathcal{S} = \{\mathbf{s}_i \in \mathbb{R}^d \,|\, i = 1, ..., n\}\,, \tag{1}$$

and the target dataset is defined as

$$\mathcal{T} = \{\mathbf{t}_i \in \mathbb{R}^d \,|\, i = 1, ..., n\}\,, \tag{2}$$

where d is the dimension of the feature vector. For any $\mathbf{t}_i \in \mathcal{T}$, a simple linear transformation that can project $\mathbf{t}_i$ to $\mathbf{s}_i \in \mathcal{S}$ is defined as

$$\mathbf{s}_i = \mathbf{A}\mathbf{t}_i + \mathbf{b}\,. \tag{3}$$

Coefficients $\mathbf{A}$ and $\mathbf{b}$ are limited by the modified sum of the squared error function with regularization terms

$$\min_{A \in \mathbb{R}^{d \times d}, b \in \mathbb{R}^d} \sum_{i=1}^{n} f_i \|\mathbf{A}\mathbf{t}_i + \mathbf{b} - \mathbf{s}_i\|^2 + \beta\|\mathbf{A} - \mathbf{I}\|_F^2 + \gamma\|\mathbf{b}\|^2\,, \tag{4}$$

where f_i is the confidence of linear transformation, $\|\cdot\|_F$ is the matrix Frobenius norm, and β and γ are hyperparameters for the regularization terms. This optimization problem has a closed-form solution for $\mathbf{A}$ and $\mathbf{b}$

$$\mathbf{A}^* = \frac{\sum_{i=1}^{n} f_i \mathbf{s}_i \mathbf{t}_i^T - \frac{1}{\hat{f}} \hat{\mathbf{s}} \hat{\mathbf{t}}^T + \beta \mathbf{I}}{\sum_{i=1}^{n} f_i \mathbf{t}_i \mathbf{t}_i^T - \frac{1}{\hat{f}} \hat{\mathbf{t}} \hat{\mathbf{t}}^T + \beta \mathbf{I}}, \ \mathbf{b}^* = \frac{1}{\hat{f}}(\hat{\mathbf{s}} - \mathbf{A}^* \hat{\mathbf{t}})\,, \tag{5}$$

where $\mathbf{I}$ is the identity matrix and

$$\hat{f} = \sum_{i=1}^{n} f_i + \gamma, \hat{\mathbf{s}} = \sum_{i=1}^{n} f_i \mathbf{s}_i, \hat{\mathbf{t}} = \sum_{i=1}^{n} f_i \mathbf{t}_i.$$

2.2. *Non-linear STM and kernel method*

We now illustrate how linear STM can be modified to non-linear STM. For simplicity, we rewrite Eq. (3) as a one-dimensional output $s_i \in \mathbb{R}^1$

$$s_i = \mathbf{w}^T \mathbf{t}_i = \sum_{j=1}^{d} w_j t_{ij}\,, \tag{6}$$

where s_i and t_i are preprocessed to have zero-mean.

The simplest way to create a non-linear transformation is to replace $\mathbf{t}_i$ with $\boldsymbol{\phi}(\mathbf{t}_i)$, where $\boldsymbol{\phi} = (\phi_1, ..., \phi_M)^T$. $\phi_j(j = 1, ..., M)$ are non-linear basis functions, which map $\mathbb{R}^d$ to $\mathbb{R}^1$. The resultant non-linear form of Eq. (6) is

$$s_i = \mathbf{w}^T \boldsymbol{\phi}(\mathbf{t}_i) = \sum_{j=1}^{M} w_j \phi_j(\mathbf{t}_i)\,. \tag{7}$$

Similar to Eq. (4), the modified sum of the squared error function with regularization terms is given as

$$\min_{\mathbf{w}\in\mathbb{R}^M} \sum_{i=1}^{n} \|\mathbf{w}^T \boldsymbol{\phi}(\mathbf{t}_i) - s_i\|^2 + \lambda \|\mathbf{w}\|^2\,. \tag{8}$$

This error function's derivative concerning the coefficient $\mathbf{w}$ will be linear; therefore, the optimal coefficient $\mathbf{w}$ to minimize Eq. (8) has the closed-form solution

$$\mathbf{w}^* = \boldsymbol{\Phi}^T (\boldsymbol{\Phi}\boldsymbol{\Phi}^T + \lambda \mathbf{I})^{-1} \mathbf{s}\,, \tag{9}$$

where $\mathbf{s} = (s_1, ..., s_n)^T$ and $\boldsymbol{\Phi} = (\boldsymbol{\phi}(\mathbf{t}_1), ..., \boldsymbol{\phi}(\mathbf{t}_n))^T$. The kernel $\mathbf{K} = \boldsymbol{\Phi}\boldsymbol{\Phi}^T$ is defined as an $n \times n$ symmetric matrix with the elements of

$$K_{ij} = k(\mathbf{t}_i, \mathbf{t}_j) = \boldsymbol{\phi}(\mathbf{t}_i)^T \boldsymbol{\phi}(\mathbf{t}_j)\,. \tag{10}$$

Equation (9) can be used to rewrite Eq. (7) as

$$s_i = \mathbf{k}(\mathbf{t}_i)^T (\mathbf{K} + \lambda \mathbf{I})^{-1} \mathbf{s}\,, \tag{11}$$

where $\mathbf{k}(\mathbf{t}_i) = \boldsymbol{\Phi}\boldsymbol{\phi}(\mathbf{t}_i) = (k(\mathbf{t}_1, \mathbf{t}_i), ..., k(\mathbf{t}_n, \mathbf{t}_i))^T$. This approach solves the non-linear regression problem by using the kernel method, and creates a way to extend it to a Gaussian process model.

2.3. *Gaussian process*

A Gaussian process (GP) extends a multivariate Gaussian distribution to infinite dimensions [28]. Let us still consider $s_i \in \mathbb{R}^1$ at first (whereas $\mathbf{t}_i \in \mathbb{R}^d$). A Gaussian process model assumes $\mathbf{s} = (s_1, ..., s_n)^T$ and follows the n-variate Gaussian distribution

$$\mathbf{s} \sim \mathcal{N}(\boldsymbol{\mu}, \ \mathbf{K}) \,. \tag{12}$$

If we have a new vector $\mathbf{t}_* \in \mathcal{T}$ and want to predict the corresponding $s_* \in \mathcal{S}$, it is assumed that

$$\begin{bmatrix} \mathbf{s} \\ s_* \end{bmatrix} \sim \mathcal{N}\left(\begin{bmatrix} \boldsymbol{\mu} \\ \mu_* \end{bmatrix}, \ \begin{bmatrix} \mathbf{K} & \mathbf{K}_*^{\mathbf{T}} \\ \mathbf{K}_* & \mathbf{K}_{**} \end{bmatrix} \right), \tag{13}$$

where

$$\mathbf{K}_* = [k(\mathbf{t}_*, \mathbf{t}_1), ..., k(\mathbf{t}_*, \mathbf{t}_n)] \,, \ \mathbf{K}_{**} = k(\mathbf{t}_*, \mathbf{t}_*) \,. \tag{14}$$

The optimal estimate of s_* will maximize the conditional probability of $p(s_*|\mathbf{s})$. This probability follows a multivariate Gaussian distribution

$$s_*|\mathbf{s} \sim \mathcal{N}\left(\mu_* + \mathbf{K}_*\mathbf{K}^{-1}(\mathbf{s} - \boldsymbol{\mu}), \ \mathbf{K}_{**} - \mathbf{K}_*\mathbf{K}^{-1}\mathbf{K}_*^{\mathbf{T}}\right) \,. \tag{15}$$

Thus, the best estimation for s_* is the mean value of this distribution:

$$s_* = \mu_* + \mathbf{K}_*\mathbf{K}^{-1}(\mathbf{s} - \boldsymbol{\mu}) \,. \tag{16}$$

In expanding $\mathbf{s}_i$ from 1 to d dimensions, let us consider $\mathbf{s}_i \in \mathbb{R}^d$, which is defined in Eq. (1). As $\mathbf{s}_i (i = 1, ..., n)$, and can be written as $(s_{i1}, ..., s_{id})$. Assume each dimension $s_{ij} (j = 1, ..., d)$ has the same covariance matrix $\mathbf{K}$ and denote $\boldsymbol{\mu}_* = (\mu_1, ..., \mu_d)$ to be the mean vector of each dimension. When the source matrix $\mathbf{S} = (\mathbf{s}_1^T, ..., \mathbf{s}_n^T)^T$ and mean matrix $\boldsymbol{\Omega}$ are matrices with n rows and d columns, then Eq. (16) becomes

$$\mathbf{s}_* = \boldsymbol{\mu}_* + \mathbf{K}_*\mathbf{K}^{-1}(\mathbf{S} - \boldsymbol{\Omega}) \,. \tag{17}$$

2.4. *GP-STM*

Based on the results in the previous subsection, we propose our GP-STM model. Considering Eq. (17), we treat the mean vector $\boldsymbol{\mu}_*$ as a rough approximation and the $\mathbf{K}_*\mathbf{K}^{-1}(\mathbf{S} - \boldsymbol{\Omega})$ term as a modification. For our model, the source vector $\mathbf{s}_*$ must be close to the target vector $\mathbf{t}_*$, whereas its style should be changed to fit the source style. Therefore, we set $\boldsymbol{\mu}_*$ to be $\mathbf{t}_*$ and the mean matrix $\boldsymbol{\Omega}$ to be the extension of the mean vector of the source vectors $(\bar{\mathbf{s}}, ..., \bar{\mathbf{s}})^T$. Then the GP-STM estimation of the source vector $\mathbf{s}_*$ would be

$$\mathbf{s}_* = \mathbf{t}_* + \mathbf{K}_*\mathbf{K}^{-1}(\mathbf{S} - \bar{\mathbf{S}}) \, . \tag{18}$$

$\mathbf{K}^{-1}(\mathbf{S} - \bar{\mathbf{S}})$ can be computed in advance and denoted as matrix $\mathbf{A}$. $\mathbf{K}_*$ is a function of $\mathbf{t}_*$, which can be written as $f(\mathbf{t}_*)$. If we write $\mathbf{t}_*$ as $\mathbf{b}(\mathbf{t}_*)$, then Eq. (18) can be written as

$$\mathbf{s}_* = \mathbf{A}f(\mathbf{t}_*) + \mathbf{b}(\mathbf{t}_*). \tag{19}$$

This GP-STM model is similar to the STM of Eq. (3), except that a non-linear function f is added. The covariance matrix $\mathbf{K}$ is defined by a kernel function, as shown in Eq. (10). There are many options for kernel functions. A widely used kernel function is the single Gaussian kernel, which is shown in Eq. (20).

Kernel 1. The Single Gaussian Kernel:

$$k(\mathbf{t}_i, \mathbf{t}_j) = \theta_0 \exp\left[\frac{-\|\mathbf{t}_i - \mathbf{t}_j\|^2}{2\theta_1^2}\right] + \theta_2\delta(\mathbf{t}_i, \mathbf{t}_j) \, , \tag{20}$$

where $\theta_i (i = 1, 2, 3)$ are non-negative parameters, and $\delta(\mathbf{t}_i, \mathbf{t}_j)$ is the Kronecker delta function. The covariance matrix $\mathbf{K}$ is composed of all $k(\mathbf{t}_i, \mathbf{t}_j)$ for $i = 1, ..., n$ and $j = 1, ..., n$:

$$\mathbf{K} = \begin{bmatrix} k(\mathbf{t}_1, \mathbf{t}_1) & \cdots & k(\mathbf{t}_1, \mathbf{t}_n) \\ \vdots & \ddots & \vdots \\ k(\mathbf{t}_n, \mathbf{t}_1) & \cdots & k(\mathbf{t}_n, \mathbf{t}_n) \end{bmatrix} . \tag{21}$$

It is also common to use the exponential kernel, as shown in Eq. (22).

Kernel 2. The Exponential Kernel:

$$k(\mathbf{t}_i, \mathbf{t}_j) = \theta_0 \exp(-\theta_1 \|\mathbf{t}_i - \mathbf{t}_j\|) + \theta_2\delta(\mathbf{t}_i, \mathbf{t}_j) \, , \tag{22}$$

is used in the Ornstein-Uhlenbeck Process to describe a Brownian motion.

If we want to incorporate a long-term trend, another example is the double Gaussian kernel, which is shown in Eq. (23).

Kernel 3. The Double Gaussian Kernel:

$$k(\mathbf{t}_i, \mathbf{t}_j) = \theta_0 \exp\left[\frac{-\|\mathbf{t}_i - \mathbf{t}_j\|^2}{2\theta_1^2}\right] + \theta_3 \exp\left[\frac{-\|\mathbf{t}_i - \mathbf{t}_j\|^2}{2\theta_4^2}\right] + \theta_2\delta(\mathbf{t}_i, \mathbf{t}_j) \, . \tag{23}$$

The only restriction on the kernel function is that $\mathbf{K}$ must be positive and semi-definite for any pair of $\mathbf{t}_i$ and $\mathbf{t}_j$ [26]. This restriction gives us more freedom to build our model.

3. Framework

3.1. *Framework design*

The framework can be considered in the context of transductive transfer learning [21]. Given the source dataset $\mathcal{S}$, a corresponding source classifier C_S, the target dataset $\mathcal{T}$, and a corresponding target classifier C_T, transductive transfer learning attempts to improve C_T by using the knowledge in $\mathcal{S}$ and C_S and a subset of the labeled data from $\mathcal{T}$.

According to customary notation in transfer learning, we denote the source dataset as the set of feature vectors from printed traditional Chinese characters, whereas the target dataset is the set of feature vectors of historical Chinese characters. A small subset of the target dataset, which is called the STM training set (see Figure 5), is used to train the parameters of the GP-STM. The remaining subset of the target dataset is referred to as the STM testing set. The characters in the target dataset are to be recognized (classified).

As shown in Figure 5, the framework is built in several steps.

(1) We use the source dataset to train a classifier that is named the source classifier.

(2) The STM training set is used with the source dataset to estimate the parameters of the GP-STM.

(3) The Target classifier consists of the GP-STM model and the source classifier for recognition. A new feature vector from the STM testing set is first transformed by GP-STM, which projects it to the source dataset and then classifies it by using the source classifier.

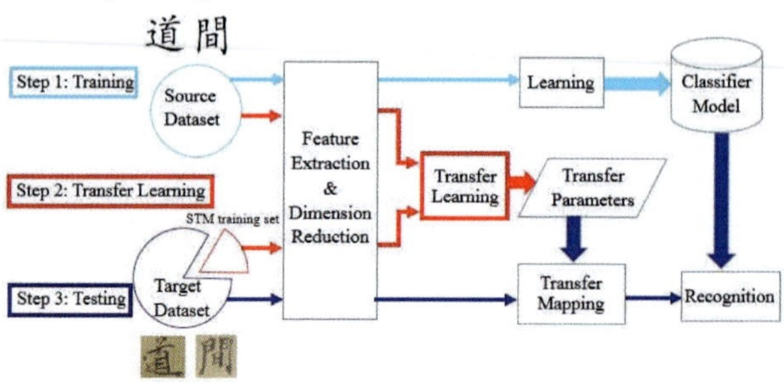

Figure 5. System framework.

3.2. *Parameter selection*

To compare with STM, we use $\beta = 0.03$ and $\gamma = 0.01$ in the STM method, as suggested by Zhang [23]. The confidence $f_i(i = 1, ..., n)$ is set to be $\frac{1}{n}$.

For GP-STM with the kernel that is described in Eq. (20), the parameter $\boldsymbol{\theta} = (\theta_0, \theta_1, \theta_2)^T$. θ_0 is the maximum allowable covariance. θ_1 controls the relation of $\mathbf{s}_i$ and $\mathbf{s}_j$; a larger θ_1 indicates more correlation between the two variables, and a smaller θ_1 leads to more independent variables. θ_2 is the noise level, which can also prevent the kernel $\mathbf{K}$ from being singular. $\boldsymbol{\theta}$ is found by maximizing the posterior $p(\boldsymbol{\theta}|\mathbf{s}, \mathbf{t})$. According to Bayes' theorem, we can alternatively maximize the log likelihood function:

$$\ln p(\mathbf{s}|\mathbf{t}, \boldsymbol{\theta}) = -\frac{1}{2}\mathbf{s}^T\mathbf{K}^{-1}\mathbf{s} - \frac{1}{2}\log|\mathbf{K}| - \frac{n}{2}\log 2\pi\,. \tag{24}$$

To accomplish this maximization, we must find the gradient of the log likelihood function concerning the parameter vector $\boldsymbol{\theta}$. In general, $p(\mathbf{s}|\mathbf{t}, \boldsymbol{\theta})$ will not be a convex function; therefore, it can have multiple maxima [26]. Another approach is to perform cross-validation. In our model, we empirically suggest $\boldsymbol{\theta}$ to be $(1, 1.5, 0.005)^T$.

For GP-STM with the kernel that is described in Eq. (23), two new parameters θ_3 and θ_4 are added to $\boldsymbol{\theta} = (\theta_0, \theta_1, \theta_2, \theta_3, \theta_4)^T$. θ_4 in the second item should be larger than θ_1, which means that the kernel considers both short distance and long distance correlation. θ_0 and θ_3 control the weight between a short and long distance. Here, we use $\theta_3 = 0.1 \times \theta_0$ and $\theta_4 = 6 \times \theta_1$.

For the exponential kernel in Eq. (22), the meaning of the parameters are the same as the parameters of the single Gaussian kernel in Eq. (20). After tuning θ_1 in the range [0, 1], we find a proper $\boldsymbol{\theta} = [1, 0.0011, 0]$.

4. Experiments

In this section, we conduct experiments on historical Chinese character recognition. Different types of features with different transfer learning models are compared by using both a smaller and a larger dataset. After this comparison, we compare different kernel functions of the GP-STM model. Finally, we directly use image pixels as features, and visualize the results of the STM and GP-STM methods.

All input character images in our experiments are binary images that are resized to 65×65 pixels, which allows us to concentrate on character recognition rather than preprocessing. The source dataset includes Kaiti font from printed traditional Chinese characters. The target dataset is historical Chinese documents that are selected from Dunhuang manuscripts and local genealogies and contains more than 11,000 characters with over 1,400 classes. The target dataset is divided into two parts. Approximately 5% of the random selected character image samples are used as the STM training set to learn the transformation coefficients, whereas the remaining 95% of character image samples constitute the STM testing set.

4.1. *STM and GP-STM*

The source classifier is trained by using the source dataset. Three types of features are extracted, including 392-dimension Weighted Direction Code Histogram (WDCH) features [32], 416-dimension Local Binary Pattern (LBP) features [33], and 395-dimension Histogram Oriented Gradient (HOG) features [34]. Fisher Linear Discriminative Analysis (FLDA) [35] is used for dimension reduction, which reduces the features to a 128 dimension. A Modified Quadratic Discriminant Function (MQDF) classifier [36] is used as the baseline for classification. Then, the transfer learning models with STM and GP-STM are compared.

We first conduct an experiments with a smaller scale dataset of 500 classes. Figure 6(a) shows the results of the recognition rate for the top 1, 2, 5, and 10 candidates with different features and models.

After these experiments, we test our model on a larger dataset. The source classifier is trained with the character set of 5,401 Level-1 BIG5 codes. The results are shown in Figure 6(b).

The results from the small character set show that the WDCH feature achieves its best classification accuracy of 51.9% with the baseline method; the LBP feature achieves its best classification accuracy with both the STM and GP-STM, at 58.4% and 67.55%, respectively. The LBP and WDCH features show small differences. In the test with 5,401 classes, the WDCH feature significantly outperforms the other two features. In the following experiments, we only use the WDCH feature.

In this experiment, the GP-STM model uses the kernel that is defined in Eq. (20). We can see that our GP-STM model results in a significant improvement over Baseline and STM. When using GP-STM, the error rate is reduced by approximately 10%, which supports the effectiveness of our model.

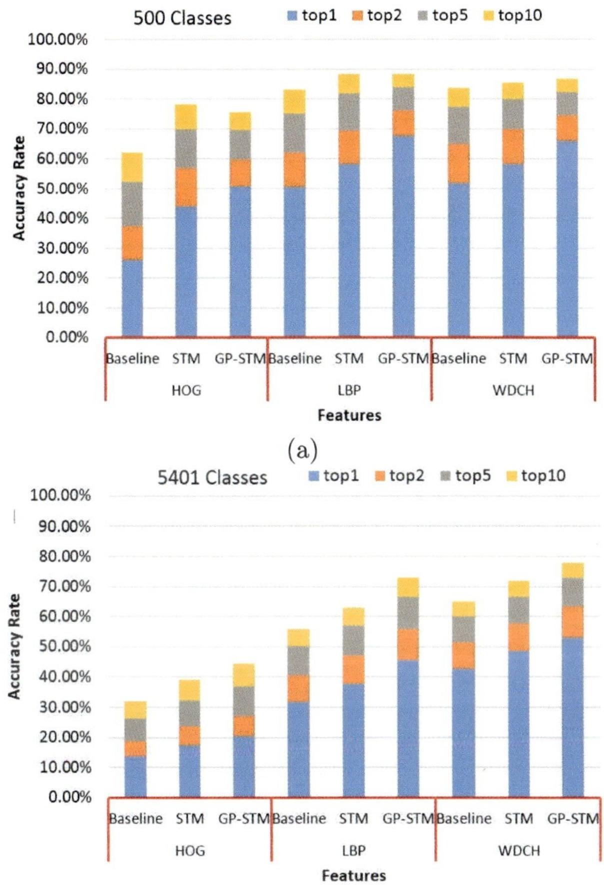

(a)

(b)

Figure 6. Comparison of different features and different models.

4.2. *Comparison of different kernels*

In this experiment, we study the kernels that are used in GP-STM. The single Gaussian kernel (Eq. (20)), double Gaussian kernel (Eq. (23)) and exponential kernel (Eq. (22)) are used. The results are shown in Figure 7.

The exponential kernel significantly outperforms the other two kernels, with a top accuracy of 57.5%, a 14.7% improvement to Baseline, an 8.33% improvement to STM and 4.83% to the other kernels. There is little difference between the single Gaussian kernel and the double Gaussian kernel.

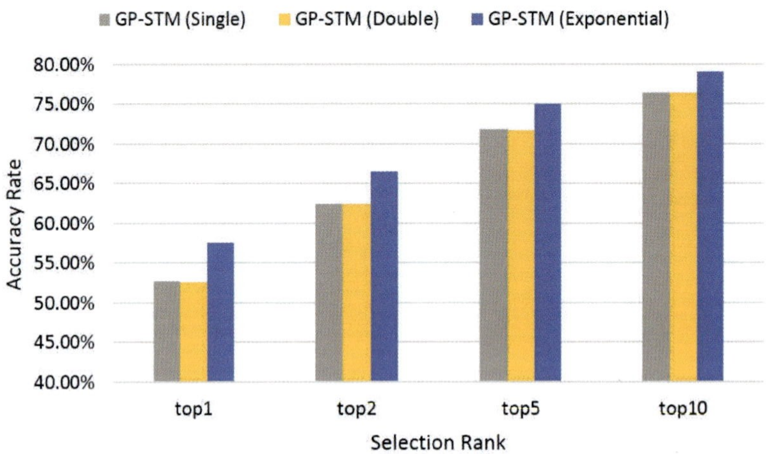

Figure 7. Comparison of different kernels.

4.3. *Visualization of STM and GP-STM*

To visualize the effect of the STM and GP-STM methods, we directly use the image pixels of the characters. Each character image is resized to 30×30 pixels, and then stretched into a 900×1 vector. The estimations of the STM and GP-STM are computed and reshaped back into 30×30 pixels, which is shown in Figure 8.

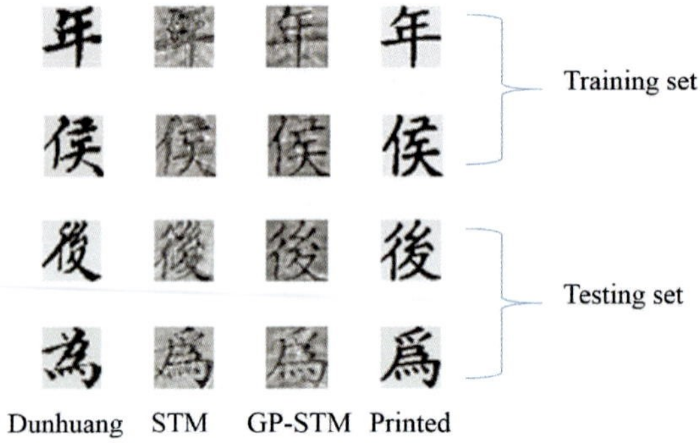

Figure 8. Visualized comparison of STM and GP-STM.

In the STM training set, GP-STM estimated characters are similar to printed characters. In the STM testing set, GP-STM estimated characters are blurred more severely, although they are more similar in detail to printed characters. GP-STM has better capabilities for style transfer than does STM, and thus has a higher accuracy rate.

As shown in Figure 9, proper parameters can successfully transform the vector in the target style to source style, such as $\theta_1 = 15$ and $\theta_2 = 0.001$. As discussed in Section 3.2, a larger θ_1 causes more transformation, sometimes with blurring. In contrast, a larger θ_2 keeps the vector more similar to its original value. The process is similar to focusing with a camera, when a proper focus distance makes the scene clearer.

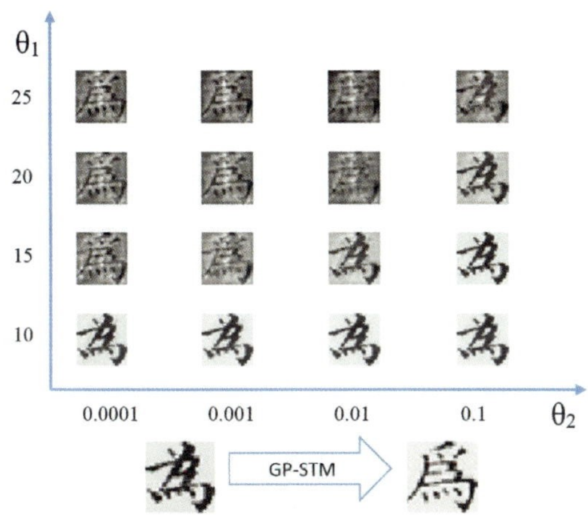

Figure 9. Visualized comparison of GP-STM with different parameters.

5. Conclusion and Future Work

The digitization of historical Chinese documents allows dusty, precious manuscripts to be presented to the public with a new look by using modern information technology, which promotes the protection and development of the nation's cultural heritage. To satisfy the growing need for electronic texts, in addition to pure digital images, significant efforts are needed to develop innovative OCR engines to satisfactorily manage the wide range of historical Chinese documents. This chapter addressed historical Chinese character recognition and provided a transfer learning-based solution to recognize commonly used historical Chinese characters that are in the same classes as printed traditional characters but in different styles. To utilize the classifier trained by the source dataset, the adopted STM method uses linear transformation to convert the feature vector of the target dataset to the source dataset. The GP-STM method extends the STM method to a nonlinear transfer learning scheme by incorporating the Gaussian process and kernel functions. The experimental results show that the recognition rate on test samples increases by using the proposed transfer learning framework and that the GP-STM method performs better than the STM method.

New methods for historical Chinese character recognition, such as deep learning, may further overcome the current barriers. In the future, webservice based OCR and collaborative proofreading will provide a final solution for the full-text digitization of historical Chinese documents.

References

1. Y. Zheng, An overview of ancient Chinese books, *The Journal of Ottoman Studies*, **41**, 411–431 (2013).
2. http://idp.nlc.cn/, 2016.
3. http://www.sikuquanshu.com/, 2016.
4. K. Lunde, *CJKV Information Processing*, O'Reilly Media, (2009).
5. H. Zhang, J. Guo, G. Chen and C. Li, HCL2000-A large-scale handwritten Chinese character database for handwritten character recognition, *Proc. 10th International Conference on Document Analysis and Recognition*, 2009, pp. 286–290.
6. T. Su, T. Zhang and D. Guan, Corpus-based HIT-MW database for offline recognition of general-purpose Chinese handwritten text, *International Journal of Document Analysis and Recognition*, **10**(1), 27–38 (2007).
7. C.-L. Liu, F. Yin, D.-H. Wang and Q.-F. Wang, Online and offline handwritten Chinese character recognition: Benchmarking on new databases, *Pattern Recognition*, **46**(1), 155–162 (2013).
8. S. Ma, Z. Jiang, Y. Xia and Y. Huang, Recognition of Chinese ancient books based on dynamic learning method (in Chinese), *Journal of Nanjing University (Natural Sciences)*, **36**(11), 255–258 (2000).
9. T. M. Rath and R. Manmatha, Word spotting for historical documents, *International Journal on Document Analysis and Recognition*, **9**(2–4), 139–152 (2007).
10. L. Likforman-Sulem, A. Zahour and B. Taconet, Text line segmentation of historical documents: A survey, *International Journal on Document Analysis and Recognition*, **9**(2–4), 123–138 (2007).
11. R. Manmatha and J. L. Rothfeder, A scale space approach for automatically segmenting words from historical handwritten documents, *IEEE Transactions on Pattern Analysis and Machine Intelligence*, **27**(8), 1212–1225 (2005).
12. L. Yang and L. Peng, Local projection-based character segmentation method for historical Chinese documents, *Proc. SPIE 8658, Document Recognition and Retrieval XX, 865800* (2013).

13. X. Sun, L. Peng and X. Ding, Touching character segmentation method for Chinese historical documents, *Proc. SPIE 7534, Document Recognition and Retrieval XVII, 75340D* (2010).
14. J. Ji, L. Peng and B. Li, Graph model optimization based historical Chinese character segmentation method, *Proc. 11th IAPR International Workshop on Document Analysis Systems*, 2014, pp. 282–286.
15. V. Lavrenko, T. M. Rath and R. Manmatha, Holistic word recognition for handwritten historical documents, *Proc. 1st Workshop on Document Image Analysis for Libraries*, 2004, pp. 278–287.
16. B. Li, L. Peng and J. Ji, Historical Chinese character recognition method based on style transfer mapping, *Proc. 11th IAPR International Workshop on Document Analysis Systems*, 2014, pp. 96–100.
17. http://www.impact-project.eu/, 2016.
18. L. Peng, P. Xiu and X. Ding, Design and development of an ancient Chinese document recognition system, *Proc. SPIE 5296, Document Recognition and Retrieval XI*, 2003, pp. 166–173.
19. R. Caruana, Multitask learning, *Machine Learning*, **28**(1), 41–75 (1997).
20. G. Tur, Multitask learning for spoken language understanding, *Proc. IEEE Conference on Acoustics, Speech and Signal Processing*, Vol. 1, 2006, pp. 585–588.
21. S. J. Pan and Q. Yang, A survey on transfer learning, *IEEE Transactions on Knowledge and Data Engineering*, **22**(10), 1345–1359 (2010).
22. R. Raina, A. Battle, H. Lee, B. Packer and A. Y. Ng, Self-taught learning: Transfer learning from unlabeled data, *Proc. 24th International Conference on Machine Learning*, 2007, pp. 759–766.
23. X.-Y. Zhang and C.-L. Liu, Writer adaptation with style transfer mapping, *IEEE Transactions on Pattern Analysis and Machine Intelligence*, **35**(7), 1773–1787 (2013).
24. C. Lu and X. Tang, Surpassing human-level face verification performance on LFW with GaussianFace, arXiv preprint arXiv:1404.3840 (2014).
25. J. Feng, L. Peng and F. Lebourgeois, Gaussian process style transfer mapping for historical Chinese character recognition, *Proc. SPIE 9402, Document Recognition and Retrieval XXII, 94020D*, 2015.
26. C. Bishop, *Pattern Recognition and Machine Learning* (Springer-Verlag, New York, 2006).
27. C. E. Rasmussen, *Gaussian Processes for Machine Learning* (MIT Press, 2006).
28. M. Ebden, Gaussian processes: A quick introduction, arXiv preprint arXiv:1505.02965 (2015).
29. N. D. Lawrence and J. C. Platt, Learning to learn with the informative vector machine, *Proc. 21st International Conference on Machine Learning*, 2004, pp. 65–72.
30. E. Bonilla, K. M. Chai and C. Williams, Multi-task Gaussian process prediction, *Advances in Neural Information Processing Systems*, 2007, pp. 153–1160.

31. A. Schwaighofer, V. Tresp and K. Yu, Learning Gaussian process kernels via hierarchical bayes, *Advances in Neural Information Processing Systems*, 2004, pp. 1209–1216.
32. F. Kimura, T. Wakabayashi, S. Tsuruoka and Y. Miyake, Improvement of handwritten Japanese character recognition using weighted direction code histogram, *Pattern Recognition*, **30**(8), 1329–1337 (1997).
33. T. Ojala, M. Pietikainen and T. Maenpaa, Multiresolution gray-scale and rotation invariant texture classification with local binary patterns, *IEEE Transactions on Pattern Analysis and Machine Intelligence*, **24**(7), 971–987 (2002).
34. N. Dalal and B. Triggs, Histograms of oriented gradients for human detection, *Proc. IEEE Conference on Computer Vision and Pattern Recognition*, Vol. 1, 2005, pp. 886–893.
35. P. N. Belhumeur, J. P. Hespanha and D. Kriegman, Eigenfaces vs. Fisherfaces: Recognition using class specific linear projection, *IEEE Transactions on Pattern Analysis and Machine Intelligence*, **19**(7), 711–720 (1997).
36. F. Kimura, K. Takashina, S. Tsuruoka and Y. Miyake, Modified quadratic discriminant functions and the application to Chinese character recognition, *IEEE Transactions on Pattern Analysis and Machine Intelligence*, **9**(1), 149–153 (1987).

Chapter 6

Handwritten Chinese Text Line Recognition

Qiu-Feng Wang*, Fei Yin and Cheng-Lin Liu

National Laboratory of Pattern Recognition,
Institute of Automation, Chinese Academy of Sciences,
Beijing 100190, China
wqfengnlpr@gmail.com, {fyin, liucl}@nlpr.ia.ac.cn

Handwritten text line recognition is difficult because the characters in text line cannot be reliably segmented prior to character recognition. This chapter introduces the general integrated segmentation-and-recognition framework for handwritten Chinese text line recognition. In the framework, on classifying candidate characters generated based on over-segmentation, candidate segmentation-recognition paths are evaluated and the optimal path is found to give the result of character segmentation and recognition. In path evaluation, we fuse the character classification scores, geometric context and linguistic context from the Bayesian decision view. In path search, we use a refined beam search algorithm to improve the search efficiency and accuracy. Moreover, we provide an unsupervised language model adaptation framework to improve the recognition accuracy for documents with domain shift from the language model. On the Chinese handwriting database (CASIA-HWDB), the proposed approach achieved a character-level correct rate of over 90 percent.

1. Introduction

This chapter describes strategies and techniques for handwritten Chinese text line recognition. Compared to isolated Chinese character recognition, text line recognition involves more issues in addition to character classification, such as character segmentation, context fusion and optimal path search. As a text line can be treated as a character string, we will refer to the terms of text line recognition and character string recognition interchangeably in this chapter.

*Current affiliation: Microsoft, Building 18, Creative Industrial Park, No. 328, Xinghu Street, Suzhou 215123, China.

Chinese character string recognition has attracted much attention and has achieved tremendous advances in the past 40 years.[1,2] However, most works focused on rather constrained application domain, such as legal amount recognition in bank checks[3] and address phrase recognition for postal mails,[4–6] where the number of character classes is very small, or there are very strong lexical constraints. Works on general character string recognition have been reported only in recent years.[7–9] The competitions in ICDAR[a] 2011 and 2013 showed a big progress,[10,11] but the reported accuracy is still not sufficient for practical application. On the other hand, online Chinese string recognition have reported higher accuracy[12,13] due to the availability of strong sequence which benefits character segmentation and discrimination.

Handwritten Chinese text line recognition is a challenge due to the character segmentation difficulty, the character classification issue, and the unconstrained language domain, see two examples of Chinese handwritten document image in Figure 1. The difficulty of character segmentation originates from the variability of character size and position, character touching and overlapping, and confusing within-character and between-character gaps, see Figures 2(a) and 2(b). The character classification issue is due to the large character set and the diversity of writing styles, as well as the confusion between similar characters. The large set of Chinese characters (tens of thousands classes) brings difficulties to efficient and effective recognition. The divergence of writing styles among different writers and in different geographic areas aggravates the confusion between different classes or in the same class, see Figures 2(c) and 2(d). Last, handwritten text recognition is more difficult than bank check recognition and mail address reading because the lexical constraint is very weak: under grammatical and semantic constraints, the number of sentence classes is infinite. Moreover, the language domain of the recognition text is variable and unknown a priori, see Figure 1 of two different domains.

Due to the infinite sentence classes of Chinese texts, character string recognition can only be solved by segmentation-based approaches to form string classes by concatenating character classes, which can be generally divided into implicit segmentation (feature sequence partition) and explicit segmentation (over-segmentation)[14] methods. Implicit segmentation is widely used in English text recognition with Hidden Markov Model (HMM),[15] while Chinese text recognition prefers explicit segmentation, which can take advantage of the character shape and overlapping and

[a]International Conference on Document Analysis and Recognition.

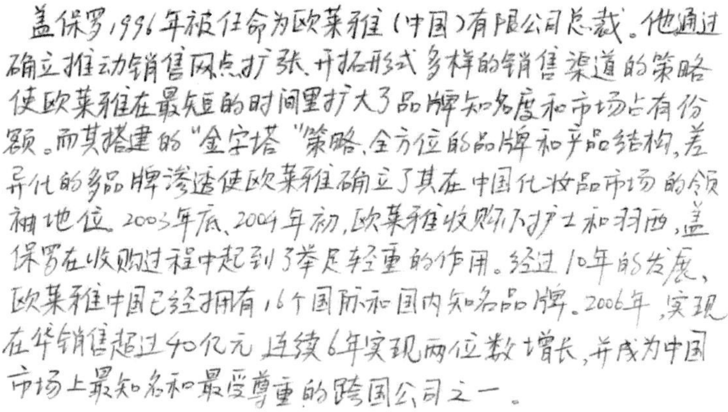

盖保罗1996年被任命为欧莱雅(中国)有限公司总裁。他通过确立推动销售网点扩张、开拓形式多样的销售渠道的策略使欧莱雅在最短的时间里扩大了品牌知名度和市场占有份额。而其搭建的"金字塔"策略、全方位的品牌和产品结构,差异化的多品牌渗透使欧莱雅确立了其在中国化妆品市场的领袖地位。2003年底、2004年初,欧莱雅收购小护士和羽西,盖保罗在收购过程中起到了举足轻重的作用。经过10年的发展,欧莱雅中国已经拥有16个国际和国内知名品牌。2006年,实现在华销售超过40亿元,连续6年实现两位数增长,并成为中国市场上最知名和最受尊重的跨国公司之一。

(a)

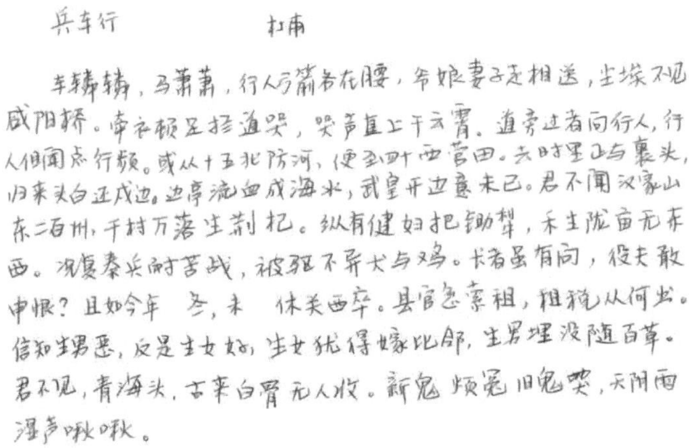

兵车行 杜甫

车辚辚,马萧萧,行人弓箭各在腰,爷娘妻子走相送,尘埃不见咸阳桥。牵衣顿足拦道哭,哭声直上干云霄。道旁过者问行人,行人但云点行频。或从十五北防河,便至四十西营田。去时里正与裹头,归来头白还戍边。边亭流血成海水,武皇开边意未已。君不闻汉家山东二百州,千村万落生荆杞。纵有健妇把锄犁,禾生陇亩无东西。况复秦兵耐苦战,被驱不异犬与鸡。长者虽有问,役夫敢申恨?且如今年冬,未休关西卒。县官急索租,租税从何出。信知生男恶,反是生女好,生女犹得嫁比邻,生男埋没随百草。君不见,青海头,古来白骨无人收。新鬼烦冤旧鬼哭,天阴雨湿声啾啾。

(b)

Figure 1. Two pages of handwritten Chinese text. (a) News domain; (b) Ancient domain.

touching characteristics to better separate the characters at their boundaries. Although Su *et al.*[7] tried to use implicit segmentation in Chinese text recognition, the reported accuracy was quite low. The result of over-segmentation is a sequence of primitive segments, each corresponding to a character or a part of a character, such that candidate characters can be generated by concatenating consecutive segments.[16] The candidate character sequences can be represented in a network called as candidate lattice,[17] and each candidate segmentation path in the lattice can be split into many segmentation-recognition paths by assigning character classes to the

Figure 2. (a) Variability of character size and position, and character touching; (b) Confusing within-character (e.g., the right arrow) and between-character gaps (e.g., the left arrow); (c) Different classes with similar shapes; (d) Same class with different shapes.

candidate characters. The result of character segmentation and recognition is obtained by evaluating the paths in the lattice and searching for the optimal path.

In integrated segmentation-and-recognition, there are two important issues: evaluation and search of candidate segmentation-recognition paths. The candidate path are usually evaluated by context fusion, i.e., combining character classification scores, geometric context and linguistic context.[14] Many efforts have been done along this direction, but there have not been a satisfactory solution. The existing methods either integrated incomplete contexts,[7,8,18] or combined the contexts heuristically without optimizing the combining weights.[19–21] In addition, one fixed general language model usually mismatches the domain of the text to recognize because the domain is variable and usually unknown *a priori*. However, there were few works on the language model adaptation (LMA) to address such domain shift problem. Only recently, Xiu and Baird[22] and Lee and Smith[23] adapted a word lexicon or uni-gram probabilities for English whole-book recognition, and He *et al.*[24] introduced a simple model combination method for language model adaptation in Chinese handwriting recognition. For the issue of path search, the beam search strategy is widely used due to its efficiency, however its pruning is usually too rough.[14] The previous works have addressed character string recognition from different viewpoints, and have contributed various techniques. However, none has investigated into these techniques comprehensively and integrated them in a high performance system for Chinese handwritten text recognition.

In this chapter, we introduce a investigate an integrated segmentation-and-recognition framework for handwritten Chinese text line recognition, describe the involved techniques with emphasis on context fusion and path search. By elaborating such techniques, we achieved significant improvements on unconstrained handwritten Chinese texts. In context fusion, we combine character classification scores via confidence transformation, geometric context and linguistic context from the Bayesian decision view, and the combining weights are optimized by a Maximum Character Accuracy

(MCA) criterion on a dataset of training text lines. In path search, a refined beam search algorithm is used to improve the search efficiency and accuracy. In addition, we propose three unsupervised language model adaptation methods to alleviate the domain problem. We evaluated the recognition performance on the unconstrained Chinese handwriting database CASIA-HWDB[25] and demonstrated superior performance by the proposed methods.

In the remainder of this chapter, we first review some related works in Sec. 2, then give an overview of our approach in Sec. 3. We focus on describing the context fusion and path search algorithm, and language model adaptation techniques in Sec. 4 and Sec. 5, respectively. After that, we report the experimental results in Sec. 6. Finally, we draw concluding remarks in Sec. 7.

2. Related Work

In the context of character string recognition, many works have contributed to the related issues of over-segmentation, character classification, confidence transformation, language model, geometric context model, context fusion (path evaluation), path search and language model adaptation.

For over-segmentation, connected component analysis has been widely adopted, but the splitting of connected (touching) characters has been a concern.[16,26,27] After generating candidate character patterns by combining consecutive primitive segments, each candidate pattern is recognized using a classifier to assign similarity/dissimilarity scores to some character classes. Character classification involves character normalization, feature extraction, character discrimination and outlier resistance. The state-of-the-art methods have been reviewed in the literature.[28–30] For classification of Chinese characters with large number of classes, the most popularly used classifiers are the modified quadratic discriminant function (MQDF)[31] and the nearest prototype classifier (NPC).[32] The MQDF provides higher accuracy than the NPC but suffers from high expenses of storage and computation.

Transforming the similarity/dissimilarity measures output by classifiers to probabilistic confidence measures can benefit fusing multiple classifiers or fusing multiple patterns, as has been demonstrated in previous works (e.g., Refs. 33, 34). In character string recognition, Jiang *et al.*[18] transformed classifier outputs to confidence values under the soft-max framework. Li *et al.*[35] used the logistic regression model for confidence transformation.

Our previous work[36] compared various confidence transformation methods in handwritten Chinese text recognition, and found a better solution.

Language models are widely used in speech recognition, machine translation and handwriting recognition.[37] The most popular language model is the n-gram model, which characterizes the statistical dependency between characters or words. Character-level n-gram models have been popularly used in character string recognition (e.g., Refs. 18–21). Word-level and hybrid language models were used in post-processing for correcting recognition errors after character segmentation,[35,38] but have been rarely used in integrated segmentation-and-recognition.[39] Recently, neural network language models[40] show promises in English handwriting recognition, but their computational cost is very large.[41]

In addition to the character classification scores and linguistic context, the geometric context also plays important role in character string recognition, particularly for disambiguating character segmentation.[19–21,42,43] Zhou *et al.* elaborated the geometric context into unary and binary, character class-dependent and class-independent models in online handwriting recognition.[13,42] Yin *et al.* elaborated the geometric models in transcript mapping of handwritten Chinese documents.[44]

To balance different models in context fusion, the combining weights were sometimes determined by trial and error.[19–21,42] Some works have applied the supervised learning approach to estimate the weights by optimizing a string recognition criterion. Recently, Zhou *et al.*[13] proposed to learn the weights by minimizing the negative log-likelihood (NLL) loss or maximizing the margin under the framework of semi-Markov conditional random field (semi-CRF). Yin *et al.*[44] optimized the weights by MCE[46] learning for transcript mapping. Zhu *et al.*[45] optimized the combining weights for handwriting recognition using the genetic algorithm (GA), which is computationally expensive and is sensitive to some artificial parameters. More discriminative learning criteria have been proposed by the community of speech recognition, such as minimum phone error (MPE) and its variant, minimum word error (MWE).[47,48]

The search of optimal path in Chinese character string recognition is not trivial because of the large number of candidate segmentation-recognition paths. The search is further complicated when using word-level language models because the word segmentation is again a combinatorial problem.[39] The speech recognition community has contributed many efficient search algorithms based on dynamic programming (DP) and some variants (e.g., beam search).[49] The beam search strategy provides a good trade-off between efficiency and accuracy. The character-synchronous beam search strategy is appropriate for lexicon-driven string recognition,[16] while the frame-synchronous (also called as time-synchronous in speech recognition) strategy is appropriate for lexicon-free string recognition.[50]

Although few works of language model adaptation (LMA) in handwriting recognition have been reported, many studies have been conducted for LMA in speech recognition,[51,52] which can be grouped into supervised and unsupervised LMA. Supervised LMA assumes that the domain of recognition task is known in advance, and meanwhile, a set of domain-specific held-out data is available to either learn the interpolation weights of several pre-defined language models[51] or train a domain-specific language model to interpolate with the generic language model.[53] In contrast, various unsupervised methods utilize recognized text to get an adaptive language model, which can be grouped into three categories: latent topic analysis (e.g., Refs. 51, 54), direct estimation of an n-gram model from the recognized text (e.g., Refs. 55, 56), and combination of multiple language models (e.g., Refs. 52, 57). Both supervised and unsupervised LMA improve the recognition performance, yet unsupervised LMA is more relevant to real applications where the topic is unknown *a priori*.

3. System Overview

This section gives a briefly overview of our recognition system for handwritten Chinese text lines. We focus on text line recognition, while the tasks of document image pre-processing and text line segmentation are assumed to have been accomplished externally.

Figure 3 shows the block diagram of the recognition system and some candidate lattice examples, and each step is introduced in the following:

(1) The input text line image is over-segmented into a sequence of primitive segments (Figure 3(b)(I)) using the connected component-based method,[16] such that each segment is a character or a part of a character;
(2) One or multiple consecutive segments are concatenated to generate candidate character patterns, forming a segmentation candidate lattice (Figure 3(b)(II)), and each path in this lattice is called a candidate segmentation path;
(3) Each candidate pattern is classified to assign several candidate character classes using a character classifier, and all the candidate patterns in a candidate segmentation path form a character candidate

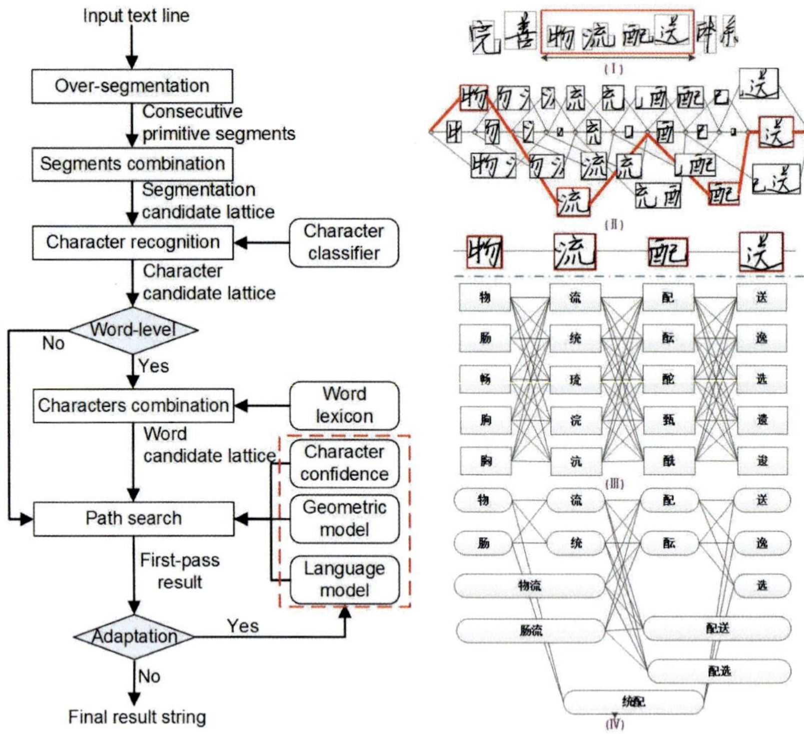

(a) (b)

Figure 3. (a) System diagram of handwritten Chinese text line recognition; (b) Candidate lattice samples: (I) Text line over-segmented to a sequence of primitive segments (each is bounded by a small box); (II) Segmentation candidate lattice of the arrowed part of (I); (III) Character candidate lattice of a segmentation path (the thick path in (II)); (IV) Word candidate lattice of (III).

lattice(Figure 3(b)(III));

(4) If a word-level language model is used, each sequence of candidate character classes is matched with a word lexicon to segment into candidate words,[b] forming a word candidate lattice (Figure 3(b)(IV));

(5) All of these character or word candidate lattices are merged to construct the segmentation-recognition lattice of the input text line, and each path in this lattice is constructed by a character sequence paired with a candidate pattern sequence, which is called a candidate segmentation-recognition path;

[b]In Chinese, a word may comprise one or multiple characters, which can explore both syntactic and semantic meaning better than a character.

(6) Each candidate segmentation-recognition path is evaluated by fusing multiple contexts (the dashed-line box in Figure 3(a)), and the optimal path is searched to give the segmentation and recognition result;
(7) If language model adaptation is needed, the recognized result is back to the step 6, otherwise it is output as the final result.

In the above, step 6 involving context fusion and optimal path search, is the core part of the recognition system, while step 7 of the language model adaptation is very useful to improve the recognition accuracy. We describe the details of these two steps in Secs. 4 and 5, respectively.

4. Context Fusion and Path Search

The task of string recognition is to find the optimal path in the segmentation-recognition candidate lattice. There are two issues in this task: First, how can we know one path is better than another, i.e., path evaluation; Once we know the evaluation score of each path, how to efficiently find the best one, i.e., path search.

4.1. *Context fusion*

Context fusion is involved in evaluating the candidate segmentation-recognition paths. We first introduce the statistical foundation of our context fusion method, then describe the probabilistic models of each context, and last, introduce the estimation method of combining weights in context fusion.

4.1.1. *Statistical foundation*

We formulate the task of string recognition from Bayesian decision view. According to Bayesian decision rule under the 0/1 loss, the optimal criterion of classification is to maximize the posterior probability of character sequence (string class) $C = \langle c_1 \cdots c_m \rangle$ given a text line image X, which is formulated by

$$\begin{aligned} P(C|X) &= \sum\nolimits_s P(C, s|X) = \sum\nolimits_s P(s|X)P(C|s, X) \\ &= \sum\nolimits_s P(s|X)P(C|X^s) \end{aligned} \tag{1}$$

where s is the segmentation path index, $P(s|X)$ denotes the posterior probability of the sth segmentation path given the text line image, and $P(C|X^s)$

represents the posterior probability of string class given the sth segmentation path. To avoid summing over segmentation paths exhaustively in Eq. (1), the optimal string class can be decided approximately by

$$C^* = \arg\max_{s,C} P(s|X)P(C|X^s). \tag{2}$$

This is to search for the optimal segmentation and string class simultaneously in the lattice.

We formulate the segmentation path probability $P(s|X)$ in Eq. (2) as

$$P(s|X) = \prod_{i=1}^{m} p(z_i^{\mathrm{p}} = 1|g_i^{\mathrm{ui}})p(z_i^{\mathrm{g}} = 1|g_i^{\mathrm{bi}}), \tag{3}$$

where m is the number of segmented candidate patterns (i.e., character number) on the segmentation path, and the two probabilistic terms correspond to the unary and binary class-independent geometric model, representing the probabilities of a valid character and a valid between-character gap (see Sec. 4.1.2), respectively.

The posterior probability of string class $P(C|X^s)$ in Eq. (2) can be obtained by the Bayes' formula:

$$P(C|X^s) = \frac{p(X^s|C)p(C)}{p(X^s)} \tag{4}$$

where the prior probability $p(C) = p(c_1 \cdots c_m)$ is given by a statistical language model $p(C) = \prod_{i=1}^{m} p(c_i|h_i)$ (where h_i is the historical characters of c_i, see Sec. 4.1.2). The likelihood function $p(X^s|C)$ can be decomposed into the product of character-dependent terms:

$$p(X^s|C) = \prod_{i=1}^{m} p(\mathbf{x}_i|c_i)p(g_i^{\mathrm{uc}}|c_i)p(g_i^{\mathrm{bc}}|c_{i-1}c_i), \tag{5}$$

where we characterize each candidate pattern in the segmentation path X^s with the intrinsic shape feature $\mathbf{x}_i$ (used in the character classifier) and the outline geometric features (unary and binary class-dependent feature g_i^{uc} and g_i^{bc}, respectively, see Sec. 4.1.2), and assume that the feature vectors are only dependent on the corresponding character patterns. Similarly, we can decompose $p(X^s)$ into terms as:

$$p(X^s) = \prod_{i=1}^{m} p(\mathbf{x}_i)p(g_i^{\mathrm{uc}})p(g_i^{\mathrm{bc}}). \tag{6}$$

Consequently, the posterior probability $P(C|X^s)$ is obtained by

$$\begin{aligned} P(C|X^s) &= p(C)\prod_{i=1}^{m}\frac{p(\mathbf{x}_i|c_i)}{p(\mathbf{x}_i)}\frac{p(g_i^{\mathrm{uc}}|c_i)}{p(g_i^{\mathrm{uc}})}\frac{p(g_i^{\mathrm{bc}}|c_{i-1}c_i)}{p(g_i^{\mathrm{bc}})} \\ &= p(C)\prod_{i=1}^{m}\frac{p(c_i|\mathbf{x}_i)}{p_1(c_i)}\frac{p(c_i|g_i^{\mathrm{uc}})}{p_2(c_i)}\frac{p(c_{i-1}c_i|g_i^{\mathrm{bc}})}{p_3(c_{i-1}c_i)}, \end{aligned} \tag{7}$$

where the three posterior probabilities can be approximated by confidence transformation of classifier outputs (see Sec. 4.1.2), and three corresponding prior probabilities $p_1(c_i), p_2(c_i), p_3(c_{i-1}c_i)$ are viewed as constants in classifier design (the un-even distribution $p(c_i)$ is considered elsewhere in the language model $p(C)$), denoted by p_1, p_2, p_3, respectively, and simply set $P = p_1p_2p_3$. Substituting statistical language model $p(C) = \prod_{i=1}^{m} p(c_i|h_i)$ in Eq. (7) gives

$$P(C|X^s) = \prod_{i=1}^{m}\frac{p(c_i|\mathbf{x}_i)p(c_i|g_i^{\mathrm{uc}})p(c_{i-1}c_i|g_i^{\mathrm{bc}})p(c_i|h_i)}{P}. \tag{8}$$

Combining the posterior probabilities of segmentation path Eq. (3) and string class Eq. (8), the optimal string class of Eq. (2) can be obtained by

$$\begin{aligned} C^* = \arg\max_{s,C}\ \frac{1}{P^m}\prod_{i=1}^{m}\Big[&p(c_i|\mathbf{x}_i)p(c_i|g_i^{\mathrm{uc}})p(c_{i-1}c_i|g_i^{\mathrm{bc}}) \\ &p(z_i^{\mathrm{p}}=1|g_i^{\mathrm{ui}})p(z_i^{\mathrm{g}}=1|g_i^{\mathrm{bi}})p(c_i|h_i)\Big]. \end{aligned} \tag{9}$$

Note that all terms $m, c_i, \mathbf{x}_i, g_i^{\mathrm{uc}}, g_i^{\mathrm{bc}}, g_i^{\mathrm{ui}}, g_i^{\mathrm{bi}}, z_i^{\mathrm{p}}, z_i^{\mathrm{g}}, h_i$ are related to the sth segmentation path, and the index s is dropped for simplification. Considering the different contribution and insufficient estimation of different probabilistic models (character recognition, geometric and linguistic models), we take the logarithm of probability (denoted by $lp_i^0 = \log p(c_i|\mathbf{x}_i)$, $lp_i^1 = \log p(c_i|g_i^{\mathrm{uc}})$, $lp_i^2 = \log p(c_{i-1}c_i|g_i^{\mathrm{bc}})$, $lp_i^3 = \log p(z_i^{\mathrm{p}} = 1|g_i^{\mathrm{ui}})$, $lp_i^4 = \log p(z_i^{\mathrm{g}} = 1|g_i^{\mathrm{bi}})$, $lp_i^5 = \log p(c_i|h_i)$, $lp^6 = \log\frac{1}{P}$) and incorporate the weights of different models to get a generalized likelihood function $f(X^s, C)$ for segmentation-recognition path evaluation:

$$f(X^s, C) = \sum_{i=1}^{m}\left[lp_i^0 + \sum_{j=1}^{5}\lambda_j\cdot lp_i^j\right] + \lambda_6\cdot m\cdot lp^6, \tag{10}$$

then $C^* = \arg\max_{s,C} f(X^s, C)$, where λ_j, $j = 1, \ldots, 6$, are the weights to balance the effects of different models.

In the above, the positive constant lp^6 is also called the word insertion penalty in the work,[58] and used to overcome the bias to short strings (without this term, the path evaluation score decreases as the path length m increases). Similar to the idea of the variable-length HMM of the work,[59] we also use the width of candidate pattern to overcome the short string bias:

$$f(X^s, C) = \sum_{i=1}^{m} \left[w_i \cdot lp_i^0 + \sum_{j=1}^{5} \lambda_j \cdot lp_i^j \right]. \tag{11}$$

This function works well because the sum of widths w_i is approximately constant for all segmentation paths, and the experimental results in our work[9] show it performs much better than that of Eq. (10) due to the imperfect estimation of lp^6.

4.1.2. *Probabilistic models of contexts*

The path evaluation function of Eq. (11) entails the estimation of one character recognition model ($p(c_i|\mathbf{x}_i)$), four geometric models ($p(c_i|g_i^{\mathrm{uc}})$, $p(c_{i-1}c_i|g_i^{\mathrm{bc}})$, $p(z_i^{\mathrm{p}} = 1|g_i^{\mathrm{ui}})$, $p(z_i^{\mathrm{g}} = 1|g_i^{\mathrm{bi}})$) and one language model ($p(c_i|h_i)$), which will be introduced in the following.

The character recognition model, ideally, the posterior probability $p(\omega|\mathbf{x})$ (ω refers to a class and $\mathbf{x}$ is the feature vector), is an important context for string recognition. Most character classifiers, however, do not output class posterior probabilities[29] (neural networks with soft-max outputs can approximate the posterior probability, but its computational cost is too large due to the very large character class set). We use a modified quadratic discriminant function (MQDF) as the character classifier, and resort to confidence transformation methods for converting classifier outputs to posterior probabilities.[36]

The sigmoidal function and soft-max function are commonly used for probabilistic confidence transformation, which are defined by

$$P^{sg}(\omega_j|\mathbf{x}) = \frac{\exp\left[-\alpha d_j(\mathbf{x}) + \beta\right]}{1 + \exp\left[-\alpha d_j(\mathbf{x}) + \beta\right]}, \quad j = 1, \ldots, M, \tag{12}$$

$$P^{sf}(\omega_j|\mathbf{x}) = \frac{\exp\left[-\alpha d_j(\mathbf{x})\right]}{\sum_{i=1}^{M} \exp\left[-\alpha d_i(\mathbf{x})\right]}, \quad j = 1, \ldots, M. \tag{13}$$

In the above, M is the total number of defined classes, $d_j(\mathbf{x})$ is the dissimilarity score of class ω_j output by the classifier, α and β are the confidence parameters. However, both functions are insufficient for character string recognition, which involves a multi-class probability and classification of non-characters (outlier rejection). To improve the sigmoidal function, we combine such two-class probabilities into multi-class probabilities according to the Dempster-Shafer (D-S) theory of evidence,[60] and the probabilities are then formulated by[36]

$$p^{ds}(\omega_j|\mathbf{x}) = \frac{\exp\left[-\alpha d_j(\mathbf{x}) + \beta\right]}{1 + \sum_{i=1}^{M} \exp\left[-\alpha d_i(\mathbf{x}) + \beta\right]}, \ j = 1, \ldots, M. \tag{14}$$

We also introduce an outlier class dissimilarity score (assuming $d_o(\mathbf{x}) = \beta/\alpha$) in soft-max confidence, and the resulting formula is the same as Eq. (14).[36] After getting multi-class probabilities, the probability of outlier class is

$$p^{ds}(w_{outlier}|\mathbf{x}) = \frac{1}{1 + \sum_{i=1}^{M} \exp\left[-\alpha d_i(\mathbf{x}) + \beta\right]}, \tag{15}$$

which is the complement probability to the M defined classes.

The confidence parameters are class-independent, which can be optimized by minimizing the cross entropy (CE) loss function on a validation dataset (preferably different from the dataset for training classifiers).[36]

There are four geometric models ($p(c_i|g_i^{\mathrm{uc}})$, $p(c_{i-1}c_i|g_i^{\mathrm{bc}})$, $p(z_i^{\mathrm{p}} = 1|g_i^{\mathrm{ui}})$, $p(z_i^{\mathrm{g}} = 1|g_i^{\mathrm{bi}})$) in Eq. (11), namely, unary and binary class-dependent, unary and binary class-independent, which are abbreviated as "**ucg**", "**bcg**", "**uig**", and "**big**", respectively. The class-dependent models help to distinguish the characters (e.g., alphanumeric characters, punctuation marks and Chinese characters) with distinct outline features[c] (e.g., size, position, aspect ratio, and within-character gap). The two class-independent models (unary and binary) are designed to indicate whether a candidate pattern is a valid character or not, and whether a gap is a between-character gap or not, respectively.

To build geometric models, we need to extract geometric features and then classify the features using a classifier. The unary geometric features are extracted from each candidate character pattern, including the size of bounding box, relative position to the vertical center of text line, and the profile-based features. Similarly, the binary geometric features are extracted from two consecutive character patterns, such as the gap between bounding boxes, differences between the outline profiles. All these features are summarized in Table 1, and the details can be found in the work.[44]

[c]These features are lost in the character classification due to the character normalization.

Table 1. Geometric features (the last column denotes whether normalized w.r.t. the text line height or not).

Models	Features	Norm
ucg/uig	Height and width of bounding box	Yes
ucg/uig	Sum of inner gap	Yes
ucg/uig	Distance of gravity center to the bound	Yes
ucg/uig	Logarithm of aspect ratio	No
ucg/uig	Size of bounding box	Yes
ucg/uig	Distance of gravity center to geometric center	Yes
ucg/uig	Means of horizontal and vertical projection profiles	Yes
ucg	Distance of upper/lower bound to text line center	Yes
ucg	Distance of gravity/geometric center to text line center	Yes
ucg	Profile-based features	Yes
bcg/big	Distance between the two consecutive bounding boxes	Yes
bcg/big	Height and width of the box enclosing two consecutive characters	Yes
bcg/big	Gap between the bounding boxes	Yes
big	Convex hull-based distance	Yes
bcg	Ratio of heights/widths of the bounding boxes	No
bcg	Size of the common area of the bounding boxes	Yes
bcg	Differences of the outline profiles	Yes

We can then build statistical models on such features. Since the number of Chinese characters is very large and many of them have similar geometric features, we cluster the character classes into six super-classes using the EM algorithm. After clustering, we use a 6-class quadratic discriminant function[14] (QDF) for the "ucg" model, and a 36-class QDF for the "bcg" model. In addition, we use a linear support vector machine (SVM) trained with character and non-character samples for the "uig" model, and similarly, a linear SVM for the "big" model. Finally, we convert both QDF and SVM outputs to posterior probabilities via sigmoidal confidence transformation in path evaluation function.

In character string recognition, the statistical language model ($p(C)$) is used to give the prior probability of a certain character sequence.[15] If the sequence C contains m characters, $p(C)$ can be decomposed by

$$p(C) = \prod_{i=1}^{m} p(c_i|c_1^{i-1}) = \prod_{i=1}^{m} p(c_i|h_i), \tag{16}$$

where $h_i = c_1^{i-1} = \langle c_1 \cdots c_{i-1} \rangle$ denotes the history of character c_i (h_1 is null). The most popular language model is the n-gram model due to its efficiency and simplicity, which only considers the $n-1$ history characters:

$$p(C) = \prod_{i=1}^{m} p(c_i | c_{i-n+1}^{i-1}), \tag{17}$$

where n is called the order of the model. In consideration of model complexity, the **character bi-gram**(cbi) and **tri-gram**(cti) are usually used:

$$p_{cbi}(C) = \prod_{i=1}^{m} p(c_i | c_{i-1}), \tag{18}$$

$$p_{cti}(C) = \prod_{i=1}^{m} p(c_i | c_{i-2} c_{i-1}). \tag{19}$$

Compared to the character-level, word-level models can better explore the syntactic and semantic meaning. Segmenting the character sequence C into a sequence of words $C = w_1 w_2 \cdots w_L$, the **word bi-gram**(wbi) model is

$$p_{wbi}(C) = \prod_{i=1}^{L} p(w_i | w_{i-1}). \tag{20}$$

Due to the large size of word lexicon (about 0.3 million words in Chinese), we only use the word bi-gram. Further, we cluster the words into a number of word classes by the exchange algorithm,[61] and the **word class bi-gram**(wcb) is calculated by

$$p_{wcb}(C) = \prod_{i=1}^{L} p(w_i | W_i) p(W_i | W_{i-1}), \tag{21}$$

where the term W_i is the class of word w_i. We found that a word class number 1,000 leads to good tradeoff between the model size and the recognition performance.[39] In addition, the word class bi-gram is often used by interpolating with the word bi-gram:[37]

$$\log p_{iwc}(C) = \log p_{wbi}(C) + \lambda \log p_{wcb}(C), \tag{22}$$

where the logarithm is used for more general purposes, and this model is called **interpolating word and class bi-gram**(iwc).

The parameters of such n-gram models are usually estimated from a lager text corpus using maximum likelihood estimation, which can be accompanished by the SRI Language Model (SRILM) toolkit.[62] In the SRILM, we use Katz back-off smoothing[63] to overcome zero probabilities of unseen n-grams, and use entropy-based pruning[64] to reduce model size.

All the above context models are summarized in Table 2.

Table 2. Contextual models summarization.

Name	Context type	Formula
Character classification	Character recognition	MQDF+Eq. (14)
Unary class-dependent geometry	Geometric context	QDF+Eq. (12)
Unary class-independent geometry	Geometric context	QDF+Eq. (12)
Binary class-dependent geometry	Geometric context	SVM+Eq. (12)
Binary class-independent geometry	Geometric context	SVM+Eq. (12)
Character bi-gram	Linguistic context	Eq. (18)
Character tri-gram	Linguistic context	Eq. (19)
Word bi-gram	Linguistic context	Eq. (20)
Word class bi-gram	Linguistic context	Eq. (21)
Interpolating word and class bi-gram	Linguistic context	Eq. (22)

4.1.3. *Fusion weights learning*

In the path evaluation function Eq. (11), the fusion weights are learned to balance the context models to optimize the recognition performance. To do this, we optimize a Maximum Character Accuracy (**MCA**) criterion, which is motivated from the idea of the Minimum Word Error (**MWE**)[47] in speech recognition. The MCA is a smoothed approximation to the accuracy of the R string samples (text line images) in the training dataset:

$$\max \Psi(\Lambda) = \frac{1}{R}\sum_{r=1}^{R}\sum_{j=1}^{N_r} P_\Lambda(C_r^j|X_r)\cdot A(C_r^j, T_r), \tag{23}$$

where N_r is the number of all segmentation-recognition paths in the lattice of the rth text line image X_r (the rth training sample), and C_r^j is the character sequence of the jth segmentation-recognition path.

In the above, the term $A(C_r^j, T_r)$ is the character accuracy score, which equals the number of characters in the ground-truth transcript T_r minus the number of errors in the jth candidate recognition result C_r^j (including substitution, insertion and deletion errors, which are calculated by aligning the C_r^j with the T_r by dynamic programming, see performance metrics introduction in Sec. 6.2). Note that the posterior probability $P_\Lambda(C_r^j|X_r)$ can be computed by soft-max:

$$P_\Lambda(C_r^j|X_r) = \frac{\exp[\xi f_\Lambda(X_r^j, C_r^j)]}{\sum_{i=1}^{N_r}\exp[\xi f_\Lambda(X_r^i, C_r^i)]}, \tag{24}$$

where ξ is a constant scaling parameter, and $f_\Lambda(X_r^j, C_r^j)$ is the path evaluation function Eq. (11) under the weights set Λ. The MCA is degenerated to the Minimum Classification Error (MCE) criterion[46] if the character accuracy score is calculated by $A(C_r^j, T_r) = \delta(C_r^j, T_r) \in \{0, 1\}$.[48]

We optimize the MCA objective (23) by stochastic gradient ascent. The gradients are difficult to calculate precisely due to the huge number N_r (growing exponentially as the length of candidate paths). Therefore, we considered only the top N paths of maximum evaluation score while viewing the probabilities of the remaining paths as zero.

4.2. *Path search*

On defining a score to evaluate each path in the candidate segmentation-recognition lattice, the next issue is how to efficiently find the path of maximum score. The summation nature of path score in Eq. (11) guarantees that the optimal path with maximum score can be found by dynamic programming (DP). However, when binary or higher-order contexts are used, the complexity of DP search is high. A beam search strategy is used to accelerate the DP search and better find an approximately optimal solution. In beam search, it is critical to make the correct partial path be retained in fewer survived paths, but a simple strategy of beam search is to retain the multiple top-rank partial paths ending at each primitive segment[14] with only one step, which is too rough to get the correct path efficiently. Hence, we use a refined beam search algorithm to better retain partial paths, and it is suitable for using high-order contexts.

For the refined beam search, we first declare some notations, then describe the details and show an illustrative example in Figure 4. After over-segmentation, the text line image is represented as a sequence of primitive segments. A candidate pattern composed of k consecutive segments and ending at the ith segment is denoted by (i, k). A node in the search space is represented as a quadruple $SN = \{CP, CC, AS, PN\}$, where SN denotes a search node, CP is a candidate pattern, CC is a candidate character of CP, and AS is the accumulated score from the root node (calculated by Eq. (11), where m is the length of the current partial path), and PN is a pointer to the parent node of SN. All nodes are stored in a list named **LIST** to backtrack the final path.

Refined Beam Search in frame-synchronous fashion:

(1) Initialize the first search node (i.e, the root) of **LIST**, $SN_0 = \{null, null, 0, null\}$, set $i = 1$.

(2) Generate nodes of $CP = (i, k)$ over k (the second level nodes in Figure 4(b), $i-k \geq 0, k \leq K$, K is the maximum number of segments to be

concatenated). For each CP, top CN (Candidate Number) candidate characters are assigned by the character classifier (the third level nodes in Figure 4(b)). In total, at most $K \times CN$ nodes are generated.

(3) Link to parent nodes for current nodes $(CP = (i,k), CC = c_{i,k})$. For multiple such parent nodes $(CP' = (i-k,k'), CC' = c_{i-k,k'})$, the current node is generated multiple copies, each linked to a respective parent node (PN) and associated an accumulated score (AS) (the fourth level nodes in Figure 4(b)). In these copies, only the node with maximum AS over $(k', c_{i-k,k'})$ is retained (the fifth level nodes in Figure 4(b)).

(4) Sort the retained nodes in above in decreasing order according to AS over $(k, c_{i,k})$, and the leading BW (Beam Width) nodes are retained and added to **LIST**, while the others are pruned to accelerate search.

(5) Set $i = i + 1$, back to Step (2) and iterate until the last primitive segment is reached (such nodes called terminal nodes).

(6) Backtrack the terminal node in **LIST** of maximum score along the pointer PN, and obtain the result character string.

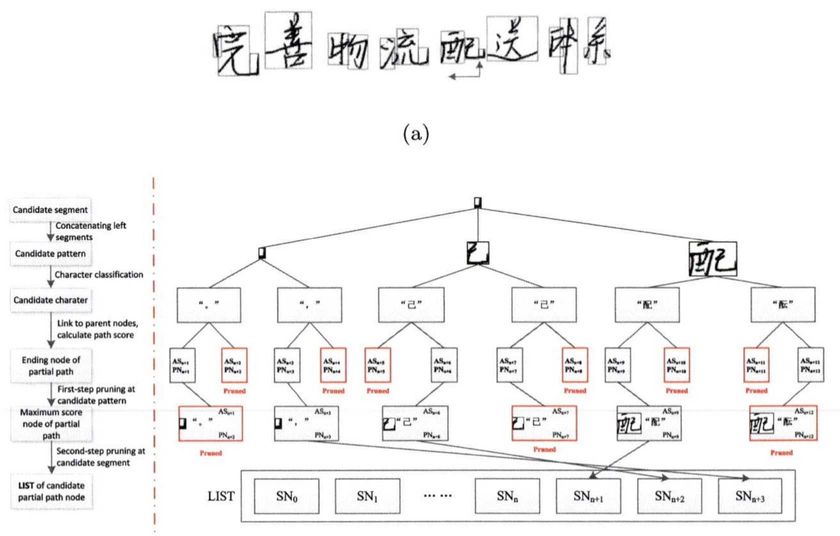

(a)

(b)

Figure 4. An illustrative example of refined beam search ($K = 3, CN = 2, BW = 3$) at a primitive segment. (a) A sequence of consecutive primitive segments; (b) Search space expansion at the pointed primitive segment of (a) (the pruned nodes are labeled), and the left part is a brief diagram corresponding to each step of the right part.

We can see that if $BW = K \times CN$, the above algorithm guarantees finding the optimal path for context models up to order 2, i.e., it is equivalent to DP. For context models of order 3 (e.g., character tri-gram) or higher, it does not guarantee finding the optimal path but significantly accelerates search compared to DP. Further, if $BW < K \times CN$, the search procedure is further accelerated. Compared to simple beam search, the two-step pruning strategy in the refined beam search algorithm has at least two advantages: (1) the first-step pruning in Step (3) observes the principle of optimality; (2) sorting the nodes has lower complexity.

If we use word-level n-grams, the search process works on a word candidate lattice, which is constructed from character lattice by combining several consecutive characters according to the word lexicon. Thus, search in word candidate lattice is very complex.[39] To accelerate this search process, we first prune the original character lattice using the above character search process (many nodes are pruned in Step (3) and Step (4)), then use it to construct a succinct word lattice. Under this strategy, the time of search process using word-based bi-gram is reduced largely, and becomes comparable to that of the character tri-gram. In addition, it improves the recognition performance due to pruning many noise nodes in character lattice.

5. Language Model Adaptation

To overcome the mismatch problem between the language model and the domain of handwritten text, we introduce language model adaptation (LMA), particularly, unsupervised adaptation because the domain of handwritten text is unknown *a priori*. In addition, we introduce language model compression techniques to reduce the storage of language models used in our adaptation.

5.1. *Unsupervised adaptation algorithm*

We usually get an adaptive language model (LM) via a two-pass recognition framework. In the first-pass recognition, we use a generic language model (LM_0) to obtain a preliminary transcript C, then we generate an adaptive language model (LM^*) that best matches the preliminary transcript, which will be used in the second-pass recognition to get the final transcript. Note that in Figure 3(a), we can see only the part of path search is processed two-pass, and the main time-consuming part (building the candidate lattice) is only one-pass, so such two-pass recognition has little additional cost compared to the baseline system.[65] To get a domain matched LM, we prepared a multi-domain LM set ($\{LM_1, LM_2, \ldots, LM_K\}$, where K is the number of pre-defined domains), and each language model (LM_k) corresponds to one specific domain (e.g., sport, business, health). In the following, we will present three methods to generate the adaptive LM from such LM set, namely, model selection, model combination and model reconstruction.

5.1.1. *Model selection*

In natural language processing (NLP), the perplexity (PP)[37] is usually used to evaluate the performance of a language model, which is calculated by

$$\mathrm{PP}(C) = P(C)^{-\frac{1}{m}} = \frac{1}{\sqrt[m]{\prod_{i=1}^{m} p(c_i|h_i)}}, \tag{25}$$

where C is a measured text containing m characters (words), and h_i is the history characters (words) of c_i. This shows that lower perplexity indicates a better model, so we can straightforwardly select the best matched LM from the pre-defined LM set (including the generic LM: LM_0) by

$$k^* = \arg\min_k \mathrm{PP}_k(C),\ 0 \le k \le K, \tag{26}$$

where $\mathrm{PP}_k(C)$ is the perplexity of the kth language model (LM_k) on the first-pass transcript C. Obviously, this criterion is equivalent to maximizing the log-likelihood. This method is simple but useful, and it works under the assumption that the domain of handwritten text can be matched well with one pre-defined LM.

5.1.2. *Model combination*

When the domain of the text to recognize is out of the pre-defined set (e.g., a hybrid of several domains), the model selection method will not work very well. To overcome this, we generate a new adaptive LM via linear combination of the pre-defined multiple LMs:

$$p(c_n|c_1^{n-1}) = \sum_{k=0}^{K} \beta_k \cdot p_k(c_n|c_1^{n-1}), \tag{27}$$

where $p_k(\cdot)$ is calculated by the kth language model (LM_k), and the parameter β_k serves as the combination weight to control the relative importance of LM_K. Since the perplexity Eq. (25) evaluates the performance of a language model on the transcript C, we can heuristically estimate these LM weights by

$$\beta_k = \frac{\frac{1}{\mathrm{PP}_k(C)}}{\sum_{i=0}^{K} \frac{1}{\mathrm{PP}_i(C)}}, \quad k = 0, 1, \ldots, K. \tag{28}$$

To learn the combination weights more accurately, we formulate this problem as a linear regression model. Given the first-pass transcript C, we can extract all the n-grams in the C to form a set of training samples. Each sample is an n-gram ($\langle c_1, \ldots, c_n \rangle$), and its features are the corresponding $K+1$ LM probabilities ($\mathbf{x} = (x_0, x_1, \ldots, x_K)^T$, where $x_k = p_k(c_n|c_1^{n-1})$ by the kth LM, $k = 0, 1, \ldots, K$). On one hand, we can set the target probability of the n-gram as $t = 1$ to hope that such n-gram will be chosen in the second-pass recognition (the path evaluation function tends to choose the n-gram with higher probability). On the other hand, Eq. (27) gives an estimated value by $y = \sum_{k=0}^{K} \mathbf{b}^T\mathbf{x}$, where $\mathbf{b} = (\beta_0, \beta_1, \ldots, \beta_K)^T$. On obtaining the target value and estimated value of each training sample, we can learn the weights by minimizing the sum of squared error (**MSE**) with the L2-norm regularization:

$$\min_{\mathbf{b}} F(\mathbf{b}) = \sum_{i=1}^{N} (t_i - \mathbf{b}^T\mathbf{x}_i)^2 + \lambda \cdot \|\mathbf{b}\|_2^2, \tag{29}$$

where N is the sample number, the vector $\mathbf{x}_i = (x_{i0}, x_{i1}, \ldots, x_{iK})^T$ denotes the features of the ith sample, and the hyper-parameter λ ($\lambda \geq 0$) governs the relative importance of the regularization term. In this formulation, the computation of $\mathbf{b}$ is a quadratic programming problem, and has a closed-form solution:

$$\mathbf{b} = \left[\sum_{i=1}^{N} \mathbf{x}_i\mathbf{x}_i^T + \lambda I\right]^{-1} \sum_{i=1}^{N} t_i\mathbf{x}_i, \tag{30}$$

where I is an identity matrix. For the tradeoff parameter λ, considering the influence of data scaling, we suggest to set λ as

$$\lambda = \frac{\tilde{\lambda}}{K+1} \sum_{j=1}^{K+1} |M_{jj}|, \tag{31}$$

where $M = \sum_{i=1}^{N} \mathbf{x}_i\mathbf{x}_i^T$, and $\tilde{\lambda}$ is selected on a validation data set.

To reduce the computational cost, we can consider a reduced number of LMs with lower perplexities while viewing the remaining LMs irrelevant to the test text, and we usually only select two or three LMs in practice.[65]

5.1.3. *Model reconstruction*

Viewing each pre-defined LM as a data sample, we can decompose such sample set into a group of orthogonal bases, then reconstruct an adaptive LM using these orthogonal bases by

$$\mathbf{s} = \boldsymbol{\mu} + U_r \mathbf{v}_r. \tag{32}$$

In the Eq. (32), the term $\mathbf{s} \in \Re^d$ is a reconstructed sample, denoting a new LM (adaptive LM), with each element representing the probability value of an n-gram, and the dimensionality d is the size of the n-gram list shared by all pre-defined LMs in the orthogonal space. The term $\boldsymbol{\mu} = \frac{1}{N_s}\sum_{i=1}^{N_s} \mathbf{s}_i$ is the sample mean, and N_s is the sample number (herein, the number of pre-defined LMs, i.e., $N_s = K+1$). The r columns of matrix $U_r \in \Re^{d\times r}$ are the orthogonal bases obtained by applying principal component analysis (PCA) to the sample set, and $\mathbf{v}_r \in \Re^r$ denotes the coefficients of the sample's projection on the orthogonal space. This idea is motivated from the work[66] for representing images of human faces, and it has been successfully used in other areas like active shape models.[67]

The computation of the orthogonal bases U_r can follow the conventional PCA, which are the first r eigenvectors of the sample covariance matrix $\Sigma = \frac{1}{K+1}\bar{S}\bar{S}^T$, where $\bar{S} = [\mathbf{s}_0 - \boldsymbol{\mu}, \ldots, \mathbf{s}_K - \boldsymbol{\mu}]$. One might wonder that how to efficiently get the eigenvectors of the large-scale matrix $\bar{S}\bar{S}^T \in \Re^{d\times d}$ (d is the order of million). Fortunately, the dimensionality of the matrix $\bar{S}^T\bar{S} \in \Re^{(K+1)\times(K+1)}$ is very small (i.e., dozen order), and its eigenvectors can be got efficiently. According to the following equations (33)–(35), the eigenvector $\mathbf{x}$ of $\bar{S}^T\bar{S}$ corresponding to eigenvalue ξ can be easily transformed to the required eigenvector $\mathbf{u}$ of $\bar{S}\bar{S}^T$ by $\mathbf{u} = \frac{1}{\sqrt{\xi}}\bar{S}\mathbf{x}$.

$$\bar{S}^T\bar{S}\mathbf{x} = \xi\mathbf{x}, \tag{33}$$

$$\bar{S}(\bar{S}^T\bar{S})\mathbf{x} = \bar{S}(\xi\mathbf{x}), \tag{34}$$

$$(\bar{S}\bar{S}^T)(\bar{S}\mathbf{x}) = \xi(\bar{S}\mathbf{x}). \tag{35}$$

On obtaining the orthogonal bases, the next issue is to compute the coefficients $\mathbf{v}_r$ in Eq. (32). Like the linear regression model in Sec. 5.1.2, we can estimate $\mathbf{v}_r$ by minimizing the sum of squared error with L2-norm regularization:

$$\min_{\mathbf{v}_r} F(\mathbf{v}_r) = \sum_{i=1}^{N}[t_i - (\mu_{\pi(i)} + \mathbf{u}_{\pi(i)}^T\mathbf{v}_r)]^2 + \lambda \cdot \|\mathbf{v}_r - \mathbf{v}_0\|_2^2, \tag{36}$$

where N is the number of n-grams in the first-pass transcript C, and $t_i = 1$ is the target value for the ith n-gram. The subscript $\pi(i)$ is the index of the ith n-gram from the C in the shared n-gram list,[d] and $\mathbf{u}_{\pi(i)}^T$ is the $\pi(i)$th row of the bases matrix U_r. In the regularization term, $\mathbf{v}_0$ represents the projected vector of the sample $\mathbf{s}_0$ in the orthogonal space: $\mathbf{v}_0 = U_r^T(\mathbf{s}_0 - \boldsymbol{\mu})$, where $\mathbf{s}_0$ is the language model via the model selection method. This means that we hope the reconstructed LM is attracted to the vicinity of the model selection result. Similar to Eq. (30), we also have a closed-form solution:

$$\mathbf{v}_r = \left[\sum_{i=1}^{N} \mathbf{u}_{\pi(i)}\mathbf{u}_{\pi(i)}^T + \lambda I\right]^{-1} \left[\sum_{i=1}^{N}(t_i - \mu_{\pi(i)})\mathbf{u}_{\pi(i)} + \lambda \mathbf{v}_0\right], \tag{37}$$

and the tradeoff parameter λ is also adjusted by considering the scaling of different handwritten texts:

$$\lambda = \frac{\tilde{\lambda}}{r}\sum_{j=1}^{r}|M_{jj}|, \tag{38}$$

where $M = \sum_{i=1}^{N} \mathbf{u}_{\pi(i)}\mathbf{u}_{\pi(i)}^T$, and $\tilde{\lambda}$ is selected on a validation data set.

Compared to the above LMA methods of either model selection or model combination, model reconstruction by the orthogonal bases can generate a more flexible LM. However it needs a longer handwritten text to estimate the optimized coefficients for an adaptive LM, and is limited to the shared n-gram list.

5.2. *Language model compression*

The above LMA methods depend on a LM set including $(K+1)$ LMs, which poses a challenge of storage in practical applications. To reduce the size of such LM set, we analyze each LM by two parts, namely, the n-gram table (a list of n-gram characters) and the probability values of each n-gram.

For the n-gram table, many prefixes are repeated, so we use the trie-structure instead of the list format to remove the duplicate storage.[68] The trie-structure originates from a hypothetical root node which branches out into the uni-gram nodes at the first level, each of which branches out to bi-gram nodes at the second level and so on. This compression is for each LM separately, and lossless of recognition accuracy.

For the n-gram probability values, all LMs are taken as a whole. We first use PCA to reduce the correlation in different LMs, then use split

[d] If this n-gram is not in the list, it is not used. So the number N is usually smaller than the length of transcript C here.

vector quantization (SVQ) technique to compress each vector in PCA decomposition, as illustrated in Figure 5. Each LM in the pre-defined LM set can be seen as a data vector $\mathbf{s}$ (see Sec. 5.1.3), and it can be projected onto an orthogonal space of low dimensionality by PCA:

$$\mathbf{v}_r = U_r^T(\mathbf{s} - \boldsymbol{\mu}). \tag{39}$$

Giving the coefficients vector $\mathbf{v}_r$, the original data vector $\mathbf{s}$ can be easily approximated according to Eq. (32). So all the $(K+1)$ vectors (d-dimensionality) can be approximated by the corresponding $(K+1)$ coefficients vectors (r-dimensionality), r bases vectors (d-dimensionality) and one sample mean vector (d-dimensionality). Since d is usually the million order, and much larger than r and K ($r < K$), such decrease of the whole LM set size is appreciable.

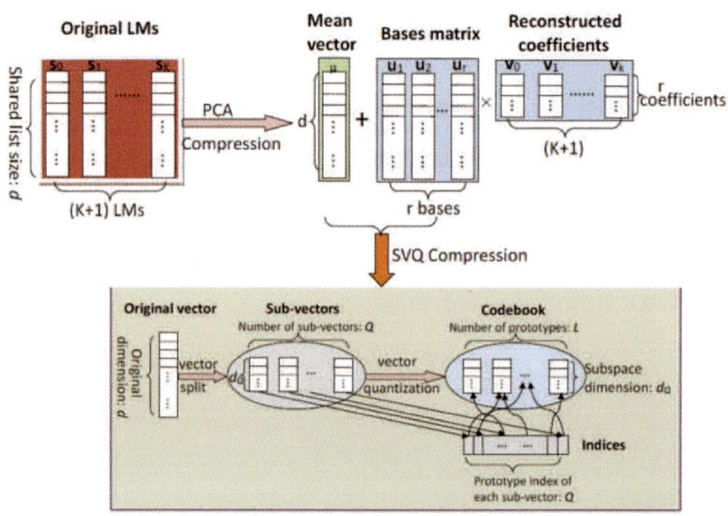

Figure 5. Diagram of language model set compression for probability values.

The sample mean vector and bases vectors in above can be further compressed by SVQ, see Figure 5. We first split the original high-dimensional vector into a low-dimensional subspace. For example, the original d-dimensional vector ($\mathbf{u_r}$) is equally partitioned into Q sub-vectors of d_Q-dimensionality $(\mathbf{u}_{r1}, \mathbf{u}_{r2}, \ldots, \mathbf{u}_{rQ})$, where $d = Q \times d_Q$.[e] Then, these sub-vectors are clustered into a small set of L prototypes by the k-means clustering algorithm to form a codebook. The codebook as well as the

[e]When d is not the integer times of d_Q, some dummy elements can be added to make d the integer times of d_Q.

corresponding indices of prototypes for all sub-vectors are stored for the original vector reconstruction. During the reconstruction, the value of one element in a sub-vector is mapped by the corresponding element of the prototype according to the index of the sub-vector. Lower mapping error can be ensured by using more prototypes (L) and lower dimensionality of the subspace (d_Q), which will lead to a larger storage size, however. Empirically, we found that $d_Q = 2$ and $L = 256$ for the compression of each LM leads to a good tradeoff between the size and recognition performance.

6. Experimental Results

We evaluated the performance of our approach on the large database of unconstrained Chinese handwriting, CASIA-HWDB.[25]

6.1. *Database and experimental setting*

The CASIA-HWDB database contains both isolated characters and unconstrained handwritten texts, and is divided into a training set of 816 writers and a test set of 204 writers. The training set contains 3,118,477 isolated character samples of 7,356 classes (7,185 Chinese characters, 109 frequently used symbols, 10 digits, and 52 English letters) and 4,076 pages of handwritten texts. The text pages have a few miswritten characters and characters beyond the 7,356 classes, which we call non-characters and outlier characters, respectively. The characters in the training text pages (except the non-characters and outlier characters, 1,080,017 samples) were also segmented and used together with the isolated samples for training the character classifier. We evaluated the text line recognition performance on the 1,015 handwritten pages of 204 test writers, which were segmented into 10,449 text lines containing 268,629 characters (including 723 non-characters and 368 outlier characters). That is to say, each test page contains 265 characters on average.

To build the character classifier, we extract features from gray-scale character images (background eliminated) using the normalization-cooperated gradient feature (NCGF) method.[69] Before feature extraction, the gray levels of foreground pixels in each image are normalized to a standard mean and deviation. The obtained 512D feature vector is reduced to 160D by Fisher linear discriminant analysis (FLDA), and then input into a modified quadratic discriminant function (MQDF) classifier. The classifier parameters were learned on 4/5 samples of training set, and the remaining 1/5 samples were used for confidence parameter estimation and confusion matrix construction. For parameter estimation of the geometric models, we extracted geometric features from 41,781 text lines of training text pages. The generic language models were trained on a large general text corpus containing about 50.8 million characters (about 32.7 million words) from the Chinese Linguistic Data Consortium. On obtaining the context models, the combining weights of path evaluation function were learned on 300 training text pages using MCA. Another 200 training text pages are used to set hyper-parameters in language model adaptation, e.g., regularization term weight $\tilde{\lambda}$ in Eq. (31) and Eq. (38) and the number of principal components r in PCA.

Table 3. Statistics of character types, recognition and segmentation correct rates on the test set of CASIA-HWDB.

	all	Chinese	symbol	digit	letter	non-character	outlier
count	268,629	233,329	26,583	6,879	747	723	368
rec (%)	83.78	87.28	60.34	69.40	77.24	0	0
top20 (%)	98.24	98.55	99.36	98.90	97.86	0	0
top200 (%)	99.18	99.58	99.64	99.40	98.93	0	0
seg (%)	95.54	95.69	96.84	86.97	83.53	94.05	92.66

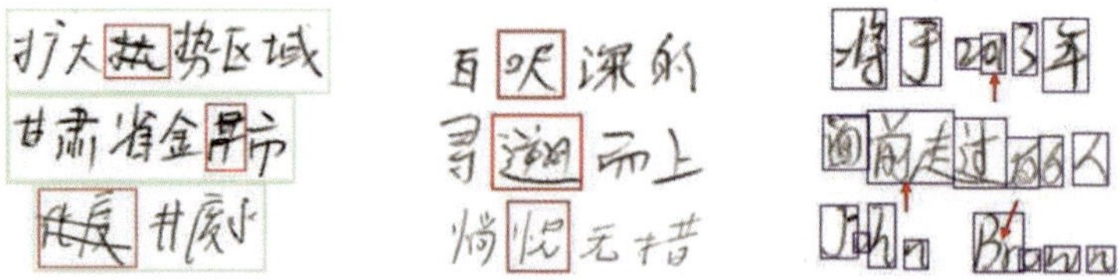

(a) (b) (c)

Figure 6. (a) Non-characters (in red boxes); (b) Outlier characters (in red boxes); (c) Over-segmentation errors (under-segmentation, indicated by red arrows).

Table 3 shows some statistics of character samples segmented from the test text pages of CASIA-HWDB. The "count" row gives the numbers of different types of characters (including non-characters and outlier characters). We can see that the majority of segmented characters are Chinese characters, and the number of symbols (mostly punctuation marks) is appreciable. Some samples of non-characters and outlier characters are shown in Figures 6(a) and 6(b), respectively. The "rec" row gives the correct rate of the segmented character recognition by the character classifier, and "top20" and "top200" are the cumulative accuracies of top 20 and 200 ranks, respectively. We can see that there are about 1.76% true character classes out of top 20 candidates. The non-characters and outlier characters cannot be recognized by the classifier, which covers a defined character set of 7,356 classes. The last row of "seg" in Table 3 shows the accuracy of over-segmentation (a character is correctly over-segmented when it is separates from other characters despite the within-character splits). We observe that 4.46% of characters were not correctly separated (i.e., they are under-segmented and cannot be correctly segmented and recognized by the subsequent character string recognition). This indicates the insufficiency of our over-segmentation method. Some examples of such errors are shown in Figure 6(c).

In language model adaptation, we extracted 14 corpora of various domains from the web pages provided by the Sogou Labs,[f] and the statistics of each corpus can be found in our previous work.[65] All the texts were segmented into word sequences using the ICTCLAS[g] toolkit for word-level LMs, and further, we clustered the words into a number of word classes using the algorithm of the work.[61] In addition, an ancient domain corpus (without word segmentation due to the unavailability of ancient domain word lexicon) was collected from the Internet.

6.2. *Performance metrics*

We evaluate the recognition performance of text lines using two character-level accuracy metrics following the work:[7] Correct Rate (**CR**) and Accurate Rate (**AR**):

$$\begin{aligned} CR &= (N_t - D_e - S_e)/N_t, \\ AR &= (N_t - D_e - S_e - I_e)/N_t, \end{aligned} \tag{40}$$

where N_t is the total number of characters in the transcript. The numbers of substitution errors (S_e), deletion errors (D_e) and insertion errors (I_e) are calculated by the aligning the recognition result string with the transcript by dynamic programming. The metric CR denotes the percentage of characters that are correctly recognized. Further, the metric AR considers the number of characters that are inserted due to over-segmentation, and is possibly negative. Vinciarelli *et al.*[15] suggested that the AR (called recognition rate there) is an appropriate measure for document transcription,

[f]http://www.sogou.com/labs/.
[g]http://ictclas.org/.

while CR (called accuracy rate there) is a good metric for tasks of content modeling (e.g., document retrieval). For analyzing the performance on different types of characters, we also give the CR for four types: Chinese characters (**ch**), symbols (**sb**), digits (**dg**) and letters (**lt**).

6.3. *Baseline text line recognition results*

We evaluate the effect of different context fusion and search strategies in handwritten text line recognition. In context fusion, we evaluated different confidence transformation (CT) methods, combinations of geometric models and language models (without adaptation). In path search, we show the results of different numbers of candidate character classes, beam widths.

6.3.1. *Comparing context models*

In the evaluation of context fusion, the search algorithm was the refined beam search with $K = 4$, $CN = 20$ and $BW = 10$. Our context fusion includes the models of character classifier (cls), geometric context and linguistic context in the path evaluation function Eq. (11), and the effects of different combinations are shown in Table 4, where "**geo**" denotes all geometric models ("ucg+uig+bcg+big"). We can see when using the character classifier only ("cls"), the string recognition performance is inferior. Adding geometric models to the character classifier, the string recognition performance is improved remarkably. By combining four geometric models, the AR is improved from 47.89% to 77.34%, and the CR is improved from 68.52% to 79.43%. It is observed that the binary geometric models yield larger improvement than the unary models. This justifies the importance of between-character relationship. Also, the class-dependent geometric models ("cls+ucg+bcg") perform better than the class-independent geometric models ("cls+uig+big"). Compared to the geometric models, the statistical language model ("cls+cti") is much more effective to yield a large improvement of AR and CR. Further, the combination of both geometric and language models to the character classifier yields the best recognition result, justifying that geometric context and linguistic context are complementary.

In the above experiments, we used by default the D-S theory confidence transformation (CT) on character classifier and sigmoidal CT. Here, we evaluate different CT methods on character classifier while keeping the sigmoidal CT on geometric models, and the results are shown in Table 5. Compared to the recognition without CT ("w/o" row, both character clas-

Table 4. Effects of different fusion of context models.

	AR (%)	CR (%)	ch (%)	sb (%)	dg (%)	lt (%)
cls	47.89	68.52	70.63	55.17	59.75	63.72
cls+ucg	69.74	76.93	78.57	71.49	56.32	58.63
cls+bcg	75.21	78.81	80.50	72.77	59.62	59.44
cls+uig	72.27	76.23	80.90	48.72	38.81	52.07
cls+big	74.00	77.08	81.09	54.15	44.19	54.22
cls+ucg+bcg	75.70	79.02	80.79	72.59	58.86	55.96
cls+uig+big	74.37	76.94	81.62	50.02	37.40	49.80
cls+geo	77.34	79.43	81.95	69.69	46.69	55.69
cls+cti	89.03	90.24	92.29	78.34	82.63	75.10
cls+geo+cti	90.20	90.80	92.94	79.10	79.63	74.43

sifier and geometric models without CT), the sigmoidal confidence improves the AR from 83.60% to 89.42%, and CR from 85.52% to 90.19%; the D-S evidence improves AR from 83.60% to 90.20%, and CR from 85.52% to 90.80%. The soft-max confidence performs inferiorly, however, because it does not consider the outlier probability. The benefit of CT (particularly, sigmoidal and D-S evidence) is attributed to the fact that the converted posterior probabilities (geometric models and character classifier) and the statistical language model are more compatible to be combined.

Table 5. Effects of different confidence transformation methods.

	AR (%)	CR (%)	ch (%)	sb (%)	dg (%)	lt (%)
w/o	83.60	85.52	87.61	74.18	75.03	57.70
sigmoidal	89.42	90.19	92.68	75.32	79.58	73.63
soft-max	74.67	74.75	79.39	49.87	31.53	17.80
D-S theory	90.20	90.80	92.94	79.10	79.63	74.43

Based on the character classifier and geometric models, we then evaluated different language models: character bi-gram ("**cbi**"), character tri-gram ("**cti**"), word bi-gram ("**wbi**"), word class bi-gram ("**wcb**"), interpolating word and class bi-gram ("**iwc**"). The recognition results are shown in Table 6, where "w/o" denotes recognition without language model. We can see that the character tri-gram outperforms the character bi-gram significantly. The advantage of tri-gram is due to its capturing long-distance text dependency. The use of second-order word dependency models, nevertheless, shows promise: the "wbi" and "wcb" both perform comparably with the "cti". Further, by interpolating the word-lavel bi-gram models, the "iwc" yields the best recognition performance.

Table 6. Effects of different language models.

	AR (%)	CR (%)	ch (%)	sb (%)	dg (%)	lt (%)
w/o	77.34	79.43	81.95	69.69	46.69	55.69
cbi	89.56	90.27	92.40	78.67	78.47	74.97
cti	90.20	90.80	92.94	79.10	79.63	74.43
wbi	90.30	90.94	93.08	79.61	78.75	71.22
wcb	90.07	90.77	92.73	80.64	79.60	73.76
iwc	**90.53**	**91.17**	93.21	80.45	79.75	72.96

6.3.2. *Comparing search strategies*

In the evaluation of context fusion, we used the default number of 20 candidate classes assigned to each candidate pattern, refined beam search with beam width 10. We compared the effects of different candidate class numbers (CN) and beam widths (BW) based on the combinations of character classifier, geometric models and character tri-gram language model. We give the processing time on all the 1,015 test pages consumed on a desktop computer of 2.66GHz CPU, programming using Microsoft Visual C++.

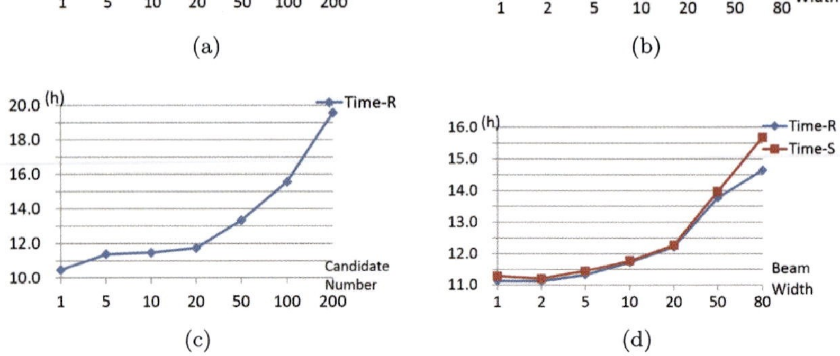

Figure 7. Accuracies of different CN and BW in two beam search methods ("-R" and "-S" denote refined and simple beam search, respectively). (a) Accuracies of different CN with $BW = 10$; (b) Accuracies of different BW with $CN = 20$; (c) Processing times of (a); (d) Processing times of (b).

Figures 7(a) and 7(c) show the effects of different CN of refined beam search algorithm, and Figures 7(b) and 7(d) show the effects of different BW of both refined and simple beam search methods. Compared to the simple beam search, our refined beam search algorithm yields much higher recognition accuracy at comparable speed. We can also see that the number of 20 candidate classes and the beam width 10 perform sufficiently well in respect of the recognition accuracy and the speed of refined beam search. Increasing CN and BW, though improves the coverage of correct path, does not improve the recognition accuracy. This is because the search algorithm does not guarantee finding the correct path in case of large number of candidate paths due to the insufficient quantitative evaluation of paths.

6.4. *Language model adaptation results*

In this section, we evaluate the effect of different methods of language model adaptation (LMA). To compare with the results without LMA in Table 6, we use the same refined beam search of $K = 4$, $CN = 20$, $BW = 10$, and only show the overall CR and AR for simplicity.

6.4.1. *Results of language model adaptation*

We show the results of three unsupervised LMA methods of model selection, model combination and model reconstruction on the CASIA-HWDB test set in Table 7. Because word-level LMs are not available for ancient domain, we use the adaptive **cti** model instead of **wbi**, **wcb** and **iwc** model in the second-pass recognition. For convenient comparison with the results without LMA, we copy those from Table 6 here as the baseline columns. We can see that both CR and AR are improved by model selection adaptation for all LM types, and the improvement of **cti** is the largest (about 1.1 percent up). This demonstrates the importance of domain-matched LM in the recognition of variable handwritten texts.

In the model combination adaptation, we selected top three LMs to be combined, and the combination weights were learned by minimizing squared error (MSE) for character-level LMs (cbi and cti). While for word-level LMs (wbi, wcb and iwc), the weighted were selected heuristically due to the insufficient number of words in the recognized text. Compared to model selection adaptation, we can see that model combination adaptation can improve the recognition accuracy more significantly, improving CR from 90.80% to 92.37% and AR from 90.20% to 91.73% for **cti**.

In the model reconstruction, the number of principal components was empirically set as 6, 3 and 3 for **cbi**, **cti** and **wbi**, respectively. Recall that we do not have a shared n-gram list to construct the orthogonal bases for **wcb**, this method does not work for **wcb**. In the **iwc** model, only the **wbi** is reconstructed, and the **wcb** uses the model of minimum perplexity. Compared to the baseline results, we can see evident improvement of recognition accuracy by model reconstruction. However, its performance is inferior to that of the model combination methods, though it is slightly better than the performance of model selection.

Table 7. Results of different language model adaptation methods.

	baseline		model selection		model combination		model reconstruction	
LM	CR(%)	AR(%)	CR(%)	AR(%)	CR(%)	AR(%)	CR(%)	AR(%)
cbi	90.27	89.56	91.26	90.59	91.69	90.85	91.39	90.71
cti	90.80	90.20	91.92	91.37	**92.37**	**91.73**	92.06	91.49
wbi	90.94	90.30	91.91	91.30	92.23	91.63	92.10	91.49
wcb	90.77	90.07	91.73	91.06	91.90	91.22	N/A	N/A
iwc	91.17	90.53	92.14	91.53	92.35	91.75	92.14	91.55

6.4.2. *Results of language model compression*

To evaluate the effects of language model compression, we compare the storage size and recognition accuracy in model combination adaptation, and the results are shown in Table 8. Because PCA compression does not work for **wcb**, there are no results (denoted as 'N/A') of **wcb** for 'PCA', and in **iwc**, only the **wbi** is compressed by PCA. In the column of combination of PCA and SVQ ("PCA+SVQ"), the original LM vectors instead of orthogonal bases are compressed by SVQ for **wcb**.

Table 8. Effects on the accuracy and Size (MB) of language model compression.

	Original		PCA			PCA+SVQ		+Trie
LMs	Size	CR(%)	AR(%)	Size	CR(%)	AR(%)	Size	Size
cbi	134	91.62	90.77	77.2	91.47	90.56	22.3	14.4
cti	470	92.18	91.55	291	92.12	91.48	102	58.7
wbi	314	92.18	91.46	227	92.10	91.34	102	68.7
wcb	81.6	N/A	N/A	N/A	91.74	90.87	38.7	28.7
iwc	396	92.32	91.58	309	92.24	91.44	141	97.4

Compared to the accuracy of model combination adaptation in Table 7, we can see that language model compression by PCA yields little loss of recognition accuracy, while the storage size is reduced significantly, and the combination of PCA and SVQ reduces the size further. This demonstrates the effectiveness of the proposed LM compression methods. The trie-structure format of n-gram table is lossless for recognition accuracy and remove about half storage size of repeated prefixes. Finally, we can see that the storage sizes of whole LM set are compressed to 14.4MB, 58.7MB, 68.7MB, 28.7MB and 97.4MB for **cbi**, **cti**, **wbi**, **wcb** and **iwc**, respectively, and the average size of each **cbi** LM is only 0.9MB for about 7 thousand uni-grams and 0.7 million bi-grams.

6.5. *Examples of recognition errors*

The string recognition errors of our approach can be categorized into three types: (1) over-segmentation failure (under-segmentation), (2) character classification error, including the failure for non-characters and outlier class, (3) path search failure. In Table 3, we can see that 4.46% of characters were not correctly separated by over-segmentation. Character classification error (about 1.76% of characters when $CN = 20$) implies that the truth class of candidate pattern is missed in the top CN ranks, so that the candidate paths miss the correct one. Path search failure is the case that even though the correct path is included in the candidate paths, it is not the "optimal" path with maximum score due to the imperfect context modeling and fusion.

Some examples of non-characters, outliers and over-segmentation errors have been shown in Figure 6. In addition, two examples of character classification error and path search failure are shown in Figure 8. In Figure 8(a), the misclassified character (indicated by the arrow) was scrawled and the correct class is failed to be included in the candidate character class set. In Figure 8(b), the candidate set includes the correct character class, but it is finally recognized wrongly due to the limitation of the character tri-gram model, which only considers short-distance context.

7. Conclusion

This chapter introduced an approach for handwritten Chinese text recognition under the character over-segmentation and candidate path search framework. The candidate segmentation-recognition paths are evaluated from the Bayesian decision view by combining multiple contexts, including

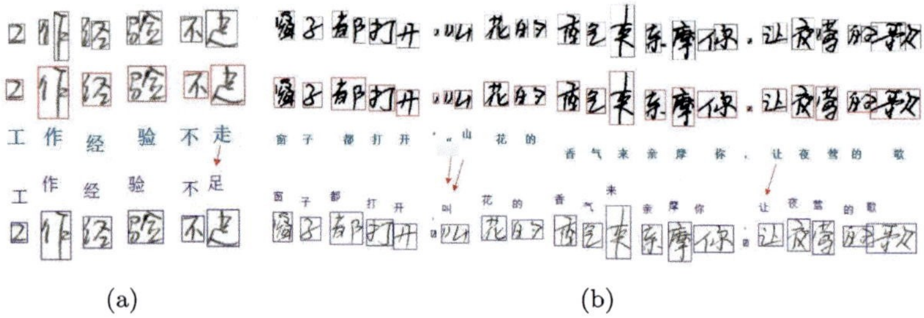

Figure 8. Two examples of recognition errors, only the part with recognition error is shown. (a) Character classification error; (b) Path search failure. Upper: over-segmentation; middle: segmentation-recognition result; bottom: ground-truth.

the character classification scores, geometric and linguistic contexts. The combining weights of path evaluation function are optimized by a string recognition objective, namely Maximum Character Accuracy (MCA) criterion. In path search, we use a refined beam search algorithm to improve the accuracy and efficiency. Considering the domain mismatch problem of language model, we proposed three unsupervised language model adaptation methods, namely, model selection, model combination and model reconstruction, which improve the recognition accuracy further. In our experiments on the large Chinese handwriting database CASIA-HWDB, the proposed approach achieved character-level accurate rate (AR) of 90.53% and correct rate (CR) of 91.17%, and language model adaptation improved the accuracy of AR and CR to 91.73% and 92.37%, respectively.

The analysis of recognition errors indicates that further research efforts are needed to improve the character over-segmentation, character classification and path evaluation. The objective of over-segmentation is to improve the tradeoff between the number of splitting points (affecting the complexity of search space) and the accuracy of separating characters at their boundaries. The objective of character classification is to improve the classification accuracy and the tradeoff between the number of candidate classes and the probability of including the true class. Compared to the baseline MQDF classifier used in this work, better classifiers include the discriminative learning quadratic discriminant function (DLQDF) that has been used in Ref. 13 and deep neural networks (paticularly, convolutional neural networks) that have yielded state-of-the-art accuracies in recent years (see former chapters in this book). For path evaluation, both the geometric and linguistic context deserve elaboration. Particularly, the real semantic context and long-distance context deserve consideration in the future.

References

1. R.-W. Dai, C.-L. Liu and B.-H. Xiao, Chinese character recognition: History, status and prospects, *Frontiers of Computer Science in China*, **1**(2), 126–136 (2007).
2. H. Fujisawa, Forty years of research in character and document recognition — An industrial perspective, *Pattern Recognition*, **41**(8), 2435–2446 (2008).
3. H.-S. Tang, E. Augustin, C. Y. Suen, O. Baret and M. Cheriet, Spiral recognition methodology and its application for recognition of Chinese bank checks, *Proc. 9th IWFHR*, 2004, pp. 263–268.
4. C.-H. Wang, Y. Hotta, M. Suwa and S. Naoi, Handwritten Chinese address recognition, *Proc. 9th IWFHR*, 2004, pp. 539–544.
5. Z. Han, C.-P. Liu and X.-C. Yin, A two-stage handwritten character segmentation approach in mail address recognition, *Proc. 8th ICDAR*, 2005, pp. 111–115.
6. Q. Fu, X.-Q. Ding, T. Liu, Y. Jiang and Z. Ren, A novel segmentation and recognition algorithm for Chinese handwritten address character strings, *Proc. 18th ICPR*, 2006, pp. 974–977.
7. T.-H. Su, T.-W. Zhang, D.-J. Guan and H.-J. Huang, Off-line recognition of realistic Chinese handwriting using segmentation-free strategy, *Pattern Recognition*, **42**(1), 167–182 (2009).
8. N.-X. Li and L.-W. Jin, A Bayesian-based probabilistic model for unconstrained handwritten offline Chinese text line recognition, *IEEE Int. Conf. on Systems Man and Cybernetics*, 2010, pp. 3664–3668.
9. Q.-F. Wang, F. Yin and C.-L. Liu, Handwritten Chinese text recognition by integrating multiple contexts, *IEEE Trans. Pattern Anal. Mach. Intell.*, **34**(8), 1469–1481 (2012).
10. C.-L. Liu, F. Yin, Q.-F. Wang and D.-H. Wang, ICDAR 2011 Chinese handwriting recognition competition, *Proc. 11th ICDAR*, 2011, pp. 1464–1469.
11. F. Yin, Q.-F. Wang, X.-Y. Zhang and C.-L. Liu, ICDAR 2013 Chinese handwriting recognition competition, *Proc. 12th ICDAR*, 2013, pp. 1095–1101.
12. D.-H. Wang, C.-L. Liu and X.-D. Zhou, An approach for real-time recognition of online Chinese handwritten sentences, *Pattern Recognition*, **45**(10), 3661–3675 (2012).
13. X.-D. Zhou, D.-H. Wang, F. Tian, C.-L. Liu and M. Nakagawa, Handwritten Chinese/Japanese text recognition using semi-Markov conditional random fields, *IEEE Trans. Pattern Anal. Mach. Intell.*, **35**(10), 2484–2497 (2013).
14. M. Cheriet, N. Kharma, C.-L. Liu and C. Y. Suen, *Character Recognition Systems: A Guide for Students and Practitioners* (John Wiley & Sons, 2007).
15. A. Vinciarelli, S. Bengio and H. Bunke, Offline recognition of unconstrained handwritten texts using HMMs and statistical language models, *IEEE Trans. Pattern Anal. Mach. Intell.*, **26**(6), 709–720 (2004).
16. C.-L. Liu, M. Koga and H. Fujisawa, Lexicon-driven segmentation and recognition of handwritten character strings for Japanese address reading, *IEEE Trans. Pattern Anal. Mach. Intell.*, **24**(11), 1425–1437 (2002).

17. H. Murase, Online recognition of free-format Japanese handwritings, *Proc. 9th ICPR*, 1988, pp. 1143–1147.
18. Y. Jiang, X. Ding, Q. Fu and Z. Ren, Context driven Chinese string segmentation and recognition, *Structural, Syntactic, and Statistical Pattern Recognition: Joint IAPR Int. Workshops*, LNCS 4109, 2006, pp. 127–135.
19. M. Nakagawa, B. Zhu and M. Onuma, A model of on-line handwritten Japanese text recognition free from line direction and writing format constraints, *IEICE Trans. Information and Systems*, **88**(8), 1815–1822 (2005).
20. X. Ding and H. Liu, Segmentation-driven offline handwritten Chinese and Arabic script recognition, in *Proc. Summit on Arabic and Chinese Handwriting*, 2006, pp. 61–73.
21. S. Senda and K. Yamada, A maximum-likelihood approach to segmentation-based recognition of unconstrained handwriting text, in *Proc. 6th ICDAR*, 2001, pp. 184–188.
22. P. Xiu and H. S. Baird, Whole-book recognition, *IEEE Trans. Pattern Anal. Mach. Intell.*, **34**(12), 2467–2480 (2012).
23. D.-S. Lee and R. Smith, Improving book OCR by adaptation language and image models, in *Proc. 10th Int. Workshop on DAS*, 2012, pp. 115–119.
24. Q. He, S. Chen, M. Zhao and W. Lin, A hybrid language model for handwritten Chinese sentence recognition, in *Proc. 13th ICFHR*, 2012, pp. 129–134.
25. C.-L. Liu, F. Yin, D.-H. Wang and Q.-F. Wang, CASIA online and offline Chinese handwriting databases, in *Proc. 11th ICDAR*, 2011, pp. 37–41.
26. L. Y. Tseng and R. C. Chen, Segmenting handwritten Chinese characters based on heuristic merging of stroke bounding boxes and dynamic programming, *Pattern Recognition Letters*, **19**(10), 963–973 (1998).
27. L. Xu, F. Yin, Q.-F. Wang and C.-L. Liu, An over-segmentation method for single-touching Chinese handwriting with learning based filtering, *J. Document Analysis and Recognition*, **17**(1), 91–104 (2014).
28. C.-L. Liu, Handwritten Chinese character recognition: Effects of shape normalization and feature extraction, in *Arabic and Chinese Handwriting Recognition*, S. Jaeger and D. Doermann (Eds.), LNCS 4768, (Springer, 2008), pp. 104–128.
29. C.-L. Liu and H. Fujisawa, Classification and learning in character recognition: Advances and remaining problems, *Machine Learning in Document Analysis and Recognition*, S. Marinai and H. Fujisawa (Eds.), (Springer, 2008), pp. 139–161.
30. C.-L. Liu, F. Yin, D.-H. Wang and Q.-F. Wang, Online and offline handwritten Chinese character recognition: Benchmarking on new databases, *Pattern Recognition*, **46**(1), 155–162 (2013).
31. F. Kimura, K. Takashina, S. Tsuruoka and Y. Miyake, Modified quadratic discriminant functions and the application to Chinese character recognition, *IEEE Trans. Pattern Anal. Mach. Intell.*, **9**(1), 149–153 (1987).
32. C.-L. Liu and M. Nakagawa, Evaluation of prototype learning algorithms for nearest neighbor classifier in application to handwritten character recognition, *Pattern Recognition*, **34**(3), 601–615 (2001).

33. X. Lin, X. Ding, M. Chen, R. Zhang and Y. Wu, Adaptive confidence transform based on classifier combination for Chinese character recognition, *Pattern Recognition Letters*, **19**(10), 975–988 (1998).
34. C.-L. Liu, Classifier combination based on confidence transformation, *Pattern Recognition*, **38**(1), 11–28 (2005).
35. Y. X. Li, C. L. Tan and X. Q. Ding, A hybrid post-processing system for offline handwritten Chinese script recognition, *Pattern Analysis and Applications*, **8**(3), 272–286 (2005).
36. Q.-F. Wang, F. Yin and C.-L. Liu, Improving handwritten Chinese text recognition by confidence transformation, in *Proc. 11th ICDAR*, 2011, pp. 518–522.
37. R. Rosenfeld, Two decades of statistical language modeling: Where do we go from here? in *Proc. IEEE*, **88**(8), 2000, pp. 1270–1278.
38. R. F. Xu, D. S. Yeung and D. M. Shi, A hybrid post-processing system for offline handwritten Chinese character recognition based on a statistical language model, *Int. J. Pattern Recognition and Artificial Intelligence*, **19**(30), 415–428 (2005).
39. Q.-F. Wang, F. Yin and C.-L. Liu, Integrating language model in handwritten Chinese text recognition, in *Proc. 10th ICDAR*, 2009, pp. 1036–1040.
40. Y. Bengio, R. Ducharme, P. Vincent and C. Jauvin, A neural probabilistic language model, *Journal of Machine Learning Research*, **3**(2), 1137–1155 (2003).
41. F. Zamora-Martinez, V. Frinken, S. E. Boquera, M. J. Bleda, A. Fischer and H. Bunke, Neural network language models for off-Line handwriting recognition, *Pattern Recognition*, **47**(4), 1642–1652 (2014).
42. X.-D. Zhou, J.-L. Yu, C.-L. Liu, T. Nagasaki and K. Marukawa, Online handwritten Japanese character string recognition incorporating geometric context, in *Proc. 9th ICDAR*, 2007, pp. 48–52.
43. M. Koga, T. Kagehiro, H. Sako and H. Fujisawa, Segmentation of Japanese handwritten characters using peripheral feature analysis, in *Proc. 14th ICPR*, 1998, pp. 1137–1141.
44. F. Yin, Q.-F. Wang and C.-L. Liu, Integrating geometric context for text alignment of handwritten Chinese documents, in *Proc. 12th ICFHR*, 2010, pp. 7–12.
45. B. Zhu, X.-D. Zhou, C.-L. Liu and M. Nakagawa, A robust model for online handwritten Japanese text recognition, *Int. J. Document Analysis and Recognition*, **13**(2), 121–131 (2010).
46. B.-H. Juang, W. Chou and C.-H. Lee, Minimum classification error rate methods for speech recognition, *IEEE Trans. Speech and Audio Processing*, **5**(3), 257–265 (1997).
47. D. Povey, Discriminative training for large vocabulary speech recognition, Ph.D. dissertation, Cambridge University, Cambridge, 2003.
48. X.-D. He, Li Deng and Wu Chou, Discriminative learning in sequential pattern recognition, *IEEE Signal Processing Magazine*, **25**(5), 14–36 (2008).

49. H. Ney and S. Ortmanns, Progress in dynamic programming search for LVCSR, *Proc. IEEE*, **88**(8), 1224–1240 (2000).
50. C.-L. Liu, H. Sako and H. Fujisawa, Effects of classifier structures and training regimes on integrated segmentation and recognition of handwritten numeral strings, *IEEE Trans. Pattern Anal. Mach. Intell.*, **26**(11), 1395–1407 (2004).
51. J. R. Bellegarda, Statistical language model adaptation: Review and perspectives, *Speech Communication*, **42**(1), 93–108 (2004).
52. X. Liu, M. J. F. Gales and P. C. Woodland, Use of contexts in language model interpolation and adaptation, *Computer Speech and Language*, **27**, 301–321 (2013).
53. D. H. Daines and A. I. Rudnicky, Implicitly supervised language model adaptation for meeting transcription, in *Proc. NAACL-HLT*, 2007, pp. 73–76.
54. D. Mrva and P. C. Woodland, Unsupervised language model adaptation for Mandarin broadcast conversation transcription, in *Proc. 7th Interspeech*, 2006, pp. 2206–2209.
55. M. Bacchiani and B. Roark, Unsupervised language model adaptation, in *Proc. 28th ICASSP*, 2003, pp. 224–227.
56. G. Tur and A. Stolcke, Unsupervised language model adaptation for meeting recognition, in *Proc. 32th ICASSP*, 2007, pp. 173–176.
57. C. Allauzen and M. Riley, Bayesian language model interpolation for mobile speech input, *Proc. 12th Interspeech*, 2011, pp. 1429–1432.
58. M. Wuthrich, M. Liwicki, A. Fischer, E. Indermuhle, H. Bunke, G. Viehhauser and M. Stolz, Language model integration for the recognition of handwritten medieval documents, *Proc. 10th ICDAR*, 2009, pp. 211–215.
59. M.-Y. Chen, A. Kundu and S. N. Srihari, Variable duration hidden Markov model and morphological segmentation for handwritten word recognition, *IEEE Trans. Image Processing*, **4**(12), 1675–1688 (1995).
60. J. A. Barnett, Computational methods for a mathematical theory of evidence, in *Proc. 7th IJCAI*, 1981, pp. 868–875.
61. S. Martin, J. Liermann and H. Ney, Algorithms for bigram and trigram word clustering, *Speech Communication*, **24**(1), 19–37 (1998).
62. A. Stolcke, SRILM - an extensible language modeling toolkit, in *Proc. 7th ICSLP*, 2002, pp. 901–904.
63. S. F. Chen and J. Goodman, An empirical study of smoothing techniques for language modeling, *Computer Speech and Language*, **13**, 359–394 (1999).
64. A. Stolcke, Entropy-based pruning of backoff language models, *Proc. DARPA Broadcast News Transcription and Understanding Workshop*, 1998, pp. 270–274.
65. Q.-F. Wang, F. Yin and C.-L. Liu, Unsupervised language model adaptation for handwritten Chinese text recognition, *Pattern Recognition*, **47**(3), 1202–1216 (2014).
66. L. Sirovich and M. Kirby, Low-dimensional precedure for the characterization of human faces, *J. Optical Society of America A*, **4**(3), 519–524 (1987).

67. T. F. Cootes, C. J. Taylor, D. H. Cooper and J. Graham, Active shape models-their training and application, *Computer Vision and Image Understanding*, **61**(1), 38–59 (1995).
68. Q.-F. Wang, F. Yin and C.-L. Liu, Improving handwritten Chinese text recognition by unsupervised language model adaptation, in *Proc. 10th Int. Workshop on DAS*, 2012, pp. 110–114.
69. C.-L. Liu, Normalization-cooperated gradient feature extraction for handwritten character recognition, *IEEE Trans. Pattern Anal. Mach. Intell.*, **29**(8), 1465–1469 (2007).

Chapter 7

Handwritten Chinese Address Recognition for Postal Automation

Shujing Lu[*], Xiaohua Wei[†], Xiao Tu[*], Yue Lu[*,†]

[*]*ECNU-SRI Joint Lab for Pattern Analysis and Intelligent System, Shanghai Research Institute of China Post, Shanghai 200062, China*

[†]*Shanghai Key Laboratory of Multidimensional Information Processing, Department of Computer Science and Technology, East China Normal University, Shanghai 200241, China*

With the rapid development of electronic commerce, the volume of parcels is keeping an annual growth of 50 percent in China, which greatly promotes the development of automatic parcel sorting system and makes it play a big role in postal automation. In this chapter, we present the details of handwritten Chinese address recognition and its application to parcel sorting system. In this system, a parcel piece is scanned by a camera when it passes through the vision module on the transmission belt. Then the image of the parcel is sent to the recognition center to extract the relevant information of the parcel for sorting and delivery purposes. Owing to the arbitrariness of parcel images in resolution and direction, SIFT features are employed to locate the express waybill affixed on the parcel, and then the address area of the waybill is extracted and input to recognition system. In address recognition phase, a word-level-tree based method is utilized for handwritten Chinese address recognition. Using this method, all the irregular handwritten Chinese addresses are mapped to normative writing formats as presented in the address word-level-tree, which overcomes the writing variation of Chinese address formats effectively.

1. Introduction

Postal address recognition is a complex task that involves image capturing, address block location, character and word recognition, database querying and association of a group of words with a delivery address[1–2]. It has been applied in mail piece sorting in many countries for more than ten years, while Chinese address recognition was firstly introduced to mail automatic sorting system since 2009 in multiple purpose sorter (MPS) produced by Shanghai Research Institute of China Post Group (SRI). Until now it has worked well on all kinds of postal (letters, parcels, flats, etc.) sorting machines. In this chapter, we introduce the details of the handwritten address recognition on parcel sorting system.

With the rapid development of electronic commerce, the volume of parcels is keeping an annual growth of 50 percent in China in recent years, which greatly promotes the development of automatic parcel sorting system. In a parcel sorting system, a parcel piece is scanned by a camera firstly while it passes through the vision module on the transmission belt. Then the image of the parcel is sent to the recognition center and the relevant information of the parcel is extracted and employed for sorting and delivery purposes.

The parcel images are much more complicated than letter images. The resolution of images is variable due to the different height of the parcels, and the directions of the parcels are arbitrary when they pass through the vision module. Figure 1 shows several examples of parcel images captured by MPF sorting machine produced by SRI. As presented in these images, there is always a form pasted on each parcel. This form is provided by an express company before a parcel is sent, then it is usually named as express waybill. The information of the senders and receivers, including address, name, postcode, phone number, etc., are required to be filled accurately in the waybill so that the parcel can be sorted correctly. Therefore, the express waybill is located firstly in the recognition system. Owing to the arbitrariness of images in resolution and direction, SIFT features are employed to locate the express waybill. Then the address area is extracted from the waybill and input to recognition system.

Handwritten Chinese address recognition (HCAR) is an important application for handwritten Chinese text recognition. One intuitive method for this problem is the bottom-up recognition method. This method first segments each character from the input image, and then recognizes the isolated characters one by one. However, there are many difficulties for this approach. Firstly, free style in handwriting and left-right structured characters will lead to inevitable segmentation errors. Secondly, offline handwritten Chinese character recognition is still a challenging task due to the diversity of writing styles, the similarity in shape, large character set (3,755 characters are used frequently in daily life and 3,008 are used sometimes), etc. Thirdly, this bottom-up recognition strategy (e.g., from single character recognition to the address) makes it difficult to utilize the address knowledge.

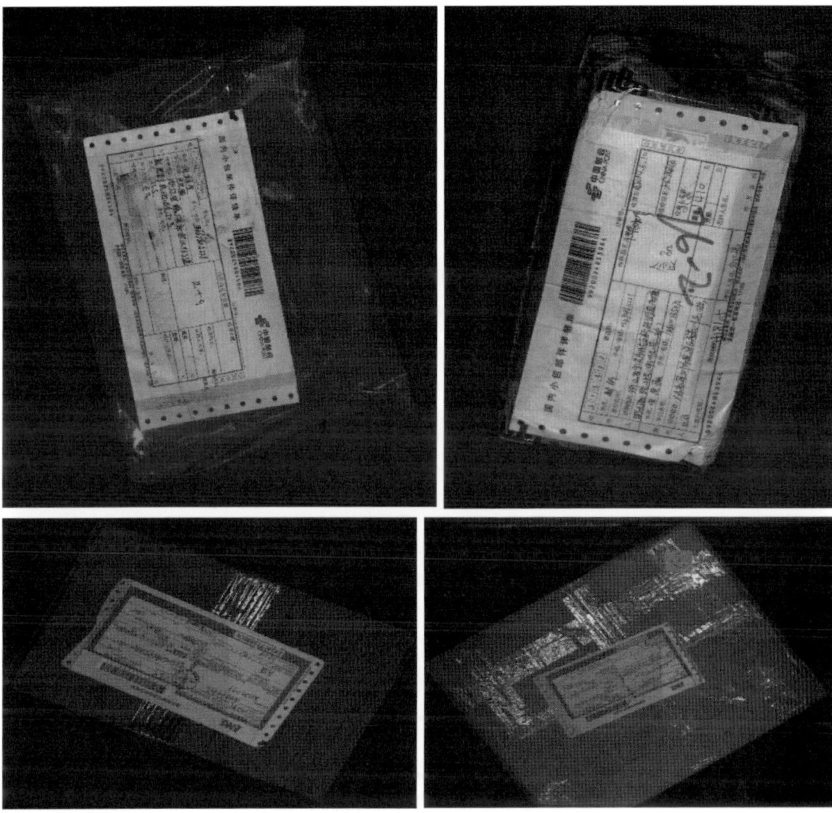

Figure 1. Examples of parcel images.

To improve the performance and practicality of HCAR, various subsystems have been proposed in the past decades, such as, lexicon-driven[3–6], recursive holistic word matching[7], confidence transformation[8] and cost-sensitive transformation[9].

In recent years, the strategy of incorporating character classification results and address lexicon into segmentation has been popularly used to improve the performance of handwritten address recognition in Chinese and Japanese. It is generally named segmentation hypothesis-and-verification approach, where the address lexicon is used in post-processing to correct the classification error or segmentation error, or to evaluate multiple segmentation hypotheses, which are generally represented in a segmentation lattice[3–6]. E. Ishidera[3] combined segmentation lattice, character recognition results and word knowledge costs into a unified function to evaluate the dissimilarities between text lines and address items. M. Koga[4] proposed a trie structure based storage for Japanese address strings. C.-L. Liu[5] proposed a trie structure to store the address phrases and a beam search strategy to match the candidate characters with all lexicon entries. Further, Y. Jiang[6] proposed a suffix tree based data structure in their HCAR system, in which suffix tree was a special case of trie, and all the suffix strings of an input string were added to trie. Every character in the string was a first character of the suffix strings. In fact, the addresses on real mails are very complicated and have great writing variations, such as omission of key characters or possession of redundant words, which greatly increases the difficulty of address recognition. To deal with this problem, a word-level-tree (WLT) based method is proposed by X. Wei[10], in which each node is correspondent to an address word, such that a path from the root to the leaf node is able to give a normative address format. Consequently, all the writing variations of an address can be mapped to its corresponding normative address format stored in the WLT.

2. Address Block Location

The direction of express waybill on a parcel image is random and the image resolution is variable due to the different height of the parcels. A key area matching method based on SIFT is proposed to acquire the location and direction of express waybill on the image. Then the address block is extracted from the waybill for address recognition, as shown in Figure 2.

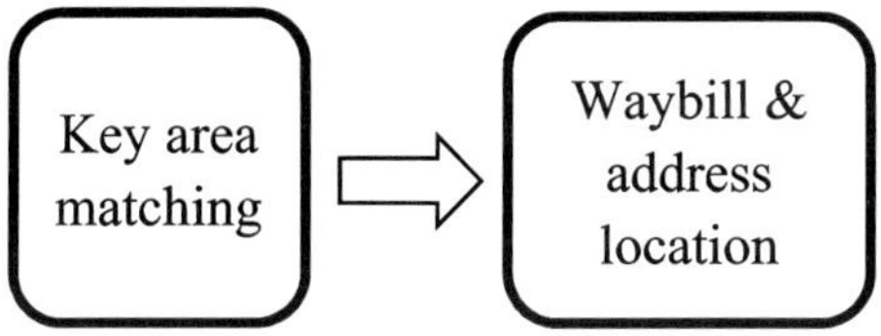

Figure 2. Framework of address location in parcel images.

2.1. *Key area matching*

As presented in Figure 1, there is always an express waybill with the information of the receiver and sender on each parcel. And we should locate the express waybill firstly in order to extract the address area of receiver in our recognition system. The resolution and direction of the waybill are unfixed for different parcels, but each waybill has its unique logo and the location of the logo on the waybill is stable. Therefore the logo area is extracted as the key area of the waybill in the location of the express waybill through key area matching.

In image matching, SIFT feature[11–13] is tolerant to image noise, changes in illumination, uniform scaling, rotation and minor changes in viewing direction. So it is used in key area matching to obtain the location and direction of the express waybill in the parcel image.

The key area matching method is divided into two stages. The first stage is the calculation of SIFT feature both in the logo image and a parcel image, mainly including the scale space extrema detection, key point accurate positioning, key points and direction distribution and SIFT feature vector generation. Each image is described as a set of SIFT features $S = \{F_i\}$. Each feature $F_i = (x, y, \sigma, \theta, d)$ has 5 elements, in which x is the horizontal coordinate of a key point, y is the vertical coordinate, σ is the scale value, θ is the direction angle and d is the feature vector of the feature points. Figure 3 presents the SIFT features of logo area in China Post express waybill in which the circles are the locations and scale values of SIFT features, and radii mean their directions. Figure 4 shows the same thing of the first parcel image in Figure 1.

Figure 3. The SIFT features in logo image.

Figure 4. The SIFT features in parcel image.

The second stage is the matching of SIFT feature vector of the parcel image with those of the logo image by using the k-dimensions tree algorithm to get matched pairs of the SIFT feature $P = \{F_{li}, F_{pi}\}$. F_{li} is a SIFT feature of the logo image, which is matched with F_{pi}, a SIFT feature of the parcel image. With the matched pairs of SIFT, the position and the angularity of logo in the parcel image can be calculated, as shown in Figure 5.

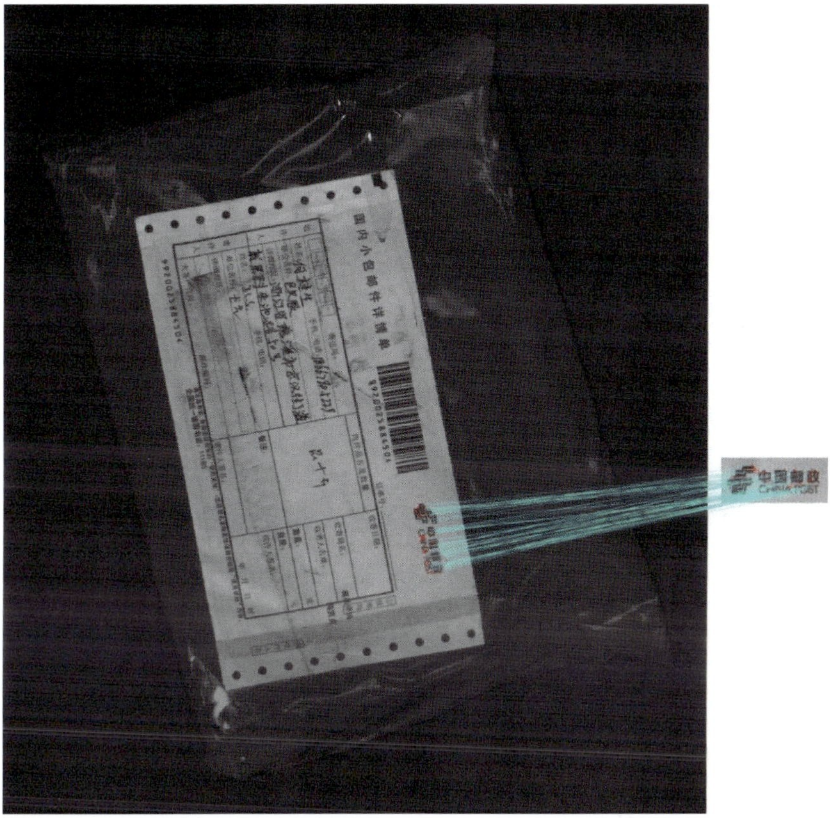

Figure 5. Logo area matching with SIFT feature pairs.

2.2. *Address location*

Since the logo's position in the express waybill is known in advance, the waybill image can be extracted from the parcel image and rotated to the obversed side through logo location. Meanwhile, the address block is fixed on the waybill, so the address block can be extracted from the waybill image based on the position information as shown in Figure 6.

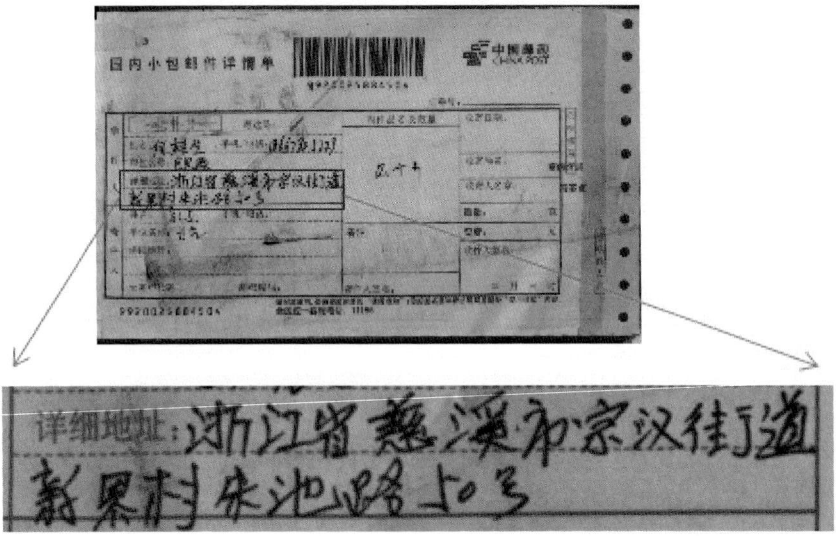

Figure 6. The waybill and address image.

3. Handwritten Chinese Address Recognition

After the address block is extracted, it will be input to the handwritten address recognition system and processed by the downstream modules, including address line segmentation, writing line removal, character segmentation, character recognition and post-processing or integration of recognition results with a real delivery address. Figure 7 describes the framework of handwritten Chinese address recognition.

3.1. *Address line segmentation*

The writing of Chinese address is usually from left to right, and there is a gap between address lines generally. Horizontal projection is an effective and fast method to segment the address lines. For an address image $I(x, y)$, $p(y)$ indicates the horizontal projection of $I(x, y)$.

$$p(y) = \sum_{x=0}^{W-1} I(x,y) \quad y = 0,1,\ldots,H-1 \tag{1}$$

where W and H represent the width and height of the address image $I(x, y)$.

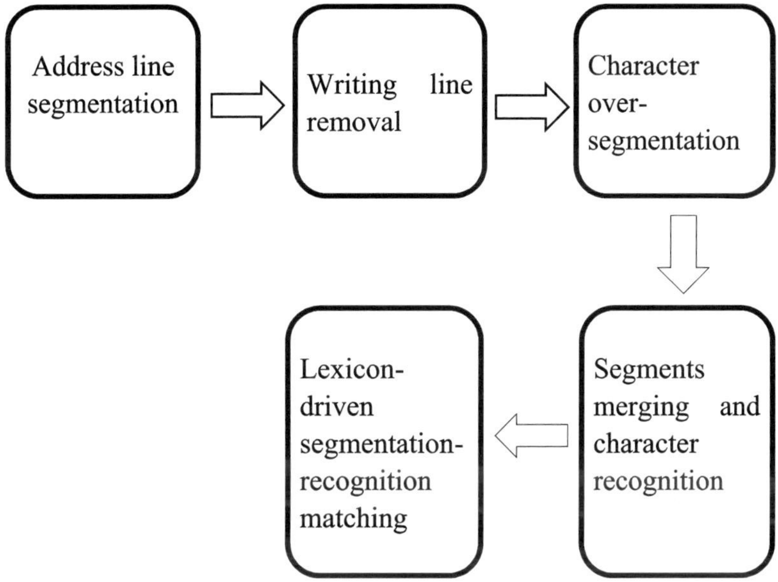

Figure 7. Framework of handwritten Chinese address recognition.

The upper and lower edges of the addresses lines are detected by the following rules:

(1) If $p(y) < \alpha$ and all $p(y+k) > \beta$ $(0 < k < LW)$, row y is the upper edge of an address line.

(2) If $p(y) > \delta$ and all $p(y+k) < \varepsilon$ $(0 < k < LG)$, row y is the lower edge of an address line.

where α, β, δ and ε are thresholds, LW and LG mean the minimum width and the minimum gap of address lines.

This line segmentation method works well on the text with clear line gap and tiny skew angle. However, when the line gap is very small and the skew angle is a little larger, it may fail to find the correct address lines. Thus, local projection is used to resolve this problem in address recognition. Firstly, the address area is divided into several blocks from left to right. Then the above segmentation rules work on each block to find all upper and lower line edges of them. Finally, the local address lines of each block are merged to address lines. Through the local projection method, we cannot only obtain the address lines, but also compute the skew angle of the address lines from the different positions of line edges in different blocks. Figures 8 and 9 show the results of line segmentation of address image in Figure 6 by global horizontal projection and by horizontal projection in blocks respectively.

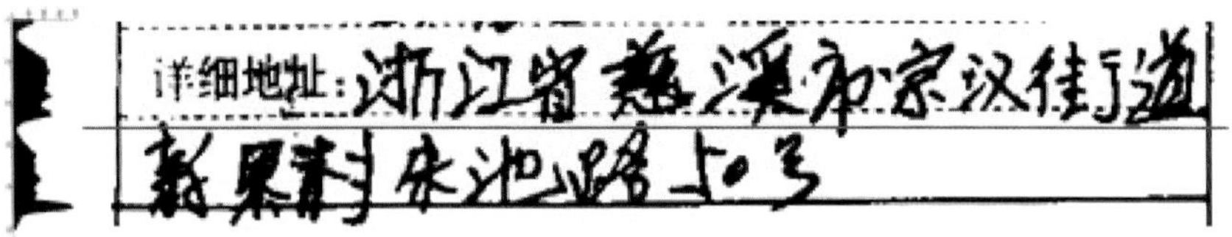

Figure 8. Line segmentation by global horizontal projection.

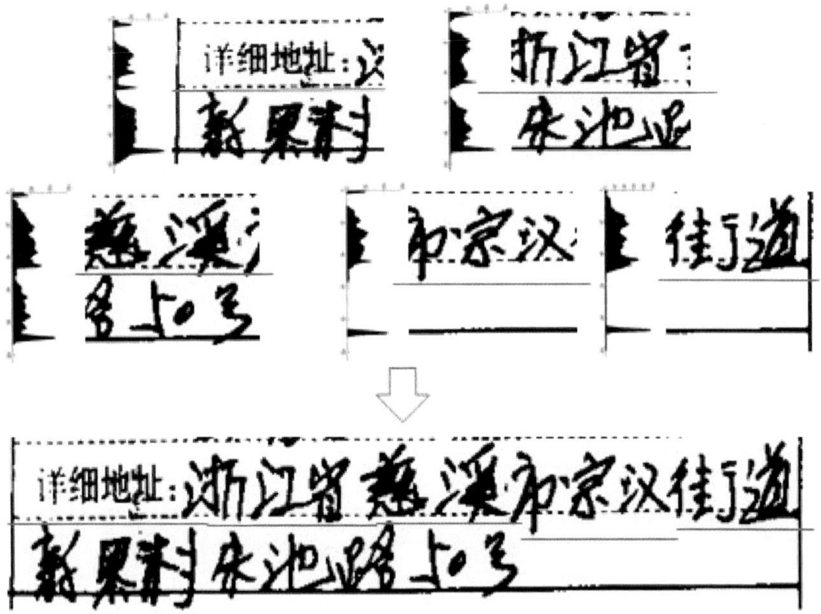

Figure 9. Line segmentation on horizontal projection in blocks.

3.2. *Writing line removal*

Ruling lines in the express waybill, categorized to writing lines and margin lines, are used to guide the writers to fill the information in an organized and size consistent way. They should be preprocessed for detection and removal prior to address recognition. In a scanned express waybill image, due to resolution effect of the scanner and quality of the express waybill in a parcel, the ruling lines along with the foreground address component would have lost their uniformity. Therefore the foreground address could be overlapped on the writing lines, while during the process of removing the background writing lines and margin lines, the foreground address characters should not be eroded.

Generally, horizontal lines are used to guide the writer and vertical line is meant to provide margin as shown in Figure 8. Margin lines are usually separated to address text and they are easily to be removed based on vertical projection. So we mainly process the horizontal writing lines in the located address area.

Here, fast Hough transform is utilized to detect writing lines from located address images. Foreground points taken from the image are divided into two subsets, feature points or not, from which feature points are selected to compute parameters in Hough space. A threshold is set such that any bin exceeding the threshold means it is a reference line and the detection will stop. The proposed Hough transform can be implemented at a fast speed with practical value. The writing lines are removed by using mathematical morphology operation while the structural element is decided according to the width of the writing line and the intersectional stroke. Character strokes are protected while the writing lines are removed.

3.2.1. *Writing lines detection*

The Hough transform can effectively detect all lines of any directions in the image. Classical Hough transformation needs to calculate the corresponding curve in the transform space of each pixel, which is equivalent to mapping all the possible lines through the pixel to the transform space. This will induce a great amount of computation and reduce the speed of line detection. Therefore, many improved Hough transforms, such as random Hough transform (RHT), have been proposed, which improved the speed of Hough transform[14].

In order to accelerate the computing speed, reduce the writing line detection time and meet the requirements of actual sorting system in real life, the Hough transform is improved as follows to detect the writing lines in address area.

(1) Writing lines are in a small range near the horizontal direction. The representation of the slope and intercept for a straight line, i.e. $y =$

$ax + b$, instead of $\rho = x\,cos(\theta) + y\,sin(\theta)$, will avoid the large amount of computation caused by sine and cosine calculation.

(2) Take the feature points instead of all pixel points for transformation. For each address line, all bottom foreground pixels are feature points as shown in Figure 10. Making Hough transform of these feature points can obtain the lower edge of the horizontal line, while the amount of computation is reduced drastically.

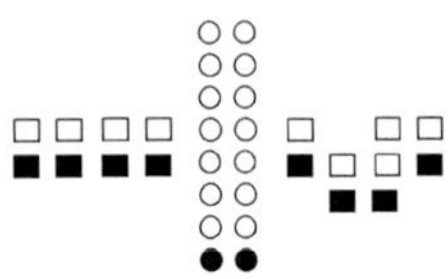

Figure 10. Selection of feature points.
(The dots represent the stroke points, the squares mean the pixels of line, black dots and squares are the feature points.)

3.2.2. *Writing lines removal*

There are several positional relations between character strokes and writing line, including disjoint, connected, intersection and overlapping (Figure 11). Disjoint (Figure 11(a)) and connected (Figure 11(b)) relationships are easy to solve. The writing line can be removed directly without eroding the address characters. For the overlapping relation of horizontal strokes and the writing line, if only part of character horizontal strokes overlapped in the writing line (Figure 11(c)), the removal of the writing line does not destroy the structure of Chinese characters. However, if character horizontal strokes completely submerged in the writing line (Figure 11(d)), recovering the horizontal strokes from the binary image is very difficult. The intersection of character strokes and the writing line is the most common relation, and intersection strokes generally include vertical, left-falling and right-falling strokes (Figures 11(e)–(g)).

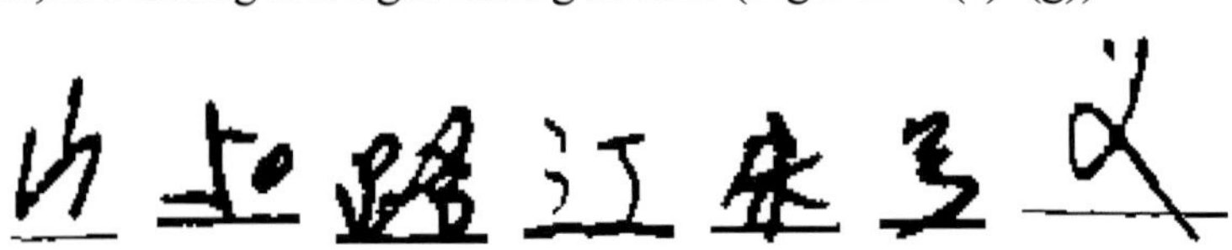

(a) (b) (c) (d) (e) (f) (g)

Figure 11. Positional relations of character stroke with writing line.

After the detection of lower edge of writing line, to compute the writing line width, the lower edge line is shifted up in the scale of one pixel. For each shift, make a statistics of the foreground pixel number in the moving line, and compare it with the number of the previous line. If the number of foreground pixel decreases dramatically, the previous line is the upper edge of the writing line. If the number of line pixel is zero, it means the address writing line is completely separate from the character strokes. In this case, all pixels between line upper edge and lower edge can be set as the background, that is, remove the writing line directly.

For the several different intersection relations of character strokes and the writing line, employing mathematical morphology open operation on the intersection area by selecting different structure elements can effectively remove the writing line, while maintaining the stroke undestroyed. Firstly, the type of the stroke crossed with writing line is detected, and then the structure element is determined according to the width of the writing line and the stroke type. The size of the structure element is determined by the width of the writing line, and the number of elements can be slightly larger than the width of the writing line. The structure of the element is determined by the type of the intersecting stroke. It is usually the same as the intersecting stroke. Figure 12 shows the structural elements, corresponding to the writing line with the width of 2 pixels, in which the strokes of intersections are vertical, left-falling and right-falling, respectively.

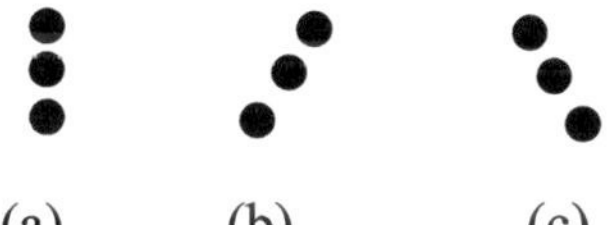

(a) (b) (c)

Figure 12. Structural component.

After ruling line removal, the address lines in Figure 9 are preprocessed to Figure 13.

(a) The first address line

(b) The second address line

Figure 13. The results of ruling line removal.

3.3. *Address line recognition*

Character segmentation of handwritten Chinese address line is very difficult due to the variability of character size/gap, touching of adjacent characters and confusion of character internal (between-radical) gap and between-character gap. It is necessary to incorporate character classification results and address lexicon into segmentation. In our system, an address line image is firstly over-segmented into a sequence of original segments using connected component analysis and touching pattern splitting methods. Then segments are merged in writing direction based on the predefined rules to generate the candidate patterns. Afterwards, each candidate pattern is input to a character recognizer and several candidates are produced to build up a character candidate lattice. Finally, the candidate segmentation-recognition paths are evaluated by a match function of candidate characters and address lexicon. And the optimal path is chosen as the recognition result of the address image.

3.3.1. *Over-segmentation of address line*

Over-segmentation is accomplished in two steps: connected component analysis and touching pattern splitting. In an address line, the connected components overlapping in writing direction are likely to compose the characters with similar size. To decide whether or not to merge two adjacent components, a normalized overlapping degree between them is computed[5]. The computation of horizontal overlapping degree is described below, while the vertical overlapping degree can be computed analogously.

The bounding box of a component is specified by the coordinates of left, right, top, and bottom boundaries. Denote the bounding boxes of two components as $(cc_1^l, cc_1^r, cc_1^t, cc_1^b)$ and $(cc_2^l, cc_2^r, cc_2^t, cc_2^b)$, respectively. Assume $cc_1^l \leq cc_2^l$ (ordered from left to right), if $cc_2^l < cc_1^r$, the two components are overlapping. The overlap and span of two components are

$$x_{ovlp} = cc_1^r - cc_2^l \tag{2}$$

and

$$x_{span} = \max(cc_1^r, cc_2^r) - cc_1^l \tag{3}$$

respectively. The normalized overlapping degree is computed as

$$x_{nmovlp} = \frac{1}{2}\left(\frac{x_{ovlp}}{w_1} + \frac{x_{ovlp}}{w_2}\right) - \frac{x_{dist}}{x_{span}}, \tag{4}$$

where w_1 and w_2 denote the widths of two components and x_{dist} denotes the horizontal distance between the centers of them. If $x_{nmovlp} > 0$, the two components are to be merged. Each component is merged recursively with the succeeding components that overlap with enough degree.

After recursive merging, each component (not necessarily connected now) is referred to as an image segment. The segments of potential touching patterns are detected and undergo splitting by recursive searching of split point.

To detect touching patterns, an estimate of the address line height (*LH*) is needed. *LH* is estimated from the histogram of image segment height after component merging. Because the heights of small segments do not well account for the character height, we temporarily merge each small segment with their succeeding segment to a temporary segment. For a temporary segment, denoting its height and width as *th* and *tw*, then the address line height is estimated as the mean value of temporary segment height

$$LH = \frac{\sum_{k=0}^{K-1} th_k \cdot tw_k}{\sum_{k=0}^{K-1} tw_k} \tag{5}$$

where *K* is the number of temporary segments. An image segment with width *sw* and height *sh* is potentially a touching pattern when $sw > \theta_{h1} \cdot LH$ or $sw/sh > \theta_{h2}$. The coefficients θ_{h1} and θ_{h2} are empirically set.

The recursive searching method of split point is derived from the observation of writing habits. In one segment with potential touching patterns, generally, a position with minimum value of vertical projection $hist(x)$ and near the middle of segment can be considered as a split point. So the position of the split point sp should satisfy the two conditions:

1. The value of $hist(sp)$ is very small;
2. sp is near to the middle of segment.

The split point sp is computed as

$$sp = argmin\big(hist(x)\big) \ \left(\left\|i - \frac{sw}{2}\right\| < \delta\right). \tag{6}$$

The coefficient δ is the threshold of distance between the split point sp and the center of segment. The results of over-segmentation of Figure 13 are shown in Figure 14.

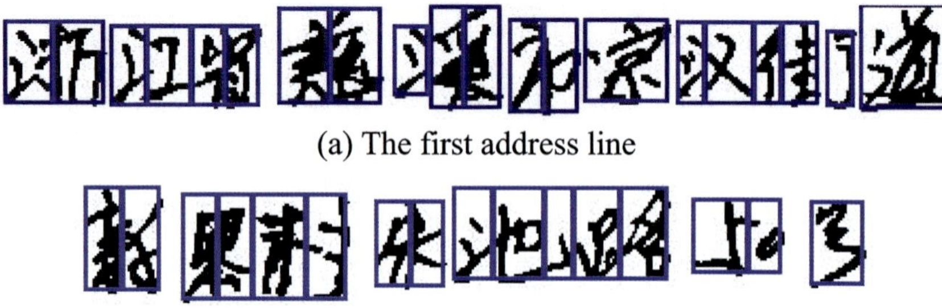

(a) The first address line

(b) The second address line

Figure 14. Over-segmentation of address lines.

3.3.2. *Segments merging and character recognition*

Consecutive primitive segments are merged to generate candidate character patterns and then the lattice of candidate character patterns is formed as shown in Figure 15. We define the candidate character patterns as a set $P = \{p_{(1,1)}, p_{(1,2)}, p_{(1,3)}, \cdots, p_{(m,n)}, \cdots, p_{(l,q)}\}$, where (m, n) is the serial number of primitive segment ($1 \leq m \leq l$; $1 \leq n \leq q$). l is the total number of primitive segments, q is the maximum number of the consecutive primitive segments grouped into a pattern, and q is set as 3 in our system. Each candidate pattern consists of one, two, or three segments subject to character size constraints. In the primitive candidate lattice, each pattern is classified into a number of candidate characters by a character classifier.

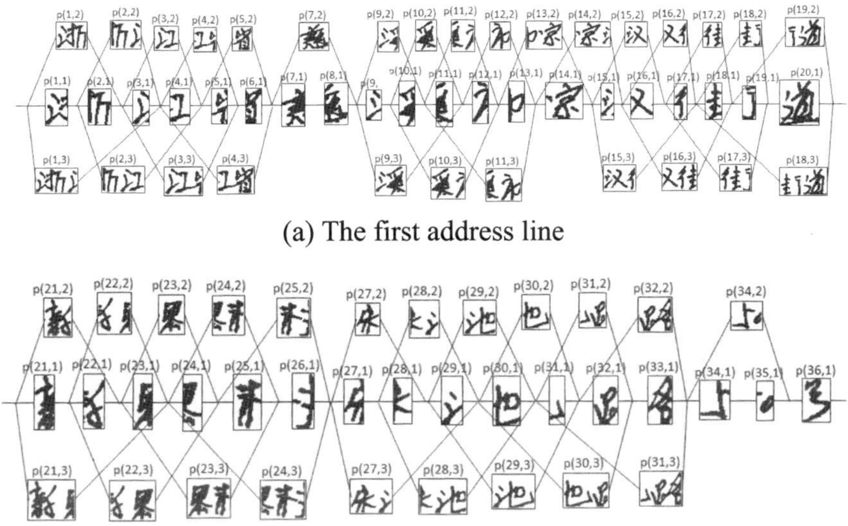

(a) The first address line

(b) The second address line

Figure 15. Segments merging to candidate character patterns.

The classification process includes two main steps: feature extraction and classification.

1. Feature extraction

In handwritten Chinese character recognition, the direction features have yielded superior performance due to the sensitivity to stroke-direction variance and the insensitivity to stroke-width variance[15]. It includes chaincode direction feature, normalization-cooperated chaincode feature (NCCF)[16], and gradient direction feature.

Chaincode direction feature:

In a binary image I, a contour pixel is a black point with at least one of its 4-connected neighbors being white. The 8-direction chaincodes of contour pixels can be decided by contour tracing, or more simply, by raster scanning. For a black pixel$(x, y)(I(x, y) = 0)$, denote the values of 8-connected neighbors in counter clockwise as p_k, $k = 0, 1, \ldots, 7$, with the right neighbor being p_0. For $k = 0, 2, 4, 6$, if $p_k = 0$, check p_{k+1};

if $p_{k+1} = 1$ (chaincode $k + 1$), the feature $f_{k+1}(x, y)$ increases by 1; otherwise, if $p_{(k+2)\%8} = 1$ (chaincode $(k + 2)\%8$), the feature $f_{(k+2)\%8}(x, y)$ increases by 1.

Normalization-cooperated chaincode feature:
For NCCF, each chaincode in the original image is viewed as a line segment connecting two neighboring pixels, which is mapped to another line segment in a standard direction plane by coordinate mapping. In the direction plane, each pixel (unit square) crossed by the line segment in the main (x or y) direction is given a unit of direction contribution. To exploit the continuous nature of line segment, the strength of line direction falling in a pixel is proportional to the length of line segment falling in the unit square.

Gradient direction feature:
In gradient direction feature extraction, the gradient vector, computed on the normalized image using the Sobel operator, is decomposed into components in eight chaincode directions. The Sobel operator has two masks to compute the gradient components in two axes. And the gradient $g(x,y) = [g_x, g_y]^T$ at location (x,y) is computed by

$$g_x(x,y) = f(x+1,y-1) + 2f(x+1,y) + f(x+1,y+1) \\ -f(x-1,y-1) - 2f(x-1,y) - f(x-1,y+1) \quad (7)$$

and

$$g_y(x,y) = f(x-1,y+1) + 2f(x,y+1) + f(x+1,y+1) \\ -f(x-1,y-1) - 2f(x,y-1) - f(x+1,y-1). \quad (8)$$

The gradient strength and direction can be computed from the vector $[g_x, g_y]^T$. The range of gradient direction can be partitioned into a number (8 or 16) of regions and each region corresponds to a direction plane. More effectively, the gradient vector is decomposed into components in standard directions. In this scheme, if a gradient direction lies between two standard directions, the vector is decomposed into two components as shown in Figure 16. The length of each component is assigned to the corresponding direction plane at the pixel (x, y).

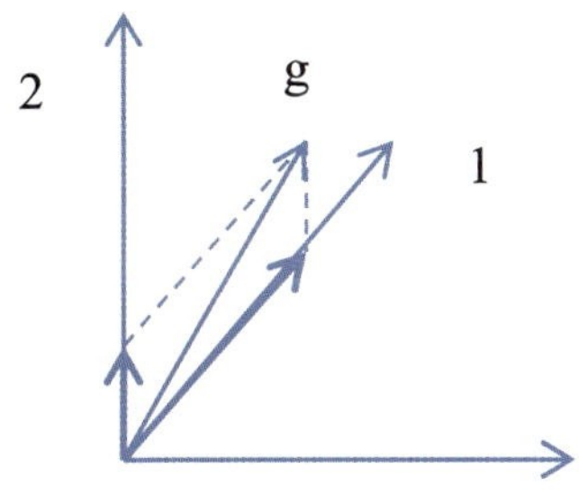

Figure 16. Decomposition of gradient vector.

2. Classification

Among a great number of methods, modified quadratic discriminant function MQDF proposed by Kimura *et al.*[17] is an excellent one and has been widely applied[18–22]. It is a modified model of QDF to improve the computation efficiency and classification performance via eigenvalue smoothing.

In Bayesian decision rule, QDF assumes that the probability density function of each class is multivariate Gaussian,

$$p(\boldsymbol{x}|i) = \frac{\exp[-\frac{1}{2}(x-\boldsymbol{\mu}_i)^T \Sigma_i^{-1}(x-\boldsymbol{\mu}_i)]}{(2\pi)^{\frac{d}{2}}|\Sigma_i|^{\frac{1}{2}}}, \tag{9}$$

where $\boldsymbol{x}$ means an input pattern, d is the dimension of $\boldsymbol{x}$, $\boldsymbol{\mu}_i$ and $\boldsymbol{\Sigma}_i$ denote the mean vector and the covariance matrix of class i, respectively. The input pattern $\boldsymbol{x}$ is classified to the class of maximum a posteriori (MAP) probability out of M classcs,

$$\boldsymbol{x} \in \arg max\ p(i \mid \boldsymbol{x}) = \arg max \frac{p(i)p(\boldsymbol{x} \mid i)}{p(\boldsymbol{x})}, \tag{10}$$

where $p(i)$ is the priori probability of class i and $p(\boldsymbol{x})$ is the mixture density function which is independent of class label. When the priori probabilities $p(i)(i = 0, 1, M - 1)$ are equal, Eq. (10) can be represented as

$$\boldsymbol{x} \in \arg max\, p(\boldsymbol{x}|i). \tag{11}$$

Substituting Eq. (9) into Eq. (11) and taking the negative logarithm, we obtain

$$x \in \arg min \left(\frac{1}{2}(\boldsymbol{x} - \boldsymbol{\mu}_i)^T \boldsymbol{\Sigma}_i^{-1} (\boldsymbol{x} - \boldsymbol{\mu}_i) + \frac{d}{2} log 2\pi + \frac{1}{2} \log |\boldsymbol{\Sigma}_i|\right). \tag{12}$$

Thus the Quadratic Discriminant Function (QDF) can be defined as

$$f_{QDF}(\boldsymbol{x}, i) = (\boldsymbol{x} - \boldsymbol{\mu}_i)^T \boldsymbol{\Sigma}_i^{-1} (\boldsymbol{x} - \boldsymbol{\mu}_i) + \log |\boldsymbol{\Sigma}_i|, \tag{13}$$

here, $\boldsymbol{x} \in \arg min\, f_{QDF}(\boldsymbol{x}, i)$, and QDF is actually a distance matric of the input pattern with the classes and the class with minimum QDF is assigned to the input pattern.

By K-L transform, the covariance matrix can be diagonalized as

$$\Sigma_i = \boldsymbol{\Phi}_i \boldsymbol{\Lambda}_i \boldsymbol{\Phi}_i^{\mathbf{T}}, \tag{14}$$

where $\boldsymbol{\Lambda}_i = \mathrm{diag}[\lambda_{i0}, \cdots, \lambda_{i(d-1)}](\lambda_{ij} \in \mathbb{R}^d, j = 0, \ldots, d-1)$ denote the eigenvalues (ordered in decreasing order) of Σi, and $\boldsymbol{\Phi}_i = [\phi_{i0}, \ldots, \phi_{i(d-1)}]$ $(\phi_{ij} \in \mathbb{R}^d, j = 0, \ldots, d-1)$ stand for the ordered eigenvectors. $\boldsymbol{\Phi}_i$ is ortho-normal (unitary) such that $\boldsymbol{\Phi}_i^{\mathbf{T}} \boldsymbol{\Phi}_i = \boldsymbol{I}$.

Inserting Eq. (14) into (13), the QDF can be rewritten in the form of eigenvectors and eigenvalues:

$$f_{QDF}(\boldsymbol{x}, i) = \sum_{j=0}^{d-1} \frac{1}{\lambda_{ij}} [\boldsymbol{\Phi}_{ij}^{\mathbf{T}} (\boldsymbol{x} - \boldsymbol{\mu}_i)]^2 + \sum_{j=0}^{d-1} log\lambda_{ij}. \tag{15}$$

Replacing the minor eigenvalues with a constant δ_i, the modified quadratic discriminant function (MQDF) is obtained as

$$\begin{aligned} f_{MQDF}(\boldsymbol{x}, i) = \sum_{j=0}^{k-1} \frac{1}{\lambda_{ij}} \left[\boldsymbol{\Phi}_{ij}^{\mathbf{T}} (\boldsymbol{x} - \boldsymbol{\mu}_i)\right]^2 + \frac{1}{\delta_i} r_i(\boldsymbol{x}) + \sum_{j=0}^{k-1} log\lambda_{ij} \\ + (d-k) log\delta_i, \end{aligned} \tag{16}$$

where k is the number of principal axes and $r_i(\boldsymbol{x})$ stands for the residual of subspace projection:

$$r_i(\boldsymbol{x}) = \|\boldsymbol{x} - \boldsymbol{\mu}_i\|^2 - \sum_{j=0}^{k-1} [(\boldsymbol{x} - \boldsymbol{\mu}_i)^{\mathrm{T}} \boldsymbol{\Phi}_{ij}]^2. \tag{17}$$

Compared with QDF, MQDF has multifold advantages. Firstly, the bias of minor eigenvalues is overcome by replacing them with a constant. Secondly, only the principal eigenvectors and eigenvalues of covariance matrices are to be stored so that the memory space is reduced. Thirdly, the computation effort is largely saved because the projections to minor axes are eliminated. But the parameters of MQDF are estimated by ML estimation, and it inevitably suffers from the estimation error from small sample size and the deviation of density model itself. To improve the classification performance, a discriminative learning quadratic discriminant function (DLQDF) is proposed by Liu *et al.*[22] During discriminative learning, the DLQDF adhered to the structure of MQDF under the Gaussian density assumption, and the parameters (mean vectors, eigenvalues and eigenvectors) are optimized under the minimum classification error (MCE) criterion.

In MCE criterion, the misclassification measure is embedded in a sigmoid function. And the loss of misclassification for the pattern $\boldsymbol{x}$ to its real class c is defined as

$$l(\boldsymbol{x}, c) = l(h_c) = \frac{1}{1+e^{-\xi h_c}}, \tag{18}$$

$$h_c = f_{MQDF}(\boldsymbol{x}, c) - f_{MQDF}(\boldsymbol{x}, r), \tag{19}$$

where r is the closest rival class ($f_{MQDF}(\boldsymbol{x}, r) = \min_{i \neq c} f_{MQDF}(\boldsymbol{x}, i)$).

On a training dataset $\{(\boldsymbol{x}^n, c^n) | n = 0, 1, \dots, N-1\}$ (where c^n is the class label of pattern $\boldsymbol{x}^n$), the misclassification loss is computed by

$$L = \frac{1}{N} \sum_{n=0}^{N-1} [l(\boldsymbol{x}^n, c^n) + \alpha f_{MQDF}(\boldsymbol{x}^n, c^n)], \tag{20}$$

where $\alpha f_{MQDF}(\boldsymbol{x}^n, c^n)$ is the regularized objective to alleviate the negative effects caused by the ML estimates (initial parameters inherited from MQDF) and α is the regularization coefficient.

On large size of training sample, discriminative learning can generally give higher classification accuracy than ML estimation. And the adherence to Gaussian density assumption renders the classifier resistant to non-characters.

The recognition results of candidate patterns in Figure 15 are presented in Table 1 partly. The first column lists the label of candidate patterns and the second column shows their corresponding candidate characters output by the character classifier. The values in the parentheses are the characters' recognition confidence.

Table 1. Recognition results of candidate patterns.

P(1,2)	浙 (0.56)，晰 (0.54)，珊 (0.51)，…，渐 (0.44)
P(3,2)	江 (0.51)，河 (0.49)，沟 (0.44)，…，努 (0.41)
P(9,3)	溪 (0.55)，演 (0.53)，赚 (0.52)，…，漠 (0.44)
P(23,2)	某 (0.54)，裹 (0.53)，界 (0.52)，…，县 (0.48)
P(25,2)	刺 (0.56)，删 (0.55)，村 (0.51)，…，削 (0.42)
P(27,2)	朱 (0.59)，味 (0.57)，来 (0.56)，…，宋 (0.51)
P(29,3)	池 (0.61)，泄 (0.58)，地 (0.57)，…，她 (0.51)
P(32,2)	路 (0.53)，酷 (0.52)，糖 (0.51)，…，酪 (0.46)

3.3.3. *Lexicon-driven segmentation-recognition matching*

Lexicon-driven segmentation-recognition hypothesis-and-verification approach is very effective to solve the difficulties of handwritten Chinese address recognition. There are two important problems in this approach: a practical address lexicon and an effective matching method between recognition results and address lexicon.

In general, an address is composed of several address words which are defined as the basic administration units. For instance, the address '广东省深圳市福田区深南中路' includes the address units '广东省', '深圳市', '福田区' and '深南中路'. The last character in each address word is the key character of the address, such as '省' (province), '市' (city), '区' (district) and '路' (road) and so on. However, the addresses on real mails are very complicated in writing variations, such as omission of key characters or possession of redundant words. This greatly increases the difficulty of address recognition. To deal with these problems, the word-level-tree (WLT) based method[10] is utilized in lexicon-driven segmentation-recognition matching phase. In WLT, each node is correspondent to an address word, such that a path from the root to the leaf node is able to give a normative address format. And all the writing variations of an address are mapped to their corresponding normative address formats stored in the WLT. The block diagram of the WLT based approach is shown in Figure 17.

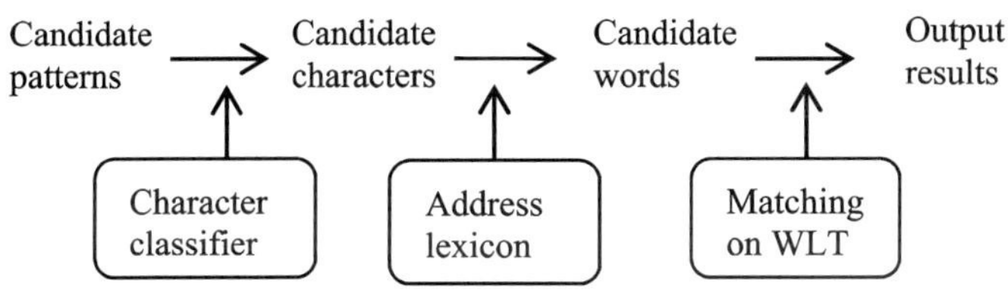

Figure 17. Block diagram of handwritten Chinese address recognition.

1. Address lexicon

The normative address in China is a top-down hierarchical structure, which typically consists of four layers representing province, city, district and road/street, respectively. Figure 18 illustrates the normative addresses represented by WLT. Here, we give the definitions of the node and path in WLT for clarity as follows:

Definition 1 (Word-level node). Each node is corresponding to an address word rather than a character.

Definition 2 (Path of normative address format). A path from the root node to a leaf node gives a normative address format.

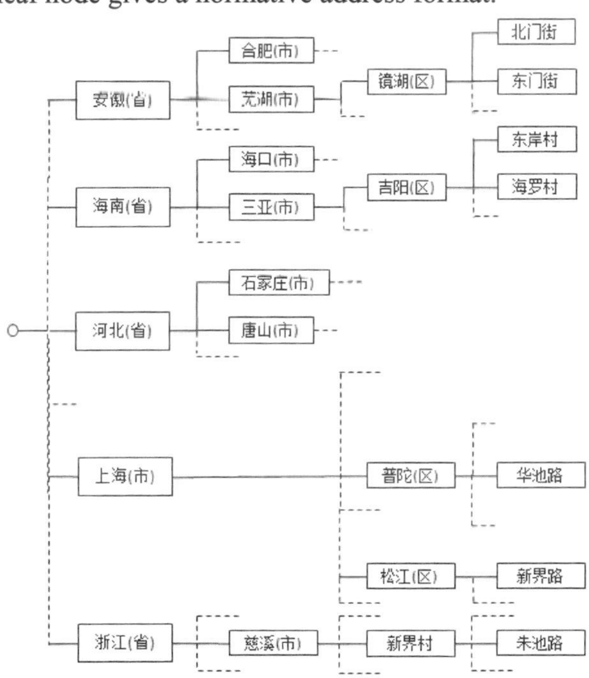

Figure 18. Representation of normative addresses using WLT.

To deal with the addresses of missing key characters, the key characters (except the key characters of road name) are set to be optional in the address words (in Figure 18, the character in the parenthesis is optional). Since the address format is various, address may be started with any basic administration units. The address may skip some nodes of certain layers. Among the four types of basic administration units, road name is most important such that it has the highest priority in this method. Once the leaf node (road name) is given, the candidate addresses containing that road name can be found.

2. Address matching

In this step, two address lines in Figure 15 are combined to search the recognition result. Specifically, all the candidate characters of two address lines are mapped to many address words on the proposed word-level-tree (WLT) address database to generate the candidate address words firstly. In addition, each candidate word is labeled by a score based on its recognition confidence and segment confidence. Then, the candidate address words build up several candidate address strings based on the inherent administrative relationship among different address words in WLT. Finally, the address recognition result is obtained by summing the scores of candidate address words in each search path.

The WLT provides a potential address word list (AW_O) that stores all of the address words, from which a list of candidate address words is generated. Firstly, according to the recognition results of candidate patterns, those address words in AW_O which do not satisfy $nr \geq nl/2$ (*nr* indicates the number of recognized characters and *nl* refers to the length of the address word) are pruned. Then considering the relative position of recognized characters in address words with its matched candidate patterns, the address words with invalid positional relationship will be pruned too. Finally, the confidence score of each address word is computed to reduce the candidate address words further. If the score of an address word is smaller than an empirical threshold, it will be pruned. After that, the ultimate candidate address words are obtained. The generated candidate address words in the segmentation candidate lattice are shown in Figure 19.

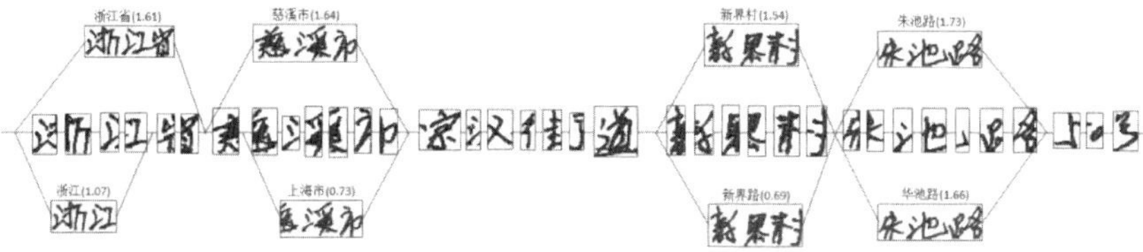

Figure 19. Candidate address words.

Each candidate address word is a node of the WLT. As the nodes corresponding to those ultimate candidate address words are determined, they are used to match the paths in the tree to generate candidate addresses. The matching starts with the leaf nodes to root node inversely to ensure that all the candidate addresses must include the recognized road name, and it is named bottom-up tree match strategy. The ultimate candidate address words are allocated to four lists PR, CI, DI and RO, which correspond to province, city, district and road, respectively.

In this method, the bottom-up tree search strategy is adopted. In the searching, a triple $TN = \{CN, PN, AS\}$ is used to represent a node in search space, where CN denotes the current node, PN is the parent node of CN, and AS is the accumulated score from the leaf node. For a candidate word W, its leftmost pattern $(lp(W))$ and rightmost pattern $(rp(W))$ are corresponding to the first matching character and the last matching character, respectively. The position between parent node and child node is valid or not depends on whether the rp of parent node is smaller than the lp of child node. Here, the position is in an ascending order from left to right on the image.

In the bottom-up tree searching, the list RO is first checked to see if it is empty. If the list RO is empty, namely, the road name is missing, then $AS = 0$ and the searching will stop. Otherwise, the address word will appear in list $RO(W \in RO)$, then the searching is started at this word. Firstly, CN and AS are initialized to the address word and the corresponding score. PN points to the parent node of the CN. There are two situations which should be considered when checking the address word of PN, that is, $PN \in DI$ or $PN \notin DI$. If $PN \notin DI$, it means that the address word of the PN is not to be found. In this case, the CN is pointed to the parent node of the PN directly. If $PN \in DI$, it means that the address word of the PN has been found. In this case, the AS is updated by adding the score of PN when the positions between PN and CN satisfy $rp(PN) < lp(CN)$. And CN is pointed to the PN. Otherwise, the AS is not updated, and CN is pointed to the parent node of the PN directly. The search is completed when PN is pointed to the root of the tree. Finally, the path from the leaf node to the root gives a candidate normative address and the score of this candidate normative address is AS. A two-tuple denoted by $RS = \{\xi, AS\}$ is utilized to store the result of this searching, where ξ stores the candidate normative address.

We can obtain several valid candidate addresses based on the WLT. The candidate address with maximum score is taken as the final recognition result. Figure 20 gives the illustrative result of path matching in WLT of the first parcel image in Figure 1. The address recognition result is '浙江省慈溪市新界村朱池路' which is signed with bold font.

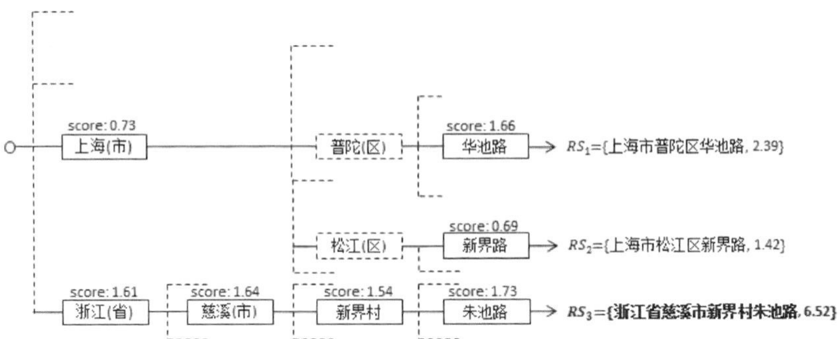

Figure 20. Address recognition results in WLT.

4. Conclusions

We present the details of handwritten Chinese address recognition on parcel sorting system in this chapter. Owing to the arbitrariness of parcel images in resolution and direction, SIFT features are employed to locate the express waybill on the parcel with address information first. Then the address area is extracted and input to recognition system. In address recognition phase, a word-level-tree (WLT) framework is employed for handwritten Chinese address recognition. In this framework, all the writing variations of address image are mapped to the normative writing form in the WLT, which facilitates the recognition of handwritten Chinese address.

With the rapid development of electronic commerce, the volume of parcels is keeping an annual growth of 50 percent in China in recent years, which means the demand for automatic parcel sorting machines is still very strong. Furthermore, besides sorting, other demands for address recognition, such as information extraction, postal inspection, etc., also require the persistent improvement of handwritten Chinese address recognition in future.

References

1. Y. Lu, X. Tu, S. Lu and P. S. P. Wang, Application of pattern recognition technology to postal automation in China, in *Pattern Recognition and Machine Vision — in Honor and Memory of Professor King-Sun Fu*, 2010, pp. 367–381.
2. X. Gao and L.-W. Jin, A vision-based fast Chinese postal envelope identification system, *Journal of Information Science and Engineering*, **28**(1), 31–49 (2012).
3. E. Ishidera, D. Nishiwaki and K. Yamada, Unconstrained Japanese address recognition using a combination of spatial information and word knowledge, in *Proc. 4th International Conference on Document Analysis and Recognition*, 1997, pp. 1016–1020.
4. M. Koga, R. Mine, H. Sako and H. Fujisawa, Lexical search approach for character-string recognition, in *Proc. 3rd IAPR Workshop on Document Analysis Systems*, 1998, pp. 115–129.
5. C.-L. Liu, M. Koga and H. Fujisawa, Lexicon-driven segmentation and recognition of handwritten character strings for Japanese address reading. *IEEE Trans. Patt. Anal. Mach. Intell.*, **24**(11), 1425–1437 (2002).
6. Y. Jiang, X.-Q. Ding and Z. Ren, A suffix tree based handwritten Chinese address recognition system, in *Proc. 9th International Conference on Document Analysis and Recognition*, 2007, pp. 292–296.
7. K. Huang, Y. Hotta and S. Naoi, A handwritten Chinese address recognition method using recursive holistic word matching and edit distance based verification strategies, in *Proc. 10th International Workshop on Frontiers in Handwriting Recognition*, 2006, pp. 292–296.
8. Q. Wang, F. Yin and C.-L. Liu, Improving handwritten Chinese text recognition by confidence transformation, in *Proc. 11th International Conference on Document Analysis and Recognition*, 2011, pp. 518–522.
9. S. Lu, X. Wei and Y. Lu, Cost-sensitive transformation for Chinese address recognition, in *Proc. 22nd International Conference on Pattern Recognition*, 2014, pp. 2897–2902.
10. X. Wei, S. Lu, Y. Wen and Y. Lu, Recognition of handwritten Chinese address with writing variations, *Patt. Recog. Lett.*, **73**, 68–75 (2016).
11. D. G. Lowe, Distinctive image features from scale-invariant keypoints, *International Journal of Computer Vision*, **60**(2), 91–110 (2004).

12. Q. Zhou and Z. Zhao, Substation equipment image recognition based on SIFT feature matching, in *Proc. 5th International Congress on Image and Signal Processing*, 2012, pp. 1344–1347.
13. S. Liu, L. Zhao, J. Li and Q. Cai, The SIFT features matching for spherical panoramic images, in *Proc. 11th International Conference on Control & Automation*, 2014, pp. 914–917.
14. L. Xu and E. Oja, Randomized Hough transform (RTH): basic mechanisms, algorithms, and computational complexities, *CVGIP: Image Understanding*, **57**(2), 131–154 (1993).
15. C.-L. Liu, Handwritten Chinese character recognition: Effects of shape normalization and feature extraction, *Arabic and Chinese Handwriting Recognition*, 4768, 104–128 (2008).
16. M. Hamanaka, K. Yamada and J. Tsukumo, Normalization-cooperated feature extraction method for hand-printed Kanji character recognition, in *Proc. 3rd Int'l Workshop on Frontiers of Handwriting Recognition*, 1993, pp. 343–348.
17. F. Kimura, K. Takashina, S. Tsuruoka and Y. Miyake, Modified quadratic discriminant functions and the application to Chinese character recognition, *IEEE Trans. Patt. Anal. Mach. Intell.*, **9**(1), 149–153 (1987).
18. C.-L. Liu, F. Yin, D.-H. Wang and Q.-F. Wang, Online and offline handwritten Chinese character recognition: Benchmarking on new databases, *Pattern Recognition*, **46**(1), 155–162 (2013).
19. Y.-W. Wang, X.-Q. Ding and C.-S. Liu, MQDF discriminative learning based offline handwritten Chinese character recognition, in *Proc. 11th International Conference on Document Analysis and Recognition*, 2011, pp. 1100–1104.
20. K. Ding and L. Jin, Incremental MQDF learning for writer adaptive handwriting recognition, in *Proc. Int'l Conf. Frontiers in Handwriting Recognition*, 2010, pp. 559–564.
21. T. Long and L. Jin, Building compact MQDF classifier for large character set recognition by subspace distribution sharing, *Pattern Recognition*, **41**(9), 2916–2925 (2008).
22. C.-L. Liu, H. Sakoand and H. Fujisawa, Discriminative learning quadratic discriminant function for handwriting recognition, *IEEE Trans. Neural Networks*, **15**(2), 430–444 (2004).

Chapter 8

Off-line Text-independent Writer Identification for Chinese Handwriting

Yu-Jie Xiong and Yue Lu

Department of Computer Science and Technology,
Shanghai Key Laboratory of Multidimensional Information Processing,
East China Normal University, Shanghai 200241, China
ylu@cs.ecnu.edu.cn

Encouraged by the strong requirements of information security, the rapid development of biometrics becomes a new focus in both academic and industrial research. Writer identification is a branch of behavioral biometrics using handwriting with a natural writing attitude as the individual characteristic for identification. Off-line text-independent writer identification is to identify a person based on the static handwritten data with unrestricted text content. We propose an effective method using the contour-directional feature (CDF) combined with the modified SIFT for Chinese writer identification. The investigation demonstrates that both features are capable of describing the characteristic of handwriting. In the stage of the modified SIFT extraction, a simple connected-component based segmentation algorithm is used to segment the handwriting image into character regions, and the modified SIFT descriptors are extracted from the character regions. Then, a codebook is constructed by K-means clustering. With the codebook, the occurrence histogram of the modified SIFT for each handwriting image is calculated. Both features are concatenated together to represent the characteristic of handwriting. Experimental results show that the proposed method is able to improve the performance and is superior to other methods in terms of identification accuracy. On the HIT-MW Chinese handwriting dataset involving 240 writers, the Top-1 accuracy is 96.3%, and the Top-10 accuracy is 99.2%.

1. Introduction

The requirements of personal authentication have placed biometrics at the center of the academic and industrial research, as it is becoming a key aspect of information security.[1] Biometrics refers to analyzing the biological phenomena and observations by means of statistical techniques for individual recognition. It is performed by comparing the biometric template measured from an unknown person with the templates linked to known persons with certainty. Depending on the adoptive traits, biometrics can be categorized into physiological biometrics and behavioral biometrics. Physiological biometrics identifies a person using a physical property of the human body (e.g. DNA, iris, fingerprint, face, and hand geometry), while behavioral biometrics considers individual traits of a person's behavior (e.g. voice, gait, signature, handwriting) for authentication. It is worth noting that handwriting is the most widespread carrier of personal behavioral information, and people have employed signatures as the legitimate means to verify an individual's identity for several centuries. Moreover, acquisition of handwriting is not invasive, and we always do some writing in our daily life which makes handwriting easy to get. For these reasons, handwriting with a natural writing attitude is an effective way to represent the individual characteristics, and plays an essential role in the set of biometric traits. In consideration of the variability of handwriting, writer identification is still an attractive but challenging research field.

1.1. *Writer identification vs. handwriting recognition*

Compared with writer identification, handwriting recognition is an older and broader research domain which has lasted for several decades.[2] The key of handwriting recognition is to obtain the invariant representation from a large number of manuscripts to eliminate the individual variations of handwriting.[3] However, the individual style of handwriting is the biometric trait for writer identification. Researchers aim to find the specificity of writing style to achieve personal authentication. From this perspective, writer identification and handwriting recognition are two totally different tasks. However, an interesting phenomenon shows that handwriting recognition system can achieve better results with the writer adaptation.[4]

1.2. *Writer identification vs. writer verification*

Writer identification and writer verification are actually very similar. As shown in Figure 1, writer verification involves a one-to-one comparison to determine whether two samples of handwriting are produced by the same person or not. Writer identification is to select the authentic author of handwriting from a group of writers, and a sorted list of candidates is

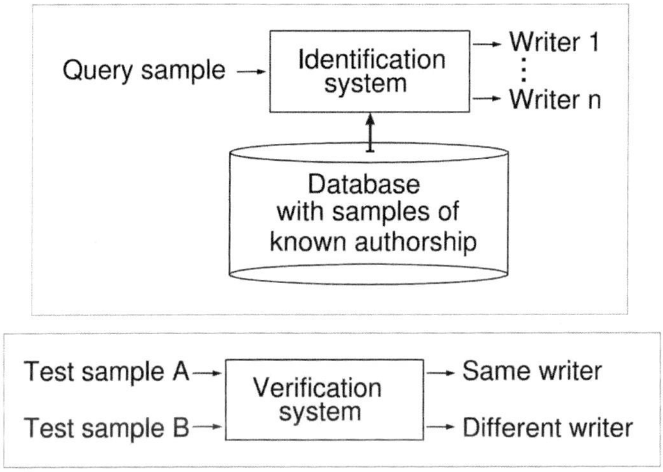

Figure 1. A writer identification system and a writer verification system.[3]

returned as the output. In addition, writer verification is also very similar to signature verification. The difference between them is the text content of input. The former is a piece of handwriting, which contains several words or a few text lines. The text content of the reference is not related to the content of the query. The latter is a signature, which means the text content of the reference and the query is the same. Furthermore, writer verification assumes that handwriting is produced naturally,[5] whereas signature verification considers different conditions, including genuine and forged handwritings.[6]

1.3. *Text-dependent vs. text-independent*

On the basis of the content of handwriting, there are two different subcategories of writer identification: text-dependent and text-independent.[7] The text-dependent writer identification is similar to signature verification. It assumes that the references and the query share the same text content. For text-dependent identification system, interactive tools are widely used to precisely find out the same characters or words. As a consequence, manual intervention makes its objectivity in doubt and its applicability is also restricted. Text-independent writer identification eliminates the restriction of text content and involves less manual work. It treats writer identification as a statistical classification problem rather than a template matching problem, so text-independent writer identification requires sufficient handwritten text of each writer to extract robust statistical feature for pattern representation. Therefore, the minimal amount of handwritten text which can satisfy the statistics assumption is of crucial importance for the text-independent writer identification.

1.4. *Recent progress in Chinese writer identification*

Writer identification is relevant to disciplines ranging from neuroscience to computer science, and it attracts a lot of interests from both academia and forensics. Plamondon and Lorette[7] summarized the progress of writer identification and signature verification in 1989. Continuing attentions and efforts have been devoted to reaching text-independent writer identification. Here we present several popular off-line text-independent approaches proposed since 2000, as a survey of recent developments of the topic of Chinese writer identification.

Zhu *et al.*[8] used the two-dimensional Gabor filtering technique to extract texture features and a weighted Euclidean distance classifier to fulfil the identification task. Shen *et al.*[9] improved the Gabor filters with the wavelet technique to reduce the excessive calculational cost, and K-nearest neighbor (KNN) classifier was utilized to identify the writer. He and Tang[10] used both autocorrelation function and Gabor filters to extract the features, and weighted Euclidean distance classifier was used to match the extracted features. He *et al.*[11] presented hidden Markov tree model (HMTM) in wavelet domain for Chinese writer identification. Compared with the two-dimensional Gabor model, the HMTM not only achieved better identification performance but also greatly reduced the elapsed time. After that, they also presented a wavelet based method with generalized Gaussian density model.[12] Zhang *et al.*[13] proposed a hybrid method combining Gabor model with mesh fractal dimension. Li and Ding[14] proposed a histogram-based feature called as the grid microstructure feature (GMF) which was extracted from the edge pixels, and the similarity of different handwritings was measured with the improved weighted chi-squared metric. It is noted that they were the winners of the ICDAR 2011 writer identification contest.[15] However, the grid microstructure feature is sensitive to pen-width variation in practical situation. Xu *et al.*[16] proposed an inner and inter class variances weighted feature matching method to solve this problem. Wen *et al.*[17] characterized the frequent structures distribution of edge fragments on multiple scales to describe the writing style of Chinese handwriting, and applied Chi-squared distance as similarity measurement. Hu *et al.*[18] employed the SIFT descriptor to describe the local directional information of Chinese characters, and KNN classifier was used to identify the author of handwriting. Instead of hard voting, they also presented two coding strategies as improved fisher kernels and locality-constrained linear for feature coding.

2. The Proposed Method

We present a new writer identification method to identify the authentic writer of the query handwriting document using the contour-directional feature and the modified SIFT occurrence histogram. The flowchart of the proposed method is given in Figure 2. The contour-directional

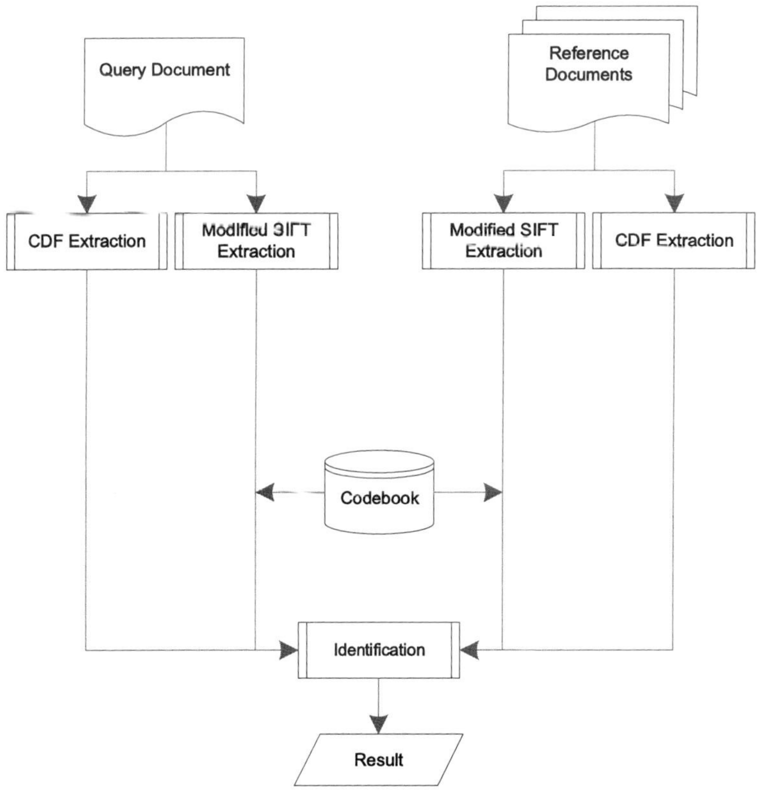

Figure 2. System flow chart.

feature is extracted from the contour image obtained by contour detection. The extraction of the modified SIFT occurrence histogram is divided into two stages: codebook generation and histogram calculation. First, a segmentation algorithm based on connected-component is used to segment the handwriting image into character regions. Then, the modified SIFT descriptors are extracted from the character regions. These obtained descriptors are used to create the codebook using K-means clustering. After that, the occurrence histogram of the modified SIFT descriptors for each handwriting is calculated with the codebook. The contour-directional feature and the modified SIFT occurrence histograms are concatenated together for similarity measurement. In the proposed method, weighted Chi-squared distance is utilized to calculate the distance of the contour-directional features and Manhattan distance is used to calculate the distance of the modified SIFT occurrence histograms. The two distances are accumulated to measure the final similarity.

2.1. *Contour-directional feature*

It is important to extract appropriate features to represent handwriting image for similarity measurement. Bulacu *et al.*[19] proposed a feature of the edge-hinge distribution which represents the changes in the direction of handwriting strokes. Experimental results showed that identification performance of edge-hinge feature outperforms all non-angular features, but the edge-hinge feature only computes the joint probability distribution of the directions of the two edge in the neighborhood. Li and Ding[14] expanded the edge-hinge feature into grid microstructure feature for Chinese writer identification. Chinese is a hieroglyphic writing. Compared with alphabetic writing (like English), Chinese characters have more complex stroke crossings. Grid microstructure feature is extracted from grids of variable sizes and records the positions of specific edge pixel pairs. But according to the definition of the GMF, if the edge pixel pairs with the same directions are located in the grids with different scales, they are regarded as different microstructures. From the perspective of directions, these pixel pairs are very similar though they have different scales. Hence, we propose the contour-directional feature, which characterizes the writing style of handwriting by the distribution of pixel pairs based on the directional information. The contour-directional feature retains local information of the character, not only the relationships of stroke structures but also the directions of pixel pairs.

The first step of contour-directional feature extraction is contour detection. We use the Sobel operators to extract the contour. An example of contour detection is shown in Figure 3.

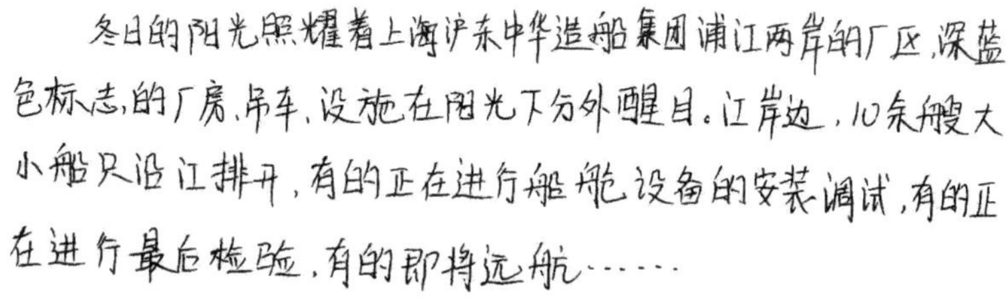

(a)

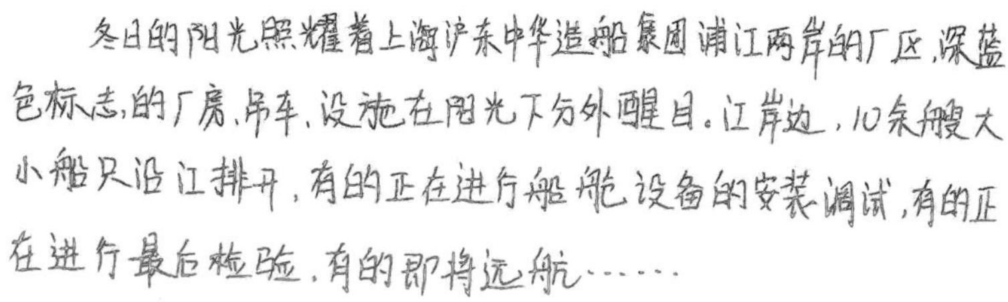

(b)

Figure 3. Original Sample (a) and handwriting image after contour detection (b).

Then, we extract the specific pairs of edge pixel from the contour image. To obtain these pairs of edge pixel, the contour image is divided into a number of blocks of size $n \times n$, and the center of each block is a edge pixel. In each block, we find all the edge pixel pairs (α, β) which satisfy the following conditions:

$$\begin{cases} \alpha \text{ and } \beta \text{ are edge pixels,} \\ G(\alpha) = A_i,\ G(\beta) = B_j, \text{ and } A = B,\ i < j, \\ \text{If } G(\gamma) = A_k, \text{ and } i < k < j, \\ \text{then } \gamma \text{ is not the edge pixel.} \end{cases}$$

As shown in Figure 4(a), it denoted a block of 5×5. The black square is the edge pixel P, and the gray squares are edge pixels connected to P. The pixel A around P is marked with the index $G(A) = Dis_i$, where Dis denotes the larger distance in the horizontal and vertical distance between A and P, and $1 \le i \le 8 * Dis$. This step is similar to the GMF.[14]

Then, we define the direction $Dir(A)$ of the pixel A in the block as:

$$Dir(A) = \arctan\left((A_y - P_y)/(A_x - P_x)\right),$$

where (A_x, A_y) and (P_x, P_y) are the coordinates of A and P. Afterwards, we redefine the index of each pixel in the block according to the pixel's direction. The new index of A is denoted as $C(A)$. The naming rule of $C(A)$ is defined as:

$$\begin{cases} \text{If } Dir(A) \text{ is unique, then } C(A) = G(A) = dis_i; \\ \text{If } Dir(A) = Dir(A_1) = \ldots = Dir(A_n), \\ dis(An) < \ldots < dis(A1) < dis(A) \\ \text{then } C(A) = C(A_1) = \ldots = C(A_n) = G(A_n) = dis(A_n)_i. \end{cases}$$

As shown in Figure 4(b), the changed indexes are labeled with red color. As a comparison, $(1_2, 1_4)$, $(1_4, 1_6)$, $(2_3, 2_7)$, $(2_7, 2_{13})$ in Figure 4(a) are recorded as the GMF, while the edge pixel pairs $(1_2, 1_4)$, $(1_4, 1_6)$, $(1_2, 1_4)$, $(1_4, 1_7)$ in Figure 4(b) are recorded as the CDF.

Every edge pixel is surrounded by the block of size $n * n$, so we record the occurrence numbers of all the specific edge pixel pairs (α, β) of each block, and accumulate them to obtain the frequency histogram of pixel pairs after normalization. In this way, we acquire the contour-directional feature vector.

2_7	2_6	2_5	2_4	2_3
2_8	1_4	1_3	1_2	2_2
2_9	1_5	P	1_1	2_1
2_{10}	1_6	1_7	1_8	2_{16}
2_{11}	2_{12}	2_{13}	2_{14}	2_{15}

(a) Find specific edge pixel pairs

1_4	2_6	1_3	2_4	1_2
2_8	1_4	1_3	1_2	2_2
1_5	1_5	P	1_1	1_1
2_{10}	1_6	1_7	1_8	2_{16}
1_6	2_{12}	1_7	2_{14}	1_8

(b) Redefine the index of pixels

Figure 4. An example of the extraction of the CDF.

2.2. *Modified SIFT*

Lowe proposed Scale Invariant Feature Transform (SIFT),[20] which has been successfully applied to object detection. The four major stages of SIFT are:

(1) detection of scale-space extrema, (2) accurate keypoint localization, (3) orientation assignment, and (4) keypoint descriptor extraction. For the problem of writer identification, we hope that the features can represent the local patterns of stroke structures. The previous work was focused on extracting the SIFT descriptors from the whole handwriting image directly. It means that a part of descriptors obtained by the global extraction are located in the background area and they should be removed. The orientation information is useful for describing the characteristics of handwriting, but it is not contained in the original SIFT descriptors. In order to obtain SIFT descriptors appropriately, we propose some modifications for the original SIFT. The modified SIFT contains six major stages: (1) character region segmentation, (2) detection of scale-space extrema, (3) keypoint localization, (4) keypoint selection, (5) orientation assignment, and (6) modified descriptor extraction.

2.2.1. *Character region segmentation*

The modified SIFT extracts the features from character regions rather than the whole handwriting image, so we need to segment the handwriting image into character regions. Given a handwriting image I, the segmentation process is described as three steps:

a. I is converted to the binary image I_b using Otsu algorithm.

b. Connected-components in I_b are labeled and their average height H_a and average width W_a are calculated.

c. Connected-components C_i and C_j are merged if they meet the following conditions: (1) overlapping area of C_i and C_j is larger than 20% of the total area of C_i and C_j. (2) overlapping area of C_i and C_j is larger than 60% of the smaller area of C_i and C_j. (3) the vertical distance of centres of C_i and C_j is less than 25% of H_a. (4) the horizontal distance of centres of C_i and C_j is less than 25% of W_a.

After the segmentation, a handwriting image is divided into many character regions.

2.2.2. *Keypoint selection*

Compared with natural scene image, handwriting image lacks gray scale variation, so the original SIFT does not work well in the handwriting image. Based on the characteristics of handwriting, we add the step of keypoint selection to overcome this shortcoming. In general, the allographic information of character exists in the stroke of the character rather than the background area. Therefore, we apply the background point elimination to remove these useless keypoints. This procedure is performed according to the following criterions: If $S_n < n-1$, p is regarded as a keypoint in the background area; if $S_n \geq n-1$, p is regarded as a keypoint in the stroke area, where p is a detected keypoint, and S_n is the number of black pixels in the $n \times n$ spatial neighbor grid of p. We remove the keypoints in the background area. Through the above operations, the remaining keypoints are credible representation of the individuality of handwriting. Figure 5 is an example of the background point elimination. Figure 5(a) is an original handwriting image, and Figure 5(b) is the image after extrema detection, in which the colorized circles with different sizes are the potential keypoints in different scales. The red circles are keypoints in the background area, while the cyan ones are keypoints in the stroke area. After background point elimination, only the keypoints in the stroke area are remained in Figure 5(c).

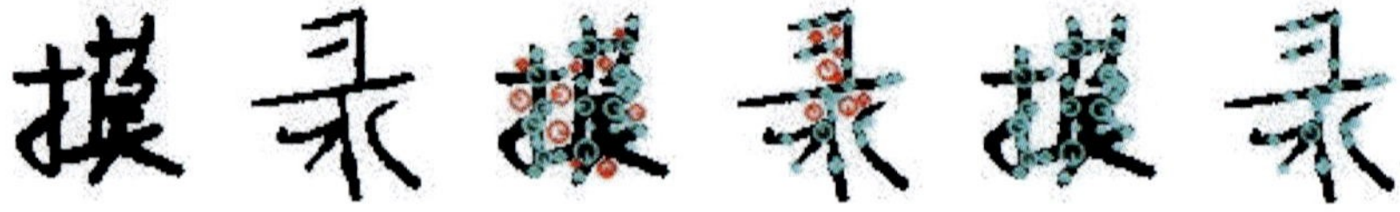

(a) (b) (c)

Figure 5. Keypoint selection processing. (a) original sample, (b) potential keypoints after keypoint localization, and (c) keypoints after background point elimination.

2.2.3. *The modified SIFT descriptor*

After keypoint selection, the modified SIFT descriptor of each keypoint is computed. The modified SIFT descriptor contains two parts: the original descriptor and the orientation of the keypoint. It is well known that by assigning a consistent orientation to each keypoint based on local image properties, the original SIFT descriptor is represented relative to this orientation and therefore achieves invariance to image rotation. However, the invariance to image rotation is not necessary for the issue of writer identification, and the orientation of the keypoint is discriminative to represent the writing style of handwriting, so we combine it with the original descriptor to create the modified SIFT descriptor. The orientation of the keypoint $L(x, y)$ is calculated as:[20]

$$\theta(x, y) = \tan^{-1}\left(\left(L(x, y+1) - L(x, y-1)\right) / \left(L(x+1, y) - L(x-1, y)\right)\right).$$

The range of $\theta(x, y)$ is $(-\pi, \pi)$, and it is quantized to 8 intervals. An example of the modified SIFT descriptor is shown as Figure 6.

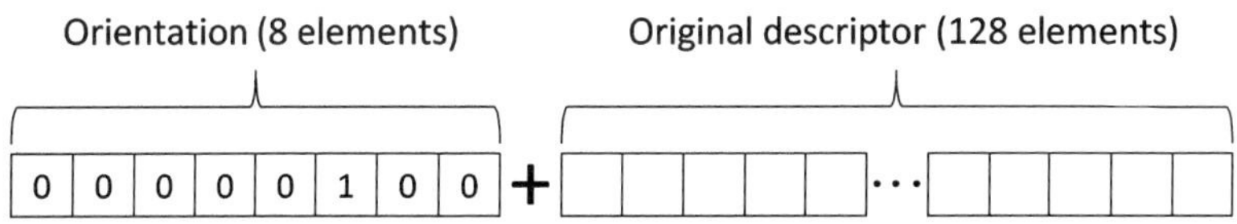

Figure 6. An example of the modified SIFT descriptor.

2.2.4. *Codebook generation and the modified SIFT occurrence histogram calculation*

Figure 7 sketches the main modules of the codebook generation: After the step of the modified SIFT extraction, thousands of modified SIFT descriptors are extracted from handwriting. It is hard to calculate the similarity of different handwritings using these descriptors directly. To solve this problem, we utilize K-means clustering to cluster the descriptors into N classes as the codebook and represent each class by its center $(C_1, C_2 ... C_N)$. In order to keep the independence of the codebook, we use the training images to create the codebook. And N is set equal to 300 empirically in our experiments.

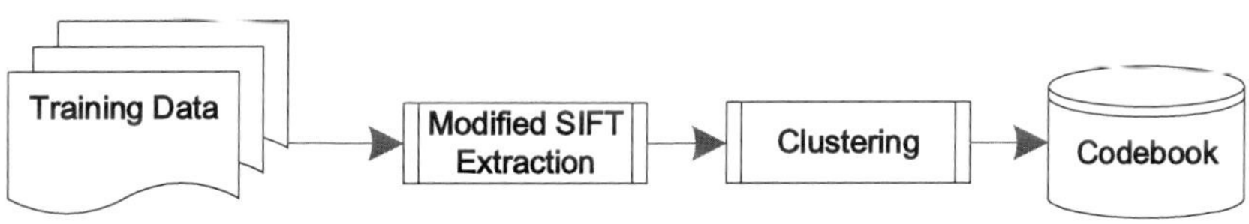

Figure 7. Codebook generation.

After the codebook generation, the modified SIFT occurrence histogram of each image are calculated. For each SIFT descriptor, we calculate its nearest cluster center $C_i (1 < i \leq N)$ of the codebook based on Euclidean distance, and the occurrence counter corresponding to C_i is incremented by one. After all SIFT descriptors are calculated, the normalized occurrence histogram is treated as feature representation of handwriting.

2.3. *Identification*

Query image and the reference image are denoted as Q and R, let $CDF_Q = \{a_1, a_2, ..., a_N\}$ and $CDF_R = \{b_1, b_2, ..., b_N\}$ denote their contour-directional features, and let $SOH_Q = \{x_1, x_2, ..., x_M\}$ and $SOH_R = \{y_1, y_2, ..., y_M\}$ denote their modified SIFT occurrence histograms. Many existed methods based on minimum distance can be used for distance measure. In our method, weighted Chi-squared distance is used to calculate the distance D_C between CDF_Q and CDF_R:

$$D_C = \sum_{i=1}^{N} \frac{(a_i - b_i)^2}{(a_i + b_i)}.$$

And Manhattan distance is used to calculate the distance D_S between SOH_Q and SOH_R:

$$D_S = \sum_{i=1}^{M} (|x_i - y_i|).$$

We summarize the two distances together to measure the final dissimilarity between Q and R:

$$D = D_C + D_S.$$

For a given query handwriting, we calculate its distance to all reference handwritings, then a distance-based candidate list is obtained by sorting the results from the most similar to the least similar handwriting.

3. Experimental Results

We evaluate the proposed method on the HIT-MW dataset and our own LPAIS dataset. The Top-N criterion is used for evaluating the identification performance. For the TOP-N criterion, we consider a correct hit when at least one document image of the same writer is included in the N most similar document images.

HIT-MW[21] is built for the off-line Chinese handwritten text recognition, but it can also be used for the research of writer identification with the writer information list. HIT-MW includes 853 documents and each document consists of at least 200 characters. Two sub-datasets are generated from the HIT-MW dataset. Set-A contains 240 documents written by 240 writers, and every writer has one document in this dataset. Set-B contains all 853 documents of HIT-MW. For simplicity, we assume that this dataset is created by 853 writers, and each writer provides one document to simulate the situation of large number of writers. As shown in Table 1, Set-A contains 480 sub-document images, and Set-B contains 1,706 images. In our experiments, each document image is segmented into two sub-images. One of them is used as the reference, and the other is used as the query. A simple segmentation algorithm based on ground truth information is utilized to segment each image into two commensurate parts.

Table 1. Overview of the experimental datasets.

Dataset	No. of documents	No. of queries	No. of references
Set-A	480	240	240
Set-B	1,706	853	853
LPAIS	400	200	200

Note: 100 images of each reference set are used to generate the codebook.

LPAIS is built for handwritten mail address analysis. It is collected from the practical mail images. LPAIS contains 400 handwritten mail address images collected from 20 Chinese writers and 20 images per writer. For each image, the address content is unrestricted. In most cases, the number of characters in the image is less than 30. Some mail address images are shown in Figure 8. Compared with images in HIT-MW, we can see that the mail address images have various layouts and few characters. This implies

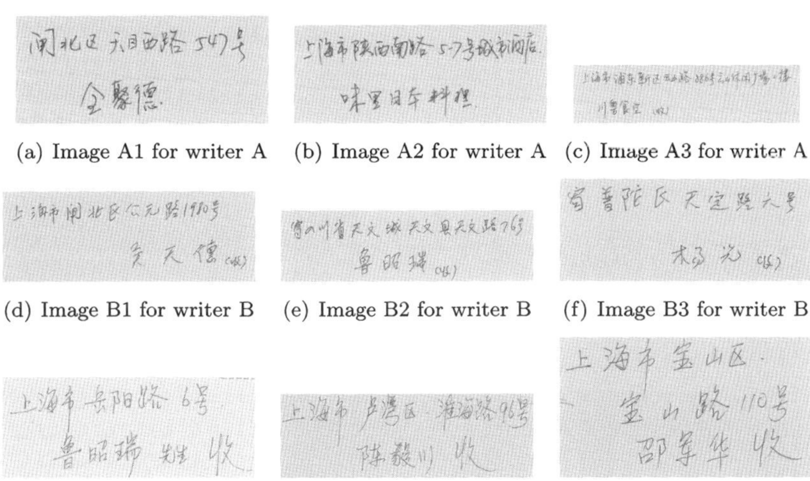

(a) Image A1 for writer A (b) Image A2 for writer A (c) Image A3 for writer A

(d) Image B1 for writer B (e) Image B2 for writer B (f) Image B3 for writer B

(g) Image C1 for writer C (h) Image C2 for writer C (i) Image C3 for writer C

Figure 8. Some mail address images from three writers.

that LPAIS is a more challenging dataset for the task of text-independent writer identification.

3.1. *Codebook size*

The size of the codebook has a significant impact on the performance of the modified SIFT. In this experiment, a range of codebook sizes are tested to find the optimal parameter of codebook size. For Set-A and Set-B, 100 samples of each reference set are used for codebook generation. Figure 9 shows that the Top-1 accuracy of identification is improved with the increasing of codebook size. When the codebook size is larger than 300, the accuracy drops slightly. So the codebook size is set equal to 300 in the following experiments.

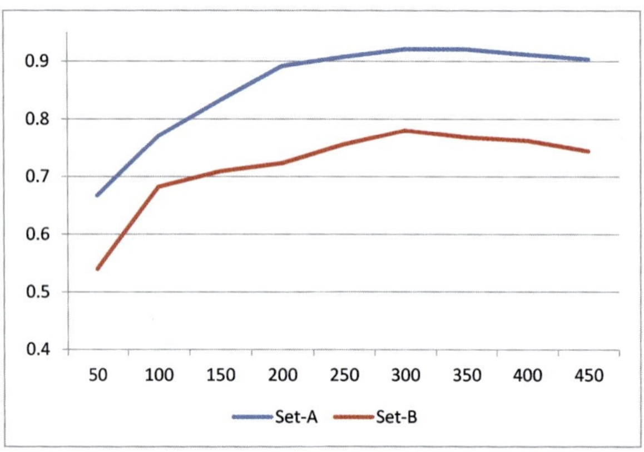

Figure 9. The identification (Top-1) performance with different codebook sizes.

3.2. *GMF vs. CDF*

Experiments are performed to validate the performance of the CDF. For each query, the distances between it and all references are calculated. The writer of the reference corresponding to the minimal distance is the most likely writer of the query. Figure 10 shows that the Top-1 accuracy and the Top-5 accuracy of the CDF are very close to those of the GMF on Set-A. When the number of writers becomes larger, the CDF performs better than the GMF on Set-B. It indicates that the CDF can be considered as an modification of the GMF, and its performance is more reliable.

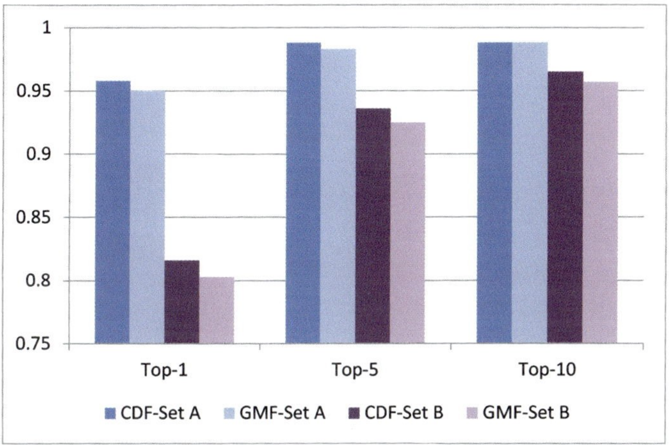

Figure 10. The identification performance comparison of the CDF and the GMF.

3.3. *SIFT vs. modified SIFT*

This experiments are used to compare the modified SIFT and the original SIFT. As shown in Figure 11, we observe that the performance of the modified SIFT method drops a lot in Set-B. The Top-1 accuracy drops from 92.1% to 78.0% and the Top-5 accuracy drops from 95.4% to 87.6%. These demonstrate that the modified SIFT is not very robust to the amount

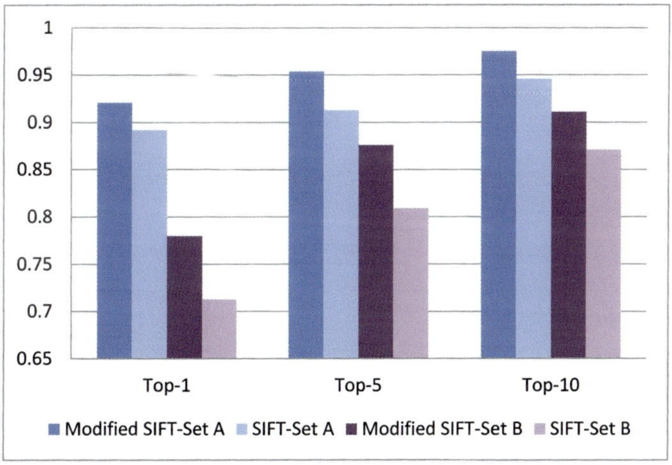

Figure 11. The identification performance comparison of the modified SIFT and SIFT.

of writers. However, the modified SIFT is much better than original SIFT on both datasets. It shows that the modified SIFT profits from the additional orientation information. The segmentation of character regions also improves the accuracy by reducing the redundant keypoints.

3.4. *Combination of the CDF and the modified SIFT*

Figures 12 and 13 show the performance of different features in two datasets. As shown in the both figures, compared with the sole CDF and the modified SIFT, the combination of both features dramatically improves the performance. It demonstrates that the proposed method can work well on the Chinese handwriting. Although the performance of the modified SIFT is not as good as that of the CDF, the fusion of them can improve the performance. The Top-1 accuracy grows from 95.4% to 96.2% and the Top-5 accuracy grows from 97.9% to 98.8% on Set-A. A possible reason is that the CDF and the modified SIFT characterize handwriting from different aspects, so the combination of the two features contributes to enhancing the performance effectively.

The results of some state-of-the-art methods on the same datasets are also provided for comparison. In Table 2, we compare the proposed method with four existing methods, the grid microstructure feature,[14] the edge-hinge distribution,[19] the multi-scale edge-hinge combinations[22] and the edge structure coding[17] on Set-A. For comparison, we also implement

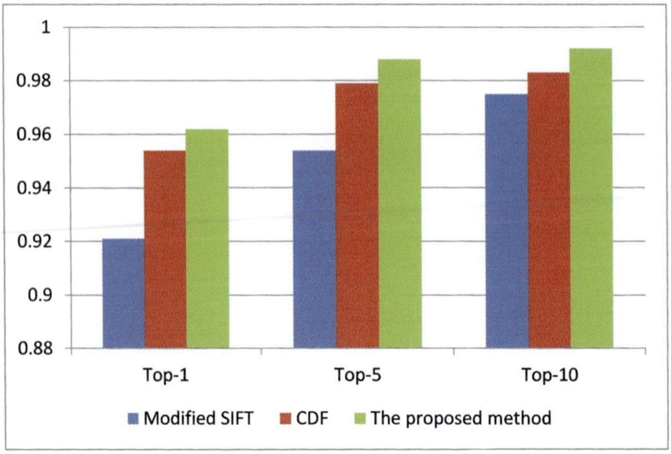

Figure 12. The identification performance of different features on Set-A.

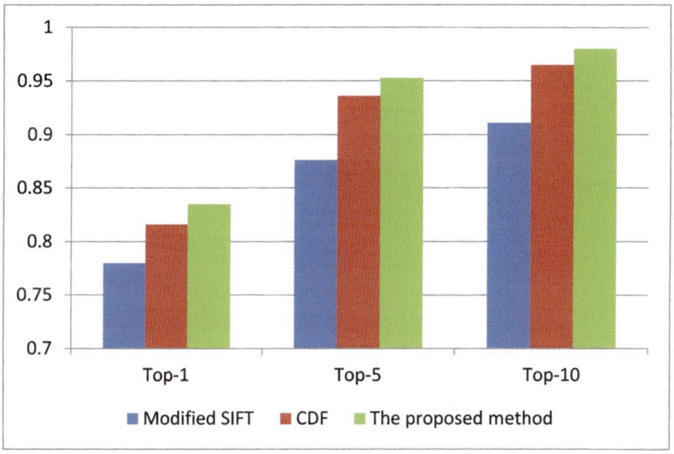

Figure 13. The identification performance of different features on Set-B.

the grid microstructure feature[14] on Set-B. The results in Table 3 show that the Top-1, Top-5 and Top-10 accuracy of the proposed method is better than that of the GMF.

Table 2. The Top-N performance of different methods on Set-A.

Methods \ Top-N	Top-1	Top-5	Top-10
Grid microstructure feature[14]	95.0%	98.3%	98.8%
Edge-hinge distribution[19]	91.7%	-	-
Edge-hinge combinations[22]	93.8%	-	-
Edge structure coding[17]	95.4%	-	-
The proposed method	**96.3%**	**98.8%**	**99.2%**

Table 3. The Top-N performance of different methods on Set-B.

Methods \ Top-N	Top-1	Top-5	Top-10
Grid microstructure feature[14]	80.3%	92.5%	95.7%
The proposed method	**83.5%**	**95.3%**	**98.0%**

To further investigate the robustness, the proposed method is tested on the LPAIS dataset. It is noted that mail address images of LPAIS have less characters and quite different layouts. Figure 14 shows the writer identification performance of different features on this dataset.

The Top-1 accuracy of the CDF is 92.5%, however the Top-1 accuracy of modified SIFT is 57.0%, and the combination of the CDF and the modified SIFT achieves only 89.0%. Compared with the sole CDF and the modified SIFT, the combination of both features dramatically degrades the performance. It indicates that the modified SIFT has adverse effect on the combination which leads to performance degradation. The reason for the poor performance of the modified SIFT is that there are too few characters in the mail address image. Essentially, the modified SIFT is based on the bag of visual words model. Without sufficient characters, we only extract few keypoints from the address image, which causes the frequency histogram of visual words cannot represent the characteristics of the writer any longer. Hence, the modified SIFT is less effective when the handwriting image only contains few characters.

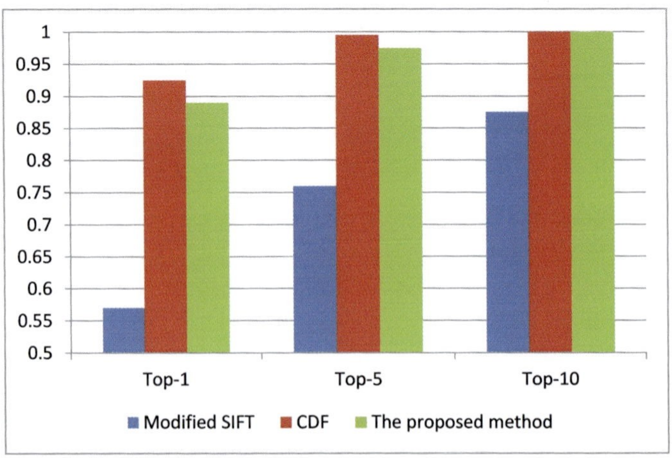

Figure 14. The identification performance of different features on LPAIS.

4. Conclusions

Biometrics is widely deployed to ensure the personal and public security in our daily life. Writer identification as a special case of behavioral biometrics is facing great challenges and chances. We concentrate on the particular issue of off-line text-independent Chinese writer identification, and propose a new method based on the contour-directional feature and the modified SIFT. Experiments on HIT-MW dataset demonstrate the effectiveness of the proposed method. The new concatenated feature is capable of reflecting the characteristic of handwriting appropriately. Experiments on LPAIS dataset also show the weakness of the modified SIFT when the number of characters is small. Without enough keypoints extracted from the handwriting image, the bag of visual words model based feature cannot provide a proper feature representation for the characteristics of individual writing style. In the feature, we will pay more attention to explore how to deal with the situation when the handwriting image contains few characters.

References

1. A. K. Jain, A. Ross and S. Pankanti, Biometrics: A tool for information security, *IEEE Trans. Information Forensics and Security*, **1**(2), 125–143 (2006).
2. R. Plamondon and S. N. Srihari, Online and off-line handwriting recognition: A comprehensive survey, *IEEE Trans. Pattern Analysis and Machine Intelligence*, **22**(1), 63–84 (2000).
3. M. L. Bulacu, Statistical Pattern Recognition for Automatic Writer Identification and Verification, Ph.D. thesis, University of Groningen, 2007.
4. X. Y. Zhang and C. L. Liu, Style transfer matrix learning for writer adaptation, in *Proceedings of the International Conference on Computer Vision and Pattern Recognition*, 2011, pp. 393–400.
5. M. L. Bulacu and L. Schomaker, Text-independent writer identification and verification using textural and allographic features, *IEEE Trans. Pattern Analysis and Machine Intelligence*, **29**(4), 701–717 (2007).
6. D. Impedovo and G. Pirlo, Automatic signature verification: The state of the art, *IEEE Trans. System, Man and Cybernetics, Part C: Applications and Reviews*, **38**(5), 609–635 (2008).
7. R. Plamondon and G. Lorette, Automatic signature verification and writer identification — The state of the art, *Pattern Recognition*, **22**(2), 107–131 (1989).
8. Y. Zhu, T. N. Tan and Y. H. Wang, Biometric personal identification based on handwriting, in *Proceedings of the International Conference on Pattern Recognition*, 2000, pp. 797–800.
9. C. Shen, X. G. Ruan and T. L. Mao, Writer identification using gabor wavelet, in *Proceedings of the World Congress on Intelligent Control and Automation*, 2002, pp. 2061–2064.
10. Z. Y. He and Y. Y. Tang, Chinese handwriting-based writer identification by texture analysis, in *Proceedings of the International Conference on Machine Learning and Cybernetics*, 2004, pp. 3488–3491.
11. Z. Y. He, X. G. You and Y. Y. Tang, Writer identification of Chinese handwriting documents using hidden markov tree model, *Pattern Recognition*, **41**(4), 1295–1307 (2008).
12. Z. Y. He, X. G. You and Y. Y. Tang, Writer identification using global wavelet-based features, *Neurocomputing*, **71**(10), 1832–1841 (2008).

13. J. J. Zhang, Z. Y. He, Y. M. Cheung and X. G. You, Writer identification using a hybrid method combining gabor wavelet and mesh fractal dimension, in *Proceedings of the International Conference on Intelligent Data Engineering and Automated Learning*, 2009, pp. 535–542.
14. X. Li and X. Q. Ding, Writer identification of Chinese handwriting using grid microstructure feature, in *Proceedings of the International Conference on Biometrics*, 2009, pp. 1230–1239.
15. G. Louloudis, N. Stamatopoulos and B. Gatos, ICDAR 2011 writer identification contest, in *Proceedings of the International Conference on Document Analysis and Recognition*, 2011, pp. 1475–1479.
16. L. Xu, X. Q. Ding, L. Peng and X. Li, An improved method based on weighted grid micro-structure feature for text-independent writer recognition, in *Proceedings of the International Conference on Document Analysis and Recognition*, 2011, pp. 638–642.
17. J. Wen, B. Fang, J. L. Chen, Y. Y. Tang and H. X. Chen, Fragmented edge structure coding for Chinese writer identification, *Neurocomputing*, **86**, 45–51 (2012).
18. Y. J. Hu, W. M. Yang and Y. B. Chen, Bag of features approach for offline text-independent Chinese writer identification, in *Proceedings of the International Conference on Image Processing*, 2004, pp. 2609–2613.
19. M. L. Bulacu, L. Schomaker and L. Vuurpijl, Writer identification using edge-based directional features, in *Proceedings of the International Conference on Document Analysis and Recognition*, 2003, pp. 937–941.
20. D. G. Lowe, Distinctive image features from scale-invariant keypoints, *International Journal of Computer Vision*, **60**(2), 91–110 (2004).
21. T. H. Su, T. W. Zhang and D. J. Guan, Corpus-based HIT-MW database for offline recognition of general purpose Chinese handwritten text, *International Journal on Document Analysis Recognition*, **10**(1), 27–38 (2007).
22. L. Van Der Maaten and E. Postma, Improving automatic writer identification, in *Proceedings of the Belgium-Netherlands Conference on Artificial Intelligence*, 2005, pp. 260–266.

Chapter 9

Chinese Word Segmentation, Syntactic Parsing and Discourse Analysis

Man Lan and Yuanbin Wu*

Department of Computer Science and Technology,
Shanghai Key Laboratory of Multidimensional Information Processing,
East China Normal University, Shanghai, P.R. China 200241
mlan@cs.ecnu.edu.cn, ybwu@cs.ecnu.edu.cn

This chapter covers several key components of Chinese Natural Language Processing (NLP). Firstly, two fundamental tasks in Chinese NLP are introduced, i.e., Chinese word segmentation and parsing. Then, discourse analysis is described as an intermediate application of the two aforementioned fundamental components, which benefits many downstream NLP applications.

1. Chinese Word Segmentation

Word segmentation is a task of dividing plain texts (sentences, passages) into words. In English and many other languages, white spaces are often good indicators of adjacent words. In Chinese, however, the basic meaningful units in texts are characters rather than words, and there are no special word delimiters in texts. Word segmentation is an initial step for most Chinese natural language processing tasks, such as part-of-speech (POS) tagging, syntactic parsing. The quality of the segmented words plays a fundamental role in those downstream applications.

In this section, we first give the definition of Chinese word segmentation task, then introduce the sequential labelling formulation, which is the dominant algorithm for solving the problem, finally we briefly give some closely related topics including joint learning of segmentation and global (high order) features.

---

*The two authors made equal contributions to this chapter.

1.1. *The problem*

Table 1 is an example Chinese sentence:

Table 1. An example Chinese sentence.

今	晚	长	安	街	流	光	溢	彩	.	
c_1	c_2	c_3	c_4	c_5	c_6	c_7	c_8	c_9	c_{10}	c_{11}

Each c_i is a Chinese character: $c_1 =$ 今 (means "now"), $c_2 =$ 晚 (means "night"), ..., etc. The adjacent characters could be grouped into words. For example, the combination of $c_1 c_2 =$ 今晚 is a word (means "tonight"). The word segmentation task takes a sentence (sequence of characters) as input, tries to group its characters and outputs a sequence of words. Table 2 is the word segmented sentence of the above example:

Table 2. The segmented sentences.

今晚	的	长安街	流光溢彩	.
w_1	w_2	w_3	w_4	w_5

Formally, we define an input $x = c_1, c_2, \ldots, c_n$ as a Chinese character sequence, the word segmentation task aims to output a word sequence $y = h(x) = w_1, w_2, \ldots, w_m$, where each w_j is a non-empty continuous subsequence of x.

1.2. *Methods*

To tackle the problem, the first proposal might be using a Chinese word dictionary. However, this simple method fails for the cases that multiple segmentation results are possible. For example, a text "今天下雨" has two possible outputs: "今天␣下雨" (today raining) and "今␣天下␣雨" (now world rain). It is hard to decide which is the more proper one if we only look at the dictionary.

The difficulty could be overcame with the help of human annotations. By building large corpus of segmented sentences and using data-driven methods, researchers can develop word segmentation systems with relatively high accuracies (95% F-value). Next, we will introduce the sequential labelling formulation, which is the dominant method for the Chinese word segmentation task.

First, we encode a word sequence with a "label" sequence. Denote that "B" indicates a begin of a word, "I" indicates inside of a word, "E" indicates the end of a word and "S" indicates a word with only one character. With the notation, the segmentation result of our running example can be represented by a equivalent "BIES" sequence (Table 3).

Table 3. Segmentation with "BIES".

今晚	的	长安街	流光溢彩	.
BE	S	BIE	BIIE	S

Sequential labelling is a machine leaning task which takes an input $x \in X$, outputs a label sequence $y = y_1, y_2, \cdots, y_n \in Y(x)$, where $y_i \in S, \forall 1 \leq i \leq n$, S is called the label set. Obviously, Chinese word segmentation could be considered as a sequential labelling task with $S = \{\text{B, I, E, S}\}$. Two popular models are often used: conditional random field and structural support vector machine. In fact, they are two important models for a more general machine learning task, called *structured prediction*. We will briefly introduce the two models in the following two subsections.

1.2.1. *Two sequential labelling models*

Conditional random field (CRF) is an undirected graphical model with a simple chain structure[1] (Figure 1).

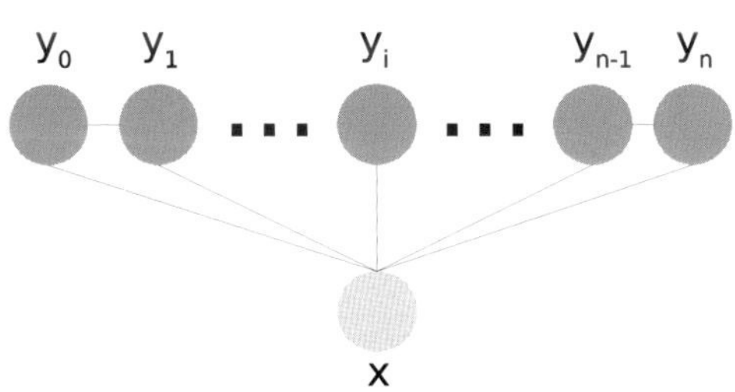

Figure 1. Conditional random field.

CRF models the conditional probability $p(y|x)$ by exponential-family distributions:

$$p(y|x)= \frac{1}{Z(x)} \exp\{w^{\mathsf{T}}\varphi(x,y)\}$$
$$= \frac{1}{Z(x)} \exp\left\{\sum_{i=1}^{n} w^{\mathsf{T}}\varphi(x,y_i,y_{i-1})\right\}, \quad (1)$$

where w is the model parameter, $\varphi(x,y_i,y_{i-1}) : X \times S \times S \mapsto \mathsf{R}^d$ is a feature function which maps the input sequence and possible adjacent label combinations to a d dimensional vector space, and $Z(x)$ is the normalizer

$$Z(x) = \sum_{y\in Y} \exp\left\{\sum_{i=}^{n} w^{\mathsf{T}}\varphi(x,y_i,y_{i-1})\right\}.$$

Structural support vector machine (Structural SVM) is a large margin classifier.[2,3] By considering the output $y \in Y$ as a class label of x, we could define the concept of margin like the multi-class SVM:

$$\gamma(x,y,\hat{y},w) \triangleq w^{\mathsf{T}} \left(\varphi(x,y) - \varphi(x,\hat{y})\right),$$

Given a training set $\{(x_j,y_j)\}_{j=1}^{N}$, the structural SVM is the following optimization problem:

$$\begin{aligned} \min.\ & \frac{1}{2}\|w\|^2 + \sum_{j=1}^{N} \xi_j \\ \text{s.t. } & \gamma(x_j,y_j,\hat{y}_j,w) \geq l(x_j,y_j,\hat{y}_j) - \xi_j, \forall j, \forall \hat{y} \in Y(x) \\ & \xi_j \geq 0, \forall j \end{aligned}$$

where $l(x,y,\hat{y})$ is a loss function measuring the different between two output sequences. An example of $l(x,y,\hat{y})$ is the Hamming loss:

$$l(x,y,\hat{y}) = \sum_{i=1}^{n} \mathbb{I}(y_i \neq \hat{y}_i),$$

where the indicator function $\mathbb{I}(x) = 1$ if x is true, 0 otherwise.

1.2.2. *Feature functions*

In both CRF and Structural SVM, the feature function $\varphi(x,y_i,y_{i-1})$ only depends on two adjacent unobserved labels y_i, y_{i-1}. This decomposition assumption (also known as the first order Markov assumption) makes learning and inference of the sequential labelling problems tractable (see the following section on inference).

Another fact about the feature is that the dimension d of $\varphi(x, y_i, y_{i-1})$ is often very high. For example, an entry of the vector could be

$$\varphi_k(x, y_i, y_{i-1}) = \begin{cases} 1 \text{ if } \ x_i = c \ \text{ and } \ y_i = \text{“B”} \ \text{ and } \ y_{i-1} = \text{“E”} \\ 0 \text{ otherwise} \end{cases}$$

where c is a Chinese character. Note that, for every possible character in the dictionary V, there is a corresponding entry (i.e., the dimension of the feature vector $d = O(|V|)$). Table 4 lists typical feature functions in Chinese word segmentation.

Table 4. Feature functions for Chinese word segmentation.

Name	Description	Example
x_i	current character	安
x_{i-1}	character at position $i-1$	长
x_{i-2}	character at position $i-2$	的
x_{i+1}	character at position $i+1$	街
x_{i+2}	character at position $i+2$	流
x_{i-2}, x_{-1}	character bigram at position $i-2$	长安
x_{i-1}, x_i	character bigram at position $i-1$	的长
x_i, x_{i+1}	character bigram at position i	安街
x_{i+1}, x_{i+2}	character bigram at position $i+1$	街流

The “Example” column contains the fired features at position $i = 5$ of the sentence in example 1.

1.2.3. *Inference*

An important problem in Chinese word segmentation (also in other sequential labelling problems) is, given the model parameter w, how to find the “best” word sequence for an input. Here, the “best” means that an output with the highest weighted sum of features. Formally, define *inference* to be a function

$$h(x) = \arg\max_{y \in Y(x)} w^\intercal \varphi(x, y) \tag{2}$$

$$= \arg\max_{y \in Y(x)} \sum_{i=1}^{n} w^\intercal \varphi(x, y_i, y_{i-1}). \tag{3}$$

Inference plays a key role in parameter estimation and prediction. For example, in CRF, the MAP (maximum *a posteriori*) estimation exactly equals to computing $h(x)$, and in structural SVM the margin constraints can be rewritten using $h(x)$:

$$\gamma(x_j, y_j, \hat{y}_j, w) \geq l(x_j, y_j, \hat{y}_j) - \xi_j, \quad \forall j, \forall \hat{y} \in Y(x)$$

$$\Leftrightarrow \gamma(x_j, y_j, h'(x_j), w) \geq l(x_j, y_j, h'(x_j)) - \xi_j, \quad \forall j,$$

where $h'(x)$ is a loss augmented inference problem:

$$h'(x_j) = \arg \max_{y \in Y(x_j)} w^\mathsf{T} \varphi(x_j, y_j) + l(x_j, y_j, y).$$

Different from binary and multi-class classification, the computation of $h(x)$ in Equation 2 is not trivial. Naive enumerating all y is impossible since the size of $Y(x)$ is huge (for a sentence x and the "BIES" tag set, $|Y(x)| = 4^{|x|}$). In order to make the inference problem tractable, one needs to take some independent assumptions. Here, we mainly focus on the first order Markov assumption (Equation 3), with which the problem of computing $h(x)$ equals to find the longest path in a lattice (Figure 2), and can be solved efficiently by the dynamic programming (the Viterbi algorithm, see Figure 3).

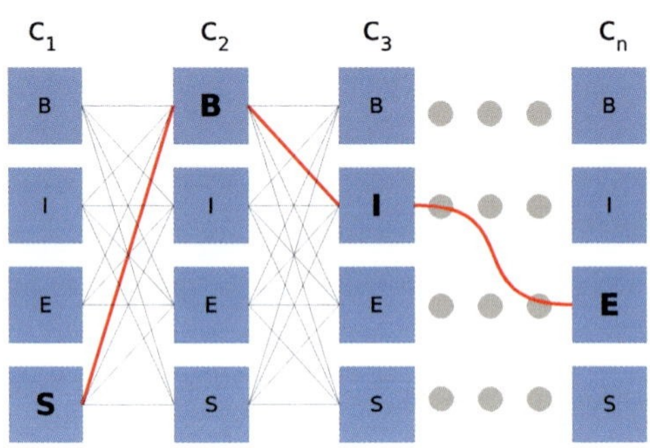

Figure 2. The inference algorithm equals to find the longest path in a lattice.

Updates

$$\text{score}(i, t) = \max_{s \in S} (\text{score}(i-1, s) + w^\mathsf{T} \varphi(x, y_i = t, y_{i-1} = s))$$

$$\text{prev}(i, t) = \arg\max_{s \in S} (\text{score}(i-1, s) + w^\mathsf{T} \varphi(x, y_i = t, y_{i-1} = s))$$

Initial values

$$\text{score}(0, t) = \max_{s \in S} w^\mathsf{T} \varphi(x, y_0 = t, y_{-1} = 0), \forall t \in S$$

Outputs

$$y_n = \arg\max_{t \in S} \text{score}(y_n = t), \quad y_{i-1} = \text{prev}(i, y_i)$$

Figure 3. Dynamic programming of the Viterbi algorithm.

1.3. *Related tasks*

As mentioned at the start of this section, Chinese word segmentation is the very first step for many Chinese natural processing tasks. Because of its importance, many works try to improve both its performance and efficiency. We briefly introduce two related research directions: global features and joint learning with other tasks.

1.3.1. *Global features*

Like other data-driven methods, features are crucial in Chinese word segmentation task. We have introduced features based on the adjacent y_i, y_{i-1} labels. The model is also called *character-based method*, since the features only rely on the labels of adjacent characters. Obviously, this first order Markov assumption might be strong in practice since the current label y_i could depend on more distant labels rather than y_{i-1}. Hence, one could involve the so-called "p-order" Markov assumption which allows the features $\varphi(x, y_i, y_{i-1}, y_{i-2}, \ldots, y_{i-p})$. At the same time, the same dynamic programming inference can be adapted (with more computation time).

On the other hand, a main problem of character-based model is it is hard to encode features such as "what is the previous *word* before position i". Such features are "global" in the sense that they could depend on any label in the sentence. Models involving this kind of features are called *word-based method*.[4] Inference with global features are intractable, and approximate inference algorithms (like beam search) are inevitable. Both character-based and word-based methods have their own advantages, and there are works trying to combine the power of the two.[5]

1.3.2. *Joint learning*

Like other pipeline systems, errors from word segmentation results could propagate to following tasks. To prevent the "garbage in garbage out" problem, one could try to do Chinese word segmentation and other NLP tasks simultaneously. For example, joint segmentation with part-of-speech tagging. The main motivation behind is that while the POS tagging is based on the result of segmentation, POS features could also help to get a more accurate segmentation sequence. The mutual enforcements among different NLP tasks attract a lot of research interests. Works related to Chinese word segmentations include Refs. 6, 7.

2. Chinese Syntactic Parsing

For a natural language sentence, syntactic parsing is a task which aims to recover a sentence from a set of compositional rules. The set of all possible rule is called a "grammar", and the rules generating a sentence are called a "derivation" of the sentence. A derivation basically describes how the words and phrases are syntactically related.

Different from programming languages, which are overall unambiguous, natural language sentences are usually ambiguous and have multiple interpretations. A syntactic parser needs to determine which one is the correct derivation. For Chinese, which is inherently more ambiguous than English, recovering the best derivation is even harder (see the following discussions).

In this section, we empirically introduce two widely-used Chinese syntactic parsing paradigms: constituent parsing and dependency parsing.

2.1. *Constituent parsing*

Constituent parsing parses a sentence into recursive phrase structures using a context free grammar. The output of parsing is a constituent tree (also called phrase structure tree). Figure 4 contains an example of Chinese constituent tree.

There are two kinds of nodes in the tree: non-terminal nodes (internal nodes) and terminal nodes (leave nodes). Terminal nodes are simply words in the sentence (for example, "中资" (Chinese companies), "澳门" (Marcau)). A non-terminal node corresponds to a phrase in the sentence, which is recursively defined by smaller phrases. For instance, the noun phrase "澳门最大的外来投资者" dominates four sub-phrases (NP, "澳门" (Marcau)), (DNP, "最大的" (largest)), (ADJP, "外来" (foreign)) and (NP, "投资者" (investors)).

To illustrate the ambiguity of the parsing, we borrow an example (NP-NP modification) from[8] (Figure 5). The ambiguity is about how different sub-phrases composite a compound noun phrase (flat or hierarchical). In the example, two possible parse trees are shown.

Because of the existence of ambiguities, existing constituent parsers always parse with a probabilistic context free grammar (PCFG), rather than the usual CFG. A PCFG assigns a probability mass function on the grammar, and a parser will try to find the best (i.e. the highest probability) parse tree among all legal candidates.

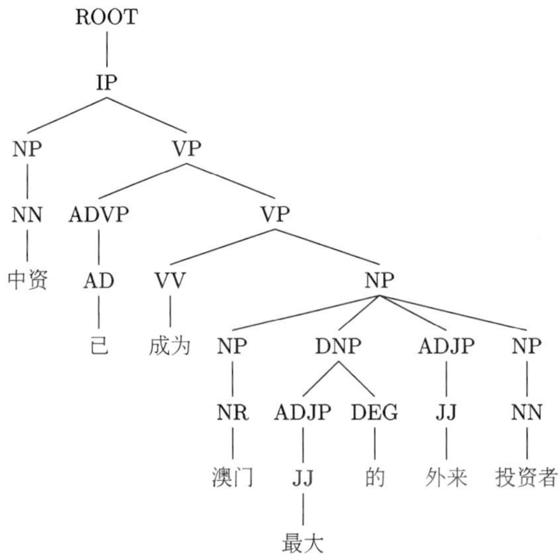

Figure 4. Example of a Chinese constituent parse tree. The sentence is "中资 (Chinese companies) 已 (have already) 成为 (been) 澳门 (Macau) 最大 (largest) 的 ('s) 外来 (foreign) 投资者 (investors)".

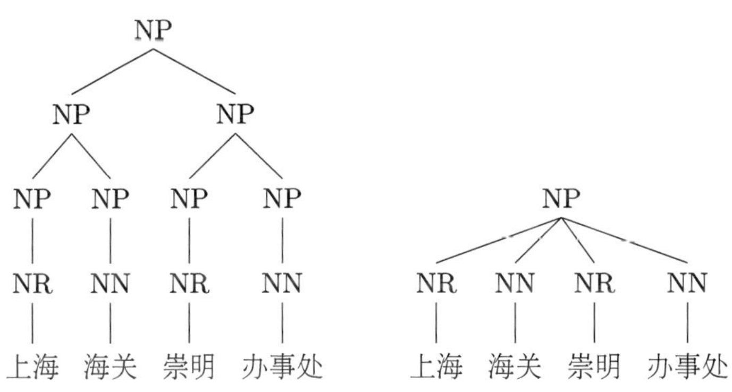

Figure 5. Two constituent trees for a same noun phrase "上海 (Shanghai) 海关 (customs) 崇明 (Chongming) 办事处 (office)".

Formally, a PCFG is defined by a quintuple $G = (M, T, R, S, P)$[a]

- M is the set of non-terminal symbols
- T is the set of terminal symbols

[a]https://en.wikipedia.org/wiki/Stochastic_context-free_grammar.

- R is the set of production rules
- S is the start symbol
- P is the set of probabilities on production rules.

The probability of a parse tree is defined to be the product of probabilities on the rules in its derivation.

We say a PCFG is in Chomsky normal form (CNF) if all production rules in R are either $A \to BC$ or $A \to \alpha$, where $A, B, C \in M, \alpha \in T$.

Given a PCFG in CNF, a sentence $x_1, x_2, \ldots, x_n$ can be parsed by the CYK algorithm, which is a dynamic programming. Specifically, we define $u(i, j, A)$ as the best (partial) parse tree of $x_i, x_{i+1}, \ldots, x_j$, with non-terminal A at root. The CYK algorithm is described in Figure 6.

Updates

$$u(i, j, A) = \max_{\substack{A \to BC \in R \\ i \le k < j}} u(i, k, B) \times u(k+1, j, C) \times p(A \to BC)$$

Initial values

$$u(i, i, A) = p(A \to x_i) \text{ if } A \to x_i \in R; 0 \text{ otherwise.}$$

Outputs

$$\arg\max_{A \in M} u(1, n, A)$$

Figure 6. The CYK algorithm.

2.2. *Dependency parsing*

Dependency grammar is another popular syntactic relation formulation. In the grammar, syntactic structures are expressed by binary relations among lexical items (words). A binary relation (h, d, l) is asymmetric and labelled, where h is the head word, d is the dependent word, l is the label of the relation. h is called the parent of d. The relations form a rooted directed tree (i.e., for each word, there is only one parent and all relations should be connected and acyclic). Figure 7 is the dependency tree of the sentence in Figure 4. In the tree, the relation (成为, 中资, nsubj) reads “中资” is the nominal subject of “成为”.

Compared with constituent parsing, the dependency parsing doesn't distinguish terminal and non-terminal nodes. The syntactic structures are

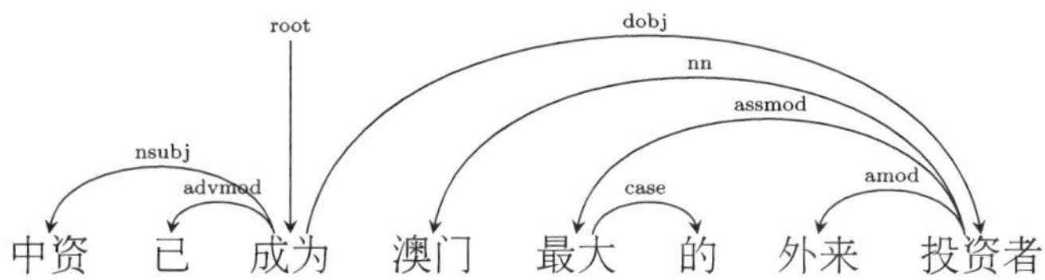

Figure 7. An example of dependency tree.

expressed by binary relations and labels. On the other hand, unlike the constituent parsing, there is no explicit phrase structure in dependency trees.

The parsing algorithms for dependency grammar include CYK-style models, transition-based models and graph-based models. CYK-style models are basically dynamic programming algorithms which are pioneered by Jason Eisner,[9] and followed by works such as Refs. 10, 11. Transition-based models define transition systems which build the dependency trees incrementally. An example of such algorithms is the shift reduce dependency parsing.[12,13] Graph-based models consider all possible dependency edges for a sentence, and output the best subgraph (tree). An example of such algorithms is the maximum spanning tree parsing.[14,15]

3. Discourse Relation Recognition

A discourse relation (or *rhetorical* relation), such as *Contrast* and *Cause*, between two segments of textual units expresses how they are logically/semantically connected to one another. Unlike previous study on semantic relation between words or phrases, discourse relation recognition is considered a crucial step for the ability to properly interpret or produce discourse. It can be of great benefit to a wide range of downstream NLP applications, such as question answering (QA),[16] text summarization,[17] information extraction (IE),[18] machine translation (MT),[19] sentiment analysis[20] and text generation,[21] etc. For example, in QA system, detecting *Cause* relation in text can help to answer *Why* question. Besides, recognizing *Restatement* relation is useful for document summarization.

3.1. *A taxonomy of discourse relations*

Discourse relation can sometimes be marked lexically by words and expressions (i.e., cue words) in the texts, such as *but* or *since*. For example[b], *because* and 因而 indicate *Contingency* relations in E1 and E2. In this case, the discourse relation and connectives are named as *explicit discourse relation* and *explicit discourse connectives* (known as *discourse markers*).

(**E1**) Longer maturities are thought to indicate declining interest rates **because** they permit portfolio managers to retain relatively higher rates for a longer period.

(**E2**) 实现保证金台帐制度后，[海关对正常开展加工贸易的企业不再征收与进口料件税款等值的风险保证金，只是在银行设立台帐时收取一百元的手续费]_$Arg1$， **因而** [将减轻企业的实际经济负担]_$Arg2$。

However, connectives are sometimes absent between sentences. In E3, *for instance* does not appear in real text, but it can be manually inserted by annotator into the text to express the *Expansion* relation between sentences without any redundancy[c]. Similarly, in E4, 然而 does not exist in real text and it can be manually inserted into the text to express the *Contrast* relation between two adjacent sentences. In this case, the discourse relation and the discourse connectives are called as *implicit discourse relation* and *implicit discourse connectives*, respectively.

(**E3**) Typically, money-fund yields beat comparable short-term investments because portfolio managers can vary maturities and go after the highest rates. [**for instance**] The top money funds are currently yielding well over 9%.

(**E4**) [五年前，中国的数字电话程控交换机市场为多种品牌的外国产品垄断，我们还担心中国能不能研制成功数字程控交换机]_$Arg1$。[然而] [如今国产的高性能电话程控交换机已占国内市场份额的百分之三十六]_$Arg2$。

As discussed in Ref. 24, although explicit discourse connectives may have two types of ambiguity, i.e., one is discourse or non-discourse usage ("*once*" can be either a temporal connective or a word meaning "formerly"), the other is discourse relation sense ambiguity ("*since*" can serve as either a

[b]The examples in this section are from guidelines in Refs. 22 and 23.

[c]According to the PDTB Annotation Manual,[22] if the insertion of connective leads to "redundancy", the relation is annotated as Alternative lexicalizations (AltLex), not implicit.

temporal or causal connective), their study shows that for explicit discourse relations in Penn Discourse Treebank (PDTB) corpus, the most general 4 senses, i.e., Comparison (Comp.), Contingency (Cont.), Temporal (Temp.) and Expansion (Exp.), can be easily addressed by the presence of discourse connectives and a simple method only considering the sense frequency of connectives can achieve more than 90% accuracy. This indicates the importance of connectives for discourse relation recognition.

However, without the information provided by explicit connectives, the task of implicit discourse relation classification has become quite a challenge.[25] Furthermore, in real world texts, discourse connectives are often missing between sentences. Actually, almost half the sentences in the British National Corpus have no discourse connective entirely.[26] Among a total of 40,600 annotated relations in PDTB, 16,053 (40%) are annotated as implicit discourse relation.[22] A recent work[27] on Chinese implicit discourse relations showed that approximately 80% Chinese texts hold implicit discourse between sentences or clauses. Therefore, improving the performance of implicit relation classification is the key to the overall performance of discourse relation analysis. In recent years, a multitude of efforts have been employed to solve this task. One approach is to exploit various linguistically informed features extracted from human-annotated corpora in a supervised framework, for example, work in Refs. 25, 28–31. Another approach is to perform recognition without human annotated corpora by creating synthetic examples of implicit relations in an unsupervised way.[32] Our recent study[33] has presented a multi-task learning framework to integrate the human-annotated corpora and synthetic examples to address the shortage of implicit examples to further improve the performance of discourse recognition.

3.2. *Discourse corpora*

The earlier work has performed discourse relation classification on unlabeled data. For example, Ref. 32 proposed an unsupervised method to recognize discourse relations, i.e., *Contrast*, *Explanation-evidence*, *Condition* and *Elaboration*, between two arbitrary segments of text. They used unambiguous patterns to generate synthetic implicit discourse relation data set from unlabeled data automatically. Based on the work of Ref. 32, some studies attempted to extend the work to improve the performance of relation classification.[26,34,35]

Later, the research work was to use human-annotated corpora as training data, e.g., the RST Bank[36] annotated based on Rhetorical Structure Theory[37] and used by Ref. 38, adhoc annotations used by Refs. 39 and 40, and the GraphBank[41] used by Ref. 42.

In 2008, with the release of the Penn Discourse TreeBank (PDTB),[43] this hand-annotated corpus has become a new benchmark data set and has been widely used for discourse relation classification by researchers.[25,28,44] PDTB is an open-domain corpus of discourse relation, which contains 2,312 Wall Street Journal articles and it is the largest corpora of discourse relation so far. Moreover, it is the first annotation framework that follows the lexically grounded, predicate-argument approach, as proposed in Webber's framework.[45] Given a sentence pair, annotators of PDTB checked whether one of the following relations holds, i.e., Explicit, Implicit, AltLex, EntRel and NoRel. The first three types, i.e., Explicit, Implicit, and AltLex relations are annotated as discourse relations, whereas the EntRel and NoRel are grouped as non-discourse relations. In PDTB, the tag set of senses is organized hierarchically with three levels, i.e., *class*, *type* and *subtype*. The *class* level contains four major semantic classes: Comparison, Contingency, Expansion and Temporal. For each class, a second level of up to 16 types is defined to provide finer semantic distinctions. For example, there are six types defined under the Expansion class: Conjunction, Instantiation, Restatement, Alternative, Exception, and List. A third level of subtypes is defined to specify the semantic contribution of each argument. However, only 9 out of the 16 types are refined into subtypes.

The PDTB style annotation benefits the researchers with a large discourse annotated corpora, using a comprehensive scheme for both implicit and explicit relations, even in other domains. For example, BioDRB[46] is a biomedical domain corpus of discourse relation, which adapts the annotation framework of PDTB. It has 24 articles selected from GENIA corpus.[47] Different from PDTB, BioDRB only has a two-level tagset of sense.

More recently, the Chinese Discourse TreeBank (CDTB) 0.5 (LDC2014T21) developed at Brandeis University as part of the Chinese Treebank Project has been released in 2014, which consists of approximately 5,500 annotation instances (73,000 words) of Chinese newswire text annotated for discourse relation.[23] The texts are selected from the newswire material in Chinese Treebank (CTB) 8.0 (LDC2013T21), specifically, from Xinhua News Agency stories. Although CDTB followed the PDTB style, there are several differences between their annotations. Firstly, CDTB only has three types of relations annotated in corpus: Explicit, Implicit and AltLex. Secondly, different from PDTB with a three-level hierarchy of multiple relation senses, CDTB has only 10 relation senses without hierarchy: Alternative, Causation, Conditional, Conjunction, Contrast, Expansion, Purpose, Temporal, EntRel and NoRel. Thirdly, unlike in PDTB in the case of Explicit connectives, where Arg2 is always the argument to which the connective is syntactically bound, in CDTB the relative positions of Arg1 and Arg2 in Explicit relation are dependent on the relation sense rather than the position of explicit connective. Fourthly, PDTB only annotated the discourse relations between sentences within one paragraph, whereas in CDTB the implicit relation can be hold across paragraphs.

Due to the difference between English and Chinese language, the annotation procedure of CDTB is different from that of PDTB. For example, since there are many punctuations in one Chinese sentence to indicate discourse relations between text spans, it is important to use them as potential indicators to indicate discourse relations. The annotation procedure of CDTB is briefly described as follows (refer to CDTB *Discourse Annotation Guidelines*).

(1) scan the text for punctuations (pause marks (顿号), commas, periods, colons, semi-colons, ellipses, exclamation points, and question marks) and judge for each punctuation whether there is a discourse relation;
(2) identify whether the relation type is one of Explicit, Implicit and AltLex;
(3) identify the relation sense;
(4) identify the order of Arg1 and Arg2. Note that the order is dependent on the sense of the relation rather than the discourse connectives, which is specified as in Table 5;
(5) label argument span;
(6) identify Attribution/meta-expressions. The attribution reveals sources of information being reported and the meta-expressions conveys author's attitudes, actions, opinions etc. with respect to the information being reported.

Meanwhile, following PDTB and RST theory, another recent work in Refs. 48 and 27 build their own manually-annotated Chinese discourse treebank (CDTB), which consists of 158 newswire documents (chtb0001 – chtb0130, and chtb0211 – chtb0240) selected from Chinese Treebank (CTB) 6.0. This corpus consists of approximate 739 paragraphs and 3,398 sentences, which hold 453 explicit relations and 1,878 implicit relations. Clearly, unlike the balanced distribution of explicit and implicit relations

Table 5. The order of arguments for each sense of discourse relations in CDTB.

Sense	Arg1	Arg2
Alternative		或者
Causation	因为	所以
Conditional	如果	就
Conjunction		而且/另外
Contrast	虽然	但是
Expansion	综上所述	例如
Progression	不仅	还
Purpose	通过	还
Restatement		换言之
Temporal	在 ... 之后/text order	在 ... 之前/text order
EntRel/NoRel	text order	

in English, the implicit relations dominate discourse relations in Chinese (about 80%). Similar with the three-level hierarchy of relation senses in PDTB, the first level consists of four semantic classes: Causality, Coordination, Transition and Explanation. For each class, a second level of seventeen types is defined to provide finer semantic distinctions. For example, there are six types defined under the Causality class: Causality, Inference, Presumption, Purpose, Condition and Context. A third level is defined as discourse connective to connect the arguments. Figure 8 depicts the statistical distribution of implicit relations in their corpus, which is borrowed from Ref. 27.

第一层	第二层	第三层	训练实例(所占比例/%)	测试实例(所占比例/%)
因果类	因果关系；推断关系；假设关系；目的关系；条件关系；背景关系	因此，所以，因为，由于……，如果……那么	297 (18.10)	67 (28.27)
转折类	转折关系；让步关系	虽然……但，即使……也	17 (1.04)	7 (2.95)
并列类	并列关系；顺承关系；递进关系；选择关系；对比关系	同时，并，并且，然后	979 (59.66)	123 (51.90)
解说类	解说关系；总分关系；例证关系；评价关系	总之，例如	348 (21.2)	40 (16.88)
总和			1641	237

Figure 8. Distribution of implicit relations in CDTB corpus.

Several previous work performed discourse relation classification on the first-level sense in PDTB.[24,25,30,31,33,49] Others presented classification on the second-level as the first-level is thought to be too coarse to be applied to other NLP tasks.[50]

3.3. *The general flowchart of discourse parser*

An end-to-end discourse parser is given free texts as input and returns discourse relations in a PDTB style, where a connective acts as a predicate that takes two text spans as its arguments. Previous work[50] constructed a full parser on the top of several subtasks, which contained multiple components joined in a sequential pipeline architecture including a connective classifier, argument labeler, explicit classifier, non-explicit classifier, and attribution span labeler. The extraction of exact argument spans and Non-Explicit sense identification have been shown to be the main challenges of the discourse parsing.[50] Following their framework, our recent work[44] presented a refined end-to-end discourse parser and achieved the best performance on all components in discourse parser released by CoNLL 2015 shared task. Figure 9 shows the general framework of our refined end-to-end discourse parser.

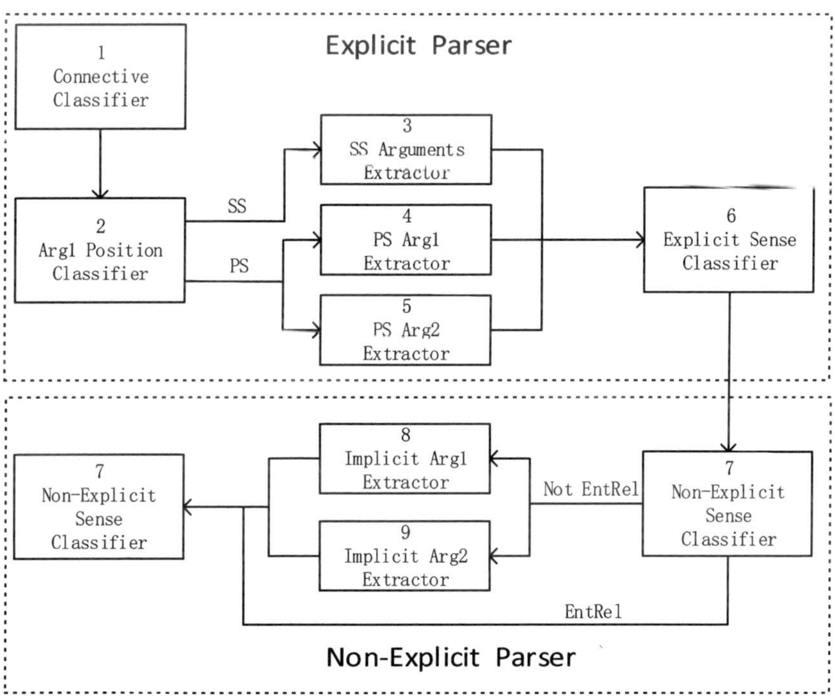

Figure 9. System pipeline for the discourse parser.

The discourse parser is designed as a sequential pipeline and consists of 9 components listed as follows.

First, for texts with Explicit connective words:

(1) **Connective Classifier** is to identify the discourse connectives from non-discourse ones.

(2) **Arg1 Position Classifier** is to decide the relative position of Arg1 — whether it is located within the same sentence as the connective (SS) or in some previous sentence of the connective (PS).

(3) **SS Arguments Extractor** is to extract the spans of Arg1 and Arg2 in the SS case.

In the PS case, we build two extractors to identify the text spans for PS Arg1 and PS Arg2 respectively.

(4) **PS Arg1 Extractor** is to extract Arg1 for PS.

(5) **PS Arg2 Extractor** is to extract Arg2 for PS.

(6) **Explicit Sense Classifier** is to identify the sense that this Explicit connective conveys.

Second, for all adjacent sentence pairs within each paragraph, but not identified in any Explicit relation:

(7) **Non-Explicit Sense Classifier** is to classify the sense of each sentence pair into one of the Non-Explicit relation senses.

Since attribution is not annotated for EntRel relations, if the output of the above Non-Explict sense classifier is EntRel, we regard the previous sentence as Arg1 and the next one as Arg2. Otherwise, we build the following two argument extractors to label Arg1 and Arg2.

(8) **Implicit Arg1 Extractor** and (9) **Implicit Arg2 Extractor** extract Arg1 and Arg2 for Non-EntRel relations in Non-explicit respectively.

The detailed descriptions of these components and feature engineering of this refined parser are presented in the following several subsections.

3.4. *Explicit discourse relations*

3.4.1. *Connective classifier and explicit sense classifier*

Since the input of the parser is free raw text, the first thing is to identify all connective occurrences in text, and then to use the connective classifier to decide whether they function as discourse connectives or not.

For each connective occurrence C, we extract features from its context, part-of-speech (POS) and the parse tree of the connective's sentence. Note that $prev_1$ and $next_1$ indicate the first previous word and the first next word of connective C respectively. For a node in the parse tree, we use the POS combinations of the node, its parent, its children to represent the *linked context.*

The features used for connective classification consist of the following: (1) Pitler's: *C string* (case-sensitive), *self-category, parent-category, left-sibling-category, right-sibling-category*, C-Syn interaction (the pairwise interaction features between the connective C and each category feature (i.e., self-category, parent-category, left-sibling-category, right-sibling-category)), Syn-Syn interaction (the interaction features between pairs of category features); (2) Lin's: C POS, $prev_1 + C$ string, $prev_1$ POS, $prev_1$ POS + C POS, C string + $next_1$, $next_1$ POS, C POS + $next_1$ POS, path of C's parent $\rightarrow$ root, compressed path of C's parent $\rightarrow$ root; (3) our three newly proposed features: the POS tags of nodes from C's parent $\rightarrow$ root, *parent-sibling-category linked context, right-sibling-category linked context.* The three new features are considered to capture more syntactic context information of the connective C for connective classification.

Since discourse connective has very close relationship with the sense of discourse relation, we also extract features from its context, POS and the parse tree of its sentence to perform the explicit sense classification. The features for explicit sense classifier consist of the following: (1) Lin's features: C string, C POS, $prev_1 + C$; (2) Pitler's features: *self-category, parent-category, left-sibling-category, right-sibling-category*, C-Syn interaction, Syn-Syn interaction; (3) our five newly proposed features: *parent-category linked context*, previous connective and its POS of *as* and previous connective and its POS of *when.* The first *parent-category linked context* feature is to provide more syntactic context information for the classification. The last four features are specially designed to disambiguate the relation senses of the connective *as* or *when*, since the two connectives often have ambiguity between `Contingency.Cause.Reason` and `Temporal.Synchrony`. As shown in following example E5, the previous connective of the discourse connective *as* is *But*, therefore the discourse connective *as* usually carries the `Contingency.Cause.Reason` sense rather than `Temporal.Synchrony`.

(E5) *But the gains in Treasury bonds were pared* <u>as</u> **stocks staged a partial recovery..**

(Contingency.Cause.Reason – WSJ_1213)

3.4.2. *Argument span labelling*

On the one hand, although two discourse arguments are assumed to be attached to an identified discourse relation, according to PDTB 2.0 Manual, there are a variety of cases in the attribution of the discourse relation or its arguments. For example, the relation and its arguments are attributed to the writer or someone other than the writer, as well as the relation and its arguments are attributed differently to different sources. Therefore, simply taking the syntactic arguments of connective to be its discourse arguments yields an incorrect semantic interpretation. Moreover, since the PDTB annotators followed the *minimality principle*, which states that the annotation should include in the argument the minimal span of text that is sufficient for the interpretation of the relation, small portions of text are deleted from or added to the spans in most cases. Thus recognizing the arguments spans within discourse relations is an important task for deriving the correct interpretation of the relations, which requires deep semantic analysis rather than syntactic alone.

On the other hand, in PDTB, discourse relations in text are realized in two types according to the existence of "Explicit" connectives. In the first type relations realized explicitly by "Explicit" connectives, the arguments of Explicit connectives are unconstrained in terms of their location, that is, arguments can be found anywhere in the text. Otherwise, the second type involves relations between two adjacent sentences in the absence of an Explicit connective. In all cases, discourse relations are assumed to hold between two and only two arguments and the two arguments to a connective are simply labelled Arg1 and Arg2. In the case of Explicit connectives, Arg2 is the argument to which the connective is syntactically bound, and Arg1 is the other argument. In the case of relations between adjacent sentences, Arg1 and Arg2 reflect the linear order of the arguments, with Arg1 before Arg2.

Note that in case of Explicit connective, a connective and its arguments can appear in any relative order, and an argument can be arbitrarily far away from its corresponding connective. Since Arg2 is defined as the argument with which the connective is syntactically associated, its position is relatively fixed once we locate the discourse connective *C*. However, the location of the Arg1 can be in any position, categorized into 4 types, as follows: (1) SS: Arg1 in same sentence as connective; (2) IPS: Arg1 in previous, adjacent sentence; (3) NAPS: Arg1 in previous, non adjacent sentence; (4) FS: some sentence following the sentence containing the connective.

To make a clear analysis, we count the distributions of the location of Arg1 in PDTB Explicit discourse relation and summarize in Table 6. We can see that the SS accounts for the largest proportion (60.9%), and PS accounts for 30.1%. Thus, we only consider the current sentence containing the connective and its immediately preceding sentence as the text span where Arg1 occurs, similar to what was done in Refs. 50, 51.

Table 6. Distribution of the locations of Arg1 of explicit connectives.

	Count
Arg1 in same sentence as connective (SS)	11236
Arg1 in previous, adjacent sentence (IPS)	5549
Arg1 in previous, non adjacent sentence (NAPS)	1666
Arg1 in some sentence following the sentence containing the connective (FS)	8
total	18459

Kong *et al.* proposed a constituent-based approach and experiments showed that this method outperformed the tree subtraction algorithm by Lin *et al.*[50] for Explicit arguments labeling[50] only focused on the SS case, and Kong *et al.*[51] treated the immediately preceding sentence as a special constituent for PS. That means, they just viewed the immediately preceding sentence as Arg1 and thus performed only Arg2 span extractor in PS case. Besides, they build a global model for both Arg1 and Arg2 extraction. Different from their work, based on our observation and analysis mentioned above, we build two different extractors for Arg1 and Arg2 separately in both cases of SS and PS. Our consideration is that the two arguments have different syntactic and discourse properties and a unified model with the same feature set used for both cases may not have enough discriminating power.

3.4.3. *Arg1 position classifier*

After identifying the discourse connectives from the texts, we come to locate the positions of Arg1 and Arg2 of the connective *C*. Since Arg2 is defined as the argument with which the connective is syntactically associated, its position is fixed once we locate the discourse connective *C*. So we only need to identify the relative position of Arg1 as whether it is located within the same sentence as the connective (SS) or in some previous sentences of the connective (PS). We do not identify the case which Arg2 is located in some sentences following the sentence containing the connective (FS), because the statistical distribution of PDTB[52] shows that less than 0.1% instances are FS for Explicit relations.

The features consist of the following: (1) Lin's: C string, C position (the position of connective C in the sentence: start, middle, or end), C POS, $prev_1$, $prev_1$ POS, $prev_1$ + C, $prev_1$ POS + C POS, $prev_2$, $prev_2$ POS, $prev_2$ + C, $prev_2$ POS + C POS; (2) our newly-proposed features: C POS + $next_1$ POS, $next_2$, path of $C \rightarrow$ root. Note that $prev_2$ and $next_2$ indicate the second previous word and the second next word of connective C, respectively.

3.4.4. *Argument extractor*

Once the relative position of Arg1 is classified as SS or PS in previous component, the argument extractor is to extract the spans of Arg1 and Arg2 for the identified discourse connectives. According to the work,[51] Kong's constituent-based approach outperforms Lin's tree subtraction algorithm for the Explicit arguments extraction. However, Lin only focused on the SS case, and Kong treated the immediately preceding sentence as a special constituent for PS, which means that they just viewed the immediately preceding sentence as Arg1 and only extracted Arg2 for PS. So we only follow Kong's constituent-based approach to extract Arg1 and Arg2 for SS. However, for PS, we build two different extractors for Arg1 and Arg2 separately. Our intuition is that the two arguments have different syntactic and discourse properties and a unified model with the same feature set used for both may not have enough discriminating power.

SS Arguments Extractor: In the case of SS, we adopt Kong's constituent-based approach[51] without Joint Inference to extract Arg1 and Arg2.

For PS, we build two argument extractors for Arg1 and Arg2, respectively, as follows.

PS Arg1 Extractor: We consider the immediately previous sentence of connective C as the text span where Arg1 occurs and then build a extractor to label the Arg1 in it. Similar to Lin's Attribution span labeler, this extractor consists of two steps: splitting the sentence into clauses, and deciding, for each clause, whether it belongs to Arg1 or not. First we use nine punctuation symbols (...,.:;?!-∼) to split the sentence into several parts and use the SBAR tag in its parse tree to split each part into clauses. Second, we build a classifier to decide each clause whether it belongs to Arg1 or not.

On the one hand, the attribution relation is annotated in PDTB, which expresses the "ownership" relationship between abstract objects and individuals or agents. However, the attribution annotation is excluded in CoNLL-2015. Therefore we borrow several attribution features from Ref. 50 in order to distinguish the attribution-related span from others. On the other hand, according to the *minimality principle* of PDTB, the argument annotation includes the minimal span of text that is sufficient for the interpretation of the relation. Since connectives have very close relationship with discourse relation, we consider to adopt connective-related features to capture text span for relation. We choose the following features: (1) attribution-related features from Ref. 50: lemmatized verbs in *curr*, the first term of *curr*, the last term of *curr*, the last term of *prev* + the first term of *curr*, and (2) our proposed connective-related features: lowercased C string and C category (the syntactic category of the connective: subordinating, coordinating, or discourse adverbial), where *curr* and *prev* indicate the current and previous clause respectively and the corresponding category for the connective C is obtained from the list provided in Ref. 53.

PS Arg2 Extractor: The PS Arg2 Extractor is similar to the PS Arg1 Extractor. However, they differ as follows: (1) in the first step, we consider the sentence containing connective C as the text span where Arg2 occurs and besides the previous nine punctuation symbols, we also use the connective C to split the sentence; (2) we adopt different features to build classifier: lowercased verbs in *curr*, lemmatized verbs in *curr*, the first term of *curr*, the last term of *curr*, the last term of *prev*, the first term of *next*, the last term of *prev* + the first term of *curr*, the last term of *curr* + the first term of *next*, production rules extracted from *curr*, *curr* position (i.e., the position of *curr* in the sentence: start, middle or end), C string, lowercased C string, C position, C category, path of C's parent $\rightarrow$ root, compressed path of C's parent $\rightarrow$ root.

3.5. *Non-explicit discourse relations*

Since most of Non-Explicit relations are annotated for adjacent sentence pairs within paragraphs, we first collect all adjacent sentence pairs within each paragraph, but not identified in any Explicit relation. We assume the previous sentence as Arg1 and the next sentence as Arg2, and then identify the sense by the features extracted from (Arg1, Arg2). After that, we use Implicit Arg1 Extractor and Implicit Arg2 Extractor to label Arg1 and Arg2 for Non-EntRel relations in Non-Explicit, and for EntRel relations, we simply label the previous sentence as Arg1 and the next as Arg2.

Moreover, as shown in Figure 9, we use the Non-Explicit sense classifier again to identify the sense on the refined arguments (extracted arguments from Implicit Arg1 & Arg2 Extractor) rather than the adjacent sentence pairs (i.e., previous sentence as Arg1, the next sentence as Arg2). Our expectation is that the overall parser performance might be improved if we extract features on refined argument spans rather than original argument spans.

3.5.1. *Non-explicit sense classifier*

According to previous work, this component is the most difficult one in the discourse parser. And the features we adopted in this component are chosen from Refs. 54–56, including: *production rules*, *dependency rules*, *first-last*, *first3*, *modality*, *verbs*, *Inquirer*, *polarity*, *immediately preceding discourse connective of current sentence pair*, *Brown cluster pairs*. For the collection of *production rules*, *dependency rules*, and *Brown cluster pairs*, we used a frequency cutoff of 5 to remove infrequent features, and for Brown cluster, we choose 3,200 classes, as in Ref. 56.

3.5.2. *Implicit Arg1 extractor*

The implicit Arg1 Extractor is performed to extract Arg1 for Non-EntRel relations in Non-Explicit, which is done similarly to the PS Arg1 Extractor. We first split the sentence into clauses and then decide each clause whether it belongs to Arg1 or not. The features extracted from the current and previous clauses (*curr* and *prev*) are: the first term of *curr*, the last term of *prev*, the cross product of the *prev* and *curr* production rules, the path of the first term of *curr* → the last term of *prev*, number of words of *curr*.

3.5.3. *Implicit Arg2 extractor*

The implicit Arg2 Extractor is similar to that of Arg1, but different features are extracted from the current, previous, and next clauses (*curr*, *prev*, and *next*), including: lowercased verbs in *curr*, the first term of *curr*, the last term of *prev*, the last term of *prev* + the first term of *curr*, the last term of *curr* + the first term of *next*, *curr* position, the cross product of the *prev* and *curr* production rules, the cross product of the *curr* and *next* production rules, the path of the first term of *curr* → the last term of *prev*, number of words of *curr*.

3.6. *Related system settings*

The main algorithms for discourse relations recognition are usually borrowed from widely-used supervised machine learning algorithms, e.g., MaxEnt, SVM and Naive Bayes, etc. Among them, MaxEnt has shown better performance than other algorithms in most components in our refined discourse parser.

In general, a discourse relation is considered to be correct if and only if: (1) the discourse connective is correctly detected (for explicit discourse relations); (2) the sense of a discourse relation is correctly predicted; (3) the text spans of the two arguments as well as their labels (Arg1 and Arg2) are correctly predicted. We use the measure F_1 (harmonic mean of Precision and Recall) to evaluate performance.

References

1. J. D. Lafferty, A. McCallum and F. C. N. Pereira, Conditional random fields: Probabilistic models for segmenting and labeling sequence data, in *Proceedings of the Eighteenth International Conference on Machine Learning*, 2001, pp. 282–289.
2. I. Tsochantaridis, T. Hofmann, T. Joachims and Y. Altun, Support vector machine learning for interdependent and structured output spaces, in *Proceedings of the Twenty-first International Conference on Machine Learning*, 2004.
3. B. Taskar, C. Guestrin and D. Koller, Max-margin markov networks, in *Advances in Neural Information Processing Systems 16*, 2003, pp. 25–32.
4. Y. Zhang and S. Clark, Chinese segmentation with a word-based perceptron algorithm, in *Proceedings of the 45th Annual Meeting of the Association of Computational Linguistics*, 2007, pp. 840–847.
5. W. Sun, Word-based and character-based word segmentation models: Comparison and combination, in *Coling 2010: Posters*, 2010, pp. 1211–1219.
6. X. Qian and Y. Liu, Joint Chinese word segmentation, POS tagging and parsing, in *Proceedings of the Joint Conference on Empirical Methods in Natural Language Processing and Computational Natural Language Learning*, 2012, pp. 501–511.
7. Y. Zhang and S. Clark, Joint word segmentation and POS tagging using a single perceptron, in *Proceedings of ACL-08: HLT*, 2008, pp. 888–896.
8. R. Levy and C. D. Manning, Is it harder to parse Chinese, or the Chinese treebank?, in *Proceedings of the 41st Annual Meeting of the Association for Computational Linguistics*, 2003, pp. 439–446.
9. J. Eisner, Bilexical grammars and their cubic-time parsing algorithms, in *Advances in Probabilistic and Other Parsing Technologies*, 2000, pp. 29–62.

10. T. Koo and M. Collins, Efficient third-order dependency parsers, in *Proceedings of the 48th Annual Meeting of the Association for Computational Linguistics*, 2010, pp. 1–11.
11. Z. Li, M. Zhang, W. Che, T. Liu, W. Chen and H. Li, Joint models for Chinese pos tagging and dependency parsing, in *Proceedings of the Conference on Empirical Methods in Natural Language Processing*, 2011, pp. 1180–1191.
12. J. Nivre and M. Scholz, Deterministic dependency parsing of English text, in *Proceedings of the 20th International Conference on Computational Linguistics*, 2004.
13. Y. Zhang and J. Nivre, Transition-based dependency parsing with rich non-local features, in *Proceedings of the 49th Annual Meeting of the Association for Computational Linguistics: Human Language Technologies*, 2011, pp. 188–193.
14. R. McDonald, K. Crammer and F. Pereira, Online large-margin training of dependency parsers, in *Proceedings of the 43rd Annual Meeting of the Association for Computational Linguistics*, 2005, pp. 91–98.
15. A. Martins, N. Smith and E. Xing, Concise integer linear programming formulations for dependency parsing, in *Proceedings of the Joint Conference of the 47th Annual Meeting of the ACL and the 4th International Joint Conference on Natural Language Processing of the AFNLP*, 2009, pp. 342–350.
16. S. Verberne, L. Boves, N. Oostdijk and P. Coppen, Evaluating discourse-based answer extraction for why-question answering, 2007, pp. 735–736, in *Proceedings of the 30th Annual International ACM SIGIR Conference on Research and Development in Information Retrieval.*
17. D. Marcu, Improving summarization through rhetorical parsing tuning, *The 6th Workshop on Very Large Corpora*, 1998, pp. 206–215.
18. P. Cimiano, U. Reyle and J. Šarić, Ontology-driven discourse analysis for information extraction, *Data & Knowledge Engineering*, **55**(1), 59–83 (2005).
19. B. Hatim and I. Mason, *Discourse and the Translator* (Routledge, 2014).
20. S. Mukherjee, P. Bhattacharyya *et al.*, Sentiment analysis in twitter with lightweight discourse analysis, in *COLING*, 2012, pp. 1847–1864.
21. E. Hovy, Automated discourse generation using discourse structure relations, *Artificial intelligence*, **63**(1-2), 341–385 (1993).
22. PDTB-Group, The penn discourse treebank 2.0 annotation manual, Technical report, Institute for Research in Cognitive Science, University of Pennsylvania, 2008.
23. Y. Zhou and N. Xue, Pdtb-style discourse annotation of Chinese text, in *Proceedings of the 50th Annual Meeting of the Association for Computational Linguistics: Long Papers-Vol. 1*, 2012, pp. 69–77.
24. E. Pitler and A. Nenkova, Using syntax to disambiguate explicit discourse connectives in text, in *Proceedings of the ACL-IJCNLP Conference Short Papers*, 2009, pp. 13–16.
25. E. Pitler, A. Louis and A. Nenkova, Automatic sense prediction for implicit discourse relations in text, in *Proceedings of the Joint Conference of the 47th Annual Meeting of the ACL and the 4th International Joint Conference on Natural Language Processing of the AFNLP*, Vol. 2, 2009, pp. 683–691.

26. C. Sporleder and A. Lascarides, Using automatically labelled examples to classify rhetorical relations: An assessment, *Natural Language Engineering*, **14**(03), 369–416 (2008).
27. Z. G. Sun Jing, Li Yancui and F. Wenhe, Research of Chinese implicit discourse relation recognition, *Acta Scientiarum Naturalium Universitatis Pekinensis*, **50**(1), 112–117 (2014).
28. Z. Lin, M. Kan and H. Ng, Recognizing implicit discourse relations in the penn discourse treebank, in *Proceedings of the Conference on Empirical Methods in Natural Language Processing*, Vol. 1, 2009, pp. 343–351.
29. W. Wang, J. Su and C. L. Tan, Kernel based discourse relation recognition with temporal ordering information, in *Proceedings of the 48th Annual Meeting of the Association for Computational Linguistics*, 2010, pp. 710–719.
30. Z. Zhou, Y. Xu, Z. Niu, M. Lan, J. Su and C. Tan, Predicting discourse connectives for implicit discourse relation recognition, in *Proceedings of the 23rd International Conference on Computational Linguistics*, 2010, pp. 1507–1514.
31. Y. Xu, M. Lan, Y. Lu, Z. Y. Niu and C. L. Tan, Connective prediction using machine learning for implicit discourse relation classification, in *International Joint Conference on Neural Networks*, 2012, pp. 1–8.
32. D. Marcu and A. Echihabi, An unsupervised approach to recognizing discourse relations, in *Proceedings of the 40th Annual Meeting on Association for Computational Linguistics*, 2002, pp. 368–375.
33. M. Lan, Y. Xu, Z.-Y. Niu *et al.*, Leveraging synthetic discourse data via multi-task learning for implicit discourse relation recognition, in *ACL (1)*, 2013, pp. 476–485.
34. M. Saito, K. Yamamoto and S. Sekine, Using phrasal patterns to identify discourse relations, in *Proceedings of the Human Language Technology Conference of the NAACL, Companion Volume: Short Papers on XX*, 2006, pp. 133–136.
35. S. Blair-Goldensohn, *Long-Answer Question Answering and Rhetorical-Semantic Relations*, PhD thesis, 2007.
36. L. Carlson, D. Marcu and M. Okurowski, Building a discourse-tagged corpus in the framework of rhetorical structure theory, in *Proceedings of the Second SIGdial Workshop on Discourse and Dialogue*, Vol. 16, 2001, pp. 1–10.
37. W. Mann and S. Thompson, Rhetorical structure theory: Toward a functional theory of text organization, *Text-Interdisciplinary Journal for the Study of Discourse*, **8**(3), 243–281 (1988).
38. R. Soricut and D. Marcu, Sentence level discourse parsing using syntactic and lexical information, in *Proceedings of the 2003 Conference of the North American Chapter of the Association for Computational Linguistics on Human Language Technology*, Vol. 1, 2003, pp. 149–156.
39. R. Girju, Automatic detection of causal relations for question answering, in *Proceedings of the ACL 2003 Workshop on Multilingual Summarization and Question Answering*, Vol. 12, 2003, pp. 76–83.
40. J. Baldridge and A. Lascarides, Probabilistic head-driven parsing for discourse structure, in *Proceedings of the Ninth Conference on Computational Natural Language Learning*, 2005, pp. 96–103.

41. F. Wolf, E. Gibson, A. Fisher and M. Knight, The discourse graphbank: A database of texts annotated with coherence relations, *Linguistic Data Consortium*, 2005.
42. B. Wellner, J. Pustejovsky, C. Havasi, A. Rumshisky and R. Sauri, Classification of discourse coherence relations: An exploratory study using multiple knowledge sources, in *Proceedings of the 7th SIGdial Workshop on Discourse and Dialogue*, 2006, pp. 117–125.
43. R. Prasad, N. Dinesh, A. Lee, E. Miltsakaki, L. Robaldo, A. Joshi and B. Webber, The penn discourse treebank 2.0, in *Proceedings of LREC*, 2008.
44. B. Wang, X. Wang, C. Sun, B. Liu and L. Sun, Modeling semantic relevance for question-answer pairs in web social communities, in *Proceedings of the 48th Annual Meeting of the Association for Computational Linguistics*, 2010, pp. 1230–1238.
45. B. Webber, D-ltag: extending lexicalized tag to discourse, *Cognitive Science*, **28**(5), 751–779 (2004).
46. R. Prasad, S. McRoy, N. Frid, A. Joshi and H. Yu, The biomedical discourse relation bank, *BMC Bioinformatics*, **12**(1), 188 (2011).
47. J. Kim, T. Ohta, Y. Tateisi and J. Tsujii, Genia corpus — semantically annotated corpus for bio-textmining, *Bioinformatics*, **19**(suppl. 1), i180–182 (2003).
48. D. B. F. S. Guodong, Explicit discourse relation parsing of Chinese text, *Journal of Chinese Information Processing*, **28**(6), 101–106 (2014).
49. W. Wang, J. Su and C. Tan, Kernel based discourse relation recognition with temporal ordering information, in *Proceedings of the 48th Annual Meeting of the Association for Computational Linguistics*, 2010, pp. 710–719.
50. Z. Lin, H. T. Ng and M.-Y. Kan, A PDTB-styled end-to-end discourse parser, *Natural Language Engineering*, 2014, pp. 1–34.
51. F. Kong, H. T. Ng and G. Zhou, A constituent-based approach to argument labeling with joint inference in discourse parsing, in *Proceedings of the Conference on Empirical Methods in Natural Language Processing*, 2014, pp. 68–77, URL `http://www.aclweb.org/anthology/D14-1008`.
52. R. Prasad, N. Dinesh, A. Lee, E. Miltsakaki, L. Robaldo, A. K. Joshi and B. L. Webber, The Penn Discourse TreeBank 2.0., in *LREC*, 2008.
53. A. Knott, A data-driven methodology for motivating a set of coherence relations, 1996.
54. Z. Lin, M.-Y. Kan and H. T. Ng, Recognizing implicit discourse relations in the Penn Discourse Treebank, in *Proceedings of the Conference on Empirical Methods in Natural Language Processing*, Vol. 1, 2009, pp. 343–351.
55. E. Pitler, A. Louis and A. Nenkova, Automatic sense prediction for implicit discourse relations in text, in *Proceedings of the Joint Conference of the 47th Annual Meeting of the ACL and the 4th International Joint Conference on Natural Language Processing of the AFNLP*, Vol. 2, 2009, pp. 683–691.
56. A. T. Rutherford and N. Xue, Discovering implicit discourse relations through brown cluster pair representation and coreference patterns, in *EACL*, 2014, p. 645.

Chapter 10

Speaker Recognition: Deep Neural Networks Approach

Xin He and Lekai Huang

Shanghai UVoice Technology Co., Ltd.,
906 Huanan Building, 1988 Dongfang Rd., Shanghai 201120, China
hex@uvoicetech.com, huanglk@uvoicetech.com

In this chapter we investigate the use of deep neural networks (DNNs) and long-short-term memory recurrent neural networks (LSTM RNNs) for a global password text-dependent automatic speaker verification (ASV) task. First, at training phase of ASV, a DNN or LSTM RNN is trained to classify speakers at the frame level. Second, at speaker enrollment phase of ASV, the trained DNN and LSTM RNN are used to extract speaker specific features from the activation of last hidden layer. The averaged top-N pooling of these speaker features, we called it improved *d*-vector, is taken as the speaker model. Finally at evaluation phase of AVS, an improved *d*-vector is extracted for each test utterance and compared to the enrolled speaker model to make a verification decision. Experimental results show the speaker verification system based on LSTM RNN achieves better performance compared to a popular *i*-vector system and DNN based system on the global password text-dependent speaker verification task, and the combined systems outperform the *i*-vector system by reducing the equal error rate (EER) 10% and 15% relative to our fixed-text ASV dataset.

1. Introduction

Voice signal conveys rich information, including language information (linguistic contents, etc.), speaker information (identity, emotion, physiological characteristics, etc.), environmental information (background, channel, etc.) and so on. While speech recognition aims at recognizing the word spoken, speaker recognition refers to identify persons from their voice [1–3].

There are two major applications of speaker recognition technologies. If the speaker claims to be of a certain identity and the voice is used to verify this claim, this is called automatic speaker verification (ASV) or authentication. Another application is automatic speaker identification (SID) which is used to determine an unknown speaker's identity. Speaker recognition system can also be divided into text-dependent and text-independent ones. In text-dependent systems which suited for cooperative users, the recognition phrases are fixed, or known beforehand. For instance, the user can be prompted to read a randomly selected sequence of numbers as described in [1, 4, 5]. In text-independent systems, there are no constraints on the words the speakers are allowed to use.

Of the two basic tasks, text-dependent speaker verification is currently the most commercially viable and useful technology [6, 7]. When the lexicon of the spoken utterances is constrained to a single phrase across all users, the process is referred to as global password speaker verification or fixed text speaker verification. In this chapter, we focus on a low-cost small footprint global password text-dependent ASV task on mobile device, which we will accompany with our on-device hot-word wakeup system.

The ASV process can be divided into three phases [8, 9]:

(i) *Training*: background models are trained from a large collection of data to define the speaker manifold.
(ii) *Enrollment*: new speakers are enrolled to obtain speaker models by deriving speaker specific information.
(iii) *Evaluation*: each test utterance is evaluated using the enrolled speaker models and background models. A decision is made on the identity claim. The value of a scoring function of the utterance and the claim speaker model is compared against a threshold. We accept if the score exceeds the threshold, otherwise reject.

There are two types of error in ASV system: false reject and false accept. The false reject rate and the false accept rate depend on the threshold. When the two rates are equal, the common value is called equal error rate (EER). We used EER to measure the performance of our ASV system, the lower is better [10, 11].

The state-of-the-art ASV systems are based on *i*-vectors [12, 13] combined with Probabilistic Linear Discriminate Analysis (PLDA). In these systems, joint factor analysis (JFA) [14, 15] is used as a feature extractor to extract a low-dimensional *i*-vector as the compact representation of a spoken utterance for ASV, PLDA is used as score function to make final decision.

Motivated by the powerful feature extraction capability and great success of deep neural networks (DNNs) and long-short-term memory recurrent neural networks (LSTM RNNs) applied to speech recognition, [16–19] proposed the DNN based speaker feature extractor referred to as *d*-vector for ASV, we simplify the DNN structure, modify the method to calculate the speaker *d*-vector and propose the improved speaker feature extractors using DNNs and LSTM RNNs.

The rest of this chapter is organized as follows. In Section 2, baseline *i*-vector/PLDA based ASV is described. In Section 3 we propose an improved DNN-based *d*-vector ASV system. In Section 4 we describe the new LSTM-based *d*-vector ASV system. Sections 5 and 6 show the experimental setups and results for our global password ASV systems. An improved DNN *d*-vector and LSTM *d*-vector based ASV systems are compared with an *i*-vector/PLDA system. We also describe improvements from combination of improved DNN *d*-vector with *i*-vector systems and the other combination of LSTM *d*-vector with *i*-vector systems. Finally, Section 7 concludes the chapter.

2. *I*-Vector Speaker Recognition System

An *i*-vector extractor [20, 21] is a system that maps a sequence of feature vectors (typically cepstral coefficients) obtained from a speech utterance to a fixed-length low-dimensional vector. Given an utterance, the speaker and session dependent super-vector M is defined as follows [22, 23]:

$$M = m + Tw \tag{1}$$

where m is the speaker and session independent super-vector comes from a speaker independent Gaussian mixture model (GMM) [24–26] denoted as universal background model (UBM), T is a low rank matrix referred to as total variability matrix (TVM), and w is a vector containing the total factors and is referred to as the *i*-vector.

In Figure 1 we show a simplified block diagram of *i*-vector extraction and scoring.

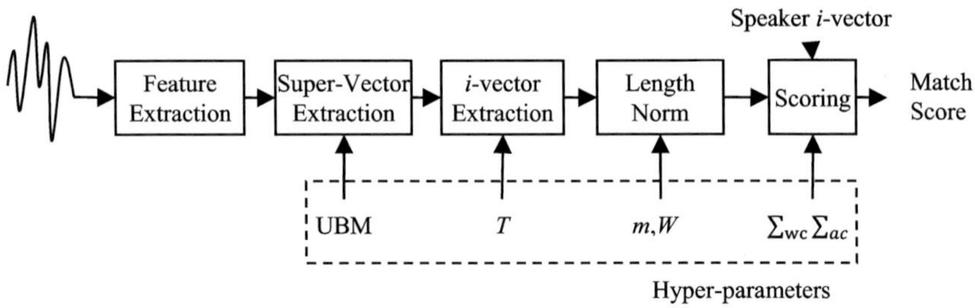

Figure 1. A simplified diagram of *i*-vector extraction and score flow.

2.1. *Acoustical feature extraction*

In ASV system, an input audio segment is first processed by voice activity detection (VAD) to find the locations of speech and to extract acoustic features that convey speaker information. Typically, 20-dimensional mel-frequency cepstral coefficients (MFCC) and first and second derivatives analyzed at 100 feature vectors per second are used for ASV system.

2.2. *Universal background model*

The UBM has been used in speaker recognition as one of the fundamental components for many years [27, 28]. In the *i*-vector ASV framework, the UBM is represented by a GMM trained on unlabeled speech data of many different speakers with EM algorithm, and the standard approach uses the Gaussians in the UBM as the classes to compute the posterior probability of each speech frame.

2.3. *I-vector extraction*

Using a UBM, the per-mixture posterior probability of each feature vector ("GMM-posterior") is computed and used, along with the feature vectors in the speech segment, to accumulate 0th, 1st, and 2nd order sufficient statistics (SS) [29]. These SSs are then transformed into a low dimensional *i*-vector representation (typically 100–600 dimensions) using a total variability matrix, *T*. The *i*-vector is whitened by subtracting a global mean, *m*, scaled by the inverse square root of a global covariance matrix **W**, and then normalized to unit length [30].

In ASV system, each training or testing utterance will be processed and represented as one *i*-vector. In enrollment stage, the speaker *i*-vector is computed as the average of *i*-vectors from the speaker's training utterance.

2.4. *Scoring function*

During evaluation stage of an ASV system, the score between a speaker model and test *i*-vector is computed. The cosine distance of simplest scoring function is between the speaker *i*-vector and the *i*-vector representing the test utterance. The current state-of-the-art scoring function, called Probabilistic Linear Discriminate Analysis (PLDA) [31–33], requires a within-class matrix Σ_{wc}, characterizing how *i*-vectors from a single speaker vary, and an across class matrix Σ_{ac}, characterizing how *i*-vectors between different speakers vary.

The UBM, *T*, *W*, *m*, Σ_{wc} and Σ_{ac} are the hyper-paramcters of *i*-vector/PLDA based ASV system and must be estimated during a system development stage. The UBM, *T*, *W*, and *m* represent general feature distributions and total variance of statistics and *i*-vectors, so unlabeled speech data from the desired domain can be used to estimate them. The Σ_{wc} and Σ_{ac} matrices, however, each require a large collection of labeled data for training. For ASV, Σ_{wc} and Σ_{ac} typically require thousands of speakers each of whom contributes tens of samples to the dataset.

Over the past few years, *i*-vector based system has achieved the state-of-the-art speaker verification performance [34]. We will use *i*-vector/PLDA ASV system as baseline in our experiment.

3. Deep Neural Networks for Speaker Verification

The model used in this sector is a deep fully connected feed-forward multi-layer perceptions (MLP), it consists of an input layer, more than two hidden layers and an output layer [35, 36].

3.1. *DNN architecture*

Each layer of the DNN has a fixed number of nodes and each sequential pair of layers is fully connected with a weight matrix. The activations of nodes on a given layer are computed by transforming the output of the previous layer with the weight matrix: $a^{(i)} = M^{(i)}x^{(i-1)}$. The output of a given layer is then computed by applying an "activation function" [37] $x^{(i)} = h^{(i)}(a^i)$ (see Figure 2). The common activation functions include the sigmoid $\sigma(z) = 1/(1 + e^{-z})$, the hyperbolic tangent $t\varphi(z) = (e^z - e^{-z})/(e^z + e^{-z})$, rectified linear units (ReLU) $l(z) = \max(0, z)$ [38] and even a simple linear transformation. When the DNN is trained as a classifier with K alternative classes, we apply a soft-max nonlinearity in an output layer of K nodes [39]. The soft-max function is as $\hat{y}_k = e^{a_k}/\sum_{j=1}^{K} e^{a_j}$ (for $j = 1$ to K). The denominator is a normalizing term consisting of the sum of the numerators, ensuring that the outputs of all nodes sum to one. For DNN classifier training, the objective function is the cross entropy between the output and the true class labels. Each output node of the DNN classifier corresponds to a class and the output is an estimate of the posterior probability of the class given the input data.

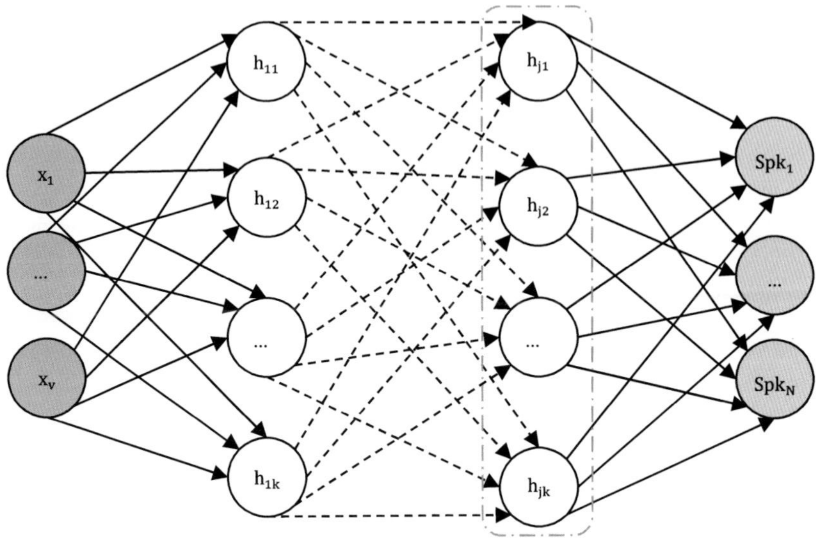

Figure 2. The architecture of DNN.

For ASV system, the input of DNN is a stacked set of spectral features (e.g., Log Mel-Filter Bank Energy, MFCCs, PLPs) extracted from short segments of speech [40]. Typically a context of 10 frames around the current input frame is used. The ReLU activation function is selected for hidden layers. The output layer of the speaker DNN is a soft-max layer corresponding to the number of speakers in the training set, *N*. The target speaker labels are formed as a 1-hot *N*-dimensional vector where the only non-zero component is the corresponding speaker identity. Each output of DNN is a prediction of the posterior probability of the target speaker for the current input frame (see Figure 2).

3.2. *DNN training*

We trained the DNN model using the mini-batch stochastic gradient descent (SGD) learning algorithm [41–43]. For better randomization of gradients in SGD and stability of training, the training utterances were shuffled and split into random chunks of the same length. We used 2 GPU machines for distributed training and in each machine 12 concurrent threads each processing a batch of 128 subsequences. In training epoch, we used an exponentially decaying learning rate of 1e-04.

3.3. *Improved DNN d-vector extractor*

After the speaker recognition DNN is trained, the parameters of the speaker DNN are fixed in enrollment and evaluation stages. We derive the *d*-vector speaker feature from output activations of the last hidden layer before the output soft-max layer.

We use the standard feed-forward propagation to compute the *d*-vector. For every input feature vector of a given utterance, we compute the output activations h_j^t of the last hidden layer j. Then we take the element-wise mean of the top-*n* maximum of activations to form the compact representation of that utterance, which is referred as the *d*-vector $\vec{d}$. The ith component of the *k*-dimensional *d*-vector $\vec{d}$ is given by:

$$\vec{d_i} = \frac{1}{N}\sum_t \text{top } N(h_i^t) \quad (2)$$

Each utterance generates exactly one improved DNN *d*-vector. For enrollment, a speaker provides a few utterances of the global password; Same to baseline *i*-vector speaker model and [25], the *d*-vector from each of these enrolling utterances is averaged together to form an improved *d*-vector speaker model that is used for ASV. During evaluation stage, we use the simple cosine distance as the scoring function between the improved *d*-vector speaker model and the improved *d*-vector of an evaluation utterance.

4. LSTM RNNs for Speech Verification

Long short-term memory (LSTM) is one of the most successful recurrent neural network (RNN) architectures, it is published [46] in 1997 by Hochreiter and Schmidhuber. LSTM introduces the memory cell, a unit of computation that replaces traditional artificial neurons in the hidden layer of a network, which overcome the problem of vanishing gradients in training earlier recurrent neural network.

4.1. *LSTM architecture*

The modern LSTM RNN architecture [47–50] is shown in Figure 3. The LSTM contains special units called memory blocks in the recurrent hidden layer. The memory blocks contain memory cells with self-connections storing the temporal state of the network in addition to special multiplicative units called gates to control the flow of information. The input gate controls the flow of input activations into the memory cell.

The output gate controls the output flow of cell activations into the rest of the network. The forget gate scales the internal state of the cell before adding it as input to the cell through selfrecurrent connection of the cell, therefore adaptively forgetting or resetting the cell's memory. In addition, the LSTM RNN architecture contains peephole connections and its internal cells to the gates in the same cell to learn precise timing of the outputs [51, 52].

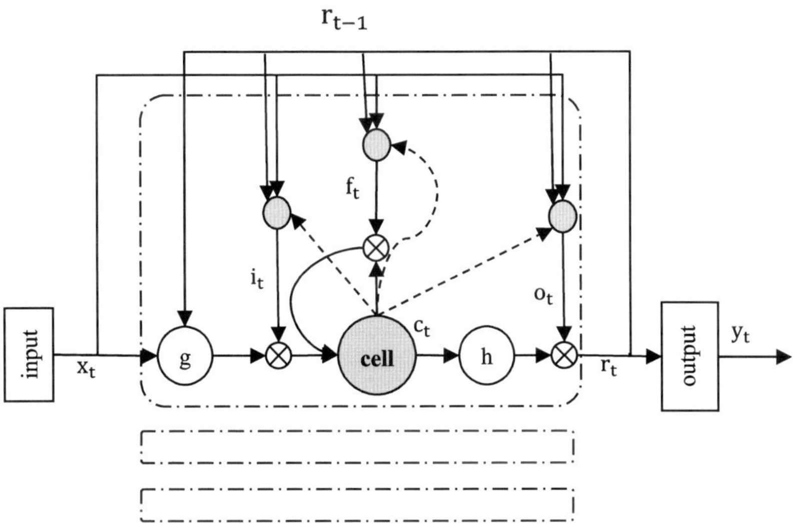

LSTM memory blocks

Figure 3. The architecture of LSTM RNN.

With this architecture, LSTM RNNs compute a mapping from an input sequence $x = (x_1, \ldots, x_T)$ to an output sequence $y = (y_1, \ldots, y_T)$. They calculate the activations for network units using the following equations iteratively from the time step $t = 1$ to T: [53, 54]

$$\boldsymbol{i_t = \sigma(W_{ix}x_t + W_{ir}r_{t-1} + W_{ic}c_{t-1} + b_i)}$$
$$\boldsymbol{f_t = \sigma(W_{fx}x_t + W_{fr}r_{t-1} + W_{fc}c_{t-1} + b_f)}$$
$$\boldsymbol{c_t = i_t \odot \varphi(W_{cx}x_t + W_{cr}r_{t-1} + b_c) + f_t \odot c_{t-1}}$$
$$\boldsymbol{o_t = \sigma(W_{ox}x_t + W_{or}r_{t-1} + W_{oc}c_t + b_o)}$$
$$\boldsymbol{r_t = x_t \odot \varphi(c_t)}$$
$$\boldsymbol{y_t = \phi(W_{yr}r_t + b_y)} \tag{3}$$

where the W terms denote weight matrices (e.g. W_{ix} is the matrix of weights from the input gate to the input), W_{ic}, W_{fc}, W_{oc} are diagonal weight matrices for peephole connections, the b terms denote bias vectors (b_i is the input gate bias vector), σ is the logistic sigmoid function, and i, f, o and c are respectively the input gate, forget gate, output gate and cell activation vectors, all of which are the same size as the cell output activation vector r, $\odot$ is the element-wise product of the vectors, φ is the hyperbolic tangent activation function for cell inputs and cell outputs, and ϕ is the softmax output activation function for the LSTM RNN models used in this chapter.

4.2. *LSTM RNN training*

We train the LSTM RNN model using stochastic gradient descent (SGD) and the truncated back propagation through time (BPTT) learning algorithm [55–57]. Activations are forward propagated for a fixed step time of 20 over a subsequence of an input utterance; the cross entropy gradients are computed for this subsequence and back propagated to its start. For better randomization of gradients in SGD and stability of training, we split the training utterances into random groups with 64 utterances per batch. We also set the same target speaker id sparsely for a chunk, 1 in every 10 frames for the experiments in this chapter. The errors are only calculated for the frames that we set a target speaker id. We used 2 GPU machines for distributed training and in each machine 12 concurrent threads each processing a batch of 64 subsequences to speed up the training. We used an exponentially decaying learning rate of 1e-05 and momentum of 0.9 for whole training.

4.3. *Proposed LSTM d-vector extractor*

Similar to DNN *d*-vector extrcactor, we derive the *d*-vector speaker feature from output activations of the LSTM layer before the output soft-max layer.

The method to extract the LSTM *d*-vector is same to improved DNN *d*-vector extractor in Section 3.3. The only one exception is there are 10 frames delay when we compute the output activations h_j^t of the hidden LSTM layer.

5. Experiment Setup

5.1. *Dataset*

The experiment was held on our fixed text ASV dataset. The dataset contains 800 speakers speaking the same phrase, "My voice is my password" in Mandarin Chinese, many times in multiple sessions recorded in different environments and with different mobile phone models. The gender distribution is balanced on the dataset. 700 randomly selected speakers are used for training the background model and the remaining 100 speakers were used for enrollment and evaluation. The number of utterances per speaker for background model training varies from 90 to 100. The average duration of each utterance is about 1.5 seconds. For the enrollment speakers, the first 20 utterances are reserved for possible use in enrollment and the remaining utterances are used for evaluation. By default, we only use the random 3 utterances of the enrollment set for generating speaker models. We used one out of 100 trials as a target trial and there are approximately 10,000 trials in total.

5.2. *System configuration*

5.2.1. *Baseline i-vector system*

In the experiments, an *i*-vector classifier, using the similar configuration as [12], was used for baseline systems.

The front-end for the baseline *i*-vector ASV system uses 20 MFCCs including C0 and their first and second derivatives for a total of 60 features. The baseline GMM *i*-vector systems use a 128 component GMM in UBM. In this case, 100 dimensional *i*-vectors are extracted from stacked mean vectors which are standardized to using diagonal Gaussian parameters. After extraction, *i*-vectors are length normalized. The TVM is initialized using PCA and further refined using 10 EM iterations, while for UBM training we used 7 EM iterations.

We evaluate the equal error rate (EER) performance of the *i*-vector/PLDA system, improved DNN *d*-vector and LSTM *d*-vector system.

5.2.2. *Improved DNN d-vector system*

The front end of DNN uses 40 MFCCs stacked over a 21 frames window (10 frames to either side of the center frame) for a total of 840 dimension input features. The DNN has 4 hidden layers of 256 nodes each. All hidden layers use a ReLU activation function. The number of nodes in output layers 700 corresponding to the speaker number in training set. The DNN training is performed on NVidia GTX780 GPU using custom software we ourselves developed.

5.2.3. *LSTM d-vector system*

The LSTM RNN front-end uses 40 MFCCs without frame stack for input features. The RNN has 1 hidden LSTM layers of 256 memory cells and the output layer has 700 nodes corresponding to the speaker number in training set. The LSTM RNN training is preformed on nVidia GTX780 GPU using custom software we ourselves developed.

6. Experiment Results

We first investigate how much the verification performance changes in the *d*-vector system with different numbers of enrollment utterances per speaker. We compare the performance results using 1, 2, 3 utterances for speaker enrollment.

Table 1. EER results of *i*-vector, DNN *d*-vector, LSTM *d*-vector ASV systems with different number of enrollment utterances.

	Equal Error Rate (EER in %)			
Enrollment Utterances		1	2	3
	i-vector/PLDA	4.05	3.14	2.08
	Improved DNN *d*-vector	3.81	3.20	2.61
	LSTM *d*-vector	3.28	2.52	1.90

Table 1 lists the EER results. It shows that all three ASV systems perform better with increasing numbers of enrollment utterances. The performance of LSTM *d*-vector system is best in all system in all conditon. The overall performance of *i*-vector/PLDA system is better than DNN *d*-vector system. We also notice that the performance of two *d*-vector systems are much better than *i*-vector/PLDA system in 1 enrollment utterance situation. This indicates that the *i*-vector system needs more data to estimate the paramters of model than the *d*-vector system.

We also investigate the performance of the system fusion of combining *i*-vector with two *d*-vector systems separately. Our preliminary results in Table 2 are obtained using a simple combination named as sum fusion, which sums the scores provided by each individual system for each trial. Results show that the two combined systems outperform the all tree individual systems. In terms of EER performance, the *i*-vector/DNN *d*-vector system outperform the *i*-vector system by 10%, the best *i*-vector/LSTM *d*-vector system beats the *i*-vector system by 15% on our fixed text dataset.

Table 2. EER results of system fusion *i*-vector/DNN *d*-vector, *i*-vector/LSTM *d*-vector.

	Equal Error Rate (EER in %)	
Enrollment Utterances		3
	i-vector/DNN *d*-vector	1.81
	i-vector/LSTM *d*-vector	1.69

7. Conclusions

This chapter describes the development of the new proposed DNN and LSTM *d*-vector system and demonstrated substantial performance gains when applying the system to the global password text-dependent speaker verification benchmarks. For our fixed-text ASV dataset the LSTM *d*-vector system was shown to reduce the error rates of the baseline *i*-vector/PLDA system by 5% for EER. Further reductions in error were demonstrated on the fixed-text ASV task using score fusion. Fusing the *i*-vector and DNN *d*-vector system scores reduces the error rates relative to the *i*-vector system by 10% for EER. Fusing the *i*-vector and LSTM *d*-vector system scores reduces the error rate relative to the baseline *i*-vector system by 15% for EER.

References

1. D. Reynolds, T. F. Quatieri and R. B. Dunn, Speaker verification using adapted Gaussian mixture models, *Digital Signal Processing*, **10**(1), 19–41 (2000).
2. P. Kenny, G. Boulianne, P. Ouellet and P. Dumouchel, Joint factor analysis versus eigenchannels in speaker recognition, *IEEE Transactions on Audio, Speech, and Language Processing*, **15**, 1435–1447 (2007).
3. P. Kenny, G. Boulianne, P. Ouellet and P. Dumouchel, Speaker and session variability in GMM-based speaker verification, *IEEE Transactions on Audio, Speech, and Language Processing*, **15**, 1448–1460 (2007).
4. P. Kenny, P. Ouellet, N. Dehak, V. Gupta and P. Dumouchel, A study of interspeaker variability in speaker verification, *IEEE Transactions on Audio, Speech, and Language Processing*, **16**, 980–988 (2008).
5. N. Dehak, P. J. Kenny, R. Dehak, P. Dumouchel and P. Ouellet, Front-end factor analysis for speaker verification, *IEEE Transactions on Audio, Speech, and Language Processing*, **19**, 788–798 (2011).
6. G. Hinton, L. Deng, D. Yu, G. E. Dahl, A. Mohamed, N. Jaitly, A. Senior, V. Vanhoucke, P. Nguyen, T. N. Sainath and B. Kingsbury, Deep neural networks for acoustic modeling in speech recognition, *IEEE Signal Processing Magazine*, **29**, 82–97 (2012).
7. T. Stafylakis, P. Kenny, P. Ouellet, P. Perez, J. Kockmann and P. Dumouchel, Text-dependent speaker recognition using PLDA with uncertainty propagation, in *Proc. Interspeech*, 2013.
8. H. Aronowitz, Text-dependent speaker verification using a small development set, in *Proc. Odyssey Speaker and Language Recognition Workshop*, 2012.
9. A. Larcher, K.-A. Lee, B. Ma and H. Li, Phonetically constrained PLDA modeling for text-dependent speaker verification with multiple short utterances, in *Proc. ICASSP*, 2013.
10. J. Oglesby and J. S. Mason, Optimization of neural models for speaker identification, in *Proc. ICASSP*, 1990.
11. Y. Bennani and P. Gallinari, Connectionist approaches for automatic speaker recognition, in *ESCA Workshop on Automatic Speaker Recognition, Identification and Verification*, 1994.
12. L. P. Heck, Y. Konig, M. K. Sonmez and M. Weintraub, Robustness to telephone handset distortion in speaker recognition by discriminative feature design, *Speech Communication*, **31**(2), 181–192 (2000).
13. H. Lee, Y. Largman, P. Pham and A. Ng, Unsupervised feature learning for audio classification using convolutional deep belief networks, in *NIPS*, 2009.
14. T. Stafylakis, P. Kenny, M. Senoussaoui and P. Dumouchel, Preliminary investigation of Boltzmann machine classifiers for speaker recognition, in *Proc. Odyssey Speaker and Language Recognition Workshop*, 2012.

15. G. Dahl, T. N. Sainath and G. E. Hinton, Improving deep neural networks for LVCSR using rectified linear units and dropout, in *Proc. ICASSP*, 2013.
16. J. Dean, G. Corrado, R. Monga, K. Chen, M. Devin, Q. Le, M. Mao, M. Ranzato, A. Senior, P. Tucker, K. Yang and A. Ng, Large scale distributed deep networks, in *NIPS*, 2012.
17. V. Nair and G. E. Hinton, Rectified linear units improve restricted Boltzmann machines, in *ICML*, 2010.
18. R. Auckenthaler, M. Carey and H. Lloyd-Thomas, Score normalization for text-independent speaker verification systems, *Digital Signal Processing*, **10**, 42–54 (2000).
19. H. Aronowitz, R. Hoory, J. W. Pelecanos and D. Nahamoo, New developments in voice biometrics for user authentication, in *INTERSPEECH*, 2011, pp. 17–20.
20. R. Prabhavalkar, R. Alvarez, C. Parada, P. Nakkiran and T. N. Sainath, Automatic gain control and multi-style training for robust small-footprint keyword spotting with deep neural networks, in *Proc. ICASSP*, 2015.
21. J. Schalkwyk, D. Beeferman, F. Beaufays, B. Byrne, C. Chelba, M. Cohen, M. Kamvar and B. Strope, 'your word is my command': Google search by voice: A case study, in *Advances in Speech Recognition* (Springer, 2010), pp. 61–90.
22. E. Variani, X. Lei, E. McDermott, I. L. Moreno and J. Gonzalez-Dominguez, Deep neural networks for small footprint text-dependent speaker verification, in *IEEE International Conference on Acoustics, Speech and Signal Processing*, 2014, pp. 4052–4056.
23. T. Stafylakis, P. Kenny, P. Ouellet, J. Perez, M. Kockmann and P. Dumouchel, Text-dependent speaker recognition using plda with uncertainty propagation, *Matrix*, **500**, 1 (2013).
24. J. Campbell, Speaker recognition: A tutorial, *Proc. IEEE*, **85**(9), 1437–1462 (1997).
25. F. Bimbot, J. F. Bonastre, C. Fredouille, G. Gravier, I. Magrin-Chagnolleau, S. Meignier, T. Merlin, J. Ortega-Garcia, D. Petrovska-Delacrétaz and D. A. Reynolds, A tutorial on text independent speaker verification, *EURASIP J. Adv. Signal Process. (Spec. Issue Biom. Signal Process)*, **4**(4), 430–451 (2004).
26. B. G. B. Fauve, D. Matrouf, N. Scheffer, J. F. Bonastre and J. S. D. Mason, State-of-the-art performance in text-independent speaker verification through open-source software, *IEEE Trans. Audio Speech Lang. Process*, **15**(7), 1960–1968 (2007).
27. T. Kinnunen and H. Li, An overview of text-independent speaker recognition: From features to supervectors, *Speech Commun.*, **52**, 12–40 (2010).
28. S. Sarkar, Robust speaker recognition in noisy environments, Master's thesis, School of Information Technology, Indian Institute of Technology Kharagpur, Mar. 2014.
29. R. Schafer and L. Rabiner, Digital representations of speech signals, *Proc. IEEE*, **63**(4), 662–677 (1975).

30. B. Atal, Automatic recognition of speakers from their voices, *Proc. IEEE*, **64**(4), 460–475 (1976).
31. D. A. Reynolds, Experimental evaluation of features for robust speaker identification, *IEEE Trans. Speech Audio Process*, **2**(4), 639–643 (1994).
32. R. Mammone, X. Zhang and R. Ramachandran, Robust speaker recognition: A feature-based approach, *IEEE Signal Process. Mag.*, **13**(5), 58–71 (1996).
33. D. Reynolds, The effects of handset variability on speaker recognition performance: experiments on the Switchboard corpus, in *Proceedings of IEEE International Conference on Acoustics, Speech and Signal Processing*, vol. 1, 1996, pp. 113–116.
34. K. S. Rao, J. Yadav, S. Sarkar, S. G. Koolagudi and A. K. Vuppala, Neural network based feature transformation for emotion independent speaker identification, *Int. J. Speech Technol.*, **15**(3), 335–349 (2012).
35. S. Furui, Cepstral analysis technique for automatic speaker verification, *IEEE Trans. Acoust. Speech Signal Process*, **29**(2), 254–272 (1981).
36. H. Hermansky and N. Morgan, RASTA processing of speech, *IEEE Trans. Speech Audio Process*, **2**(4), 578–589 (1994).
37. D. Reynolds, W. Andrews, J. Campbell, J. Navratil, B. Peskin, A. Adomi, Q. Jin, D. Kluracek, J. Abramson, R. Mihaescu, J. Godfrey, D. Jones and S. Xiang, The supersid project: Exploiting high-level information for high-accuracy speaker recognition, in *Proceedings of IEEE International Conference on Acoustics, Speech and Signal Processing*, 2003.
38. H. Hermansky, Perceptual linear prediction (PLP) analysis for speech, *J. Acoust. Soc. Am.*, **87**, 1738–1752 (1990).
39. L. Rabiner and B. H. Juang, Fundamentals of Speech Recognition, 1st edn. (Prentice-Hall, Englewood Cliffs, 1993).
40. V. Mitra, H. Franco, M. Graciarena and A. Mandal, Normalized amplitude modulation features for large vocabulary noise-robust speech recognition, in *Proceedings of IEEE International Conference on Acoustics, Speech and Signal Processing*, 2012.
41. A. K. Vuppala and K. S. Rao, Speaker identification under background noise using features extracted from steady vowel regions, *Int. J. Adapt. Control Signal Process*, **27**(9), 781–792 (2013).
42. A. K. Vuppala, K. S. Rao and S. Chakrabarti, Improved speaker identification in wireless environment, *Int. J. Signal Imaging Syst. Eng.*, **6**(3), 130–137 (2013).
43. K. S. Rao, S. Maity and V. R. Reddy, Pitch synchronous and glottal closure based speech analysis for language recognition, *Int. J. Speech Technol.*, **16**, 413–430 (2013).
44. T. Kristjansson and B. Frey, Accounting for uncertainity in observations: A new paradigm for robust speech recognition, in *Proceedings of IEEE International Conference on Acoustics, Speech and Signal Processing*, 2002, pp. 61–64.
45. C. H. Lee, On stochastic feature and model compensation approaches to robust speech recognition, *Speech Commun.*, **25**, 29–47 (1998).

46. T. Quatieri, D. Reynolds and G. O'Leary, Estimation of handset nonlinearity with application to speaker recognition, *IEEE Trans. Speech Audio Process*, **8**, 567–584 (2000).
47. H. A. Murthy, F. Beaufays, L. P. Heck and M. Weintraub, Robust text-independent speaker identification over telephone channels, *IEEE Trans. Speech Audio Process*, **7**(5), 554–568 (1999).
48. R. Teunen, B. Shahshahani and L. Heck, A model-based transformational approach to robust speaker recognition, in *Proceeding of the Annual Conference of the International Speech Communication Association*, 2000, pp. 495–498.
49. J. Gauvain and C. Lee, Maximum *a posteriori* estimation for multivariate Gaussian mixture observations of Markov chains, *IEEE Trans. Speech Audio Process*, **2**(2), 291–298 (1994).
50. C. Leggetter and P. Woodland, Maximum likelihood linear regression for speaker adaptation of continuous density HMMs, *Comput. Speech Lang.*, **9**, 171–185 (1995).
51. D. A. Reynolds and R. C. Rose, Robust text-independent speaker identification using Gaussian mixture speaker models, *IEEE Trans. Acoust. Speech Signal Process*, **3**(1), 72–83 (1995).
52. D. Reynolds, T. Quatieri and R. Dunn, Speaker verification using adapted Gaussian mixture models, *Digit. Signal Process*, **10**(1), 19–41 (2000).
53. D. Zhu, B. Ma and H. Li, Joint MAP adaptation of feature transformation and Gaussian mixture model for speaker recognition, in *Proceedings of IEEE International Conference on Acoustics, Speech and Signal Processing*, 2009, pp. 4045–4048.
54. V. Digalakis, D. Rtischev, L. Neumeyer and E. Sa, Speaker adaptation using constrained estimation of Gaussian mixtures, *IEEE Trans. Speech Audio Process*, **3**(5), 357–366 (1995).
55. S. Kozat, K. Visweswariah and R. Gopinath, Feature adaptation based on Gaussian posteriors, in *Proceedings of IEEE International Conference on Acoustics, Speech and Signal Processing*, 2006, pp. 221–224.
56. K. K. Yiu, M. W. Mak and S. Y. Kung, Environment adaptation for robust speaker verification, in *Proceedings of the European Conference of Speech Communication and Technology*, 2003, pp. 2973–2976.
57. M. J. F. Gales and S. J. Young, Robust speech recognition in additive and convolutional noise using parallel model combination, *Comput. Speech Lang.*, **9**, 289–307 (1995).

Index